SHARING WELLNESS

PSYCHOSYNTHESIS FOR HELPING PEOPLE: THEORY AND APPLICATIONS

A COLLECTION OF CLASSIC ARTICLES

EXPLORING ISSUES IN THERAPY AND
TREATMENT, SELF-CARE, MEDICINE, SPIRITUAL
LIFE, EDUCATION, ENVIRONMENTAL DESIGN,
ORGANIZATIONS, COMMUNITIES, SOCIETY,
AND PSYCHOSYNTHESIS THEORY

CHESHIRE CAT BOOKS

SHARING WELLNESS

Psychosynthesis for Helping People: Theory and Applications

A Collection of Classic Articles Exploring Issues in Therapy and Treatment, Self-Care, Medicine, Spiritual Life, Education, Environmental Design, Organizations, Communities, and Psychosynthesis Theory

Edited by Jan Kuniholm

Written by
Robert A. Anderson, MD
Judith Bach, PhD
Joan Cannon Borton
Molly Young Brown, MA, MDiv
Jack Canfield, MEd
Helena Davis, MA
Kathleen Denison, MA
Marco J. De Vries, MD, PhD
Piero Ferrucci, PhD
Mary Greene, PhD
Vivian King, RN, PhD
Bruce McBeath, PhD
Anita R. Olds, PhD
Rachel Naomi Remen, MD
Chris Robertson, MPhil, DipPsych
Richard Schaub, PhD
Bonney Gulino Schaub, RN, MS
Kay Lynne Sherman, PhD
Victoria Tackett, PhD
Rev. Jane Vennard, MA, MDiv
John Weiser, PhD
Anne Eastman Yeomans, MA
Thomas Yeomans, PhD

Published by Cheshire Cat Books
P.O. Box 599
Cheshire, MA 01225-0599
www.Cheshire-Cat-Books.com
Book and Cover Design by Jan Kuniholm

The material in this book is intended for educational purposes only. No expressed or implied warranty is given or liability taken as to the use of this material. Users of this book are advised to seek professional assistance, guidance or support should they encounter any difficulty in applying the material herein.

ISBN 978-0-9882024-1-2

Library of Congress Control Number: 2018967192

Contents

Part IV. Spiritual Life

Part V. Education

Part VI. Environmental Design

Part VII. Organizations, Communities, and Society

Part VIII. Psychosynthesis Theory

Preface

Thomas Yeomans

Background

In June of 1983 the Ontario Institute for Studies in Education in Toronto, Canada, hosted an international conference on psychosynthesis that drew over 500 participants from all over North America and from several European countries. John Weiser, who was a professor at OISE, and I were the conference co-coordinators, and our purpose was to bring together practitioners to share their work in psychosynthesis in a wide range of fields, stretching from psychotherapeutic and educational to organizational and global work. The conference was very lively and inspirational and sounded a note of renewed cooperation between the various psychosynthesis centers in North America and also with those in Europe.

John and I used the proceeds of this conference to publish three books over the next years—*Psychosynthesis in the Helping Professions (1984)*, *Readings in Psychosynthesis, Volume I (1985)*, and *Readings in Psychosynthesis Volume II (1988)*. All three books included articles from the fields of Psychotherapy, Self-Care, Education, Medicine and Health, Religion, Organizational Development, and World Order. As we had with the format of the conference, with the books also we wanted to make known the wide range of application of the principles and practice of psychosynthesis, and to inspire people to keep utilizing, and expanding further, this orientation to human development, in whatever field of work they found themselves.

For a number of reasons the books got "lost" in the '90s and did not get the wide circulation that they deserved. A few centers included them in their professional training programs, but the wider audience that might have picked them up and made good use of them did not materialize. By the beginning of the new century, they were mostly out of print.

This Book

Always in the back of my mind was the idea that perhaps the books could be resurrected in some form and the valuable material they contained be shared more widely. In 2014 I mentioned this dream to Jan Kuniholm, editor of the online *Psychosynthesis Quarterly*, and to my great joy he took me up on it. He engaged Judith Broadus, co-director of the Kentucky Center of Psychosynthesis, to work with him to select those articles still most pertinent to work in psychosynthesis, and to edit and publish one volume to hold them all. Thus this book came to be.

John Weiser had passed away in the last years, so Jan asked me if I would write a preface, and I happily agreed. It is a great pleasure to see these articles in print again and to think that they might be read by this and future generations of practitioners in the field. And I can see my co-editor and dear friend, John, smiling as I write these words.

Psychosynthesis: A Unique Orientation

The articles speak for themselves and range over the same spectrum of applications they did in the earlier books. What I want to do here in introducing them is to speak to the unique context within which they exist—a truly radical conception of the human being and the process of human development.

At the end of his life (1974), Roberto Assagioli, the first formulator of psychosynthesis, in an interview with Evart Loomis, spoke of this approach, not as a school, or a theory, but as an attitude, or orientation, toward human development. Psychosynthesis started, he stated emphatically, with an assessment of the unique existential situation of each person, or group, or organization, and then proceeded to discern how the natural "process of psycho-synthesis" was at work in this situation. He saw this process as tending always toward what he called "an organic unity," characterized by the harmonious integration and synthesis of all elements involved without any loss of difference and diversity of the elements themselves. This process could be blocked, or stunted, or slowed, but it was inherent in the human being and could therefore be freed up and supported by conscious attention and work.

The attitude that we needed to cultivate in order to do this, he posited, was to be curious and receptive as well as keenly present. It might be focused on different aspects of the personality, or different members of a group, or different departments in an organization, or even different countries on the planet. The key, however, was to discern clearly and accept the unique existential situation, without any theoretical or methodological pre-suppositions, and then to work, using whatever technique, or method, was best indicated and at hand, in cooperation with this natural process of psycho-synthesis toward integration, healing, development, and transformation.

More radical, he held that this natural process was guided by what he termed the "Higher Self," or soul, and his conception of the human being included this deeper organizing principle and force in human life. In positing this he was including the spiritual dimension as real and active in the growth and developmental process and was exploring how it could be integrated into the bio-psycho-social aspects of human experience.

This was a radical vision at that time (1910 — 1974) and it still is, for it holds that there is no "right," orthodox, way to use psychosynthesis; rather it is an inclusive and sometimes quite unorthodox approach to the human issues we face that seeks, above all, alignment with the forces for health and well-being inherent in each and all of us, including the Higher Self. I have often said in my teaching that "psychosynthesis is, in essence, Life seeking to live itself more deeply and wholly." The challenge of this way of working, I believe, is to discern how to best support this "living more deeply" at any particular moment in each unique person, or situation, as well as to call upon the innate wisdom and power of the soul in doing this. This is the context for the work described in these articles.

The World Now

I hope this book will stimulate and inspire further exploration and experimentation in the application of the principles of psychosynthesis to the great needs that we face now as individuals, groups, and species. In his introduction to his book *Psychosynthesis* (1965) Assagioli says,

> *I should not want by any means to give the impression that it is, or that I consider it as, something already fully developed or satisfactorily completed. On the contrary, I consider it as a child—or, at the most as an adolescent— with many aspects still incomplete, yet with a great and promising potential for growth... Let us feel and obey the urge aroused by the great need of healing the serious ills which at present are affecting humanity; let us realize the contribution we can make to the creation of a new civilization characterized by an harmonious integration and cooperation, pervaded by the spirit of synthesis.*

Fifty years later I can join Roberto in encouraging us all to be bold in expanding further this orientation to human growth and development and continuing to refine this powerful and humane way of working with others for the betterment of the world at all levels.

Thomas Yeomans, PhD, *is the founder and director of* The Concord Institute *and co-founder, with Russian colleagues, of the* International School, *a post-graduate training institute in St. Petersburg, Russia. In 1974 he completed training in psychosynthesis, which included work with Roberto Assagioli in Florence, Italy. Since then he has worked as a psychotherapist, teacher, and trainer of professionals in psychosynthesis and spiritual psychology throughout North America and in Europe and Russia and, more recently, as a spiritual guide/mentor. He has published writing on psychosynthesis and spiritual psychology, as well as three volumes of poetry. He is also a painter and musician. Currently he maintains a private practice in spiritual guidance/mentoring in Shelburne Falls, MA and teaches occasional training workshops.*

Introduction:
A Framework for Understanding
the Human Condition
and for Helping People

Jan Kuniholm

Of all the students who studied Freud or Jung and eventually went beyond psychoanalysis, the Italian Roberto Assagioli, MD, (1888-1974) created perhaps the most wide-ranging framework for understanding the human condition and for helping people in a variety of settings. His *psychosynthesis* originally was conceived as adding "height" to the depth psychologies of Freud and Jung, and so its origins lie in the realm of psychology. However, Assagioli soon found that a full understanding of a human being required more than analysis, more than mental constructs. And the purview of psychosynthesis soon burst the bounds of "psychology."

Psychosynthesis is a well-rounded, inclusively scientific approach to the human being. By "inclusively scientific" I mean that its approach is open to and founded upon *evidence* of every type of phenomenon, at whatever level human experience may encounter it. Assagioli's approach to understanding the human being was based upon the full range of human *experience*, rather than a selected, controlled, narrowly-defined set of conclusions that conform to a given theoretical orientation. He had little use for "pure theory," and believed that the modern use of the word "theory" was a degeneration from the original meaning of "direct knowledge from experience." He, like William James before him, insisted on a conception of "science" that fearlessly explores the full range of phenomena available for human investigation and considers all evidence without *a priori* limitations.

The works of Freud and Jung are far more widely known than those of Assagioli and seem more amenable to academic and medical interest. Why is this? My sense is that the difference lies precisely in Assagioli's reluctance to be a "theoretician," as well as his refusal to create a controlling organization or an "orthodoxy" of thought. He was not so concerned to leave a body of written work — in fact, the books he did leave behind were written with the assistance of others and only produced in the last decades of his life, only after his major life's work was largely completed. Reading his major works, one gets the sense that he was not a gifted writer. Perhaps this is because his books attempt to condense a huge area of investigation and practice into a few hundred pages. But if we attend to the ideas that are contained in his books[1] and other written articles we find that the ideas are deep, broad, and yet eminently practical. His books are aimed at application, not at the erection of a theoretical edifice. A quick reading gives the sense that these books are merely summations.

There is a reason for this: The written word was intended to be only an introduction to his work. Psychosynthesis is not just a set of "ideas." It cannot properly be taught in a typical modern academic setting, because it is not an "intellectual discipline" — it is best taught and transmitted in experiential *training*, rather than by academic or literary instruction. Assagioli's work always included an awareness of all the levels of human being: physical, emotional, mental, and spiritual. His models of the human being, the map of the various psychological functions, and the topology of conscious and unconscious, his description of the nature of the will and the stages of willing, including his elucidation of "psychological laws," all point toward understanding a multifaceted being whose levels, aspects and functions are intricately interrelated. For Assagioli, "understanding" is not merely mental or intellectual; it must flow experientially through all of a person's psychological functions: thought, emotion and feeling, sensation, imagination, impulse and desire, and intuition — or at least as many of them as possible. Understanding is a function of *being*, not merely of thinking (thinking being actually only one of the psychological functions). And at the core of human being, in Assagioli's understanding, are awareness and will.

Assagioli's conception of psychosynthesis owes some to the conceptions of Feud and Jung in its genesis, but his understanding added a "breadth" and "height" to the "depth" of his predecessors' work, enabling psychosynthesis to become a framework for working constructively in many arenas beyond "psychology." The roots of psychosynthesis, however, are deeper. Assagioli studied the psychological and philosophical outlooks and practices that were embedded in the great psycho-spiritual traditions of east and west, and derived his framework of understanding from a remarkable variety of sources, both ancient and modern. I do not think Assagioli thought he was presenting something absolutely "new" but rather a modern, more comprehensive formulation and synthesis of knowledge that had existed in bits and pieces for millennia, and whose original import was largely lost to modern people.

The new paradigm in science that is implicit in psychosynthesis discards the Cartesian dualism that has reigned in the west for centuries as a result of the split between science and religion. Since Descartes' time in the early 1600s, scientists have largely limited their investigations to things they can quantify — following the lead of this famous French mathematician. Assagioli discovered that there was a treasure trove of scientifically valid data buried within the spiritual traditions of both east and west, and available for study and use. Western scientists, in particular, have largely avoided "the soul" and other concepts and practices that have for over 400 years been "reserved" for religious thinkers, with the result that they have not investigated phenomena that are described in minute detail — with the eyes of scientists — in the writings of many ancient traditions.

Not having the language, modern scientists have not known how to interpret data that has been reported by these traditions, nor have they been able to develop modern techniques that utilize knowledge that has been "hidden in plain sight" for centuries. Furthermore, many of these traditions also insisted upon an experiential basis for knowledge and understanding; experience that went beyond attempts at "objectivity" and included the action of so-called "subjective" states on a level that has only recently been explored in the realm of quantum physics. Assagioli's holistic approach is one that resonates with many cutting-edge thinkers of our time.

In his Preface to this work, Tom Yeomans, who has been a prominent teacher/trainer of psychosynthesis in North America since before Assagioli's death, has given a summary of the genesis of this book as well as a summary of psychosynthesis as "an orientation." In fact, a great many of the people who have trained in psychosynthesis in North America in the past 40 years have not proceeded to "practice psychosynthesis" *per se*, but have taken its orientation into other fields and disciplines, and have thus "seeded" psychosynthesis concepts and practices into a variety of currents in the Western cultural stream.

Psychosynthesis concepts and practices lie hidden (and often unacknowledged) within many books and organizations in North America, Europe, and elsewhere. Concepts such as subpersonalities were developed for clinical use in modern times by Assagioli, and are now widely used by many others. It could be argued that the entire field of transpersonal psychology might not exist without his work, which cross-fertilized with the work of Maslow and others to form the "fourth wave" in psychology. While Assagioli would be pleased that his orientation is putting down roots, and while we too are happy that this work is finding fertile ground for germination, still we wanted to provide the public with some of the ideas in their original context.

The works presented here were written by students of psychosynthesis in the wave that gathered momentum soon after Assagioli's death in 1974. Some of these authors were direct students of Assagioli, others learned from them. All were riding a tide of enthusiasm for this new approach to human experience that had been brought to North America with Assagioli's founding in 1957 of the Psychosynthesis Research Foundation (PRF). The PRF presented papers and encouraged research in Maryland and New York until its closure in 1976, after which psychosynthesis was taught and promoted by centers in New York, Massachusetts, Kentucky, Minnesota, Illinois, Missouri, California, Québec, Ontario, and elsewhere. From the 1950s on there has been a cross-fertilization of psychosynthesis ideas and practices between North American and European practitioners, and this volume reflects that reality. Perhaps because of our choice of the English language (in which some of Dr. Assagioli's works initially appeared), the North American writers are more numerous among those presented here.

The writers whose work is contained herein had a luxury that Roberto Assagioli did not have when he was writing his books — they were not trying to distill the entirety of psychosynthesis. They were able to concentrate on specific areas of concern and address issues in their particular manifestations, and develop techniques and practices that were direct applications of psychosynthesis. The original versions of these pieces originally appeared in three books edited by John Weiser, PhD, and Thomas Yeomans, PhD, in the 1980s.[2] The reader may well detect signs of the times in some of these articles, which reflect their origins. But we have selected these particular pieces with the conviction that the essence of their messages has stood the test of time — they can still talk to us and teach us. We had to limit our selections to a number that could fit into a single volume, and chose those that we believed would be most valuable at this time. We hope that readers will find them illuminating and useful.

Psychosynthesis is a framework that can used to understand and help people in a wide variety of contexts. Although perhaps the largest number of psychosynthesis students have used it in clinical settings, as social workers and therapists, this volume is a demonstration that psychosynthesis has a truly global reach — it provides a practical framework for activities in psychiatry, therapy and self-care, medicine, treatment of addictions, education, social action, prison work, systems and organizations, theology and spirituality; and a philosophical framework to understand reality and the human condition.

When we reviewed these articles, written and published over 30 years ago, we were struck by how *advanced* were some of the thinking and practice — and are still. Many of these articles pointed toward a future that is still unrealized. They make connections in physics and medicine, education and psychology, criminology and spirituality that resonate with the most advanced thinking and scientific endeavors of our time. Even though psychosynthesis draws upon knowledge that was discovered and developed over the millennia, these threads of perennial wisdom must be updated for each culture. Psychosynthesis promises to break open the closed system of western thought, to provide help and healing in many areas of human endeavor.

Much of mainstream western culture has remained in ruts that are familiar and profitable. We feel that presenting these works in a fresh format may provide today's readers with insights that will not fade with time, that will indeed provide "tools for the journey" for thoughtful and committed people, now and into the future.

We hope that these articles may stimulate renewed interest in psychosynthesis. These articles, for the most part, do not present the basic concepts and practices of psychosynthesis, which are to be found in Roberto Assagioli's books cited earlier, and elsewhere.[3] The works here build on Assagioli's work and show some of the threads of its current and future development. The reader who is interested in pursuing the depth, profundity and versatility of psychosynthesis is directed to Assagioli's books and to one of the many training centers for this remarkable framework to be found in North and South America, Australia and New Zealand, and in Europe[4] where it can be studied independently for private enlightenment or as part of professional training at the graduate level.

I want to thank Judith Broadus, PhD, and Rhonda Barnett, of the Kentucky Center of Psychosynthesis, for helping to make the difficult choices of which works to include in the volume; Anne Yeomans and Bonney Kuniholm for assistance in making some artistic choices about the layout; Thomas Yeomans, PhD, for the initial impetus for this project and for his ongoing support of it; and the Association for the Advancement of Psychosynthesis for material and moral support to bring this book to the public.

Notes

[1] *Psychosynthesis: A Collection of Basic Writings* (1965); and *The Act of Will*

(1974). Also many shorter works exist in article format, published or reprinted by many of Assagioli's students and the centers established by those students.

[2] *Psychosynthesis in the Helping Professions: Now and for the Future (1984); Readings in Psychosynthesis: Theory, Process, & Practice, Vol.1 (1985) and Readings in Psychosynthesis: Theory, Process, & Practice, Vol.2 (1988).* All original articles are reprinted in this volume by arrangement with the authors or authors' heirs, and many articles have been revised by the authors for this publication.

[3] A bibliography of significant works on psychosynthesis is to be found at the end of this volume.

[4] See a partial listing of psychosynthesis centers at the end of this volume.

Jan Kuniholm *was an active member of* The Association for the Advancement of Psychosynthesis from *2004 to 2018, serving in many capacities including as Cochair of its Steering Committee, and was founder and editor of the online journal* Psychosynthesis Quarterly. *He is the author of* The Gospel Within Us, *a psychosynthesis-oriented study of the Gospel According to Mark. He is retired and lives in Cheshire, MA.*

Part I.

Helping Applications:
Therapy and Treatment

The Untrodden Regions of the Mind

Piero Ferrucci

In the *Conference of the Birds*, a poetical work written by the Sufi mystic Attar, birds of all types met one day to discuss their situation and future destiny. Things looked bleak, and the winged community was in a state of confusion. At some point, however, the most authoritative bird announced that there was a powerful King, called Simurg, living in a far away, wonderful place, who would be able not only to help everybody deal with their predicament but also to bring them to the highest state of consciousness. This was a sublime place to go, the most desirable in the whole universe. All the birds were interested in the proposal to fly out to the Simurg; but when the time came to make a decision, the majority found excuses or reacted in other negative ways. The nightingale, for instance, was in love with a rose in her backyard, and didn't want to leave it for such a long and perilous journey; the peacock was too busy being proud of its own beauty; the hawk protested that he, and not the Simurg, was the true king; the pelican was just too depressed to even think of starting; and to the duck, the local pond was much more real and enjoyable than any promise of cosmic reward; the owl was too attached to the treasures he had kept among the ruins of an abandoned house; the sparrow was blocked by a nagging feeling of inferiority; and so on with many other birds. So only a part of the community started out on the long flight.

The trip was long and difficult, and it required the utmost powers of attention and dedication. The birds had to leave behind everything they had that was dear to them, and meet with dangers of all kinds. Many of them died or lost their way: some fell in the ocean, exhausted; others died of thirst or were devoured by tigers; others, weary due to the heat, became mad and attacked each other; others disappeared in the desert; some just couldn't make it and gave up, or let themselves be misled by some local attraction; others still, who had started out enticed only by a vague yearning for pleasure or by gratuitous curiosity, died without even knowing what they had been looking for.

Of the original thousand who had started, only thirty birds arrived at their destination, and after a hundred curtains were opened, saw a splendor like a thousand suns. In this state of wonder and contemplation, they saw that the Simurg was *them*, and they were it. They understood that they and the Simurg,[1] the Light of Lights, the supreme good, were and had always been one and the same since the beginning of time.

This story describes well the nature and the difficulties of the spiritual search, and it points at the end to the paradoxical truth that this, the longest of all journeys, ends with the nearest of all aims: ourselves. We are and have always been that which we are so eagerly looking for. And it is precisely for this reason that the mysterious and radiant reality described in this story, as in so many other tales and myths, is a legitimate field of inquiry not only for metaphysics or theology but also for psychology, the science which aims to study and explain human experience.

The notion of a higher unconscious source of illumination, inspiration, and vivifying energy was at first ignored by modern day psychology. Later, the phenomena of the superconscious (as we call it in psychosynthesis) were considered as defense mechanisms, wish fulfillments, or just straight pathology.[2] Meanwhile, pioneers such as Jung, Maslow, and Assagioli considered the spiritual dimension as a subject with a dignity and a function of its own, not to be explained away in terms of other functions. In the late sixties and the early seventies, the idea spread to a committed minority, and gave birth to groups, centers, journals, books and bookshops, conferences, and activities of various kinds. The "transpersonal"—a word already used by Jung, and by Mircea Eliade, and later adopted by Maslow and Assagioli—was born: ecstasy, liberation, and unlimited joy were there (and so, at times, was inflation) as long as you followed certain rules and used certain techniques. Experiments with psychedelic drugs facilitated the exploration. People did genuinely get high. The interest was directed toward the existing psychotechnologies that enabled individuals to reach such desirable states. The *Book of Highs* (1973) listed 250 ways of "altering your consciousness." This was a collective turn-on. Meanwhile, both in psychosynthesis and in the wider field of transpersonal psychology, ways were gradually found in which higher levels of our being could be present in some degrees in therapy.

Transpersonal Issues

My aim here is to consider those issues of the transpersonal which need most attention. After all, because of its otherness, the transpersonal realm is the easiest to misrepresent; because of its undiluted goodness, the most subject to exploitation; because of its purity, the most liable to be violated; because of its vastness, the most apt to lose us; and yet, because of its power, the most likely to destroy us.

In dealing with the transpersonal, we should often go back to basics. Not only that, we should also question these basics and see how successful they are as working hypotheses. For if we don't face them clearly, we will end at best in theoretical confusion, at worst in folly. I will mention briefly a definition of the transpersonal and its function in therapy. Then I will focus on the dangers engendered by the transpersonal.

To begin then, what are the criteria defining "transpersonal?" This term has often been used in a rather loose way to mean *great, good, powerful, unusual, or very pleasant,* as a psychological superlative rather than as the indication of the difference in nature between this and other realms of experience. Roberto Assagioli's definition of "superconscious" was that region from which "we receive our higher intuitions and inspirations—artistic, philosophical or scientific, ethical "imperatives" and urges to humanitarian and heroic action. It is the source of the higher feelings, such as altruistic love; or genius and of the states of contemplation, illumination, and ecstasy. In this realm are latent the higher psychic functions and spiritual energies" (1965, p. 17).

I propose to add the following distinctive criteria:

Intensity — The spiritual experience strikes us and involves us intimately. By its own power, it changes what we feel we are. Its intensity is not just given by the potency of what we see and feel, but rather by the fact that we are presented with a reality structurally different from the one in which we usually live. The response evoked may be one of wonder but also surprise, awe, even terror.

Universality — The higher we ascend into the superconscious, the greater the range of our vision. The reality we perceive belongs to everybody, and as we cease feeling isolated or separated, selfishness becomes in our eyes an absurd, awkward attitude. Take, for instance, these words of Einstein, describing the state of scientific or artistic contemplation:

> In the first place, I agree with Schopenhauer that one of the most powerful motives that attract people to Science and Art is the longing to escape from everyday life with

its painful coarseness and unconsoling barrenness, and to break the fetters of their own ever-changing desires. It drives those of keener sensibility out of their personal existence into the world of objective perception and understanding. This motive force is similar to the longing which makes the city dweller leave his noisy, confused surroundings and draws him with irresistible force to restful Alpine heights, where his gaze covers the wide expanse lying peacefully before him on all sides, and softly passes over the motionless outlines that seem created for all eternity. (Moszkowski, 1972, p. 58)

Incidentally, this, and not emotional abreaction, is what I would call the true catharsis.

Rightness — The intrinsic value of the transpersonal reality is self-evident and needs to be neither explained nor justified. This is not a logical or legal or technical or even ethical rightness. It is complete rightness, and we need no outward authority to put its seal of approval on it. Take, for example, the words of Jean Jacques Rousseau written in the *Rêveries du Promeneur Solitaire* (1782):

If there is a condition in which the soul finds a poise so still that it is able to truly rest and gather its whole being, without the need of remembering the past nor aiming at the future; in which time is nothing for it, and the present lasts forever, beyond any trace of rhythm or sequence, without any feeling of lack or joy, of pleasure or pain, of desire or dread, except the sense of one's own existence, and with only this awareness filling it completely; as long as this state lasts, whoever experiences it can be called happy; and this is not an imperfect, needy, or relative happiness such as the one we meet with in life's plea-sures, but a happiness which is plentiful, perfect, and complete, and does not leave in our soul any empty space crying to be filled. Such is the state which I experienced in the island of Saint Pierre, during my solitary day-dreaming, now lying on my boat as it drifted on the water, now sitting by the restless sin-face of a lake, or elsewhere, on the bank of a river or a stream murmuring as it runs on the stones. What does one enjoy in such a situation? Nothing external, nothing except oneself and one's own existence; and as long as this state lasts one is self-sufficient as God is.

Noetic value — As William James put it, the true transpersonal experience is not just a rapturous state of emotional exaltation. When it happens, we know something we did not know before, although this knowledge, not being discursive, is hard to communicate with words.

Unity — Whether it is in the harmony of a work of art or the coherence of a scientific vision, in the oneness perceived by the great seers of all ages or in the coincidence of opposites described by the alchemical tradition, or even in the psychological integration of contrasting inner forces, unity is an unmistakable mark of superconscious production. The clashing of opposites or the fragmentation of heterogeneous entities gives place to wholeness. There is often a sense of great simplicity in the perception of an underlying design, the emerging of a connection between two apparently extraneous realities, or the ecstatic insight into the oneness of all things.

Social effectiveness — There is no private salvation, and a spiritual experience is not truly such unless it reaches out instead of remaining within the boundaries of individual enjoyment. This influence takes place in a variety of ways: a transpersonal experience may clarify a situation and therefore stimulate action; it can be felt as a beneficial atmosphere and therefore facilitate interpersonal cohesiveness and communication; it can inspire individuals by offering them a vision to be anchored in historical reality; and it can concretize into some structure (a symphony, a mathematical theorem, an invention, etc.) which can serve and uplift people for a longtime. On the other hand, a transpersonal experience which is not fully grounded may even be harmful to psychological health, as we shall see later.

These could perhaps be considered the main criteria. Yet many states and experiences may still be considered transpersonal even though they do not include all of these factors. Perhaps, here, Wittgenstein's model of family resemblance can help us. Imagine a family, he says, in which everybody has some traits in common, but no feature appears in each one without exception. For instance, many individuals in this big family have red hair, but not all; the majority has a hooked nose, but not everyone does; many have blue eyes, but some don't; almost all of them are tall, but there are a few exceptions; and so on. So you cannot find one single trait held in common with everybody, and yet there is a general resemblance, so that you can easily see that all these people belong to the same family. I believe we can say the same about transpersonal experiences. The superconscious can account for a wonderfully extended variety of "family members." Several authors and spiritual leaders have tried since time immemorial to subdivide these experiences into levels, and you often see diagrams with various layers symbolizing states of increasing universality and formlessness. Some of these classifications are useful and convincing, but as Assagioli used to say, we shouldn't think of the higher levels of the mind as being rigidly compartmentalized like floors in a building. I may add that it is useful to keep in mind the visible biological world, where there is no cut-and-dried differentiation, but rather infinite variations, resemblances, and echoes, expressing the power of an immensely creative intelligence.

If we apply all these ideas to the field of therapy, we can easily see how the transpersonal element is not just an intense, occasional aspect, but rather the decisive factor. Ignoring it would be like trying to understand the solar system without mentioning the sun. I would like to go through briefly the benefits I have seen offered by the transpersonal dimension in psychosynthesis therapy:

- It changes the client's self-image, and gives him or her a wider and more truthful sense of identity.
- It heals hurts and past traumas, evoking beneficial energies, and redeeming wrongs and violations which our personal psychological equipment would not be able ordinarily to handle.
- It changes one's perspective and helps one to perceive reality in an entirely different context.
- It gives guidance in the basic choices of our life, a guidance such as only the wisest of spiritual teachers can offer. And finding this inner guidance means recovering our own personal autonomy.
- It integrates experience and transforms a chaos of piecemeal, free-floating fragments into a cosmos, a harmonious order.
- It reveals meaning and value in one's life, even in the most trying or apparently absurd situations.
- It helps us to transcend our narrow sphere of petty concerns, and become immersed in a universal outlook.
- By elevating us above fragmentary realities, it offers us the healing, harmonizing perception of cycles: the cycle of life and death, the cycles of nature and the universe.

- It evokes a caring solidarity with the human race at large and with all life, thus dissipating all fear of solitude.
- It leads us to experience the fundamental goodness of the universe, in an undiluted, unconditional sense.

There is no *guarantee* that the spiritual dimension may inevitably offer these benefits. This depends very much upon the psychological makeup, the stability, the purpose, and the general situation of the individual involved.

Also, there may be serious harm, causing what I have called the pathology of the sublime.

Dangers of the Transpersonal Reality

After the first waves of enthusiasm generated by spiritual awakening, to their dismay, many people start to discover that the transpersonal dimension can oppress, torture, confuse, and even annihilate if it is not approached with adequate psychological equipment. Moreover, the way we relate to it tends to determine the way we relate to each other; and if our attitude to higher consciousness is immature, we can actually violate each other in the name of the spirit. Whereas in the past, the spiritual dimension was entered through specific procedures and rhythms, and one was in some way protected by a number of cultural devices, this is not so in our case: in our age innumerable prohibitions and other structures have fallen, and circulation of information is maximized. The "numinous" is not protected as it was in the past, and we are on our own, entering free, naked, and vulnerable into a world of energies unknown.

In the past, myths obscurely warned against immature attitudes toward the transpersonal dimension. The story of Phaeton is an example of this. As in so many Greek and Roman myths, Phaeton was born of a god and of a mortal. His mother was a woman, Clymene; his father was the sun. Phaeton was a young boy, and his peers would often hurt and make fun of him, refusing to believe that his father was, in fact, the sun. So Phaeton went to the sun's radiant palace, and taking up his father's promise to give him anything he requested, asked for the privilege to take his place for one day in his ride through the sky. At this request, the sun wanted to retreat from his promise. The wish of his son was the most dangerous mistake imaginable. But now that he had given his word, it was too late to take it back. So the little boy, Phaeton, went on the carriage with the horses, and started his rise, ascending toward the heavens, bringing everywhere fire and light. For a little while, he felt like the lord of the sky: what sudden power, what a dazzling sense of majesty! But soon, he lost command, and as the horses felt a weaker presence at the reins, they started darting in all directions, up and down the sky, getting too close to the earth and setting it on fire, drying up the rivers, and creating all sorts of disasters. At this point, Jupiter, the king of the gods, decided to strike Phaeton with a bolt of lightning, causing the horses to fall into the river Eridanus, and Phaeton to die.

This story pictures the rage we feel when our true being is not acknowledged for what it actually is, but is instead undervalued, ridiculed, or denied. This humiliation engenders feelings of revenge and may stimulate an individual to identify with the spiritual world with the purpose of using it to compensate for his loss of ego image and his profound sense of inferiority—and seek the ultimate self-affirmation. The message coming from the rest of the story is clear: access to realms for which we are not ready entails loss of control, an upsetting of the psychological balance, and disaster.

Some relevant work concerning these matters has been done in psychosynthesis during the past few years. Alberto Alberti, for instance, in his work with psychotics, found that schizophrenia in some cases is the result of stepping in the spiritual world while still identified with some unresolved subpersonality. There are, in other words, correct and incorrect ways of experiencing the same reality. According to Alberti, the remedy is humility, not as a moralistic imposition from the part of the therapist, but rather as a natural function that is spontaneously growing or needs to be skillfully evoked. The word "humility," like "human," comes from "humus," the Latin word indicating the soil.

For example, Alberti has people imagine walking down from the top of the mountain, instead of up to it, as in the traditional visualization exercise symbolizing ascent toward the Self. The strength that comes from admitting one's own humanness and limitations, genuinely being conscious of one's biological roots while fully realizing the importance of time and of natural rhythms, is highly beneficial and is a necessary prerequisite for an authentic and balanced spiritual growth.

In France, Martine Sandor points out that many people with insufficient self-knowledge tend to project on the Self all kinds of parental images and fantasies. For example, many individuals form an idealized image during their infancy of the "good mother," a mother who is always present, fulfils their needs, and will never betray them. The less fit the real mother, the greater the compensation offered by this fantasy. Later, the fantasy seeps into the unconscious and remains there unfiltered; but it can be projected onto the Self, which is then ineffectively and dangerously forced within the boundaries of this projection. Or to give another example, an individual may feel the Self as a tremendous power, full of thunder and explosions—images reminiscent of the infantile image of a violent father.

In England, Diana Whitmore has worked on our habit of attributing to the Self the traits of a severe "top dog" or an intolerant Victorian moralist. Try asking participants in a group, she says, to engage in a gestalt chair dialogue with their Self. Chances are that the room will fill with rage, pain, and guilt. And why is that so? It is because we understand the transpersonal realm in terms of our guilt feelings. We experience the Self by comparing ourselves with it; and thus we turn it into a tyrant.

In Italy, Stuart Miller and others have pointed out several risks present for anyone who in some way deals with the transpersonal dimension, and with psychosynthesis in particular. These risks include the belief in the omnipotence of the will or an excessive confidence in its power; "Stalinism of the spirit," or the risk of becoming militant, authoritarian, and dogmatic; the temptation of holism, or the illusion of having reached a complete and consistent vision of human affairs and life in general; and finally, the danger of creating too strong a polarity between the spiritual and the material.

I have noticed this last problem especially in my therapeutic work, and would like to comment on it. The beauty of the vision is in sharp contrast with the narrow world of our actual condition, and this contrast, rather than fulfilling its natural function of stimulating us in our evolution, pushes us into depression and despair. One feels hopelessly imprisoned in a meaningless and ugly world, and the superconscious, while experienced with great intensity, is nevertheless far away, a beautiful essence whose wonderful perfection can only be unintentionally, but ironically, offensive. At this point, one just wants not to be here on earth, and suicidal thoughts are not uncommon. Being human means then being part of unregenerated matter, and thus prey to illusion, perpetual violation, decay, and pain. Moreover, this situation may well extend to relationships between a person and the society to which she or he belongs.

In a short story by H.G. Wells, "The Country of the Blind," there is a land forgotten and concealed among the Andes in Peru. Following a series of earthquakes and other catastrophes occurring in the remote past, the people in this place become isolated from the rest of the world. Moreover, because of a mysterious illness, they start, very slowly, to lose their sight, and their babies are eventually born completely blind. Before everybody loses their sight, however, they become accustomed to their new condition, and gradually develop a new system of living, adapting themselves and surviving; they are able to solve their economic and social problems, to create a new culture and a series of myths and beliefs. This goes on for many generations until the last memory of vision and the external world becomes blurred, surviving only in children's tales. Then one day, a mountain guide by the name of Nunez, who lives in a nearby valley, falls down a precipice, and becomes the first man from the outside world to meet this community of the blind in a very long time.

The story goes on to narrate the meeting of this man with the blind people. They think that Nunez is abnormal, and claim that he was formed out of the rocks. When he speaks about seeing and vision, they say he is uttering nonsense words. And when he tries to convey to them the wonders of the visible world beyond that valley—the sky, the clouds, and the stars—they think he is having delusions.

At first, Nunez feels powerful and confident, but gradually the blind people indoctrinate him with their beliefs. Little by little, he finds himself believing them, almost forgetting who he is and what he can do; vision is, after all, just a dangerous hallucination.

At some point, Nunez falls in love with a blind woman, and his ties with the community become stronger. Since he is believed to be a rather insane individual, however, the only way in which marriage is permitted to him is for him to undergo (voluntarily) an operation to remove his sight. The theory of the community's doctor is that if he takes away what he thinks are hypertrophied glands, Nunez' brain will not be irritated any more, and all his delusions will cease.

Nunez initially accepts this plan for intervention, but then decides to follow his heart's nostalgia for the lost beauty of the world and to leave the blind people. He climbs back from where he had fallen, and regains his freedom and vision.

I think this story aptly illustrates the violation, the solitude, and the "divine homesickness" of individuals aware of realities greater than the ones accepted by the culture in which they live.

A Case History

Let us now consider a case history that illustrates many of the points I have been making. This is the case of a woman whom I shall call Esther. Esther had already been working with me for a while. I won't go into the details of her situation except to say that she had often suffered from periods of depression leading to plans of suicide. At the same time, she was open to the superconscious, and her aesthetic sensitivity was highly developed. In fact, it was precisely the nostalgia for unity that made her feel like an exile imprisoned in matter in an unbearable situation.

One day, she started a session by telling me that she wanted me to help her decide whether she wanted to live or to die. At that time, her bias was toward dying. A clean, painless suicide was a strong temptation: what she imagined to be an effortless avenue back to unity. I must confess now, as I did to Esther at the time of the session, that I could not remain neutral in front of such a dilemma, and that if she were to choose to die, I would collaborate with this. Books could actually be written on the ethical implications of this issue. Nevertheless, I decided to play the game according to her rules; yet, I had the feeling of walking on a tightrope. I felt the request to be genuine. Esther meant business, and hers was an open question; neither of us knew what the answer was going to be.

We agreed to explore the reality of death and the reality of life in sessions scheduled closely together. I asked her at first to close her eyes and imagine a door with "DEATH" written on it. Behind that door, I told her, was the world of death, which she could now look into.

When this door opens, as if by itself, Esther finds herself already on the other side. She doesn't see any floor and, at first, does not quite feel at home in this foreign environment. Then, she realizes she is actually floating in a gray mass of fog and that music is playing. At each note, the fog in which she is immersed becomes more present and more real, and also wider, as if each note added a dimension to this space. She also feels more extended. This immense and opaque space is liberating. The door behind her becomes smaller and smaller, and finally disappears.

The process continues; she feels that she is growing larger, but at the same time, while floating with an increasing sense of freedom, finer and lighter. No longer encapsulated and oppressed by matter, she experiences this wide expanse as healing and soothing. And as she becomes lighter, the fog becomes less gray and less dense. More light filters in, and soon she is floating in a medium that is becoming finer and more luminous.

This light increases Esther's sense of liberation. She feels herself becoming almost weightless, like a soap bubble, and becoming transparent and full of light. This process, which is slow in the beginning, becomes faster. The music is now gone, as it belongs to the world of fog which is now far below her.

With the waxing of the light, everything floats upward, including her. Already the light is present everywhere. There isn't anything but radiance, and it starts to become scintillating. There is great beauty in this, and Esther feels surrounded by thousands of explosions. These explosions become so intense that they start bothering, almost hurting, her. She has the feeling that if they continue, she as well is going to explode. She is now identified with a soap bubble and in it she discovers wonderful light colors: lilac rose, emerald green, a very fine red. At the beginning, they are so faint that they are almost non-existent: perfumes of the colors, rather than colors themselves. And in this discovery of gradually emerging colors, the fear of the explosions disappears. In its place, there is now wonder. Esther is aware of a world of colors in herself, and sees them all around, feeling herself become increasingly red.

Imperceptibly, Esther leaves her bubble form and becomes color: she becomes a flaming red entity, ascending toward a universe in which a thousand colors are floating. She sees other reds coming toward her, attracted by each other, and together converging to form a pattern, and she feels a strong temptation to join in. At this point, however, she is afraid, because she knows that if she lets herself go and fuses with this universe, she could lose her own form, perhaps even her own self-consciousness, without any way back. She feels already far away from the starting point, and the idea of going back is strange. The prospect of losing herself frightens Esther, but then she makes up her mind and plunges into this "red immensity," becoming one with this great flame.

Suddenly, this pattern of red entities, this "us," as Esther calls it, is taken by a great storm of incredible force, which projects it very far away in cosmic space, thousands of galaxies away from where they were before. It is as if cosmic forces were playing ball with them and throwing them here and there across interstellar space. After the first feelings of astonishment, Esther becomes joyous, like a child playing. Now, she can see other spheres or balls dancing around, as if brought by strong winds. There is this great feeling of being projected in a space of total freedom.

Esther now experiences this amazing event in its totality: red, blue, yellow, green spheres, which she perceives as living beings, moving in a great dance of which she is herself a part. Suddenly, she knows why she is so joyous; this is a feast. It is a great cosmic feast in which she is accepted, involved, dancing, happy. And beautiful.

At this point, I ask her to have a dialogue with these entities. We often find this kind of inner dialogue useful in psychosynthesis. If it is done with images representing something joyous, high, and beautiful, the answers can have a high cognitive value; they can guide and uplift a person, and give everybody concerned relevant messages. But with Esther, something apparently goes wrong. Here is how she describes what happens:

> Piero disturbs me with this question. All of a sudden I
> feel separated. I don't feel that I am one with them

anymore. I experience my own difference, because these beings don't have to ask questions.

I remember that this is an exercise and I have to follow instructions. It is very difficult for me to separate myself from them. Before, I was them. But then I come to this separation, and I ask the question. I then hear their answer: this is a feast. And then I hear the explanation of this statement: life and death are the same thing. At first this answer seems to be very evident. But then a faint memory reminds me of how I feel down there on earth, my misery, my tears. And I say: how can I find this feast on earth? I cannot see all this great beauty down there in life. It also seems to me that with these questions I separate myself more and more from the feast. Already, I am not dancing any more with them. I am standing still with these hard questions, looking at them. They keep dancing, and do not seem in the least concerned with me or my problems. I have a great desire of forgetting about all these questions and joining with them again, but Piero insists. There is in his voice something that touches me, and which makes me feel conscious of their detachment towards me. They are neither kind nor negative—they are beautiful, intensely beautiful, and in no way worried about me.

Behind my voice, Esther hears the voice of her children, caring for her, wanting her not to die, wanting to be with her on earth. This realization gives her some strength to ask again why she doesn't see any of that beauty on earth, in her life. What should she do? She hears no answer: we live in beauty, in total beauty. She goes on:

After this answer the desire to join them again becomes so strong that I start crying and I tell Piero that I don't want to go back. I remember my promise given at the beginning of the session, to remain as objective as possible, that is, to not let myself be sucked in by images or to listen to them as absolute messages. I keep my promise, and start coming back; I try to bring back those luminous beings with me, and now they are like a circle of fire; their colors become smaller like petals of a flower, and I try to bring them in my own heart. But seeing how they are becoming small, I cry again. I feel myself coming back, but I am very, very sad.

I remind Esther of the answers to her questions, but she feels filled with what she has experienced, and questions and answers are a disturbance of an experience that she knows to be inexpressibly happier and more beautiful than her present situation. To come back is torment:

> I see the danger of this exercise, I see how much such an ecstasy makes me feel closer still to my temptation of suicide. I feel aggression against my instinct to live, which makes me continue the way I continue. It is a river of unconsciousness: eating, sleeping, breathing, getting dressed. But they, those beings of light that were dancing, they said that both realities are one and the same thing. There are no two realities, according to them, the one of living and the one of death. Why not, then, choose for life after death? Since it is the same thing, why this difficult, painful path full of suffering? I remember now that I forgot to ask them about suffering. This was so far away from them that I didn't think about it anymore. I was so far away from earth, from my own inner life, that I had become so much one with lightness, freedom, bright color, joy. What is suffering? It is being separated from them. Separation from joy, from light, from weightlessness, from beauty especially. And separation without knowing why. Suffering without meaning. Like a beast, like an idiot, because that is the way life is, and one just has to be in it. This is revolting. If suffering were a means of getting in touch with them on earth, then it would all be different.
>
> But what guarantee do I have? One can become sour, dead inside, because of suffering. I feel like I am dying inside and the only way of escaping is by this project that I have had; it is the resolution of going there as soon as possible.

We end the session here, on this note of torment, which words in no way can heal. Esther feels that her choice for death is increasingly energized. This is a very clear example of how the superconscious, if it is only perceived and not fully realized, can at times generate very painful situations.

At home, however, the process keeps working by itself, and Esther encourages it by repeating the inner dialogue. She is struck by the renewed contact with the beings of light. This experience seems to be decisive, and she consciously makes the decision of, as she calls it, "incarnation." Her situation is now transformed:

> I make my choice of being here among people, of accepting suffering and love which will come to me in all their shapes. I am a human being, and I want to live on earth among human beings. I feel brotherhood with them, with everything and everybody. Love and suffering are human values. Both allow that timeless light to emanate and express itself.
>
> Only here, on earth, the colors of that world become love, warmth, tenderness, and also suffering and evil. This is necessary for making love, strength and light emerge. It is that way, and it is good that it is that way. I want it like that. I feel solidarity with this great work. I take on my own little part. I want to be here.

To sum up, the transpersonal world is what we make of it, even though it is not our construction and has a reality of its own. Let us not make it into an unreachable standard that separates us from ourselves and from others; or into a means to vengefully affirm superiority and grandeur; or into a way to evade the hard issues of life; or into an excuse for vicariously fulfilling immature needs; or into a reassuring but oppressive parent.

References

Assagioli, R. (1965). *Psychosynthesis.* New York: Hobbs & Dorman.

Attar, F. (1971) *The Conference of the Birds (Matiq ut-tair).* Boulder: Shambhala

Moszkowski, A. (1972). *Conversations with Einstein.* London: Sidgwick & Jackson.

Rosenfeld, E. (1973) *The Book of Highs: 250 Methods of Altering Your Consciousness Without Drugs.* Chicago: Quadrangle Books.

Rousseau, J. (1782), *Reveries of the Solitary Walker* (French: *Les Rêveries du promeneur solitaire*) reprint in English available from Penguin 1980.

Wells, H.G. (2007)"The Country of the Blind," in *The Country of the Bind and Other Stories.* New York: Penguin Classics

Notes

<hr>

1. "Simurg" means "30 birds" in Persian—*Ed.*
2. For the purpose of this paper, terms such as superconscious, transpersonal, spiritual, and Self will be considered synonymous.

Piero Ferrucci, *psychotherapist and philosopher, studied with Roberto Assagioli. He is the author of many articles and books, including* What We May Be: Techniques for Psychological and Spiritual Growth Through Psychosynthesis; Inevitable Grace: Breakthroughs in the Lives of Great Men and Women: Guides for Your Self-Realization; Beauty and the Soul: The Extraordinary Power of Everyday Beauty to Heal Your Life; The Power of Kindness: The Unexpected Benefits of Leading a Compassionate Life; *and* Your Inner Will: Finding Personal Strength in Critical Times. *He lives in Florence, Italy.*

Changing the Context of Change

Chris Robertson

My purpose in this paper is to explore the common ground between psychosynthesis and systemic therapies in developing a new psychology and a new epistemology of change. If you will start by considering two questions, the following discussion will be related to your experience. First, "Have you ever changed?" And second, "Have you ever stopped changing?" You may also want to be aware of your reactions as you consider these two questions. In doing so, you may experience some dissonance between the questions. This will be resolved when you realize that your answers are not contradictory but rather point to different levels of change. In any organization—chemical, biological, psychological—some levels may change while others remain stable. In the case of the human body, the content (the cells) are changing constantly, yet the form remains the same. Similarly, it is possible for you to have been involved in many changes and yet meet an old friend who says, "You haven't changed at all!"

In exploring the nature of change, we should bear two ideas in mind. First, we cannot easily describe change without specifying the level at which the change is occurring. Second, change is not something contradictory to stability. Change and stability always exist together as complementary polarities. I will develop this theme later, but first I want to expand on the idea of levels.

Levels of Change

Gregory Bateson (1973) gave a lot of attention to this idea in the area of education, suggesting that there were logically different levels of learning, each involving a different sort of change (p. 250). The basis for his theory was Russell's theory of logical types that pointed to the logical distinction between the member of a class and the class itself. Thus, in any hierarchy, we must be careful not to confuse levels within the hierarchy. For instance, to talk about changing a family and changing one of its members is to talk about different sorts of changes. In much the same way as Bateson did for education, I try below to set out a simple hierarchy of therapeutic change:

Level 1 is a change in a specific behavior such as practiced in behavior-modification techniques. As Bateson points out in relation to Pavlovian experiments, there is always a context for this simple kind of change, which makes it meaningful. In therapy, this context is the "why" of "why change?" At level 1, this context will be a belief or a construct of how life would be better with this change.

Level 2 is a change in a set of behaviors, which are controlled by a belief or a construct about how to operate in the world. An example of such a set might be "good manners." But, once again, there will be a context for this belief, and when this context is no longer adaptive; a person may need therapeutic help to understand what has happened. Insight or cognitive therapy is effective at this level, not just because it helps people make their beliefs more adaptive to their environment, but because it creates a larger context within which they can see their behavior as maladaptive.

Level 3 is a change in a set of beliefs, which are held within a worldview or paradigm. An example of such a change is the crisis experienced by a devoted mother when her children leave home and establish their own lives. Her sense of meaning in life and her identity, which may have been taken from mothering, are lost. Most depth therapies operate in this area. Although they use different methods, they follow the psychosynthesis principle of "disidentification"—that is, stepping back from a limiting identification (being a mother in this case) to arrive at a more inclusive sense of self that allows for new meanings to emerge. What many therapists miss, however, is access to the next level of context (level 4), which would provide some guidance as to what method would be suitable for this unique individual. By operating only at level 3, they are forced to classify the person's symptoms according to a certain category and treat him or her accordingly. Yet this is to commit an error of logical type. The only way to understand or reflect on level 3 is from a meta-level (i.e., level 4). For instance, mothers' experiences of letting go of their children are different and cannot be predicted from the situation. The meaning of the experience exists in relation to the mother's unique context, and this can only be understood from the meta-level.

Level 4 is a change in a set of paradigms or worldviews. Some have called this a meta-paradigm, but I believe this is a mistake because it still implies some identification, however inclusive. Level 4 is about not being identified in any worldview but rather being truly oneself. Work at this level does not strictly involve "therapy" so much as a spiritual discipline such as meditation. But level 4 is vital for therapists who wish to facilitate deep changes within a person in that it gives a context for changes at level 3. Of course, there is no logical reason to stop at level 4, though there is a problem of communicating in ordinary language what might lie beyond it. An example of level 4 change is provided by Arthur Deikman (1982) who relates the story of the man who knocks on God's door seeking admission:

> "Who is there?" God asks.
> "It is I."
> "Go away!" God replies.
> Sometime later, the person returns and knocks again.
> "Who is there?" God asks.
> "It is thou."
> "Enter," God replies.

Looking back over this scheme, we can see that not only is each higher level the context for the level below but that a change at a lower level need not affect this context. Thus a person may wish to change a particular belief that is causing a problem without wishing to change his or her whole worldview. Appreciating the different levels of change can help us as therapists to see both at what level clients want to change and at what level they want to remain the same. It may also help to clarify this for our clients, because when caught in a problem, they cannot easily move to the meta-position (the disidentified place) from which to "see" the problem. In fact, this limited perspective, I suggest, is what makes their issue "a problem." Often, moving levels to the larger context is enough for the issue to cease being "a problem" even if something still has to be done about it.

Guidelines for a New Psychology

That it is *the context*—or the lack of it—that creates the problem is an important idea in the new psychology of change. Watzlawick (1974) and the Palo Alto Group have described this as the "Gentle Art of Reframing." A lot of their brief therapy consists in dissolving problems by redefining the context in which the problem has originally been perceived. For the traditional therapists, it may seem that nothing has really changed—no insight, no catharsis, no working through—yet often there is a clear difference for the clients.

What Watzlawick shows is that a problem cannot be isolated because it is part of an interconnected pattern that is maintaining itself (see Weakland, Fisch, & Watzlawick, 1974). Problems become "problems" either because they have been developed to some advantage or because previous attempts to solve them have actually exacerbated the issue, making it a "problem." Thus the therapist's straightforward attempts to help are usually met by so-called resistance. For instance, any attempt to help a depressed client see the positive side of life is liable to increase the client's depression. This is true even when the client seems to want to cooperate with the therapist's help. "Resistance" to therapeutic change often occurs when the therapist has accepted the problem as defined by the client rather than understanding the wider system to which the "problem" belongs.

In order to change the working of such a system, its underlying assumptions need to be gently shifted. Although Watzlawick does consider the therapist's attitude and assumptions to be part of the system, he does not take this far enough. I suggest that there is an underlying cultural assumption about the nature of change that maintains a collusive system in many therapeutic relationships. Most simply put, this assumption is that the therapist is an agent of change who can somehow work on the patient to produce the desired effect. This Newtonian notion of change is deeply rooted in our Western consciousness, and through the rise of technology, it has achieved remarkable success. Yet, in the practice of therapy, it contains three fallacious conceptions. These underlie the old psychology of change:

1. that entities can be separately isolated
2. that there can be a linear sequence of cause and effect; and
3. that the Self is an object.

Within the new psychology of change, these conceptions can be reformulated as powerful guidelines to therapeutic practice:

4. that the therapist is always part of the system he or she is attempting to change. This means that the therapist needs to be willing to evolve with the system and to be aware of the strange position he or she holds—being both within the system and outside it. As Bateson says, "The evolution of the horse from *eohippus* was not a one-sided adjustment to life on the grassy

21

plains ... Turf was the evolving response of the vegetation to the evolution of the horse. It is the *context* which evolves" (Weakland et al., 1974, p. 178). So it should be in the therapeutic relationship—the context evolves through reciprocal interaction between therapist and client.

5. that the client's problem is not caused by some past event but rather is maintained in the present. Thus, no one is to blame for the problem, and the norms of pathology are not helpful in understanding the client's need for the problem. More important still, therapy is not a game the therapist can win by defeating the "resistance" of the client. At the least, this means that the therapist needs to get out of the way of the evolving process, and at best, that he or she can cooperate with what Peggy Penn (1982) has called "co-evolution."

6. that the Self is not an object whose behavior can be predicted by Newtonian laws. As Bateson (1973) points out, what is being transferred from one human being to another is not energy but information, and the way this information is received is unpredictable. Thus, as therapists, we need to beware our tendency to impose our solutions, our expectations, as to where our clients should be going. Whereas therapists can often get away with their "helpful" solutions when operating on levels 1 and 2, they become mere obstacles on levels 3 and 4. Deikman (1982) has suggested an interesting polarity between the "object mode" and the "receptive mode" of awareness (see also Assagioli, 1974, p. 128). The receptive mode, dealing with process, non-realization, simultaneity, and paralogic, thus seems more in keeping with the new psychology of change. It means the therapist needs to be more receptive to the emerging or evolving context, using his or her presence as the major tool for transformation.

As useful as receptivity is in practice, it does not take us to the central issue. We know that the Self is the subject, and yet how can we express the causality of this subject (free will) without falling back into old epistemological errors? By dealing with the Self as only an "observing Self," Deikman limits its characteristics to those of awareness. The Eastern mystical traditions from which he draws have always placed the accent on the introspective character of the Self, whereas in the West, we have focused too exclusively on its dynamic character. Within the old paradigm, this has given us the notion of isolated egos in competition with other egos in the "survival of the fittest." But to move into the paradigm does not mean we have to give up the conception of our own causality; rather, it means we have to see it within a new context.

The Therapist's New Position

Assagioli, in *The Act of Will* (1974), is careful to point out the value of unique individual expression as participation in a universal state of being. He quotes Radhakrishnan as saying: "The peculiar privilege of the human self is that he can consciously join and work for the whole and embody in his own life the purpose of the whole" (p. 128). Embodying the whole within a part is a well-known phenomenon in groups and has recently been given a lot of attention in the use of Bohm's "holographic" metaphor. Yet, within systemic therapy, there is still a tendency to exclude the individual factor as if it were a fall-back to the old paradigm. It is as if some systemic thinkers had seized on the "system" as an exclusive truth rather than as a more inclusive context for perception. This is evident in the way the "Milan Model" can become rigidified around the concepts of "circularity" and "neutrality." Thus the Milan Group writes: "That which we call circularity is therefore our conscious-ness, or better yet, our conviction of being able to obtain from the family authentic information only if we work with the following fundamentals: (1) information is a difference and (2) difference is a relationship" (Selvini, 1980). While it may be true that in families, which want to keep the appearance of "sameness" (such as the schizophrenic families studied by the Milan Group), information will be in differences and this will help to define relationships, one can easily imagine other families where *similarities* provide information about relationships.

The Milan Group's concept of neutrality fits well with my third guideline with respect to not imposing any expectation and not trying to make anyone change; however, it can become a defensive stance, which actually prevents the therapist from making significant contact. It is as if in their efforts to avoid linear thinking and the enmeshment of the therapist, they become controlled by the very thing they wish to avoid.

The point I am making is that the new psychology of change cannot be "achieved" through exclusion or attempting to build methodologies which technically simulate how therapists "ought" to be. No therapist can truly remain at a meta-level as the Milan Group would like. Nor should we attempt to exclude the Self of the therapist, for that is the most valuable tool at his or her disposal. What we need to understand is the nature of the therapist's involvement in the new paradigm.

Psychosynthesis has a lot to offer this new way of thinking about the therapeutic relationship through its understanding of the Will. Assagioli has written of the therapist (or guide)[1] as the external unifying center for the client. The question is: Center of what? In levels 1 and 2, and to some extent 3, this may be taken to mean the center of the personality. Within the old paradigm, this meant a new, more positive approach to the phenomenon of transference—the therapist acting as an ideal model (ego ideal) for the client. But when we come to the transition between levels 3 and 4, this no longer makes sense. We can only understand "Center of what?" within the new paradigm. The therapist/guide acts as a center for the new context, which remains "implicate" (David Bohm's concept) for the client. He or she becomes, as it were, the channel for this new context to become "explicate" and thus for new opportunities to become available to the client. Thus, we could say that the therapist/guide is attuned to the evolving context, or the means by which it can start to express itself.

The skill of evoking the emerging property (the *nova*) in any system is not something that can be made technical. It comes through the individual therapist's own sensitivity to the developing context of the therapeutic relationship. It also comes with the shift in the therapist's experience of Will from that of a separate causative agent toward that of the impulse of wholeness. Thus, the effectiveness of this new position for the therapist does not rely on individual power but on cooperating synergistically with the direction of change.

It is strange that it has taken a physicist, Ilya Prigogine, working with unstable chemical systems, to remind us that living systems evolve toward less probable states. As Paul Dell (1982) pointed out, living systems are not controlled by the cybernetic notion of homeostasis. They do have an ordering principle but it is not a cybernetic one because it evolves to higher states of order through non-equilibrium. What I am suggesting is that the *transpersonal will* is this non-equilibrium ordering principle.

Assagioli (1974) notes that the integrative and organizing capacity of Will is its most important function. Giving the example of the body as a system, he asks, "What is the unifying principle that makes this possible? Its real nature escapes us; we can only call it *Life*; but something can be said of its qualities and ways of operating. These have been variously called co-ordination, interaction, or organic synthesis." Assagioli goes on to talk about syntropy and negentropy as being both the mathematical descriptions of this principle and the specific characteristics of the Will. He writes, "We need not discuss how the unifying synergetic force operates at biological levels. What matters is to realize that we can be aware of its higher manifestations in the conscious human being, and also at transpersonal levels" (pp. 32-34).

This area is obviously a fruitful one for further thinking and research by those involved in systemic therapy and in psychosynthesis. What I hope to have shown in this short paper is that the evolution of living systems cannot be considered a random process any more than it can be considered a linear program. Yet some systemic therapists seem so frightened of the old teleology that they fail to see the purposeful direction of unfolding that characterizes human beings. Thus what we need to work toward is not so much a circular epistemology as a spiral one (see deVries, 1981). For whereas a circular approach to change (i.e., a non-change approach) may well unblock resistances developed by clients to previous therapeutic attempts to produce a change, it thereby only sets the scene for a transformation. Important though this is, it is not a purposeful context for change. In fact, its effectiveness comes from its lack of "purpose," or "goal directedness," as it used to be referred to in the old paradigm. To really change the context of change, we need not only to break out of the old paradigm; we need to be born into the new one. This certainly means letting go of our old conscious "purposes," but it also means opening to the transpersonal purpose that is attempting to break through in all evolving systems.

References

Assagioli, R. (1974). *The Act of Will*. Colorado Springs: Wildwood.

Bateson, G. (1973). *Steps to an Ecology of Mind*. Boulder: Paladin.

Deikman, A, J. (1982), *The Observing self—Mysticism and Psychotherapy*. Boston: Beacon.

Dell, P. (1982). Beyond Homeostasis. *Family Process*, 21.

De Vries, M. (1981). *The Redemption of the Intangible in Medicine. Psychosynthesis Monographs*. London: Institute of Psychosynthesis.

Penn, P. (1982). Circular Questioning. *Family Process*, 21, 267-280.

Selvini, P. B. (1980). Hypothesizing—Circularity—Neutrality: Three Guidelines for the Conductor of the Session. *Family Process*, 19,3-12.

Watzlawick, P. (1974). *Change: The principles of Problem Formation and Problem Resolution*. New York: W.W. Norton.

Weakland, Fisch, Watzlawick, & Bodin. (1974). Brief Therapy: Focused Problem Resolution. *Family Process*, 13, 141-168.

This article was slightly revised by the author in 2017.

Note

---

[1] "Guide" is perhaps a more appropriate concept for the worker in the new paradigm as the original meaning of *"therapia"* as service has become degenerate in modern usage.

Chris Robertson, MPhil, DipPsych, *has been a psychotherapist and trainer since 1978. He is the co-author of* Emotions and Needs *(OUP 2002), a co-founder of* Re-Vision *and co-creator of* Borderlands and the Wisdom of Uncertainty, *which in 1989 became the subject of a BBC documentary. He works in London, is involved with the* Climate Psychology Alliance *and in developing psychotherapy's relevance to culture change. He authored the chapter "Dangerous Margins" in the anthology* Vital Signs *(Karnac 2012) and the articles "Ecopsychology's Wilding" (PPI 2013), "The Numinous Psyche" IJP (Vol. 18, 2012), "Hungry Ghosts" (Self & Soc. 2014) and "Well-being of Misfortune: Accepting Ecological Disaster" (CPA 2015).*

Treating Mental and Emotional Abuse

Victoria Tackett

Much clinical counseling work consists of alleviating the mental anguish and emotional suffering inflicted on individuals in their interpersonal relationships. If the client is female, her self-esteem has very often been damaged by a multitude of sexist insults and societal misassumptions about her appearance, ability, potential, and worth. If the client is male, he may have been judged as lacking, measured against stereotypically high expectations, or emotionally injured by the cultural admonition against the male expression of a full range of feelings. In a society that claims to value and encourage individuality, individuals are denied their inalienable rights at home, at school, and at work—sometimes in subtle and insidious ways. In a society that claims to love its children and support the family unit, homes and families are dissolving at an alarming rate. Add to this the overwhelming visage of nuclear destruction, planetary pollution, and economic instability and it is no wonder that the stress has made us apathetic toward one another. And yet, the problem of psychological abuse and alienation in America is of such major proportions that it must be addressed if life is to be worth living at all.

Socially inflicted hurts and rejections occur with such frequency that they are now considered an expected part of daily life. Marriages have become battlegrounds. Children are not adequately cared for. Authoritarian professors, physicians, and bosses are endured. Politicians are assumed to be dishonest. Television producers parody these situations and sell them as entertainment. Comedians attempt to make us laugh about it. And we all know, from our own experience, that the situation is critical.

The problems of physical separation, loneliness, and alienation have become extreme—so much so that Ma Bell has found it necessary, as well as lucrative, to encourage us to "reach out and touch someone." [1] The problem of mental abuse is so commonplace that a nationwide bank promotes its services with the statement: "We'll treat you with respect, concern, and understanding. But don't worry, you'll get used to it." And the dire problem of emotional abuse of children in the United States prompted a national media campaign to remind us that "it shouldn't hurt to be a child." Apparently, we had forgotten.

To anesthetize these interpersonal wounds, we are rapidly becoming a nation of addicts. Across the nation people confess addictions to everything from alcohol, to cigarettes, to illicit and prescription drugs of all kinds, to food, to work, to jogging and other sports, to power, to sex, and even to love—all attempting to ease the need for personal support and spiritual sustenance and block the psychological pain of alienation and abuse. When this pain cannot be suppressed, some react by becoming even more psychologically abusive, while others, seeing no solution for their pain, take their own lives. Human beings are much more sensitive and complex than we care to admit.

Although our courts do not, as yet, consider mental and emotional abuse as crime, counselors see the crippling results in their offices on a daily basis. Even when physical or sexual abuse is also reported, the associated mental and emotional injury is often what lingers on and remains in need of healing. The matter-of-fact way in which innocent young hearts and minds are ridiculed, hurt, and betrayed results in producing apparently functional adults who are unable to trust, love, or provide stable home environments for their own children.

It is difficult to admit the extent of this problem in human relations because we have all been wounded, and we have all hurt someone else at some point in our lives. We are able to admit complicity after we have changed our point of view and can re-examine the interaction, and our participation, in a new light. Then we may experience shame, remorse, and the desire for forgiveness or reconciliation. Only then can honest apologies and amends be made to those we have hurt through ignorance. When we are humbled by the recognition of our past mistakes toward others, to have our apology accepted acts as a natural healing agent for ourselves and for those we have hurt. These wounds do not seem to heal simply with time. Interpersonally inflicted wounds are best healed within an interpersonal context of love and genuine care.

Forms of Abuse

Ultimately, the line between healthy and abusive interaction is not merely one of degree, but of quality and kind. Healthy interactions are different from abusive ones; that difference can be felt and understood. However, acknowledging that difference is a matter of social awareness, education, personal sensitivity, and environmental support. Those social assaults to the mind and feelings that are inflicted intentionally, those that are extreme or acute, or those that are subtly insidious and are repeated over time can all be defined in the clinical setting, without question, as psychological "abuse."

For purposes of clarification and study, psychological abuse can be stated as taking two forms: (1) mental abuse and (2) emotional abuse. In daily interactions, mental and emotional abuse most often occur simultaneously, and may be expressed either verbally or non-verbally. As well as being a betrayal of the body, physical abuse, rape, and sexual molestation always have with them a psychologically abusive component. Alternatively, when one's highest ideals, religious convictions, or spiritual experiences are ridiculed or refuted, this increases self-doubt and it is then that spiritual orthodoxy becomes psychological abuse. Below, examples of mentally abusive tactics are given, followed by examples of emotionally abusive behavior.

In mentally abusive interactions, people are harmed by being treated as objects, or by being lied to or otherwise deceived. Mental abusiveness creates extreme cognitive dissonance. It is often based on things that individuals cannot change such as their race, gender, sexual orientation, appearance, weight, body type, age, disability, intelligence, financial status, or ethnic heritage. Racism, sexism, homophobia, bigotry, and other class distinctions are all forms of mental abuse. They are used to rationalize mistreatment, unfair employment practices, and inequity. At best, this prejudice is personally demeaning; at worst, it leads to genocide, homicide, and suicide.

The Western overvaluation of the scientific method, rationality, and analytic thinking—besides limiting creative possibilities—becomes abusive when it is used to discredit visionary or intuitive functioning. Many minds are wounded in our educational institutions: bright and intelligent people are judged as stupid because they are able to think synthetically, seeing first the whole, then extrapolating the relationship between levels and parts, rather than coming to conclusions in a step-by-step analytic fashion. Intuitive thinking is often met with skepticism and misgiving, causing considerable pain and rejection of visionary insight at a time when the world is in need of new visions.

Lies and deceptions are the most common form of mental abuse used in everyday interpersonal interactions. Being blatantly lied to—whether by advertisers, politicians, or loved ones—is a cause of confusion, anguish, and mistrust. Lying behavior may also take indirect forms such as evasiveness, secrecy, duplicity, withholding information, chronic ambivalence, and the use of covert statements that make the truth hard to ascertain. Not knowing the truth, it is difficult to take affirmative action. Widespread fear, uncertainty, and insecurity may be a natural reaction to this pervasive cultural habit of lying.

Other techniques of mental abuse include extreme mental dominance, callous arrogance, and unrelenting one-upmanship. Overcontrol, the enforcement of impossibly rigorous expectations, obsessive or convoluted stories designed to "win" at all costs, brainwashing methods, and semantic rigidity used against another to limit inquiry are but a few more examples.

To be lied to, or persecuted, or refused respect is very damaging. Such mental abuses, commonplace in interpersonal relationships, educational and professional institutions, and social groups of all kinds, are unjust and painful. In our culture, this pain is seldom acknowledged. Yet widespread mental abuse points to a crisis in our personal and cultural values. If, as individuals and as a society, we value only youth, then one automatically loses one's value early, after youth has passed. If it is popular to believe that one can be neither too rich nor too thin, then we look down on those without money and create a climate where cosmetic surgery and fad diets are a major industry and young girls die of anorexia. As a nation we spend millions of dollars on non-essentials while many of our neighbors are homeless, hungry, and destitute. If we remain intent on looking out for "Number One," then who is to care for the children and for those who are temporarily unable to care for themselves? If we only value life in the fast lane, then we are bound by frenetic activity in which there is no place for a rich and meaningful inner life. As we lose a sense of deeper values, addictions and abuses flourish. In this context, the existence of pervasive mental abuse demands a conscious re-examination of, and change in, popular cultural values.

While mental abuses tend to discount, confuse, or demean, emotional abuses are experienced more personally—on the feeling level. They are frequently described in the same language and metaphors used to describe physical wounds. This may be due, in part, to the fact that emotionally abusive interactions evoke and are accompanied by physical indicators such as instantaneous headache, nausea, the breath being held, a feeling of being "hit" in the solar plexus, the heart "breaking," or heartbeat racing in fear. Why is it that emotional abuse has such an overall effect? It is because humans are feeling beings.

In emotionally abusive interactions, the natural feeling bond that takes place between human beings is either denied, misused, severed, ignored, or negated. Some studies indicate that this human bonding is necessary for survival. Infants have been known to die without it. In adulthood, the lack of such bonds appears to weaken the immune system. We are indeed feeling beings, and as such are bonded to one another—for better or for worse.

Emotional abuse is particularly hurtful and unsettling when it occurs within the intimate bonds of trust inherent in marital and familial relationships. We are harmed when we experience threats to these emotional bonds in the form of insults, degradation, cruelty, ridicule, criticism, "put-downs," verbal assaults, and intimidation from those who are supposed to love us. It is unfortunate that the family is often the place where emotionally abusive behavior is first learned. Emotional abuses experienced in childhood become a devastating legacy for the entire nation—for the betrayal of trust between parent and child leads the abused child to re-create similarly dysfunctional relationships in adult life, and the problem of emotional abuse expands exponentially.

Dominance and forced submission, harassment, and public or private humiliations are psychologically abusive and lower self-esteem. Both mental abuses and emotional threats may seem relatively minor when assessed incident by incident; they may even seem a normal part of growing up. But when taken collectively, or when repeated with recurrent frequency over time, they definitely become injurious. Emotion-laden projection, volatility, moodiness, inconsistencies, emotional manipulation, violent, chaotic, and unpredictable behavior are all ways in which the emotional bonding between individuals is misused. The withholding of love or approval, ignoring another, refusing affection, threats of abandonment, forced isolation, and other emotional deprivations are examples of how this natural human bond is negated or denied.

In situations or relationships in which emotional abuse is prevalent, there are typically periodic demonstrations of the abuser's superiority, of coldness, of anger, or of the potential for violence. These displays are coupled with occasional indulgences and periods of kindness and affection. Unfortunately, in the context of emotional tyranny, these indulgences prove to be abusive rather than kind—they feed the illusion that the emotional bonding has not actually been damaged or severed by the abuse, when, in fact, it has.

The pervasiveness of psychological abuse in our culture calls us to reexamine not only our societal values, but all of our social relations—whether between governments, co-workers, family members, or women and men—in light of our socially moral and ethical stance. Throughout the world, the United States is perceived, not as a democratic society, but as a capitalistic society that values money above all else. It is revealing that most of the words in the English language that exemplify an ethical or moral commitment to other human beings have fallen into disuse in everyday conversation. Words like loyal, kind, courteous, just, moral, conscientious, decent, principled, honorable, faithful, reliable, ethical, constant, integrity—all seem to describe a bygone era in which life was both simple and (to us?) boring. Are we, as a people, so addicted to the new, the improved, and the exciting that we have lost a sense of interpersonal ethics? Have we become blind to the effects on human life of our self-gratifying choices? If we are to put an end to further psychological abuse so that the quality of our lives is improved, these questions must be honestly answered.

It is now recognized that psychological abuse can occur in any human interaction in which there is a real, or perceived, power difference. Mental and emotional abusiveness by those seen as more powerful, and compliance by the others in the system, has been widely accepted as the norm. In counseling offices across the country, a multitude of abuses of social and personal power are being revealed by those who have been personally injured and are in need of healing. Resignation to the "pecking-order" is currently being challenged, and hierarchical structures of all kinds are being scrutinized for abuses of power.

When amends are not made, understanding and compassion are often sought by individuals in counseling sessions. Sadly, mentally and emotionally abused clients also report abuses from professionals they have previously consulted. It is therefore extremely important that the therapist, teacher, priest, physician, attorney, or other professional, acting for a time as mentor, take great care not to further victimize the client through a misguided (though well-meaning) attitude, belief system, language, style, or approach.

Treating Abused Clients

An individual whose trust has been repeatedly betrayed by being lied to, humiliated or demeaned is no longer sure of what is true. Once labeled as "neurotic," the abused client comes to counseling in a state of pained confusion and low self-esteem now clinically defined as "learned helplessness." Self-esteem is a result of having confidence in one's own perceptions, feelings, and sensations. Psychologically abused individuals who live within a culture that denies abuse commonly enter treatment with low self-esteem.

Some presenting symptoms that can alert the clinician to possible psychological abuse are self-condemnation, doubt, hopelessness, depression, lack of confidence, low energy, lack of direction and motivation, and a variety of physical complaints such as breathing difficulties, headaches, or digestion problems. These symptoms may appear to the professional to be due to any number of personal intrapsychic problems.

Often, these clients have already consulted physicians who can find no physiological basis for their symptoms. They may have been prescribed mood-altering medications as a palliative measure. The possibility of psychological abuse has probably been ignored. All of the presenting symptoms may, however, appear wholly as a result of abusive acculturation, and are not necessarily a sign of neurosis or personal psychological disturbance. In these cases, the counselor would do well to inquire into the possibility of mental or emotional abuse as a causative factor.

If abuse is suspected, the counselor should begin whatever detective work is necessary to uncover the source of the difficulty. It is important to find out who abused the client—parent, spouse, sibling, co-worker, friend, therapist, boss, neighbor, or other intimate—when, and how. It is then valuable to acknowledge the source of abuse and actually name it as abuse so that denial can be overcome and the client can know that his or her report is believed. This acknowledgement builds self-esteem because, when correctly ascertained, it corresponds to the client's lived experience, thus providing the previously missing validation. Only after the outer abuse is acknowledged can questions of inner compliance be intelligently addressed.

The validation of factual information is empowering simply because it acknowledges the truth of what actually happened. From admitting the truth, the client again begins to build trust and self-esteem. Feelings of self-worth re-emerge. The power that the abuse has held over the individual's life is recognized, thus enabling him or her to become the "survivor" of the situation. He or she no longer feels compelled to be a part of the cultural conspiracy of silence that surrounds psychological abuse. Sometimes the client is able to confront the abuser. Even when confrontation is not possible or appropriate, these clients learn that they need no longer tolerate psychological abuse from others.

Stages of Healing

The social interactions of modem life afford many opportunities both for psychological enrichment and for psychological injury. Some people are able to withstand such injuries to a greater degree than are others. These people generally have a support system of understanding friends to help them through difficult times. Others, however, reach a limit in which their former ability to cope with recurrent insults and rejections is no longer adequate. As a general rule, these people close down emotionally, become cynical, withdraw from intimate social contacts, or become abusive themselves. Or they seek help through counseling hoping to deal with their problems and put an end to the pain.

Like those with physical wounds, those with psychological wounds go through various stages in the process of healing. In treatment, an individual may stay several months (or even years) in one stage, be in a different stage from one session to the next, or change stages within a single counseling session. Counseling interventions, to be helpful, must be stage-specific, as will be explained below. I have observed seven distinct stages of healing in my 15 years of practice as a psychosynthesis guide. They are offered here as a guideline for psychologically abused individuals, as well as for those who counsel them. The need for mental and emotional healing that is being addressed here presupposes the occurrence of an intolerable number of interpersonal wounds in an individual's life.

Stage 1—The first stage of healing can be called "Coping." This is the stage in which survival is the major motivator. Typical in this stage is a sense of overresponsibility, self-blame, denial, guilt, shame, fear, silent grief, extreme stress, attempts to gain control, or an inappropriate grandiosity in which the abused individual imagines having greater power over the situation than is possible. When clients enter counseling at this stage, the issues to be addressed are very basic ones: personal safety, elimination of self-blame, physical health, nutrition, exercise, social support systems, work, and financial stability.

Stage 2—The second stage is that of "Awakening" to the abuse. In this stage, there is a need for a great deal of honest self-disclosure, and for a reporting of wounding experiences in a non-judgmental environment. In Stage 2, clients admit, perhaps for the first time, that they have been abused. They often need to ventilate feelings of anger, outrage, and sadness. In this stage of the healing process, it is appropriate for clients to condemn the abuser, become active on behalf of themselves and others in similar situations, and express open grief for what has been lost. Self-validation is begun at this point. New injuries experienced when the client is in this stage of healing are deeply felt, and can serve to keep the client in Stage 2 for an extended length of time. This stage of emerging awareness is clearly marked by a recognition that things are not the way they seem. This is the stage that breaks through the pattern of denial.

Stage 3—In the third stage, "Patterning," the intrapsychic patterns of the client's life are recognized and addressed. These can include issues of truthfulness, trust, control, co-dependence, responsibility, love, self-esteem, boundaries, spontaneity, risk, commitment, will, assertion, spiritual surrender, patience, forgiveness, and self-nurture. This is the stage in which the major personal therapeutic work is done, assisting abused clients to discover their own self-limiting patterns and to come to an understanding of their own truths.

Stage 4—The fourth stage can be called "Transformation." This is the stage in which the slow process of self-acceptance is begun in earnest. The client comes to accept both limitation and potential in Stage 4. Forgiveness toward the abuser may occur, accompanied by the realization that this forgiveness releases resentment and is a part of the healing process. A spiritual perspective naturally emerges when this stage is not prematurely forced. With this comes a suspension of old belief systems and a greater acceptance of life as it is.

Stage 5—In the fifth stage, "Integration," the patterns worked through in Stage 3 come up again to be fully integrated into the client's daily life, but in a new way. This stage can be disheartening when it is not understood. There is a tendency to mistake it for a setback. In fact, in psychosynthesis counseling work, the fifth stage results in active co-operation with the will of the Self and is considered quite positive. At this stage of healing, it is useful for the counselor to help the client cultivate a sense of proportion and the capacity to hold paradox.

Stage 6—The sixth stage is that of "Synthesis." In this stage, individuals who have been mentally and emotionally abused begin to see their relationship to the abuse in a new way, and the problem is then perceived as the "gift" that has led them on the path of self-discovery. The former abuse, though remembered and important, is no longer an issue. At the sixth stage, there is a gratitude for the truth and the new life that has emerged from the abusive experience. There is a deepening and greater appreciation of life. Here real acceptance takes place.

Stage 7—In the last stage, "Healing," the abuse is just one of many events of the past. The client's focus is now on the present and the future. Taking the lessons learned about themselves, other people, and the world, clients go forward, with greater wisdom, acceptance, and capacities for discernment. At this stage, the healing cycle is complete.

However well-meaning, counselors can be harmful to psychologically damaged clients by remaining unaware of the stages outlined here. Some approaches to therapy that utilize a specific technique or method are excellent for clients in a particular stage of healing, but may prove detrimental if the client is in another stage. For instance, a Stage 3 therapy intervention is not really useful for a client still at Stage 1, as it only magnifies the tendency to overresponsibility and self-blame. In addition, interventions appropriate for a client at Stage 6 are wholly inappropriate for a client currently at Stage 2. Counseling is rarely initiated at Stage 4 or 6, so methods useful at these stages are not immediately beneficial for beginning work-even when the client aspires to view life from a "spiritual" perspective. It is important to remember that an intervention which is not stage-specific can, in fact, be harmful.

When we contemplate abuses in counseling, we first think of sexual seduction or financial misconduct. However, clients more often report abuses of a psycho-social nature. Counselors are only human. In a sexist society, they must be consciously trained to view social interaction in nonsexist terms. In a hierarchical society, they must learn egalitarianism. These things are not often learned in the context of professional training, nor are they required for licensing. They must be learned in the field.

Some counseling trainees are still taught in school that the recipient of abuse is, in all probability, the covert victimizer. Those who are abused are considered responsible for the abuse by "asking for," encouraging, or, in the popular theory of secondary gain, even enjoying being abused. The social inequity in which the abuse is taking place is not seen as relevant. If not considered directly responsible for their own abuse, mentally and emotionally abused clients are judged responsible indirectly for putting up with it. Those who "blame the victim," as this attitude is now termed, subtly collude with the abuser, and by doing so, further damage the self-esteem of an already psychologically abused individual. Such outdated notions are not in line with current findings and are in need of revision.

Even in the newer transpersonally-oriented counselor training, there are certain philosophical assumptions that prove detrimental to clients who have been previously mentally or emotionally abused. Particularly troublesome is the concept, "there is no victim, no victimizer." The idea of no-fault abuse is, for the wounded client, blatantly untrue and adds to the ever-present tendency to deny and repress. This idea is often elaborated to suggest that all experiences, no matter how horrible, were, in fact, "chosen" by the client, and that he or she is 100 percent responsible for creating the abusive reality. The intention of this philosophy is self-empowerment. However, in practice with psychologically wounded clients, this attitude actually is the spiritualized version of "blaming the victim." For those clients not yet free from the effects of abuse, this concept leads to further self-flagellation, frustration, depression, self-doubt, guilt, diminished self-esteem, and feeds into the inappropriate grandiosity common within the early coping mechanisms that deny that abuse is a problem. Others question why they have chosen to "draw to themselves" such abuse. Accepting the idea of a completely self-created reality, abused clients label themselves hopelessly neurotic. As part of the denial, they may continue an abusive relationship, imagining quite unrealistically that they have the power to change it since they created it, that they can transcend the pain, or that when they "get" what they need to learn from the situation, the abuse will stop. While a positive attitude can always be of help, the truth is that with greater tolerance, psychological abuse does not stop—it escalates over time. Psychosynthesis theory would suggest that total responsibility is simply the polarity of no responsibility, and that the truth is found elsewhere.

Responsibility is said to be "response-ability," or the ability to respond. Clients who have been chronically abused have a weakened or diminished ability to respond on their own behalf, and so they seek assistance. They must be listened to and given appropriate help, without imposed concepts.

Victim-blaming attitudes are not new. They were originally incorporated into western psychology by Freud, who blamed incest victims for their own seduction, and discounted reports of familial rape as fantasized wish-fulfillment, leaving the more powerful adult beyond reproach, and the child-victim psychologically victimized as well. We now know that forced incest is a social reality, yet the absurd conclusion that the child is somehow responsible for its occurrence is still held as valid in orthodox psychoanalytic practice. Even more insidious, and more difficult to prove otherwise, are victim-blaming attitudes toward those who have been psychologically raped. Unfortunately, in our society, and therefore in our traditional graduate training of professional counselors, those who exploit the less powerful are not usually considered the problem.

There is never any reasonable justification for mental or emotional abuse, no matter how provocative one might judge the child or adult victim to be. It makes us all uncomfortable to admit the possibility that there might be abusive people among us, that our own abusiveness may not have been justified, that as adults we really are accountable for our own behavior. We seem to have a kind of "emperor's new clothes" mentality, protecting powerful individuals by denying their nakedness. Because of this, attitudes which blame the less powerful for their own abuse are pervasive in our culture. Those who are called upon to intervene therapeutically, in abuse cases in particular, must be completely free of all victim-blaming attitudes.

Similarly, because mentally and emotionally abused clients have been injured by those who have taken a position of dominance over them, approaches in which the counselor acts as the "expert," the authority, the harsh confronter, or the behavior-modifier are not useful. Abused clients need to be drawn out with compassion and respect; not pushed, confronted, or told what to do. They must learn to become their own authority.

The Psychosynthesis Approach

Because mental and emotional abuse is so pervasive, and because its scars are invisible except in times of stress, it is not easy to recognize or to understand it. Through its broad-based, client-centered, non-judgmental approach, psychosynthesis counseling can provide this understanding. In Psychosynthesis, the client remains his or her own expert. Over 75 years of clinical research continues to convince psychosynthesis practitioners that even the most eloquent theories are only guidelines for actual clinical work. Every case is unique; practitioners learn from each client.

Psychosynthesis practitioners are called "guides," as that most accurately describes the facilitative work that is done. The guide simultaneously leads and follows the healing process, being actively present to this process without attempting to modify or control it. In addition to clinical counseling and psychotherapy, psychosynthesis-oriented consultants work within many vocations such as education, medicine, business, the arts, law, social services, international relations, and the clergy. If we are to alleviate mental and emotional abuse, this multidisciplinary approach is invaluable.

Psychosynthesis guides are trained to evoke and to trust the individual's inner guiding principle, called the Self, as the expert witness in his or her life. By referring to the Self, the guide is always able to see hope, no matter how frightening, painful, or horrific the client's experience of abuse. The guide remains aware that there is much more to the individual than his or her history of victimization. For psychologically abused clients, this perspective itself, which accommodates the pain of abuse while adding a broader context, is healing.[2]

The characteristically broad perspective of Psychosynthesis encourages self-help through self-acceptance. The elimination of denial and the development of self-acceptance are crucial in healing psychological wounds for both victims and perpetrators of abuse. With recognition and acceptance, the stages of the healing process are allowed to unfold in their own time and in their own way. Trusting the individual process of each client rather than following one particular method proves, paradoxically, to be an efficient method of treatment. Change has been observed to occur in a timely fashion when the natural rhythm of each person is honored. Clients who have been repeatedly mentally and emotionally battered are not accustomed to this degree of loving interest and respect. They are nourished by such treatment and are quick to respond.

Because the psychological wounds of each person are different, there is no universal formula for treatment. The psychosynthesis approach proves especially effective for victims of mental and emotional abuse in its recognition of this fact and in the multiplicity of techniques available for use within the counseling session. The techniques specific to Psychosynthesis, learning self-trust and disidentification, balancing and synthesizing polarities, and developing a sense of personal values, are particularly meaningful to these clients. Guides are taught many methods for centering the Self and for accessing their own inner guidance. These techniques are described in the psychosynthesis training literature.

Though individual guides may be more proficient with, or prefer using, some techniques over others, they are not wedded to a specific method and to its limitations. Inner dialogue, visualization, meditation, guided imagery, grief work, assertion training, gestalt technique, couples counseling, interpersonal communication, family systems work, art therapy, feminist education, massage, will training, spiritual development, and existential dialogue have all been used successfully in the treatment of the wounds of psychological abuse,

I have also had success with the few self-defined abusers I have had the opportunity to counsel. As they proved to have been abused as children, they benefited from comparable methods of treatment in their psychosynthesis sessions. Their greatest need was to heal from the psychological scars of their own childhoods. Except in cases of genuine social pathology or dire biochemical imbalance, abusive behavior may be a reaction to previous abuse, and can be considered a learned behavior. Some of these clients also displayed addictive/co-dependent tendencies. Both addictive and enabling behaviors may be ineffective means for trying to cope with psychological abuse and alienation. Through psychological introjection, this could also be the case with psychologically self-abusive behaviors such as excessive self-criticism, guilt, and perfectionism. When these wounds are healed, positive changes take place.

Stopping Abusive Interactions

Mental and emotional abuse is ultimately stopped by a change within the abuser, not by a change within the abused. As in any system, change on the part of one participant does have some effect; when abusers are reported or rejected by their victims, they do take notice of that fact. However, victims of abuse do not have the power themselves to change abusers or to change their psychologically abusive behaviors.

In cases of reported physical or sexual abuse, the perpetrator is most often an adult male. However, in cases of mental and emotional abuse, both men and women have been shown to be abusive. They may justify their abusiveness by seeing themselves at the mercy of outside provocation, or of uncontrollable moods. They believe that if others acted in line with their often unreasonable demands, there would be no need to be abusive to them. With this belief system in place, those who are repeatedly abusive continue to injure loved ones, employees, and even strangers, denying the need for change and refusing offers for intervention. This leaves those who must deal with them in a difficult position: stay and be abused, or leave the relationship. There is rarely room for negotiation.

Psychosynthesis may view the abusive individual as "stuck," perhaps for very understandable reasons, in a limiting personal identification. The pattern may often be one of emotional abuse in childhood resulting in a lost sense of integrity, values, and meaning. While seeking respect and needing love, they become isolated from others and are atheistic or spiritually empty as a result of their experience. They display either frozen or volatile feelings, causing others to act fearfully around them, offering co-dependent contrition. Rarely are they met straightforwardly as persons. Those abusers I have seen were very outwardly focused and seemed to lack introspection. They were reared in dysfunctional families or attended schools where they were severely punished or abused in the ways they abuse others. Those who become abusive are in need of deep healing. For most, unfortunately, this healing never takes place.

One abusive client who was assisted through a psychosynthesis approach was a black male in his forties, initially referred to me for counseling with his wife who complained of his violent temper, and worried that his harsh punishment of their adolescent son might cause permanent psychological scars. At work, the man was competent and personable, a top salesman for a major company, and reported no interpersonal problems there. Since the problem of his abusive behavior seemed to be focused on his family, counseling was done with this man individually, with him and his wife together, and with their seven-year-old daughter. The adolescent son refused to come.

The turning point occurred in a session in which a spontaneous form of guided hypno-therapeutic regression was utilized to access the history of the client's abusive behavior. In deep relaxation, he recalled that he had been physically and emotionally abused as a child. With deep feeling, he fully accepted this wounded Inner Child. He then remembered that his parents had been similarly abused, as were his grandparents on his mother's side of the family. (This information came from piecing together personal experience, family stories, and subconscious connections.) He revealed that both his great-grandparents and his great-great-grandparents were African slaves of American Confederate tobacco plantation owners in the South. As slaves, they were beaten and degraded and were, in turn, abusive to their own children. He then realized that the abusive behavior of his ancestors served their children as a form of insurance for survival on the plantation and in the slave markets into which they were sold or abducted. Those blacks who were strong-willed, independent, outspoken, or otherwise "uppity" were, in fact, killed. The client further became aware of the fact that, although the Emancipation Proclamation was signed over a century ago, his children were, in actuality, the first generation of his family to have the education, freedom of speech, and equality promised by the Constitution. His own children, unlike himself, were at last freed from the restraints of segregation and it was, therefore, no longer necessary for their survival to keep them "down." He experienced deep relief when he received this internal message.

Through the awareness gained in this psychosynthesis session, this client was able to stop his abusive behavior and ask forgiveness of his wife and children. It must be emphasized that this man had been personally damaged by cultural racism and that this most certainly contributed to his behavior toward his family. Recognition of that fact served to raise his self-esteem, allowed him to acknowledge his abusive behavior, and gave him more control over his own life.

Abusive interactions can sometimes be stopped by helping abusers become accountable for their mentally and emotionally abusive behaviors. Although not responsible for the abuse they received in childhood, they become responsible for the abuse they inflict on others in adulthood. Avoidance and denial serve no one. Some among us have become unwitting tyrants. If given socially sanctioned alternatives, a percentage of these people do take the opportunity to change unworkable patterns. Psychosynthesis, with its emphasis on developing potential, proves to be a particularly useful approach for those ready for self-responsible change.

Case Study

The case history that follows is taken from a psychosynthesis session with a 32-year-old woman who had a long history of both mental and emotional abuse. The woman had recently relocated to the area following a particularly difficult divorce, and had not, as yet, established a support system of friends. She was an active Catholic, and a feminist, and had already spent several years in Stage 2 of her healing process.

This was her fourth psychosynthesis session, and the first session in which she was able to imagine the healing of her psychological wounds. At this juncture, the technique of guided affective imagery was used. As this excerpt illustrates graphically, it is not atypical for those who have been mentally and emotionally abused to experience their wounds as though they were physical injuries. Psyche and soma are more intertwined than we generally acknowledge.

Guide: Close your eyes and allow an image to come of your injured self...

Client: Female, my age, and all bent over on herself, holding her entire front body, from chin to knees . . . it is all injured.

Guide: Would she be willing to allow us to see the extent of her injuries?

Client: Yes. She opens up just to show us. Ooow! It is all red and raw, all the flesh from chin to knees. Seems just like a shark or some huge beast had taken a bite right out of the front of her! (Pause) It really is a bad open wound. She needs to close up now because the air makes the wound sting.

Guide: Does actually seeing the wound give you any further information?

Client: Just one thing. About rejection. And my mother. Seeing the wound somehow made me see that my mother rejected every one, not just me—that the rejection wasn't personally directed at me. I understand that now, but that doesn't really change the wound. It's too late for that . . .

Guide: Yes, it is a bad wound, (pause) Can it be healed?

Client: No, it can't. It's a fatal wound.

Guide: I see. (pause) Has there ever been a cure for such a wound, or will there be a cure in the future?

Client: Well, yes. There will be a cure in the future. Medical technology will one day be able to extract from fatality victims the pure essence of love, just as they now take eyes and hearts and lungs for transplant . . . Love is the only cure for a   wound like mine. Just as they can tell the good eyes and lungs from the bad ones, they will be able to tell which   people have good love—like children and loving parents— and they can remove it from the person and distill it into its   pure essence. Then injured people, like me, can be treated with this pure essence of love.

Guide: Can you imagine that you are in that future time and receive the love treatment for your wounds?

Client: Yes. (pause) Yes. The treatment works so that I live. I am left with rather thick scar tissue, but I am alive.

Guide: What's it like to have this scar tissue?

Client: Well, it's rather sobering to know that I'll never be as freely joyful, as open, as trusting, as naive, or as vulnerable as I was before. It's as though my childhood purity is really gone for good now, (pause) —they have been gone for a long   time, actually, I feel a little sad about that. But mostly, I'm glad to be alive—even with the scar tissue . . . and loss of innocence.

Guide: What is sad about the loss of innocence?

Client: Well, you know, (pause) It would be better if we could live in a world that lets us stay innocent and pure. It's such a sweet feeling. But it seems that isn't really possible in this   world, so I'm glad to be alive.

Guide: Even with the loss of innocence, you are grateful to be alive.

Client: Yes, very grateful. Very thankful. I know I'm going to be okay now.

And she was right. The full extent of her mental and emotional wounds were then recognized and acknowledged. She realized for the first time that these wounds were not fatal, and began moving through further stages of healing.

After five months of psychosynthesis counseling, this client, who had been repeatedly psychologically abused and betrayed both in childhood and as an adult, went on to establish new and supportive relationships. She was able, at last, to allow herself to be loved and then love in return. By reaching out in her own way, she once again began to trust in love. By coming to psychosynthesis counseling as her own best expert, she initiated the process that would eventually cure her wounds. With guidance, and the support of her friends, she was able to move through all seven stages of the healing process in a relatively short time. As her counselor, I must conclude that she seemed to have known all along, "Love is the only cure for a wound like mine."

It is our clients that make the view from the counselor's chair one of hope rather than despair. Though the pain is difficult to witness, the fact that mental and emotional abuses are beginning to be acknowledged and healed gives hope for a brighter future. Perhaps psychological abuses will not be routinely passed down to future generations if we continue the work of healing the wounds of those who have been abused—and if we encourage abusers to change their behavior and make amends—now.

Surveying the popular press and media, there are a few examples of groups and individuals beginning to work together in mutually empowering ways. In addition, the therapeutic and educational work of psychosynthesis guides and other consultants, the socially supportive work of various 12-Step programs, and the work of a few popular entertainers and musicians give nation-wide exposure to the ethic of positive human values and relationships. We need more healing and more popular examples if we are to change our cultural values and personal ethics in such a way that we may freely relate to one another, without fear of being oppressed or psychologically abused.

I end this article with a pertinent reminder from the originator of Psychosynthesis, the late Dr. Roberto Assagioli:

> We are constantly influencing others, whether we are conscious of doing so or not, whether we desire to do so or not. And the more we are aware of this, the more we can see to it that our influence is beneficent and constructive.

Notes

[1] At the time this article was written, the telephone service in the United States was a monopoly in the hands of a single company, American Telephone and Telegraph Co., founded by A.G. Bell, and whose various subsidiaries were collectively known as "The Bell System," often colloquially referred to as "Ma Bell." *Reach Out and Touch Someone* was one of the company's sales slogans. —*Ed.*

[2] Guides must be careful not to minimize the problem by treating victims of mental and emotional abuse as though the problem were merely an unruly victim subpersonality to be integrated. The client may have developed certain subpersonalities to cope with aspects of the abusive situation. These can be worked with in Stage 3. Prior to that, victimization can be considered a social reality, not just an intrapsychic phenomenon. One must be very sensitive to those who have become mentally and emotionally disabled through psychological abuse in their interpersonal relation-

ships, and take care not to minimize the problem.

Victoria Tackett, PhD, *(1947-2015) was the founding Director of* Synthesis Institute of Palo Alto, CA. *She taught at John F. Kennedy University, and was in private practice since the 1970s in Palo Alto, Chapel Hill, NC and Bay St. Louis, MS.*

The Core Personality: Treatment Strategies for Dissociative Identity Disorder

Mary Greene

Practitioners of Psychosynthesis are familiar with a perspective of the personality which holds that it is a constellation of subpersonalities centered around an "I." James Vargiu's (1974) article "Subpersonalities" gives an excellent account of the inner multiplicity of an individual and the therapeutic process leading toward integration and synthesis. Therapeutic principles such as accepting the subpersonalities and meeting their needs have also been found to be applicable to clients with Dissociative Identity Disorder (DID). The subpersonalities in these clients take the form of alternate identities (alters).

Experience in working with subpersonalities can be very helpful in working with alters, while working with alters can help us to better understand subpersonalities. Additional principles of Psychosynthesis such as the "I", the Higher Self, presence, and the relationship of various of the consciousness take on an expansion of meaning in working with this unique group of individuals.

Characteristics of Dissociative Identity Disorder

DID is unusual, but contrary to common belief, not rare. Probably each full-time therapist is seeing at this moment one or more clients with this disorder. The condition is frequently misdiagnosed because of lack of experience with the symptoms. Once therapists at the Kentucky Center of Psychosynthesis, for example, learned to diagnose the condition, they found at least one person in their client load who fit the diagnosis.

The difference between clients with subpersonalities and clients with alters is largely a matter of degree. Alters have more autonomy and are more distinct but can be more difficult to recognize because of the presence of an amnesic barrier. Many clients with DID are unconscious of their alters and have learned to ignore the symptoms that indicate their existence. Some of these symptoms might be finding themselves somewhere and not knowing how they got there or finding articles of clothing, food, and so on they do not remember buying. They may be told by friends of things they said or did that they do not remember saying or doing and they may even be aware of spans of time elapsing for which they cannot account. Headaches and other psychosomatic symptoms are commonly reported by individuals with alters as well as periods of extreme emotional disturbance for which they have no adequate explanation. In interacting with the individual, one can sometimes observe dramatic changes in facial expression, voice, movement, and handwriting.

Alters are apparently formed in the same manner as subpersonalities, but when the individual must dissociate either the emotional, mental, or physical content of an experience in order to survive or to maintain sanity, then an alter is formed. In general, dissociation occurs only under extremely stressful or traumatic circumstances and continues when adequate support is not given the individual following the trauma.

An example of dissociation could be the shock that people experience after a severe automobile accident. The mind might dissociate into separate parts which are capable of dealing with a specific aspect of the event but not with the total event. For instance, one part may hold the terror of anticipating the accident, another may hold anger at the driver of the other car, and another may hold the pain and hurt. There might be another part that has no emotions at all but was able to get out of the car and get some help. And then one part may just be numb, not be able to remember anything of the accident, and eager to go on with life as if nothing had happened. By distinguishing the parts of the personality which deal with only one aspect of the experience, we can identify various alters. In this particular example, the one who does not remember the accident would be the core personality. The alters are created to absorb the trauma and thereby protect the core personality.

Most individuals, including those with DID, have a core personality, a state of mind relatively free of defense mechanisms which can be infused with spiritual values and can experience heightened states of consciousness and will. For example, if someone suggests that we are rationalizing or projecting our experience, we can either become defensive or we can step back and sincerely acknowledge our behavior. It is possible, in other words, to move into a relatively centered, balanced state which is more than observational and which brings with it an increased awareness of both oneself and the world. This state includes mind, feelings, and physical sensations and is accompanied by an experience of being able to make and act on choices. In this state, we can check our experience to see whether or not it is influenced by defense mechanisms. Just as we can distinguish between being "real" and being controlled by defense mechanisms, people with DID can distinguish between their core personality and the alters that have resulted from dissociation. This does not imply that alters cannot be genuine, centered, and objective, but that it is more difficult for them to stay this way.

The Core Personality and the Alters

In treating DID, it is essential to consider all of the alters as important and valuable, even though they differ in characteristics, capabilities, and functions. Whereas the alters may have originally served an adaptive, survival, or defense function, the core personality has a broader function which is to live, love, be aware, choose and evolve as a human being. The attributes of this function are replicable by alters so the individual is not bereft of them in cases where the core personality has regressed.

A careful history of the dissociations with the help of the "memory trace," an alter whose purpose is to remember the history of the individual (Wilbur, 1984), usually reveals the core personality. Also, core personalities experience themselves realistically as to age, gender, or physical appearance and recognize themselves in a mirror while alters may not. A sense of morality is frequently manifested in the core, such as a general social awareness and concern for other people's feelings, awareness of family responsibilities, striving for honesty, and feelings of existential shame and guilt. At the beginning of therapy, the core personality is mostly amnesic of the alters, and may confabulate to maintain a sense of continuity. Alters, however, are usually aware of the core personality and can be strongly affected by its experiences (Ludwig, 1972). For example, experiences such as seeing an instrument that was used in abuse, can easily stir up traumatic experiences in the alters. This may cause the alter to take over and act out the emotional experience, or covertly create emotional turmoil which makes the individual feel "crazy." The core personality is generally willing to learn and to take responsibility for actions and mistakes. However, it is easily over-whelmed and has a tendency to give up, requiring the alters to take over.

It is not unusual for the core personality to be depleted and for some alters to be stronger, better adjusted, more aware, and more energetic. That is, it is not the actual ability to cope that determines the core personality, but historical development and the potential to function fully and realistically. In cases of a dormant or weak core personality, one or more alters may stand in for the core personality until it is able to develop.

Alters may take on any imaginable form or identity. They frequently see themselves as having the age and appearance of the individual at the time of dissociation. They may take on the identity of the aggressor in an abusive situation. They develop an imaginary identity consistent with an aspect of the experience of the trauma.

It is helpful to be aware of three types of alters: yang alters, yin alters, and inner self helpers. Yang alters present themselves as predominantly independent and power oriented. Yin alters present themselves as oriented toward love and harmony. The yang alters are initially more dominated by feelings of anger, rage, pride, or jealousy, whereas yin alters are initially more controlled by feelings of fear, hurt, depression, or inadequacy. Although the yin alters may be needy and helpless, they tend to accept and co-operate with the core personality. The yang alters, however, can be very resistant to working on their traumas and tend to intimidate and reject others, including the therapist. These alters can be better accepted if perceived as protectors. They almost always protect or stand up for some higher good or value, even though this may not be apparent at first sight. For instance, one of the very young alters of a client who had suffered severe infant abuse would appear hitting herself, "the baby," in the belief that if she hit "the baby" enough the abuser would stop hitting her. Another alter tried to die in an effort to preserve the existential choice to live or to die. This alter would say: "Me die, him not 'die' me."

The inner self helpers are a unique group of alters which have a special function in the personality. They are known for their knowledge of the system, their wise comments, and their loyalty to the individual (Comstock, 1985). Some of the inner self helpers never come into the body. Their function is similar to that of the Wise Person[1] and they can learn to perform mental functions that can be accomplished through hypnosis. Inner self helpers should not be confused with the Higher Self, since they have limitations related to the life experiences of the individual and specific functions for which they were developed. They hold little or no emotional aspects of the trauma. Their function is in the inner life of the individual.

Distinguishing Types of Core Personality

While the therapist is getting to know and understand the different alters, helping them to work through their traumas, and deal with their conflicts, distinguishing the core personality is helpful in understanding how the process of the alters actually represents the complex intrapsychic dynamics of a single individual. It also helps the therapist to structure and evaluate the progress of therapy. The strength of the core personality can be used as a prognosis for the mental health of the individual. For heuristic purposes one can identify three groups of core personalities which more or less fall on a continuum ranging from minimum strength to maximum strength. While a person's core personality may belong to one group, circumstances and stress can temporarily place that person in a different group.

The first group contains individuals with a dormant core personality. The core personality may have had sporadic life experience but is absent most of the time. Sometimes prenatal, infant, and/or massive dissociation, followed by continued trauma, can keep the core personality from further development. It may have tried at times to emerge, but was not successful due to a lack of strength. In these cases, the alters must make all of the decisions in life to the best of their abilities and understanding. It can, however, be hard to implement any long-term decision because of switching among the alters. For instance, yang-alters may be convinced that the core personality cannot survive in this world or they may not want to give up their perceived power. With a dormant core personality the most competent alter usually takes over the management of life with the others assisting and attempting to meet their needs

In the second group are individuals with a functional core personality. These individuals have developed a true identity and are able to cope with ordinary life situations. However, they are amnesic of certain traumas and some or all alters. They only know they have unusual experiences, and emotions they cannot understand. When situations become too difficult, the core personality disappears and an alter takes over.

In the third group are individuals with a responsible core personality. These individuals may have had a strong core personality pre-trauma, may have had trauma that was not too harmful to the personality, or they may have worked their way to this state. They have a core personality which is able to relate to the alters and can help them meet their needs in a constructive way. Usually enough co-operation has been achieved to make the individual's condition less problematic. The core personality has developed the ability to express and to tolerate a range of emotions and to implement decisions guided by inner values. Individuals in this group may come to experience alters as parts of the self, as subpersonalities, or ego states (Watkins, 1979) rather than as independent and semi-autonomous alters.

We have learned from clinical experience to adjust the therapeutic strategies and the pacing of the therapy to the strength of the core personality. Depending on the client, we may prefer not to introduce the concept of a core personality until he or she has reached a certain stage of acceptance of the alters. Yet we have found that it is not necessary to discuss the core personality with the client in order to work with the concept. Essentially, the therapy is conceptualized as a process of strengthening the core personality: as therapy progresses, a core personality becomes stronger, and the individual moves to the next group.

Therapeutic Interventions

Clients with a dormant core personality may need a guardian or a hospital to rely on. Trust needs to be developed in both tangible and intangible ways and the trustworthiness of the therapist is subjected to numerous tests. The therapist must stand in for the core personality when working with the alters. Much of the work involves reclaiming and working through traumas. This work includes the release and acceptance of emotions, reframing attitudes, and learning new ways of coping. Essential skills and attitudes of relating to themselves, each other, and other people may also need to be taught. Alters can learn to monitor the therapy session so that they can benefit from one another's therapeutic experience.

The integration of the alters may be accomplished, especially in cases where this involves an integration of personality fragments. When the alters start making progress in dealing with their emotions, and the stress on the whole person diminishes, energy becomes available for the core personality to develop. The development of the core personality needs to be planned by the therapist. For instance, if the core personality is a fetus, it may be best to work through the infant and early childhood traumas before introducing the core personality to the world. Advice and recommendations from Inner Self Helpers can be helpful in this matter. Once the core personality has emerged, sometimes with the use of a birth ritual, the core personality may need age-appropriate forms of parenting and education in order to facilitate emotional growth. This may include bottle feeding, comforting, learning to play, and so on for a limited period of time. In this stage, some alters may need help in adjusting to the presence of the core personality.

Clients with a functional core personality have had some positive experiences and have learned to cope with ordinary life situations. Therefore, they require less effort on the part of the therapist in providing for a protective and nurturing environment. Hospitalizations can be avoided with this group by timely recognition and by working through traumas from the past that are triggered by present events. The therapist needs to help the core personality understand and accept DID. It is helpful for the core personality to know about the symptoms of DID, the presence of alters, and the reasons for switching. Facilitation of an emotional acceptance of DID is frequently an ongoing process related to an increase in the strength of the core personality. It is useful for some of the therapeutic interventions to deal directly with strengthening the core personality. The core personality needs to be made aware of the tendency to give up as a way of coping with an intolerable situation. It needs to learn alternative ways of coping, to become aware of moments of choice, and to practice making choices using the new coping skills. The core personality benefits from an increased awareness of positive inner qualities.

In working directly with the core personality, the therapist needs to consider its limitations so that it is not overwhelmed with new responsibilities. The therapist continues helping the alters work through their traumas and improve their relations with each other. This work is not only beneficial for the alters but is also a vicarious learning experience for the core personality. The therapist needs to encourage the core personality toward co-consciousness and to cultivate the ability to deal with emotions that arise as a result of working with the alters. Teaching ways in which the core personality can help the alters greatly improves mutual acceptance. For example, the core personality may buy a stuffed animal for a child alter and give him or her time to play with it in a safe situation.

Clients with a responsible core personality may still have problems with their emotions but they are less likely to act them out in a harmful way. They can take more responsibility for their life and for the work done in the therapy sessions. Their dissociations are often intentional and are done for a therapeutic purpose. Generally, enough spiritual development is present for the core personality to be aware of and willing to act on values such as altruism, love, honesty, and courage. In combination with increased coping skills, this greatly enhances the self-acceptance and strength of the individual.

In this group, the experience of the alters is more available to the core personality. Usually, the core personality can begin learning to image the alters instead of dissociating into them. Through the image, the core personality is able to share in the experiences of the alters, re-parent them, provide them with the needed nurturing and protection, and help them reframe their attitudes. Thus the alters can come to be experienced by the core personality as its parts, or subpersonalities, with wants and needs that the core personality can meet. When these needs are met, the alters become more co-operative and more united in their intentions. At this point, integration and fusion occur naturally.

Summary

We have conceptualized an approach to DID that focuses on strengthening the core personality. If the core personality gains enough strength to cope with the traumatic history on an emotional, attitudinal, and behavioral level, the defense mechanism of dissociation is no longer needed. The person regains the freedom to make life decisions and to express him or herself in ways that are both aligned with inner values and appropriate to external circumstances.

References

Comstock, C. (1985), *Internal Self Helpers or Centers.* Paper presented at the Second International Conference on Multiple Personalities and Dissociative States, Chicago.
Ludwig, A. M., Brandsma, J, M., Wilbur, C. B., Bendefeldt, F., & Jameson, D. H. (1972). *The Objective Study of Multiple Personality.* Archives of General Psychiatry, 26, 298-310,
Vargiu, J. (1974). *Subpersonalities.* Synthesis, 1, 59-90.
Watkins, J. G., & Watkins, H. H. (1979). *Ego States and Hidden Observers,* Journal of Altered States of Consciousness, 5, 27—31.
Wilbur, C. B. (1984). *Treatment of Multiple Personality.* Psychiatric Annals, 14, 27- 31.

Suggested Reading

Diagnosis

Coons, P. M. (1980). *Multiple Personality: Diagnostic Considerations.* Journal of Clinical Psychiatry, 41, 330-336.
Schafer, D, W. (1986). *Recognizing Multiple Personality Patients.* American Journal of Psychotherapy, 4, 500-510.

Treatment

Kluft, R. P. (1984). *Treatment of Multiple Personality Disorder.* Psychiatric Clinics of North America, 7(1), 9-29.

Braun, B, G. (1986). *Treatment of Multiple Personality Disorder.* Washington, DC: American Psychiatric Press. (For copies write to: APA, 1400 K St. NW, Washington, DC 20005.)

Etiology

Kluft, R. P. (1985). *Childhood Antecedents of Multiple Personality.* Washington, DC: American Psychiatric Press.

General

Proceedings of the International Conference on Multiple Personality and Dissociative States. (1984/85/86/87). (For copies write to: Dissociative Disorders Program, Department of Psychiatry, Rush University, 1720 West Polk St., Chicago, IL 60612.)

This article was revised in 2018 by the author.

---

[1] "Wise Person" refers to a psychosynthesis exercise in which the client is directed in a guided imagery to discover a "wise person" who will provide the assistance or guidance that is sought.

Mary Greene, PhD, *was a co-founder and director of the* Kentucky Center of Psychosynthesis. *She is a psychologist who devotes much of her private practice to working with dissociation and DID. She has developed seminars for the Center's Professional Training Program and has assisted other professionals in their work with dissociative identity disorder.*

Grief Is More Than Crying

Kay Lynne Sherman

John Bowlby (1980) makes this observation:

> Loss of a loved person is one of the most intensely
> painful experiences any human being can suffer. And not
> only is it painful to experience but it is also painful to
> witness, if only because we are so impotent to help. To
> the bereaved nothing but the return of the lost person
> can bring true comfort; should what we provide fall short
> of that it is felt almost as an insult. That, perhaps,
> explains a bias that runs through so much of the older
> literature on how human beings respond to loss.
> Whether an author is discussing the effects of loss on an
> adult or a child, there is a tendency to underestimate
> how intensely distressing and disabling loss usually is
> and for how long the distress, and often the disablement,
> commonly lasts. Conversely, there is a tendency to
> suppose that a normal healthy person can and should
> get over a bereavement not only fairly rapidly, but also
> completely.

In this article, I would like to offer to the psychosynthesis community
my understanding of the process that grief takes, based on my personal
experience, my work with grieving clients, and on the research I have
done in the area. I believe that this is a timely subject for us, because I
see some essential changes occurring in psychosynthesis.

Historically, writers and practitioners in psychosynthesis have
tended to emphasize the spiritual qualities of the work, out of excitement
for a psychotherapy which acknowledges and co-operates with Spirit.
Much of the work has been connected to the growth movement, guiding
people to greater awareness of Self and of purpose in life. Recently,
psychosynthesis practitioners with whom I have been in contact, as well

as many of our psychosynthesis trainers and writers have been looking at ways in which we can deepen our understanding of Assagioli's work and apply it to the serious crises and pathologies that present themselves in clinical practice.

In my practice, and in my area of research, I have concentrated on the issues of bereavement trauma, and the grief process. I have found it interesting that grief, which is such a universal human experience, is absent in many training programs for therapists. Or in the programs where it exists, often a restrictive formula is given for what "correct" grieving should look like. In addition, grief is an area of great ignorance and discomfort for many people in our culture. However, grief work at its best can result in an experience of transformation and an expansion of the Self; psychosynthesis offers a very suitable framework in which to do this work.

I pay particular attention below to the symptoms of grief since these often appear without conscious connection to loss. Recognizing the symptoms for what they are can open the door to healing and transformation in our personal lives and in our work with clients. Following a description of the phases or "tasks" of grieving, I discuss therapeutic approaches to the grief process and how they relate to the psychosynthesis approach.

The Grief Process

After the death of her husband Prince Albert, Queen Victoria continued to order servants to lay out his clothing and shaving gear daily, and often she was seen speaking to "him" as she made her palace rounds. As a model for behavior in her time, she no doubt influenced mourning practices greatly. To what extent do we continue to be influenced by her model? Where today do we look for guidelines on how to grieve?

Traditionally, mourning rituals have been determined by the dominant culture; priests and priestesses handled the ceremonies as well as the counseling. However, as our own culture changes, it no longer provides clear guidelines for mourning, and the bereaved are without wise counsel. Queen Victoria's behavior is as likely a model for mourning as were the awkward responses of those around her a standard guideline for sympathy. In much of Western culture, where the subjects of death and loss are generally avoided, the bereaved not only are deprived of guidelines on how to handle their loss, but are also apt to find themselves a social embarrassment. The grieving person, with no information or guidelines, may regard symptoms as signs of physical or psychological illness, and in an attempt to suppress the process may indeed manifest illness.

How would we, as helping professionals or as friends, have responded to the Queen in her grief? How do we respond to our own friends and clients? How, in fact, do we deal with our own grief? It is sometimes difficult to know what to do or say when we come in contact with someone who has been bereaved. Conflicting ideas about what healthy grieving consists of, as well as our own lack of comfort with the subject, can immobilize us. Often we are really not sure that our actions have been appropriate or helpful.

Much has been done in recent years to transform dying into a meaningful rite of passage. Now, what of those who are left to grieve the death? And what of those who have suddenly lost a loved one through homicide or suicide, drug overdose, military action, or community violence and face their mourning with an additional burden to bear? Bereavement takes so many forms: loss of a partner as they fade into dementia or terminal illness, loss of friends or family members through estrangement; loss of a sense of place, as cities, groups and wildernesses are altered forever. And the list goes on . . . Our grief is testimony to how deeply we have loved.

By recognizing that the grief process itself has the potential to be more than just pain, that it can potentially be a transformative experience, we can better understand and provide a caring response to those facing this crucial passage.

Attachment

> [For the greylag goose] the first response to the disappearance of the partner consists in the anxious attempt to find him again. The goose moves about restlessly by day and night, uttering all the time the penetrating trisyllabic long-distance call . . . The searching expeditions are extended farther and farther and quite often the searcher itself gets lost, or succumbs to an accident . . . All the objective observable characteristics of the goose's behavior on losing its mate are roughly identical with human grief (Lorenz, as quoted in Parkes, 1972, p. 40)

At the root of mourning is attachment to another human being. If we were not deeply connected, the loss of a loved one would not matter. British psychiatrist John Bowlby has produced a monumental work on the subject of attachment and loss. He sees attachment as a normal form of behavior, distinct from feeding behavior and sexual behavior and of at least equal significance (1980, pp. 39-41). Among all species, attachments develop for survival reasons. Obviously, our attachments to one another have motivations and aspects other than survival, but I think it is helpful to realize that the pain which is felt at separation has very deep instinctual roots.

According to Bowlby, attachment behavior in humans is any form of behavior which has to do with attaining proximity to a preferred person. Affective bonds and attachments are present throughout the life cycle and are closely connected to our emotions of joy or sorrow. Attachment behavior is mediated by behavioral systems which early in development become goal corrected; the baby soon learns which behavior best elicits the affection of the care-giver. In many species, mourning responses arise out of specific attachment behavior; we can better understand the response if we appreciate the attachment behavior which is behind it. So the bereaved greylag goose continues to search for its dead mate because in earlier experiences that searching brought forth reunion. Many widows continue to search for their husbands long after there is any rational hope of finding them, feeling compelled to do so and at the same time fearing that they may in fact be going mad.

To better understand the normal human reactions to loss, let us first explore the typical grief symptoms.

Physical Expressions of Grief

> No one ever told me that grief felt so like fear. I am not afraid, but the sensation is like being afraid. The same fluttering in the stomach, the same restlessness, the yawning. I keep on swallowing, (C. S. Lewis, 1961)

In one of the earliest works on the subject, Erich Lindemann (1979) describes the symptoms experienced by 101 bereaved people, many of whom were survivors of those lost in a disastrous fire at The Coconut Grove night club. He describes acute grief as consisting of sensations of somatic distress occurring in waves lasting from 20 minutes to an hour at a time, a feeling of tightness in the throat, choking with shortness of breath, need for sighing, an empty feeling in the abdomen, lack of muscular power, and an intense subjective distress described as tension or mental pain.

In his highly sensitive work describing the many aspects of bereavement, Colin Murray Parkes (1972) quotes an Australian study which found the following symptoms: headaches, dizziness, fainting spells, blurred vision, skin rashes, excessive sweating, indigestion, difficulty in swallowing, vomiting, heavy menstrual periods, palpitations, chest pains, shortness of breath, frequent infections, and general aching. In his own study of London widows, Parkes observed alarm reaction, an urge to search for the lost person in some form, anger and guilt, feelings of internal loss of self, and identification phenomena—the adoption of traits, mannerisms, or symptoms of the lost person.

It is possible that the physical symptoms caused by grief are due in part to the poor diet and disturbed schedule that often follow the death of a loved one. Occasionally after bereavement, however, physical symptoms become chronic or serious and, indeed, can become cause for concern. Bowlby first became interested in grief and loss when he noticed that the majority of the patients in a study he was doing on colitis were recently bereaved. Parkes quotes several studies which show that the incidence of death is higher among the bereaved (1972, p, 16). Interestingly enough, as Parkes points out, the most frequent cause of death among the recently bereaved is heart disease. Perhaps it is possible to die of a broken heart.

Occasionally, people enter therapy directly after a loss, particularly if the loss has been a sudden or shocking one. In general, however, it is more common for people: to enter therapy or to seek medical help considerably later, and it is very likely that the connection is not made between the loss and the current physical symptoms. Using an intake questionnaire does not always serve to discover significant losses because they have actually disappeared from the conscious mind. A client I was working with who had been experiencing an extended depression mentioned to me in one session that she had been suffering from colitis attacks. Knowing that colitis has been observed as an indication of repressed grief reaction, I asked her whether she had lost anyone close to her recently. Initially she responded that she hadn't; then suddenly her face changed, and she began sobbing. She recalled that shortly after her husband and she had separated, her mother-in-law, whom she loved very deeply, had died of cancer. Because of the somewhat bitter circumstances of the divorce, she had not been able to attend the funeral, see her mother-in-law's body, or express her grief. We began working at that point on her grief, which was a part of what had contributed to her feelings of depression. By being aware of the physical symptoms of grief, we can sometimes discover grief that has been repressed and that would otherwise have gone unnoticed.

Kay Lynne Sherman

Cognitive Expressions of Grief

In addition to physical symptoms, cognitive changes also occur. Worden describes these as disbelief, confusion, preoccupation, sense of presence, and hallucinations (1982, p. 24). Particularly in the first hours and days, a sense of disbelief, of unreality, is prominent. If the death has been sudden, the disbelief is stronger; if it has been a violent death, stronger still. Even though persons of authority have said that a loved one has died, even though the body has been viewed and bid adieu, the sense remains that some mistake has been made and that the beloved person will somehow (joyously!) still be alive. Each day the bereaved person must let in a little more of the reality that the lost one is truly gone. The dissonance between the momentous change the bereaved is undergoing in his or her own life and the normal progression of the world can be highly disorienting. As one of my friends said after the death of her father, "You go to the supermarket and you can't believe that everyone is just buying their food as normal. Don't they know that the whole world has changed?"

Confusion takes hold as the mind struggles to process the over-whelming impact of the change. The job of healing the wound caused by a death initially takes every bit of available thought. The necessary decisions regarding such things as funeral arrangements, personal belongings, and business affairs may deplete all of the decision-making ability. Preoccupation with thoughts about the dead person may nearly amount to an obsession. Often these thoughts center around how to recover the lost person. In some cases, the confusion and disorientation may last well beyond those intense first days. This seems to be a diagnostic sign that the grief work is still in process and that it is necessary and appropriate for the bereaved person to continue drawing inward for a while longer.

A sense of the presence of the lost person is often reported by the grieving person. This may include actual hallucinations of both the visual and auditory type. In light of the results of recent research on near-death experiences in which participants report a continuation of existence after death, it is entirely possible that the dead loved one might in fact be available for completion of the relationship and that those grieving, and the alert practitioner, may be able to sense this presence. It is also possible that the sense of the loved one's presence after death may be the result of a desperate wish that it be so. Whatever the cause, in my own work as a therapist, I have indeed on occasion felt a presence in the room while working with a grieving client and have used the opportunity to help him work on any unfinished relationship issues with the deceased. Common themes that emerge are anger, apology, and forgiveness.

Richard Kalish refers to another cognitive expression of grief: the tendency to go over again and again all the events that led up to the death:

> "When I saw him last Saturday, he looked as though he were rallying."
> "Yes, but the next morning, the nurse told me he had had a bad night."
> "Do you think it might have had something to do with his sister's illness?"
> "I doubt it, but I heard from an aide that he fell going to the bathroom that morning."
> "That explains that bruise on his elbow. "
> "No wonder he told me he was angry because he couldn't seem to do anything right."
>
> And so it goes, the attempt to understand why someone who was rallying on Saturday was dead on Wednesday. (1985, p. 189)

Kalish continues by remarking;

> When a death is caused by an accident or a disaster, the effort to make sense of it is pursued more vigorously. The bereaved want to put the death into a perspective they can understand and accept—divine intervention, a curse from a neighboring tribe, a logical sequence of cause and effect, whatever it may be.

I would add two additional aspects to this need to make sense of a death. The first is a form of magical thinking: if we can discover why the person died, perhaps we can avoid such a fate in our own lives. The kidnap and murder of a child in a presumably safe neighborhood threaten the security of many people, and minds race to try to find a reason why this particular child met that fate. There is the sense that if we can find a reason for the tragedy, and if the reason cannot possibly apply to us in any way, then we may be able to avoid such an event in our own lives. Senseless events give us a sense of impotence, and it becomes very important to re-order our world so that it seems predictable and controllable once again.

Second, in some cases, a death can severely disrupt the bereaved's entire world view, and the need to make sense of the event is intense. When people have been loving, gentle, and kind, a violent death is not supposed to befall them. Good children who are loved and cared for are not supposed to die. People who meditate every day and surround themselves with light are supposed to be protected from harm. The discovery that life doesn't abide by these standards can be shattering.

Behavioral Expressions of Grief

Worden has listed major changes in behavior accompanying grief: sleep disturbances, appetite disturbances, absent-minded behavior, social withdrawal, dreams of the deceased, avoiding reminders of the deceased, searching and calling out, sighing, restless overactivity, crying, or visiting places or carrying objects that belonged to the deceased (1982, p. 24).

It is common that those who are suffering from a grief reaction may awaken every morning at an early hour, often just after a dream of the deceased. Usually, their thoughts will be centered around the lost loved one and the events of the death. It is possible that the tendency to awaken early in times of crisis is healthy, and that those hours are in fact the best time for doing the transformative work of the grief process. Monastic orders often make a practice of rising in the early morning hours to pray or to meditate. Perhaps the body tells the grieving person to wake up and partake of that very special time, when spiritual energy seems most available, to write of dreams and thoughts, to cry undisturbed, to pray or meditate, to begin to say good-bye.

Appetite disturbances are also common for the grieving person. A few years ago my fiancée was killed, and one of my clearest memories of that time involved absolute lack of appetite. When I took the first bite of breakfast the next day I found that I could not taste it at all; it tasted like straw. I, who for years had found one of life's greatest joys in preparing and eating food, found that it was months before I could taste again and actually about two years before I could do any decent cooking.

Absent-minded behavior is also very much a part of the grief process. Worden tells the story of a patient who on three separate occasions drove across the city in her car, and by the time she had completed her business, had forgotten that she had driven herself and returned home via public transportation (1982, p. 25). For people who are accustomed to maintaining very demanding schedules, this sort of absent-mindedness can be especially exasperating and at times frightening.

Social withdrawal is a common phenomenon among the grieving, and to a certain extent it can even serve the healing process. There may be people who should be avoided after a loss, and often the grieving person has a very acute sense of who those people are: friends and family who are insensitive to the issues of grief may cause further pain. In addition, the grieving person often simply does not feel very social and finds a great incongruity between his mood and that of others on social occasions. If friends are uncomfortable with death and grief issues, there may also be a tendency on their part to try to negate the reality of what has happened for the sake of their own comfort. Under such circumstances, it is understandable for the grieving person to isolate him or herself. However, it can be, and very often is, a problem if carried too far. Participating in support groups with people who share a similar experience can be a solution. It is healing to laugh and to cry with others who also awaken every morning at 5 a. m. or who forget the way to work.

Recently I spent a weekend with friends who had just had a stillborn child. They had decided to attend a gathering of old friends, in spite of their grief, and were very open in sharing what had happened with those present. During the weekend, they cried, they laughed, they danced, they held another baby who had been born at nearly the same time as theirs. Their openness and their acceptance and consideration of those attending the gathering made it possible for all to participate in the healing of their sorrow. This seems to me an ideal way to process grief, though it does take special people and a special awareness.

Grieving people often have recurring dreams of the deceased, and significant grief work can be accomplished in this way. Forgiveness can occur; relationships can be altered; anger, fear, and love can be expressed. A great deal can be learned about the progress of the grief work by questioning the bereaved about the content of dreams.

Grieving people seem to alternate between trying to re-establish contact with the deceased and to separate from the relationship. Often, both activities are pursued with real passion. One day the bereaved person may be putting pictures of the deceased all over the house, wearing a favorite shirt, carrying objects that were meaningful. The next day the pictures may all be down, and the bereaved may not even want to mention their loved one's name. In this way, the process of gradual separation takes place.

Emotional Expressions of Grief

Worden lists the following emotions as the most common in grief response: numbness, guilt and self-reproach, sadness, anger, anxiety, loneliness, fatigue, helplessness, shock, yearning, emancipation and relief (1982, pp. 20-22).

Initially, it is very common for the bereaved person to be nearly without feelings; generally, the more massive the shock, the longer it is before feelings return. Even though my father's death was not a great shock, I experienced something of this delayed response. Since he had been ill for some time, we had been able to prepare for the death. At the memorial service, my brothers and sisters and I sang the old canon that for years we had sung as a family for grace, and we rejoiced in his memory, and felt complete in our grieving. Much to my surprise, four months later, during a meditation retreat, I found myself in the woods, sobbing my heart out over my father.

Very often people marvel at the composure of the bereaved at a funeral; they may be very relieved that they are "taking it so well." However, it may be weeks or months before the bereaved even begin to grasp the reality of the changes in their lives, and at that point feelings may be nearly overwhelming. Unfortunately, by that time, they may not receive the support they need because, based on their earlier composure, friends and family have assumed that they have somehow finished with grieving.

Closely aligned with this initial numbness are the physical symptoms of shock. Especially when the death is unexpected or violent, the grieving person may experience dizziness, cold chills and hot sweats, adrenaline rushes, diarrhea, and convulsive shaking. This is especially intense in the first few hours after the death is discovered, but may recur later when a memory is evoked.

Guilt can be a big factor in the grief process, particularly if the relationship with the deceased was troubled, or if the death was by suicide. But in every grieving process, when guilt is felt it is often more intense than would seem reasonable. The impression I have gained in working with grieving clients is that there is a very strong need to regain power over the world at a time when the world seems very much out of control. For example, accepting the blame for not taking someone to the hospital in time to prevent a death at least lets the grieving person feel as if he or she were in control of fate. It is very difficult for some people to accept that life and death may in fact really be out of their control.

Sadness, yearning, and loneliness are the feelings that we more commonly associate with loss of a loved one so they generally do not come as a surprise to a grieving person. Perhaps only the intensity of the feelings is unexpected.

Anxiety and helplessness are closely related to one another and are usually a source of bewilderment for the grieving person. Normally competent people find themselves suddenly fearful of all sorts of things and unable to handle the everyday problems of life. Shortly after my fiancé was killed, the roof on my house developed a leak, and water was actually running down the wall inside the dining room. I had previously restored that house, doing much of the work myself and had never faced a problem that I could not solve. However, when the roof started leaking this time, it terrified me. Months went by before I finally had the roof fixed; the water continued to run down the dining room wall, and I felt incapable of fixing it. It is a humbling and sometimes confusing experience to find oneself so stripped of normal capabilities.

Another emotion that is difficult for the grieving person to deal with is anger. While it doesn't seem to make sense to be angry after a death—unless there is an obvious culprit such as a drunken driver or a murderer—grieving people often experience a great deal of anger: anger at life, anger at God, anger at fate, anger at their own impotence. Unfortunately, it is the rare person who can identify this anger and express it appropriately. It is generally directed at others—a hospital or doctor who is believed to have caused the death, or the person at the cleaners who lost the laundry—or at oneself to surface later in physical symptoms.

Finally, grieving people often experience emancipation and relief after a death. Especially if the dying period has been long and painful, the survivors may welcome a chance finally to resume their lives. This is sometimes a source of guilt for the grieving person who may not think that such positive feelings should be part of the grieving period, yet these feelings can be used to great benefit for recovery from the grief.

Grief Following Violent Death

My fiancé was murdered, apparently by burglars who entered the house. I was in another town at the time, and when the police called to notify me, my initial reaction was overwhelmingly physical. I walked into the bathroom and the entire contents of my digestive system turned to diarrhea. Then the convulsive shaking began, and alternate cold chills and hot sweats lasted for days and nights. I felt as though someone had whirled around with a very heavy board and had caught me in the mid-section with it; it took my breath away for months. Tears were the last thing on my mind. Rather, I felt as though I were riding a bucking bronco called my body, with a new surprising symptom every few minutes.

The ensuing months were no less of a surprise. Total numbness set in. Fear stalked me as I realized in agony that the police were in fact not going to catch the culprits. The world no longer seemed to make sense. If someone could murder a kind and gentle man such as John, how could anything make sense? What had I done to bring this into my life? The questions were deep and endless. My family and friends tried to do what they thought would help, which in many cases definitely did not help, but in fact added to my pain. Then I began the process of rebuilding myself and my life.

Most of the research that has been done on grief has used older widows and widowers as the subjects of study. For this reason, relatively little information is available on the nature of the grief process when death has occurred due to violence. In 1981, murder was the tenth leading cause of death in the United States (Federal Bureau of Investigation, as quoted in Rynearson, 1984).[1] Under any circumstances, losing a loved one is difficult enough, but when the event is due to murder, there are some additional psychological problems which present themselves. Dr. Edward Rynearson of the Mason Clinic in Seattle has conducted a study of family members of victims of homicide who had also lost family members due to non-homicidal death. It was their unanimous observation that the psychological processing of homicide was accompanied by reactions that differed from the previously experienced forms of bereavement.

Rynearson makes the observation that in the case of murder, death is violent and transgressive. He observed that all family members of homicide victims noted the presence of intrusive, repetitive images of the homicide. Since none of them had actually witnessed the murder, these images drew from the reports of witnesses, the police, or their own imaginations. Because of these recurring, intrusive images, which often also filled dream life, the subjects' concentration and thought sequencing were disrupted daily or weekly for a period of six to eighteen months. All subjects reported a pervasive fear that lasted in most cases six to eight months. For a few of the subjects, the fear never subsided:

> Compulsive behaviors of self-protection were so intense during the first year of bereavement that the subjects' usual range of territorial and affiliative behaviors was constricted; unfamiliar surroundings were circumvented, home became a protected fortress, strangers were avoided, and there was a compulsive need for the proximity and tangible assurance of the safety of remaining family members ... All subjects noted anger directed toward the murderer ... and all subjects noted behaviors directed toward retribution. (Rynearson, 1984, p. 1453)

Family members of suicide victims also report recurring images of the victim's death, increased feelings of guilt, and occasional feelings of being drawn toward committing the same act themselves. The reasoning seems to go as follows: if my family produced one person who committed suicide, perhaps it will produce another. As one of my clients wrote after the suicide of her sister:

> Once it has been done within the same constellation, within the same family, as close as the sister's psyche (scrambled eggs in bed), it is possible for me. Next. A conceivable route, a possible way. The little sister looks to see what the big sister points out, with admiration. Am I supposed to admire this? And suppose that it is an answer? I am caught by conflicting answers.

At the same time as the bereaved is working to separate from the deceased, there is also a strong tendency to identify with the deceased. This represents a particular problem in the case of homicide and suicide because the survivor has an internalized identification with someone who has suffered a very violent act. Encouraging the process of separation—seeing oneself as different from the deceased and not controlled by the same fate—is especially important in these cases.

When I first wrote these words in the 80s, there was not much treatment available for trauma. Fortunately, in the intervening years there has been a great deal of progress. The development of highly effective treatment, such as EMDR among others, has made it possible to resolve and lift many of the severe symptoms of trauma. My experience working with traumatic loss has shown me that the trauma work often must come first; until the trauma is lifted, the grief often lies hidden. It is not surprising for clients to find that years later after they have done some trauma work, (even after an unrelated trauma) suddenly the grief is there in full force. This can be disconcerting and feel like one is going backwards, but in my experience it seems to be the course that the work often may take. It is helpful if the therapist can normalize the experience and facilitate the full grieving, even if years after the event.

Spiritual Aspects of Grieving

Because bereavement brings up many life and death issues, the mourning period can be a profound time. The bereaved person's whole system is working overtime to heal the shock of the death, and the grieving may be remembered as one of the times of being most in touch with the essence of life and of Self, even for people who have had no previous spiritual awareness at all. The bereaved person readily perceives certain profound truths during the grieving process.

At the same time, because the mourning person may be in a terrible argument with God and with life, he or she may alternate between moments of sublime union and moments of deep doubt and anger. If the death has been shocking or seemingly unjustified, the grieving person may be in the process of questioning his or her most basic beliefs. Following the untimely death of his wife, C. S. Lewis wrote:

> Not that I am (I think) in much danger of ceasing to believe in God. The real danger is of coming to believe such dreadful things about Him. The conclusion I dread is not, "So there's no God after all," but "So this is what God's really like. Deceive yourself no longer."
> (1961, p, 5)

For Lewis, as for many bereaved people, making peace again with God is part of the grief process. Psychosynthesis is ideally suited to dealing with these spiritual aspects of grieving because its conceptual framework already acknowledges Spirit and suggests ways to work with it. To dialogue with the Self when one is greatly at odds with and distrustful of it opens a door to the radiance of the Self which may overcome pain and assist in healing wounds.

Stages and Tasks of Grieving

Several writers have divided the aspects of grieving into stages. Bowlby describes the stages thusly (1980, p. 85):

Phase 1—numbing that usually lasts from a few hours to a week and may be interrupted by outbursts of extremely intense distress and/or anger.

Phase 2—yearning and searching for the lost figure, lasting some months and sometimes for years.

Phase 3—disorganization and despair.

Phase 4—greater or lesser degree of reorganization.

Parkes (1972, p. 7) also divides grieving into stages, and calls them numbness, pining, depression, and recovery.

Freud (1917, p. 244) talks about the "work" of mourning. The objective is to recognize gradually the reality of a death that has occurred and to withdraw one's attachment to the deceased.

An understanding of the phases one is likely to pass through in the mourning process is helpful as long as one does not get caught in the belief that phases must be experienced in a precise order. Many people seem to be in several phases simultaneously. One explanation I might use in psychosynthesis work is that each of the subpersonalities must pass through all of the phases, and each may have a different rate in doing so.

It is also helpful to know that grief work, except in the very early stages, does not go on all the time. The bereaved person may have hours or days of intense grieving interspersed with relatively normal times. It is important to remember that people grieve in different ways, and what is normal for one should not be expected from another.

A balance is required in grief work between moving too slowly and moving too quickly. In the early stages after a death, the whole system may shut down because there is simply too much to take in all at once. There may be a reluctance to open up to the material again because earlier it was so overwhelming. Yet without opening to the grief, it cannot be successfully processed.

In his work on grief counseling and grief therapy, Worden (1982, pp. 11-16) presents a slightly different view of the phases of grieving. He affords the grieving person a far more active role by addressing what he calls the "tasks" of grieving. I find this approach, in which the Will can assist in the healing, to be very helpful. According to Worden, the tasks are as follows:

Task 1— to accept the reality of the loss. The searching behavior mentioned earlier is part of this task. The bereaved person must leave no stone unturned until he or she is completely convinced that the loved one is truly gone. Only then can he or she begin the next task.

Task 2— to experience the pain of grief. Parkes (1972) suggests that anything that allows the person to avoid or suppress the pain of grieving can be expected to prolong the course of mourning. He questions the appropriateness of using drugs for this reason. Worden notes, "There may be a subtle interplay between society and the mourner which makes the completion of Task 2 more difficult. Society may be uncomfortable with the mourner's feelings and hence may give the subtle message, 'You don't need to grieve.'

This interferes with the mourner's own defenses, leading to denial of the need to grieve" (1982, p. 13). Bowlby comments, "Sooner or later, some of those who avoid all conscious grieving break down—usually with some form of depression" (1980, p. 158). This is most likely to occur on the anniversary of a death that has not been mourned, or at the time of another loss, even if of a relatively minor kind, or upon reaching the age of a parent who has died.

I suggest an addition to Worden's Task 2—namely, healing and transforming the wound. I think it is important not only to express and experience the pain of grief, but also to acknowledge that in that very experience an alchemical process can occur which transforms the pain and makes us deeper and more insightful as human beings. The negation of Task 2 is not to feel; experiencing the pain of loss enables one to move on to the next task.

Task 3 — to adjust to an environment in which the deceased is missing. This may involve learning new skills and taking on new roles. In many cases, this may open up a whole new world of possibilities for the bereaved so that even though the task may be frightening it offers great rewards.

Task 4 — to withdraw emotional energy and re-invest it in another relationship. At the right time, it is necessary to move on to new relationships. Resistance may occur, either because it appears to indicate infidelity to the one who has died, or because there may be fear of entering something which could lead to a similar loss. Some people realize years later that they lost a certain ability to love after the death of a loved one. The successful completion of Task 4 lies in opening again to the full depth of love.

The Role of Friends and Therapists

> The person who is most valued [at the time of bereave-ment] is not the one who expresses the most sympathy but the person who "sticks around,' quietly gets on with day-to-day household tasks and makes few demands on the bereaved. Such a person must he prepared to accept without reproach the tendency of the bereaved person to pour out feelings of anguish and anger, some of which may be directed against the helper. In fact, it may be

necessary for the helper to indicate to the bereaved that he or she expects such feelings to emerge and that there is no need for them to he "bottled up." The helper should not "pluck at the heartstrings" of the bereaved until breakdown occurs any more than he or she should connive with the bereaved in endless attempts to avoid the grief work. Both probing and "jollying along" are unhelpful. The bereaved person has a painful and difficult task to perform which cannot he avoided and cannot he rushed. True help consists in recognizing this fact and in helping the bereaved person to arrange things in whatever way is necessary to set him or her free for the task of grieving. (Parkes, 1972, p. 161)

Friends can help most by understanding the nature of the grief process the bereaved is undergoing and by supporting it. This is most possible for those who have dealt with their own grief issues.

Principles of Grief Counseling

Worden (1982, pp. 39-48) has offered some very helpful principles for working with grieving clients. In the following section, I would like to adapt these principles for the use of the psychosynthesis practitioner. The principles stated are Worden's; the techniques suggested to implement each principle are my own, based in psychosynthesis.

Principle 1—Help the survivor to actualize the loss. When the loss seems too overwhelming to comprehend or when it doesn't even seem that it happened, the counselor can serve as a reality check, affirming that the death has in fact occurred. And when the grieving person is overwhelmed with the actuality of the loss, the counselor can provide a sense of perspective: yes, there has been a loss, but it is not the only factor in the bereaved person's life. In order to integrate the reality of the loss that has occurred, the subpersonality which best grasps the reality can explain to the other subpersonalities what has happened. The others can then express the sense of unbelief. In the ensuing dialogue, the more protective subpersonalities can be encouraged to allow the fearful subpersonalities to experience sorrow.

When the pain of the sorrow is too great, the practitioner can use disidentification exercises in order to draw back from the pain: "I am experiencing pain, but I am not that pain." On the other hand, when the client has lost a sense of the reality of the event, the practitioner can help by asking such questions as, "Tell me when it happened," or "Who was present at the last moments?" A bit of gentle questioning is usually all that is needed to allow the bereaved person to begin to talk about the experience. There is always a balance between moving too fast and moving too slow in actualizing the loss. The grieving person has his or her own inner rhythm which dictates how fast the work can be done.

Principle 2—Help the survivor to identify and express feelings. Because of the perceived necessities of living, the grieving person may bury feelings so much that they are difficult to access, even in a counseling session. Gentle non-verbal techniques, such as drawing, listening to music, singing, and lying on one's back, are often able to dislodge the expression of feeling. Sometimes the grieving person just needs some time and a safe space in which to cry. Sometimes levels of rage are felt which can astonish and frighten the individual. To help clients express rage, the technique which I use (for which I would like to credit Elisabeth Kubler-Ross) involves destroying a telephone book with a rubber hose. Among my clients, the record for the number of telephone books destroyed in a single session is held by a grieving woman who succeeded in totally disintegrating three large telephone books in less than an hour. Rage must be given a voice and an expression if the client is to move through the grief.

Principle 3—Assist the survivor in living without the deceased. This may mean assisting clients with very practical problems, such as exploring the possibility of living in less expensive accommodation, overcoming the fears around looking for a job, and making decisions as a single parent for the first time. Because the bereaved person may have a great number of practical tasks to accomplish at once, and because he or she may feel less capable than ever at performing these tasks, he or she may need assistance in thinking problems through and deciding on a plan of action. As the grieving person begins to perform new tasks, old subpersonalities also die and must be mourned; new ones are being born and must be nurtured and welcomed. A client who lost her husband had difficulty in welcoming a new more independent version of herself because, after over 40 years of marriage, she had developed an apparent disdain for self-reliant women. So as one part of her enjoyed new-found strengths, another part blamed herself for growing "unfeminine."

Principle 4—Facilitate emotional withdrawal from the deceased. This can be done through talking about lost loved ones, and on occasion dialoguing with them in another chair. This must be handled with sensitivity because the bereaved will alternate between needing to remember the deceased, needing to complete the relationship, and needing to move on to other relationships. The counselor must respect the current phase, and know that its complement will present itself in time.

Principle 5—Provide time to grieve. This may mean suggesting that the grieving person take time off work, drop some responsibilities, or go back to a familiar and comforting place. Leading the client in a guided imagery exercise along a path which goes "back home" may give some clues as to where the grieving person is most likely to receive comfort.

Principle 6—Interpret "normal" behavior. After a significant loss, many people have the sense they are going crazy. It is reassuring to clients to know that their symptoms, while uncomfortable, are at least normal for grief process. Helping clients to construct an ideal model for their grief process allows them to choose to participate in the process rather than to be bounced around by what appears to be craziness.

Principle 7—Allow for individual differences. All people do not grieve in the same way. Encourage the client to validate his or her own experience regardless of what others may be saying or experiencing.

Principle 8—Provide continuing support. Even though clients may terminate therapy, or move on to other issues in their lives, from time to time the grief will surface again. Very often the grieving person will have a recurrence of symptoms around the three-month, one-year, and two-year anniversary of the death, and around other significant times, such as birthdays, wedding anniversaries, holidays, and so on. When a client is experiencing a renewal of symptoms, the counselor should ask if the date is significant.

Principle 9—Examine defenses and coping styles. Since coping styles such as substance abuse, overwork, overeating, or denial will be heightened after loss, this is a good time to examine their effectiveness. The counselor should also encourage positive coping techniques such as meditation, healthy eating, exercise, and time spent with good friends. Clients have a unique opportunity to observe how their customary practices serve them in a time of stress.

The Psychosynthesis Context

What is of even more importance than techniques is the framework in which the therapeutic work is done. Psychosynthesis offers a unique approach which acknowledges the spiritual qualities of the client. For its practitioners, the Self, that spark of Divine Essence, is always at work, no matter how bleak the situation may appear. This means that they know that they are not alone in providing relief. Because inside each grieving person there exists a core of being which knows, therapeutically, the right thing to do, the work of the practitioner is to support grieving people by honoring what is true for them and by acknowledging that their feelings, beliefs, and intuitions are probably more accurate at this time in their lives than they have ever been. It is my experience that grieving people are more likely than other kinds of clients to have a strong sense of what is needed for healing, and so the work of the practitioner is to validate these feelings. The grieving person's own sense of what to do may often fly in the face of what society says is correct or what friends and family advise. But my belief, founded in psychosynthesis, is that the healing force within each person is to be recognized and supported.

As psychosynthesists, we are also uniquely able to validate the spiritual experiences that the grieving person may be having. In the grief experience, there is often a re-arranging of priorities, a sense of new values emerging, and in many cases a sense of being in touch with profound spiritual energy. It is of great value for the practitioner to "normalize" these occurrences, especially for clients who have no prior experience of such things. The psychosynthesis practitioner who has developed a spiritual discipline can at once support and encourage the spiritual insights that occur in a time of grief, and can serve as a reality check when the bereaved person becomes "ungrounded" and needs to deal with the more mundane parts of the grieving task.

At the same time, one of the traps the psychosynthesis practitioner needs to be aware of in working with grieving clients concerns the subject of spirituality. In working with clients who are having profound spiritual insights with great regularity, psychosynthesists, because of their general inclination and the historical tendency of their discipline, may be tempted to collude with them in spending too much time on spiritual issues as a way of avoiding the terribly painful therapeutic work that eventually must be done. The clues are usually there when the client needs to move into other arenas. The alert practitioner who is comfortable with dealing with difficult issues will be able to read them.

The greatest gift that the practitioner can give to sorrowing clients is to both fully share their burden, their loss, and their horror, and to maintain contact with Spirit, to help them discover that in the darkest moments healing is present. It has been my experience, in both my work and in my personal process, that unearthing buried griefs can bring new freedom to the soul, new depth to the experience of life, and a greatly expanded ability to love. Recognizing the symptoms of grief, and understanding the nature of the tasks to be completed, can facilitate the healing and transformative potential in the grieving process. As psychosynthesis practitioners and as human beings, we have much to gain from embracing the grief that comes to us.

I am deeply aware that all of Life is a gift, if we choose to see it that way; experiences of loss can be the most profound of teachers.

References

Bowlby, J. (1980), *Attachment and Loss: Loss, Sadness and Depression.* New York: Basic Books.

Freud, S. (1917). *Mourning and Melancholia* (Vol. 14). Standard Edition.

Kalish, R. (1985). *Death, Grief and Caring Relationships.* Monterey, California: Brooks/Cole Publishing Company,

Lewis, C. S. (1961). *A Grief Observed.* New York; Seabury Press.

Lindemann, E, (1979). *Beyond Grief: Studies in Crisis Intervention.* Northvale, NJ: Aronson,

Parkes, C. (1972). *Bereavement: Studies in Adult Grief.* New York. International Universities Press.

Rafael, B, (1982). *The Anatomy of Bereavement.* New York: Basic Books.

Rynearson, E. (1984). "Bereavement after Homicide: A Descriptive Study." American Journal of Psychiatry, 141 (11).

Steiner, R. (1930). *Between Death and Rebirth.* London: Rudolf Steiner Press.

Tatelbaum, J. (1980). *The Courage to Grieve.* New York: Harper & Row.

Worden, J. M. (1982), *Grief Counseling and Grief Therapy: A Handbook for the Mental Health Practitioner.* New York: Springer.

This article was revised by the author in 2017.

Notes

---

[1] By 2017 murder was the 15th leading cause of death for the overall population

of the United States; however it was more significant for some segments of the population; for example, it was the leading cause of death for African-American males between the ages of 15-34—*Ed.*

Kay Lynne Sherman, PhD, *was first introduced to psychosynthesis while living in the spiritual community of Findhorn in the 70s and early 80s. Piero Ferrucci and Diana Whitmore came to the community and presented an introductory intensive. Upon leaving Findhorn, Kay Lynne pursued more psychosynthesis training in the San Francisco area with Tom Yeomans, Phillip Brooks and Steven Kull, among others. At the same time she was pursuing a PhD in Clinical Psychology with the idea of changing careers from teacher to Psychologist. All these years later, years spent as a psychosynthesis trainer and coach, licensed Psychologist in private practice, narrator for the award-winning documentary* Grief is More than Crying, *hiker, musician, world traveler, she still regards the understandings of psychosynthesis as a foundation for much of what she does.*

Psychosynthesis and Recovery from Addictions

Richard Schaub, PhD
Bonney Gulino Schaub, MS, RN

Introduction

Addiction is a mental obsession that leads to a physical compulsion (Alcoholics Anonymous, 1976). Roberto Assagioli stated it succinctly in his first psychological law: "Images or mental pictures tend to produce the . . .external acts that correspond to them" (Assagioli, 1974).

This article refers to alcoholism as our clinical example of addiction, but of course there are many others drugs that people become addicted to. Use of cocaine, heroin, marijuana, anti-anxiety agents (e.g., Valium, Xanax), painkillers (e.g., Oxycontin, Vicodin) can develop into mental obsessions that lead to compulsive abuse. In addition, there are obsessive and compulsive syndromes without alcohol or drugs, including bulimia, anorexia, gambling, pornography and sex addiction, which follow the same dynamic of pre-occupying, driven, obsessive thoughts leading to predictable, repetitive, compulsive physical actions.

Despite their differences, all addictions have one factor in common: their pathway to recovery and healing. In this article, we show how psychosynthesis principles and practices empower the pathway of recovery from addictions.

The Beginning of an Obsession

The mental obsession with alcohol has its origins in a client's early experience of alcohol as a "medicine" for the relief of anxiety and vulnerability. In the histories of so many people in recovery, they remember the first time when alcohol took away their apprehensions and uncertainty and made them feel "normal." Stated with humor but seriously meant, a man in recovery said, "By the time I got to kindergarten, I knew I needed a drink."

This theme of *needing something to feel normal*, and then finding it in alcohol, is the early basis for the attachment of the person to alcohol. It is then relied upon in any situation in which the client feels vulnerable. Social events, tests, job interviews, difficult family matters all become more *manageable* with drinking alcohol as a behavior to calm them down or make them feel more confident. Life certainly provides us with countless occasions of vulnerability, and so alcohol as the answer may be reinforced repeatedly. Once the attachment and obsession with alcohol as a source of comfort is established as a brain pattern, the compulsion to act on it is set in motion. A physical compulsion can have no limit: if it is physiologically possible, some alcoholic clients will drink all day long every day. In Dante's *Inferno*, Cerberus in the realm of gluttony is the precise picture of insatiable compulsion (Schaub & Schaub, 2003).

Why Do Some People Become Addicted?

Most people can enjoy the relaxing effects of alcohol without becoming obsessed by it. What makes the alcoholic different? To answer this, we need to review the theoretical models of addiction.

Models of Addiction

There are at least eleven theoretical models of addiction (Schaub & Schaub, 1997).

> *The Medical Model:* The client has been consuming significant amounts of alcohol over a long period of time. Deprived of it, the client's central nervous system goes into a state of physiological craving (withdrawal). To suppress the craving, the client must continue alcohol consumption.

> *The Genetic Disease Model:* The client has a genetic, bio-chemical predisposition to alcoholism. The predisposition is activated by the use of alcohol.

> *The Self-Medication Model:* Perhaps due to trauma, the client experiences an intolerable degree of fear in daily life. He uses alcohol to soothe his anxiety.

The Dysfunctional Family Model: The client learned from people in his family that one copes with anxiety and/or depression by consuming alcohol.

The Psychosexual Development Model: The infant did not experience adequate nurturing at the oral phase of development and becomes psychologically fixated at that stage. The adult form of the oral fixation is the consuming of alcohol.

The Ego Psychology Model: Deprived of adequate nurturing and mirroring as an infant, the client has weak ego strengths and cannot tolerate the pressures of life. Alcohol relieves the pressure.

The Character Defect Model: An early model offered by the 12-Step program of Alcoholics Anonymous, it proposed that alcoholics are morally and characteriologically "defective" and require alcohol to pacify their "self-centered fears."

The Instant Gratification Model: Alcoholics are people who have a low threshold for frustration and need instant satisfaction of their impulses. This impulsiveness is reinforced by the hurried pace and materialistic craving of modern life.

The Trance Model: This is based on the pleasure principle. Once the brain has experienced the pleasure of intoxication, it stores the experience like a hypnotic suggestion and desires to repeat it.

The Transpersonal-Intoxication Model: Based on the observed connection between artists and alcoholism, this model's thesis is that the alcoholic "thirst" is really a spiritual thirst for expanded consciousness.

The Transpersonal-Existential Model: This model accepts that (1) the human condition is innately vulnerable and anxious and that, (2) alcoholics are people who experience this existential anxiety more acutely.

These models are greatly simplified. Their theme, though, is clear. Essential feelings of vulnerability cause or contribute to the development of addiction. This emphasis on vulnerability is verified for the authors by thirty-five years of clinical experience with hundreds of people in recovery in rehabilitation centers, outpatient clinics, and individual and group psychotherapy in private practices. Clients repeatedly described that their addiction temporarily solved the problem of feeling disturbed by the demands of daily life. Therefore, therapeutic attention must be given to the client's underlying vulnerability in order help him recover successfully.

Early Treatment Principles

No therapist has the power to stop an alcoholic from drinking. Other factors—the family, the client's doctor, the employer, the use of rehabilitation centers—must be involved in the initial confrontation of the alcoholic. The therapist becomes significant when the actual drinking has stopped and the client has detoxified.

Once detoxified, the alcoholic is technically a client in the recovery process. But an alcoholic without alcohol is now exposed to the pain of life without his "medicine" and will return to alcohol for relief from his vulnerability. This accounts for the many early failures in alcohol treatment. "Relapse"—the return to drinking—is an unfortunate but typical part of the early recovery process. Neither the client nor the therapist should be disheartened by relapse. It is understandable in view of the enormous life-change the alcoholic is beginning.

What does it take to finally stop? In the 12-Step programs, they refer to that moment as "hitting bottom." Edward, known in the community as a successful business executive, came out of the liquor store and accidentally dropped four bottles of Scotch whiskey on the sidewalk. With the shattered glass at his feet and people staring at him, he was completely humiliated. He knew from that moment on that alcohol had taken away his dignity, and he screamed inside his mind *Never again*.

Stopping drinking does not mean that the obsessive thoughts stop. On the contrary, the thoughts will often grow more insistent when they are not responded to by the compulsive action. Early therapy therefore needs to be behavioral and psychoeducational, teaching the recovering client new ways of behaving when the old, deeply habituated thoughts of alcohol become stimulated.

The individual therapist may be capable of accomplishing this if the client is seen frequently during each week. If this is not feasible, then the therapist should have the client engage in the 12-Step program of Alcoholics Anonymous or another group psychoeducational process. The basis of success of the 12-Step programs is that they offer an accepting community in which the behaviors of sobriety are repetitiously taught. For example, when the recovering client notices that he is again obsessing about alcohol, he is taught to call another person in the 12-Step program—a "sponsor"—and to go to a 12-Step meeting as soon as possible. By doing so, he breaks down the old syndrome of obsessive thought leading to compulsive action by replacing the action with a new, healthier action.

If the client accepts the 12-Step guidance, he literally begins to build a new pattern in his personality: that of a "sober" person. He doesn't yet *feel* like a sober person, but he accepts that he must imitate the behaviors of a sober person in order to save his life. It is the "as if " technique: he needs to practice thinking and behaving "as if " he is a sober person.

Case Vignette: Edward

In the case of Edward, he did not accept much involvement with the 12-Step approach. He went to a few meetings but felt too much conflict about revealing his feelings in such a public place. In addition, his status in the business community made him worry that the 12 Step meetings might lead to someone gossiping about him and ruining his professional reputation. He started psychosynthetic therapy with the need to build and strengthen his new identity as a sober person.

This new sober pattern needs to become strong enough to create a conscious choice in the client: the new sober pattern versus the old, established alcoholic pattern of thinking and behaving. In psychosynthesis terms, Edward would be learning how to identify with (i.e., direct energy toward) his new sober self and to disidentify (withdraw energy) from his alcoholic self. If successful in building the new pattern, Edward would be able to literally hear and feel the two sides—the new sober pattern and the old alcoholic one—arguing in his mind and emotions.

Because of his early sobriety of only three months when he started therapy, Edward was referred by the therapist for acupuncture to help balance out his nervous system. He also required a quick-acting, non-addictive herbal supplement for moments of anxiety and vulnerability which, in the past, would have been quieted by drinking. These are simply examples of the holistic outlook that should be involved in the recovery process.

At the start of therapy, Edward was 45 years old with a 25 year history of drinking alcoholically, "a habit I picked up in college." Despite this, he was married, had two teenage children, and was a major figure in a large Manhattan bank. For years, he had fooled himself into believing that "everyone drinks," but eventually he became aware that he drank differently than other people. Out at dinner, he would watch other people drink and then stop, a behavior which would baffle him. He, after all, wanted to continue drinking until he was drunk. He wondered what the "switch" was that allowed other people to turn off the desire to keep drinking. The early goal of our psychotherapy became the development of that "switch" before he even had a single drink. Our goal together was not controlling the amount he drank but stopping it entirely.

The two psychosynthesis psychotherapy practices that proved extremely helpful at this stage of his recovery were the strengthening of the observing self, and the therapeutic use of imagery.

Assagioli was far ahead of his time in emphasizing the centrality of the observing self—the "I" space—in any therapeutic work. His view is now verified by the many studies that confirm the therapeutic effectiveness of mindfulness meditation, a practice in which the observing self is specifically cultivated.

The observing self, awareness itself, consciousness, attention, etc. are all terms to describe the aspect of our nature that ceaselessly notices our experience. Our observing self notices our anxiety but is not anxious; observes our anger but is not angry; observes our thoughts but does not think. The special characteristics of our observing self make it a great ally in not getting involved in obsessive thoughts. By strengthening our observing self, we can notice obsessive thoughts rising in our mind, not identify with them, and watch them fall away. The latest brain research confirms that strengthening our awareness in this way literally, physiologically, builds stronger integrative fibers in the executive center of our brain which modulates fear and reactivity (Massachusetts General Hospital, 2011).

Utilizing the observing self practice, Edward began to recognize more clearly the thoughts and feelings that were associated with the urge to drink. The following are the techniques that were used to accomplish this:

Stream of Consciousness (verbalized out loud)

This is most effective if you, the therapist, demonstrate it first. By doing so, clients see the simplicity and low demand of the technique. Your willingness to practice in front of them also communicates a spirit of collaboration on this journey into meditative experiences.

Steps
1. Make yourself comfortable in your chair and close your eyes ...
2. Now begin to say out loud whatever comes into your awareness ... Don't need to explain it ... just name it ...

After you have demonstrated it, elicit any questions the clients have, and then ask them to try it. Let clients do this for two minutes and then ask them to stop and to open their eyes.

Discussion: As simple as the technique may appear, you are actually introducing a profound teaching to your clients. The act of noticing that things come into awareness, to then be shortly replaced by the next thing that comes into awareness, to then be replaced by the next thing, etc., demonstrates the flux of the mind and sensations. While the client may identify with thoughts and body sensations and think of them as " me" and "mine," in fact they are passing in and out of existence all of the time.

Through demonstrating this flux to your client, you are introducing an inner resource that is deeper than the passing thoughts and sensations — the ceaseless presence of awareness itself. Thoughts, feelings, urges, and sensations all come and go, come and go, and yet your awareness it always there, always present. You can tell a client this, and they may intellectually understand it, but the goal here is to have the client experience it personally.

Stream of Consciousness (verbalized in the mind)

This is a variation of the previous technique. The client will do the same noticing and naming practice, except this time they will only verbalize it in the privacy of their minds.

Steps
(The instructions you give)
3. Make yourself comfortable in your chair and close your eyes...
4. Now begin to notice whatever comes into your awareness and name it in the privacy of your mind . . . Just notice it and name it and then wait to see what comes next . . . If nothing comes, that's fine . . . Nothing special to do here . . . Nothing has to happen . . . Just noticing and naming . . .

(**Wait two minutes** and then ask them to stop and to open their eyes.)

We generally think of an obsession as a demanding, driven inner state of urgency, but it can also become a quieter voice in the mind, offering a gentle nudge, a "reasonable" argument for drinking again. The client's self-observation skills need to be able to detect and disidentify from this subtler level of the obsession since it does remain a destructive force.

Edward took well to the Stream of Consciousness techniques. He could observe in his mind what Alcoholics Anonymous calls the "insidious logic" of addiction, i.e., the many ways that the obsessive thought pattern advocates for the person to act on the obsession to drink again. The specific thought in Edward's mind that logically argued for his return to drinking was this: *Now that you have stopped drinking, you have proven you can do it. Go ahead and drink when you feel like it—after all, you can stop anytime you want to.*

Uncertain that he would be able to resist drinking again, Edward could both spot the absurdity of this addictive logic and yet feel tempted to follow its advice. This led to our use of a second psychosynthetic skill: therapeutic imagery.

Therapeutic imagery can positively reinforce a client's identification with the new sober self by imaginally rehearsing sober thinking and sober behaviors in the various scenes of his current life. Imagery can also be used as a negative reinforcement, imaginally rehearsing what life will become if the client returns to alcohol. In the 12-Step programs, they call this negative reinforcement "thinking through a drink."

This "thinking through a drink" was the form of imagery that Edward originally employed to counteract the insidious logic of addiction. He would notice the logic advising him that it was safe to drink, and he would then switch in his mind to an image of a moment of humiliation connected to his drinking days.

With the psychosynthesis practices of 1) strengthening the observing self to disidentify from obsessive thoughts when they arise and, 2) the therapeutic use of imagery to positively reinforce the new sober self and negatively reinforce the consequences of returning to drinking, Edward had the basic inner skills to counteract the obsession to drink. At this point, attention to a client's vulnerability needs emphasis. Despite everything he is learning in early recovery, it would be intolerable feelings of vulnerability that could cause Edward to relapse and return to alcohol.

Fight/Flight Symptoms

The observing self, awareness itself, consciousness, attention, etc. are all terms to describe the aspect of our nature that ceaselessly notices our experience. Our observing self notices our anxiety but is not anxious; observes our anger but is not angry; observes our thoughts but does not think. The special characteristics of our observing self make it a great ally in not getting involved in obsessive thoughts. By strengthening our observing self, we can notice obsessive thoughts rising in our mind, not identify with them, and watch them fall away. The latest brain research confirms that strengthening our awareness in this way literally, physiologically, builds stronger integrative fibers in the executive center of our brain which modulates fear and reactivity (Massachusetts General Hospital, 2011).

To assist the therapist in discerning the client's degree of vulnerability, the following list of fight and flight symptoms can be helpful. Fight and flight symptoms are of course the two primal instincts of any human being when we feel unsafe and vulnerable. The recovering alcoholic, no longer using alcohol to medicate his feelings, will display many intense symptoms of fight and/or flight. The client will not be able to describe the subtleties of vulnerability, but he will be able to tell you that he wanted to beat up his boss (fight) or that he ate a half gallon of ice cream and became ill (flight) after his girlfriend argued with him.

The list describes the typical fight/flight patterns in the recovering alcoholic. As the therapist hears some of the listed fight/flight symptoms in his client, he will be hearing the indicators of vulnerability.

Fight

Mental Patterns of Fight: Rigidity, obsessiveness, lack of creativity, black and white thinking, judgmentalism, intolerance, fanaticism, hypervigilance, arrogance, manipulativeness.

Physical Patterns of Fight: Hypertension, headaches, gastrointestinal disturbances, chronic muscle tension, rigid diets, body armoring, workaholism, forcing the body to exceed limits (e.g., risk taking, extreme exercise).

Emotional Patterns of Fight: Constricted affect, rigid control of feelings, grandiosity, fake performance of feelings, denial of vulnerability, overly aggressive, rageful, domineering.

Spiritual Patterns of Fight: Self-righteous, fundamentalism, dogmatism, attempts to control other people's inner lives, negation of spirituality.

Flight

Mental Patterns of Flight: Chronic refusal to decide, numbed mental processes, disconnection, dissociation, self-deprecation, victimized thinking, unthinking acceptance of others' opinions and demands, indifference, inability to focus, self-pity, self-absorption.

Physical Patterns of Flight: Low energy, compulsive TV watching, repetitive self-soothing, overeating, immobilization, avoidance, isolation, lack of self-care.

Emotional Patterns of Flight: Helplessness, hopelessness, emotional flooding, guilt and shame, unworthiness, co-dependence.

Spiritual Patterns of Flight: Magical thinking, narcissistic theology, nondirected, superficial spiritual dabbling, emptiness, lack of relatedness to a larger vision of life, lack of trust in his own experiences, lack of meaning or purpose.

When a pattern of fight and/or flight is recognized, the therapist can then explore the incident that triggered the fight/flight reaction. Predictably, the incident will reveal a vulnerable moment.

The client who wanted to beat up his boss was asked to go back into his memory and to see what triggered his impulse to fight. He saw in his memory that his fight reaction was the result of a mild criticism from the boss. The client who ate a half gallon of ice cream saw in his memory that his flight reaction was triggered the moment his girlfriend appeared bored with him. Gaining recognition of the impact of criticism or inattention moves the therapy toward the core issue of vulnerability itself, rather than staying focused on the incident with the boss or girlfriend.

Emotional Development in Recovery

The therapist's focus on the client's experiences of vulnerability will in time help the client to recognize those vulnerable moments for himself. With this increased self-knowledge as the groundwork, the client then needs to learn new, healthier responses to his moments of vulnerability, rather than continue in patterns of fight/flight reactivity.

The therapist should not assume that the client will know any healthy adaptive responses. The client was medicating himself with alcohol all the years when others were learning how to cope with the anxieties that inevitably come with being alive. There is a formula: the age at which the client began heavy drinking is the age of his arrested emotional development. For example, if he was drinking heavily by age sixteen, your client may be chronologically forty-two years old but he is emotionally a sixteen year old in terms of emotional skills. This formula is descriptive, not judgmental, and is meant to be a starting place for new development.

Five Emotional Developments for Recovery

There are five important developments in the process of recovery. The first two are concepts that can be taught and discussed until the client can integrate them.

The first development is the recognition that "feelings aren't facts." This is borrowed from the 12-Step programs. It establishes that, although you may feel unsafe and vulnerable in a certain situation, it does not mean that you are in fact unsafe. The concept tries to modify the trigger between vulnerability and fight/flight. It tries to calm down the client's instinctive reactions and to increase the client's ability to choose his responses to feeling vulnerable.

The second development is the recognition of the normalcy of shifting feelings. The normal moment-to-moment flow of changing thoughts and moods can feel too unstable to the client in recovery. He needs to recognize and be reassured that the flux of change is normal and not a cause for worry. His years of alcoholism have prevented him from learning this fact of emotional life. He may, for example, report that he got very upset and didn't know what to do. The "normal" person knows that he or she can get upset and that he or she will survive it. The recovering alcoholic interprets being upset as a danger signal and an indication that he can't live without alcohol.

The third development is learning stress management skills. One of the benefits of Assagioli's work is that he encouraged therapists to be psychoeducators, to literally teach and train clients in self-care and therapeutic skills. As the mind-body medicine movement has grown, and skills such as meditation and imagery have been scientifically validated, more therapists are now including such teaching in their work with clients. As only one example, if a client walks into the office feeling very anxious, one possible response is to inquire about the anxiety and quite another is to teach the client in the moment how to reduce their stress and anxiety. Both responses have their value, but teaching the client pragmatic skills empowers them to take care of themselves.

Most anxiety-reducing and stress management skills are variations on meditation and imagery, but they must be chosen for their ease and practicality so that the client can utilize them anytime, anyplace. Yoga postures will not be possible on the bus, but a simple breathing technique will work well and go unnoticed by their fellow passengers. Many of our clients like this simple phrase which they repeat silently in their mind: "_____ (their first name), let go." In the post-traumatic stress of September 11th many of our Manhattan clients used this phrase as they entered the subway, crossed a bridge, rode in an elevator, or reacted nervously to a plane in the sky.

There are many stress management skills. In the psychosynthesis spirit of working collaboratively with a client, the therapist and client can try out many skills to discover which ones work best. To do this teaching, the therapist must him- or herself be a serious student of such skills.

The fourth development is the recognition of the need for a second recovery. It is the need to recover from trauma. In the authors' experience, the majority of alcoholics have significant trauma in their early years of development. This second recovery has not been typically dealt with in drug and alcohol treatment centers, but needs to be part of the psychotherapeutic work in recovery from addictions.

This second recovery from trauma is of course a long-term process. It is aided by the repeated corrective experiences the client can have with a psychosynthesis therapist whose training inclines him or her to work from a holistic view of the client's innate possibilities and sees the "alcoholic" as only one part of the client's nature.

The fifth development is spiritual practice and growth. Spirituality has long been a confusing subject in the world of psychology, but this has never been true in the treatment of alcoholics in the 12-Step movement. The illuminative experience of one of its founders, Bill Wilson, proved to be the basis for his own full recovery after many years of failed treatment (Cheever, 2005).

Many alcohol treatment centers incorporate spiritual development as part of the recovery process and usually defer to the 12-Step version of spirituality with concepts such as having a *higher power* which can restore you to sanity and praying to *God as you understand God.* In our professional experience, many clients in recovery are comforted by these ideas but have no direct experience of what the ideas actually mean. As a result, clients in recovery often go seeking beyond the 12-Steps to find a way of spiritual development that is right for them.

Psychosynthesis offers several advantages at this stage of recovery. Psychosynthesis is not a spiritual system itself but has the concepts and methods to help people to identify their own natural path to spirituality.

Case Vignette: Miriam

Assagioli observed that just as some cultures and societies may repress sexuality, modern scientific culture has encouraged us to repress the transcendent aspect of our being. One of his students called this "the repression of the sublime"—the denial, neglect, or negation of innate human spirituality (Haronian, 1967).

Miriam was a 62 year old woman who had started drinking heavily after the death of her husband ten years ago. Up until that time, she had been a social drinker. Six months ago, she stopped drinking because she was frightened by the forgetfulness and confusion she was experiencing.

Miriam had difficulty participating in AA because she felt too different from the people there. She was older than most of them, and her drinking had never interfered with her life until recently. She was also very turned off by the talk of spirituality. She said she was not at all interested in religion or spirituality. In fact, she had an active hatred of it. She had no use for God since God let her father and brother be killed in a Nazi concentration camp.

Miriam did a lot of traveling after her husband's death, using a large portion of her limited funds to do this. She traveled with passion and fervor. She went to France and sought out Gothic cathedrals. She adored the stained glass windows, especially the rose windows. She expressed being awed by the beauty of these places, but purely on an aesthetic level. She insisted it had nothing to do with the spirituality of the places.

Miriam traveled to India, not on a tour, but as a single woman on her own, because there were very particular places she wanted to visit. She had seen pictures of these places in travel books—especially an island where there were caves filled with Buddhas. While in India, she arranged for a young guide to bring her to the caves, and this too was a wonderful aesthetic experience.

Miriam also went to Mexico to visit the pyramids. She described experiencing a sense of timelessness and also a sense of familiarity as though she belonged there. She felt embraced by the sun and delighted by the colors and scents of this ancient place.

You can listen to Miriam and hear the quest of a woman searching for spiritual experiences through art and sacred places. When the psychosynthesis therapist explained that Miriam was actually practicing one of the classic spiritual paths—the path of aesthetics and beauty, Miriam felt released from her negativity toward spirituality. This was her path, on her own terms, and at the same time it was one of the universal ways that people choose to go beyond their ego self. This psychosynthetic reframing of her choices opened her to the entire subject of spirituality in a new way. It gave her hope that there were more experiences to come.

A client's spiritual search may go in many directions over the course of a lifetime. The psychosynthesis therapist can be helpful to, as Assagioli put it, "lead the client to the door" (Assagioli, 1965).

Summary

The following steps summarize a psychosynthesis approach to the process of recovery from addictions:

1. Addiction is an obsessive-compulsive cycle of thinking and behaving driven by vulnerability.

2. All people are vulnerable, but people who feel a greater degree of vulnerability are drawn to addiction as a remedy.

3. The first step in recovery from addiction is detoxification. Then psychoeducation and psychotherapy are possible.

4. The first task in psychoeducation and psychotherapy is the building of a new sober self.

5. Since the addiction was suppressing vulnerability, the end of addiction will cause vulnerability to be a primary issue again. People in recovery can begin to heal by gaining recognition of their vulnerability as it is revealed in their fight/flight reactions.

6. The client's continued recovery is based on developing new, healthier responses to vulnerability.

7. These new responses are concepts and methods that can be learned and practiced through a collaborative effort between client and therapist.

8. Stronger recovery includes spiritual development, and psychosynthesis offers insights and practices that can introduce the client to their natural spirituality.

The treatment of addictions is a complex process but well worth the effort. Even in the many frustrations of dealing with people in recovery, the therapist should remember this single point: addiction can be completely cured. People can lead the rest of their lives without addiction. The therapist gets the opportunity to participate with the client in the transformation of suffering into a purposeful life.

References

Alcoholics Anonymous (1976). *Alcoholics Anonymous: The Big Book, 3rd Edition.* New York: Alcoholics   Anonymous World Service.

Assagioli, R. (1965). *Psychosynthesis: A Manual of Techniques.* New York: Penguin.

Assagioli, R. (1974). *The Act of Will.* New York, NY: Viking Press.

Assagioli R. (1991). *Transpersonal Development.* London: Crucible.

Cheever S. (2005). *My Name is Bill: Bill Wilson – His Life and the Creation of Alcoholics Anonymous.* New York, NY: Washington Square Press.

Haronian, F. (1967). *Repression of the Sublime.* Psychosynthesis Research Foundation. Retrieved March 30, 2018 from http://www.synthesiscenter.org/articles/0130.pdf

Massachusetts General Hospital (2011, January 21). *Mindfulness meditation training changes brain structure in eight weeks.* Science Daily. Retrieved March 30, 2011, from http://www.sciencedaily.com/releases/2011/01/1101211440 07.htm

Schaub B & Schaub R. (1997). *Healing Addictions: The Vulnerability Model of Recovery.* Albany, NY: Delmar.

Schaub B & Schaub R. (2014). *Dante's Path: Vulnerability and the Spiritual Journey.* Huntington, NY: Florence Press.

This article was re-written and re-titled by the authors in 2018.

Richard Schaub, PhD, *is counseling psychologist and a professional member of the American Psychological Association and the New York Mental Health Counselors Association.*

Bonney Gulino Schaub, RN, MS, PMHCNS-BC, NC-BC, *developed Transpersonal Coaching from 40 years of work in mental health and holistic nursing as a clinical practitioner, educator, and author. She is a recognized leader in the integration of transpersonal practices into healthcare including training clinical staff at a Veteran's Administration hospital and presenting at integrative health conferences.*

Richard and Bonney Schaub *are co-founders and directors of the Huntington Meditation and Imagery Center and the New York Psychosynthesis Institute and have trained health professionals internationally. They are author or co-author of five books:* Healing Addictions: The Vulnerability Model of Recovery *(1997);* The End of Fear: A Spiritual Path for Realists *(2009);* Transpersonal Development: Cultivating the Human Resources of Peace, Wisdom, Purpose and Oneness *(2013);* Dante's Path: Vulnerability the Spiritual Journey*(2014) and numerous articles and book chapters on meditation, imagery, and coaching. They both have served on the Steering Committee of the Association for the Advancement of Psychosynthesis.*

Imagery and the Search for Healing

Rachel Naomi Remen, MD

My practice is with people who have chronic problems and their families, with people who have terminal illnesses and their families, and at least a third of my patients are "burnt out" health professionals. These are all people in search of healing, and it seems appropriate to share with you some of their stories and some of their experiences with imagery as they have gone about this search.

Wholistic Assumptions

I would like to begin by reviewing some of the wholistic assumptions that underlie the work I will be describing to you. "Wholism" means different things to different people, and I want to be sure we are thinking within the same frame of reference. Perhaps the most basic wholistic assumption is that the word "human being" is not a noun; it is a verb. Each one of us is a dynamic process—a process of both being and becoming.

The best example I could find, as I was working on this at two o'clock yesterday morning, was something that happened to me many years ago when I was invited to speak about health to a group of children, ranging in age from about six to twelve. I began with a rather arrogant statement: "Hello, I'm a doctor. I'm here to answer any questions you may have about your body." We were sitting outside on the grass and the children began to ask me questions that interested them, such as "When I see red, am I seeing the same thing that you see when you see red?" and "Where do I go when I go to sleep?" And of course, I was prepared to talk about the importance of diet and brushing your teeth, and they very quickly established the limit of my expertise ... and lost interest. One bored little boy, of about six, picked a yellow flower out of the grass and handed it to me saying, "Have a dandelion." The others immediately jumped on that, saying, "Oh, come on dummy, that's not a dandelion," and a girl picked a fluff ball out of the grass and said, "This is a dandelion; have a dandelion;" and of course, that started a whole argument that went back and forth, and someone else picked two little leaves and said, "This is a dandelion." And then another child said, "None of these things is a dandelion. A seed is a dandelion. A little seed, that's a dandelion." By then, the whole group was interested. Someone else said, "Dummy, a seed is nothing. It has nothing. That's not a dandelion." Finally the discussion was brought to an abrupt halt by one child who said, "No, you're all silly—none of those things is a dandelion. A dandelion is something that's happening at a time and place in the world." (I just want to tell you that child was a girl.) And of course, that's a way of looking at us all.

We are all something that is happening at a certain time and place in the world. And what is this human happening that we are all involved in? Well, it's a certain kind of growth—not just a change in size, but a change in essential nature. An acorn just doesn't become a bigger acorn. It becomes an oak tree. That's something different—a fullness of expression, a change in essential nature. Let me just follow this a little more and talk a bit about what it means to work from this kind of perspective—to work actively with this process of growth in people. If you see people as acorns, you must then imagine an acorn trying to understand itself by studying itself. Imagine it brooding about how heavy it is, how hard it is, how brown: pointed on one end and flatter on the other. All of these things are true. Yet an acorn really cannot make sense of itself without knowing about the oak tree. Furthermore, just knowing about the oak tree is not enough; the acorn must also know that somewhere inside of itself is something waiting to unfold that knows exactly how to become this. An acorn is a seeker. Every acorn seeks only the proper conditions. Conditions of soil, moisture, space are all that are needed; the mechanism is there waiting.

In each of us, there is such an impulse, a yearning toward wholeness, toward fulfillment. Obviously, I am not only talking about physical wholeness. I am talking about complete wholeness. Now, not only do we have this yearning, but we are also always moving in this direction. Our wholeness exists in us now. When we talk about consciousness, time is not linear. Or if you insist that time is linear, you can simply say that the future has as much impact on the present as the past. Our wholeness exists in us now. It can be evoked. And we have all experienced this. There are certain situations in which we have experienced greater love, greater compassion, more wisdom, and more healing than we are experiencing at this moment.

This wholeness within has been conceptualized in many different ways: Jung and Assagioli spoke of the Higher Unconscious. Others refer to the Atman, the NaShuma, The Divine Spark, the Organizing Principle, the Soul. How we talk about this is not important. What is important is that it can be available to us as a resource and a source of healing.

Many other cultures have understood that we refine the quality of our adulthood throughout our lives. Our culture is a little late in recognizing this. So, it is not surprising that other cultures have studied the conditions that evoke wholeness with much more thoroughness than we have. And many conditions seem to evoke wholeness: fasting, chanting, meditation and ritual, and prayer; also psychotropic plants, and other chemicals and drugs. What I am about to propose to you as a wholistic assumption is that one of the conditions that evokes wholeness is illness. This may, at first, seem very strange, but let me develop it through the remainder of the paper.

Illness may even be a Western form of meditation. It is a way that we, perhaps for the first time, connect with our healing and the healing in other people. What does it mean to practice within this kind of a perspective? It means you do not fix things; you do not rescue people. Not everything can be fixed. Not everything that appears to need fixing is broken. It also requires us to reverse the very training of most medical fields, which is hard because we spend many years in this kind of training. As physicians, we are trained to make people aware of what is wrong with them. As psychiatrists, we uncover conflicts and old traumas. As internists, we uncover wounds and disease processes. People go to a doctor to find out what is wrong. And then of course, the doctor "fixes" it. With this kind of medical training, it is easy to forget that there is a process in people that is moving them toward a greater wholeness; that healing is natural. It is not magical; it is not mystical. It is the very ground of being. We forget this, as physicians, and people forget it too, especially people who are ill. Many of them have lost touch with the healing inside of themselves. They feel helpless and frightened.

No matter which techniques we use to empower people, it is important to hold people large. Let me say what I mean by that. Life seems to be increasingly a struggle not to become smaller, not to become a number on somebody's list, not to disappear as an individual. We can help each other in this struggle if we recognize that the way we perceive people affects them. If I see an acorn as a little woody piece of stuff, I will feel differently about it than if I see it as the seed of an oak. I communicate this in many subtle ways—by the tone of my voice, my body posture, by what I say, and by what I do not say. Even without saying anything, we can convey a sense of possibility to people. For example, I have an aunt who has known me since I was a little girl, and when I rapidly outgrew her by six or seven inches, she got the idea that I was very awkward and clumsy, which indeed I was at the time. And she believes that I am awkward and clumsy still. When I am with her, I am always spilling water glasses, tripping over nothing, and it infuriates me. Try as I might, I cannot help but fulfill her firmly held and unspoken expectation of me. Well, this reverses. If one holds people large, if one is alive to possibility, this also affects people. This does not mean making demands on people. As a matter of fact, it means making no demands, but simply being open to possibility. As Thoreau said, "We must awaken and stay awake, not by mechanical means, but by the constant expectation of the dawn." Such expectation is an environment in which to work.

Lastly, what are the wholistic assumptions about the work? What is it that we do? I do not "do imagery." People do imagery. What we do is create conditions that foster wholeness, that make the manifestation of wholeness more possible. We do this with our skills, our questions, with our attitudes, and most important, with our love. There is a Hindu greeting which people have become more aware of since the "Gandhi" movie. People put their palms together and say "Namaste, namaste." "Namaste," paraphrased, means "I salute, I greet, the soul within you." I propose that this is a position from which to practice health care. As a matter of fact, it is a position from which to practice life. It may be the only framework large enough to allow healing.

Imagery as a Healing Technique

Imagery is not the favored way of thinking in this particular culture; but it is a major way in which we think. It is very natural; it is probably uniquely human; we do it all the time. Generally, the first thing you need to do with people is help them *stop* doing their imagery, because a lot of their imagery is negative. It comes in the form of worry. In this form, it drains their energy. They use their energy to deal with things that have not happened and may never happen. So the unharnessed imagination is a problem for ill people.

What else is imagery? It is a tool. It enables us to tap into our potential, to tap into the unconsciousness, both the lower unconscious, which is behind its use in psychotherapy, and the higher unconscious. There are many definitions of imagery. It is the language of the body. Suppose I were to ask you to increase your heart rate. If I simply asked you, "Close your eyes and increase your heart rate," most of you could raise it a little bit. But if I start to tell you a horrifying story, all of you could raise it a lot. Especially if the story had verbal pictures, or images. The body responds to this wordless language. It is the language of the body. Now I am going to offer a definition for imagery that is perhaps unique to my work. I see imagery as related to that process of movement toward wholeness mentioned above. It is that process made visible. The process will cloak itself in pictures that are not random. They are unique to each individual; they are purposeful. They come from within the person. Perhaps they come from the soul. Because, it seems to me, much illness is a result of not being transparent to the soul. The friction of the soul on the body may contribute a great deal to illness. Thus, imagery is the process of movement toward wholeness made visible. We do not cause it, but we can nurture it and enable people to remove the barriers, often habitual, that they have erected to their own healing.

Now there are many uses of imagery that I am not going to discuss, even though I use them. I am basically a therapist, I have trained for many years in psychosynthesis, and I am deeply influenced by it. I am not going to discuss fixing habits, or stopping smoking. You can use imagery for that. I am not going to discuss increasing performance time, or learning to run a four-minute mile. You can use imagery for that. I am not going to talk about using imagery for psychotherapy, or evoking new perspectives, or the use of imagery in decision-making or in relaxation. Rather, I want to take this opportunity to talk on a different level: I want to talk about the use of imagery in evoking healing, in enabling people to find healing. I will be sharing with you a number of case studies to present this particular use of imagery.

Let me describe, first of all, the use of imagery in physical healing. The whole field of psycho-immunology is involved with this, and there is a rapidly growing interest in it now. Perhaps there are certain states of consciousness which affect the immune system, which affect the body, which enable a greater physical wholeness. If this is so, the premise that I work from is that such imagery must be unique to each individual. The immune system is that part of our physiology which is the guardian of our identity—the boundary between self and not-self on a physical level. It is logical that the handles of each immune system, the handles of our personal healing, are unique; and so the processes of imagery that evoke healing in the individual are unique as well. Often healing may require people to reimagine their life-long relationship with their physical self.

One of my patients was a highly intellectual young man, a brilliant analyst, who came seeking help after a diagnosis of cancer. Early in our first session it became clear how distrustful and angry he was with his body. His body was the problem. It was interfering with his relationships, his work, and with his life. This sort of anger is common in some people after their initial diagnosis, and suggests to me that they may be out of touch with the ability of their body to heal. When one is in touch with the natural healing potential of the body, the body is not seen as the problem.

The body is part of the solution if you understand that the body has the power to heal. And so I decided to work with imagery to see if I could help him be in touch, directly, with a sense of healing, without any idea of where this would lead him. So I asked him, "Do you have any scars?" He said, "Are you kidding?" I said, "What's your most recent one?" And he said, "I have a biopsy scar here where they found out that I had cancer." I asked him how old the scar was. "About three weeks," he told me. "Are you willing to use a little imagery to get a sense of the process by which your scar is healing?" He said, "Sure." I said, "Good, close your eyes. In your imagination, examine the scar and describe it to me." He described it, at first, from the outside. "It's sort of pink, a thin line but angry looking." And he went on in great detail because he was, after all, a trained observer. I said, "Good, now go a little deeper. What's going on below the surface?" He started to describe how the fat and the connective tissue had come together so you could hardly see where the incision had been made. Then I began taking him backward in time. "Let's go back a week. Keep watching. What does the scar look like now?" He spontaneously described a scene where a great many little people, like workers, were working; they were very, very busy. He was really struck by how many there were and how busy they were, and yet, they seemed to have a certain pattern in their movement, a sense of order. This kept coming up over and over again in his imagery. There was this sense of order. The workers were doing something, and he did not know what it was. He tried to get their attention to find out what they were doing and they did not pay any attention to him. His pride was a little offended. All this activity was happening in his body without his knowledge. He said that it was like a dance, very ordered, very busy. I suggested that he move backward another week and look again, "Now, there are even more little workers." Again, he was struck by the "purposefulness" of their patterned movement and his inability to get their attention to find out how it worked, how they each knew what to do. So I suggested he go back even further, to the moment of the surgical incision. He said, "There's a burglar alarm going off like a car alarm." (Imagery is so exquisite. At the moment of incision, a boundary is invaded and this is signaled by a burglar alarm.) He started to shout, "To the battle stations, to the battle stations!" Then he opened his eyes and commented that a lot of Simonton imagery (a mind-body approach to healing cancer that he had read about) has to do with warfare, but that this somehow did not seem real to him. It was not his style. So I encouraged him to close his eyes again and simply stay with what was happening. He said, "Where is everybody?

There's silence." "Stay with what is happening." I suggested he listen carefully—that he listen to the silence. After a while, he said, "Oh, interesting. There's a sound." I asked him to describe it, and he said, "It's very strange." I said, "Is it inside you?" And at first he said, "Yes." Then he said, "No. It's inside and outside ... it doesn't make sense anymore . . . inside . . . outside, it's everywhere. It's all the same . . . it fills everything." And I said, "What's it like?" It's kind of a humming sound. It's not exactly a sound, it's more like a vibration." "Just allow yourself to experience it as fully as you can—let it grow." He sat still for a while. Then he said, "I understand." I said, "What?" He said, "The dance. That explains the dance." I said, "Say more." "You know, when you make a sound, a glass will start to vibrate until it too makes that sound, until it's at one with the sound. That's how all those workers know the order. They are dancing, vibrating to the sound." And I said to him, "Can you make this sound?" He said, "Yes, it's sort of like a 'hommmmmmm'." He was sitting there, with his eyes closed, humming.

I sat in silence for some time until he fell silent, and then I suggested that he watch the wound as he made the sound, that he let it reverse and go forward in time to today, and tell me what was happening. And very carefully, slowly, and inevitably, the wound healed. He opened his eyes and he was furious, absolutely furious. (This happens a lot when people have had a very powerful experience) He said, "What does this have to do with my cancer? I came here to use imagery with my cancer; what does this have to do with my cancer?" And I just said it back to him: "What does this have to do with your cancer? Close your eyes and reflect on that a moment." After a while, he said, "You know, what is cancer? Cancer is something that has escaped the order. Perhaps this sound can help it remember—can bring it back home." And so he found this imagery, which is his personal imagery—a sound imagery, not a warfare imagery. He has done this imagery daily for the last year and a half and his remission persists. This imagery is easy for him to do—it makes sense to him.

You may have noticed that I have been talking about imagery and imagination, not visualization. Not everybody visualizes. Forty percent of people do not. I am one of them. I do a lot of imagery and I have never seen anything. I hear things. If you want to lead me in an imagery and you take me for a walk in the woods, it is best if you do it in terms of hearing: "Listen to the leaves rustling, the sound of your feet." Then it becomes vivid for me. If you talk about "watching the sunlight through the leaves," it's not very real—I have to translate that into sound imagery in order to make it more alive. For some people, it is not sound; it is touch. And others just sense things without any sensory cues at all. Not everybody has this powerful an experience of healing directly. It is not really necessary. What seems important is putting people back in touch with their capacity to heal, reminding them that this is natural for them.

A good example of this happened recently. A woman with whom I had worked before came to see me. She was 39 and had a chronic illness for 28 years. She had Crohn's disease—a very significant disease of the intestine, for which she has been operated on about 12 times. Of course, changes or complications become greater with each operation; and there were many complications and much recovery; and she had struggled back and forth over and over again. About a week before she saw me, she felt jaw pain and had gone to her dentist who found an abscess in her jaw. He told her he needed to open the bone and do a root canal on one of her teeth—a short procedure to let that pus out. She became extremely upset, refused therapy, left his office, went home, and just sat in the living room. Her husband called me to see if I could see her. When she came she seemed in despair. She said, "This is too unfair. After all of that, now this! Why me? It's just not fair. I can't do it, I just can't do it, I'll never survive it." One might even say she had become a "victim." Many people with chronic illness are vulnerable to the victim state—feeling hopeless and helpless. And yet, every victim is a survivor who does not know it yet. This is a very important principle of healing.

I knew this woman; I knew her process; her higher self was very available to her. So I did something very simple with her. I said, "Well, let's see what's going on here. Sophie, close your eyes." And she did. I said, "Imagine that I am holding a mirror in front of you, and describe the mirror to me." She said that it was round, and it had an oak rim. "Now look into it and you will find something there that will help you. Just look into the mirror and see what's there."

All we need to do is give inner wisdom and the higher self an opportunity. It always surprises me that a very simple intervention like this will yield a very complex and rich response. This response has nothing to do with the complexity of the intervention itself. It is the complexity of the human process we are tapping into. We do not make the outcome happen, we simply open a door to the inner process and offer the higher self an opportunity to be heard.

And she looked into this mirror, and she began to see her whole 28 years' experience of illness. She watched herself have the initial attack of her disease during which she almost died, ending up in a coma for six months. As the imagery unfolded, she watched herself go through surgery after surgery, complication after complication. She recovered time and time again only to face another relapse and disappointment. My rational mind, of course, was saying, "How can this be helpful? This will really activate her 'victim'." She had reached the present, and suddenly her energy shifted and she burst out laughing. "Root canal, schmoot canal, this is nothing—I can do this. This is no problem, this is nothing. I can do this with one hand tied behind my back." Basically, once she saw it in this way, all together as a whole, she was able to see the thread that runs through it all, which is her own strength and her ability to heal herself again and again.

Now with this woman, the imagery happened spontaneously. With others, I make an opportunity for it to happen, if it will. When people come in, often I am their eighth or ninth doctor, and many have said to them, "This is hopeless, you've got to live with this." Or perhaps, "You are going to die with this." I ask them to tell me their story. And they start, and they usually talk very fast, and I slow them down and tell them to take all the time they need to tell their whole story. And people tell their stories for an hour or two, and usually they are very powerful stories, stories of heroism, but people rarely realize that. I just listen, and when they get close to the end of it, I ask them a question, "What is it that keeps you alive? What is it that has kept you alive?" Often people do not quite understand what I am talking about at first. They are much more in touch with their pain. And I ask them again. And maybe again. Eventually, they start talking about it. "There is a certain stubbornness I've got, somehow I always seem to find hope that it's going to be better," or something like this. As they are talking about this, I ask them to close their eyes and to get in touch with the place within them which experiences this. It has no words, the words are coming out of this place, but the place itself has no words. I suggest they move toward the center of this experience. Often, this is a very powerful experience for chronically ill people. This place, this experience, is very strong in them. They are very close to it, but they may not have noticed it before. Illness almost evokes the experience of healing in people. This experience is as real as the pain, as real as the illness itself. It is almost like refocusing one's attention. The pain and the illness and the suffering are loudest in us, but what is loudest in us is not necessarily what is most real in us. It is very easy for people to be in touch with what has kept them alive because it is alive in them and working hard for them, if they have serious illnesses.

Sometimes, reminding people about healing is very simple. I recently was asked to help supervise a practicum in an imagery course that a colleague was teaching. The practicum task was to help people gain insight into a physical problem by using imagery. The students began doing their practice imagery with each other, and I walked around for a while to answer questions. I saw one woman sitting by herself and said, "What happened?" And she said, "I'm an odd number and I don't have a partner." I said, "Good, be my partner." We sat down, and during the imagery she did with me I got a very interesting personal insight. Then I did an imagery with her. She was a 40-year-old lawyer and she had had endometriosis, a woman's problem, for many years. It had been controlled by taking birth control pills. Now recent research had indicated that prolonged estrogen therapy was dangerous. During her last visit, her physician told her that she needed to have surgery. She said that she couldn't do it, she couldn't even consider it, and she was feeling very trapped. I said, "You're caught in the decision." "Yes, I don't know how to decide." And I said to her, "Let's do a simple imagery—a standard 'climb a mountain' imagery."

I had her imagine that she was climbing a mountain, carrying a box with her whole problem in it. At the top of the mountain, I directed her to find a presence which embodied her own wisdom and represented to her a part of herself that had wisdom about these matters. Not surprisingly, she found a wise old woman. I suggested she discuss the box and what was in it with the wise old woman. And the wise old woman said to her, "Your fear is about the fact that 20 years ago, you had a stillborn child. At the time that happened, you went into a depression that lasted close to a year. You were all alone, it was very difficult for you and you were very young, and you are worried that you couldn't survive that now if it happened again." This was something she was not in touch with at all. She had not connected it at all to the question of her surgery. I suggested she ask the wise woman more about this, that she get the wise old woman's sense of how it was now? The wise old woman said, "Well, you're a mature woman, you have a husband, you have children, you're much stronger than when you were 19 years old. You have many more resources to survive this. You can consider this possibility because you have grown resources."

Then I did something I often do. I suggested she ask the wise old woman for something to remind her of the message. And her wise old woman gave this very tough lawyer a magic wand with a star on its tip. I said, "Good, gradually come back into the room, bringing the wand with you. Allow your eyes to open and let's discuss this. What do you think a wand means? What does that mean to you, a wand?" She said, "You can make things happen in the world with a wand." "Good. What does it mean to you that a part of yourself gave you that?" She said, "Well, I can make things happen." I said, "What sorts of things happen with a wand?" "You can turn frogs into princes." "Right. What kind of change is that?" She said, "Well you know, sort of what they call transformation." And I kept pursuing it because, you see, that symbol was loaded with energy. "What does that mean to you that you can do this, that a part of you can do this?" And suddenly, her eyes filled with tears and she said, "It means I can heal, I can heal myself from this surgery." And she cried with relief.

Healing and Death

The great healer is perhaps death itself. More and more of my patients are in hospice care, a time when the higher self and its perspective may become exceedingly clear, sometimes for the first time. One of the earliest hospice patients I worked with was a 40-year-old man with cancer of the pancreas. He was referred by his oncologist, who told me, "Look, I have done everything. I have nothing more to offer him. I'm willing to talk to him, but I really have nothing more to offer him." His unspoken message was that he could use his time better with people he could do something for, people he could help. "Are you willing to see him?" he asked me, "Just to let him talk to you, once a week? Is that all right?" And I said, "Sure."

I first spoke to John on the phone. He was formerly in construction and had a company that did roofing. He wanted to come on a day when not many people were around. I practice on Wednesday, and everyone else in our office takes Wednesday off. So I said, "Come Wednesday." He was an exceptionally tall man, and at the time I first saw him he weighed only 130 pounds. I found out that he wanted to come when no one else was there because it took him an hour to climb the eight stairs to my office (this was before the ADA). He did not want anyone to watch him do that. And so we started our sessions. We talked about his bitterness, his resentment, his anger, and his unwillingness to share his thoughts and experiences with anyone. Slowly, after five or six sessions, he began to talk a little more to others, but in a very limited way. Once or twice, his family came and we all talked. It was helpful. And one day, he came and he said, "Look at me. I'm shaky. I'm sweaty. I can feel my heart pounding. I haven't been able to sleep for two nights. I'm so anxious." I asked him, "Any idea why this is?" "I have no idea," he said, "but give me something, give me a tranquillizer. I can't live like this. I can't deal with this. I can barely sit in the chair." I said, "I could do something like that, but let's try something else first to see if we can find out more about what's going on. Are you willing to do that?" He nodded. I suggested that he close his eyes, take a few deep breaths, and allow an image to come that related to his anxiety. He got an immediate image of a ravenous beast pursuing him. He started to run and his anxiety grew. In the next ten or fifteen minutes I did everything I knew to bring him into relation-ship with this imaginary beast, to alter the configuration of his running and its chasing him. Nothing worked. "Become invisible." "It can see me." "Hide behind something." "It knows where I am." "Talk to it." "It won't answer me." And slowly it was gaining on him. So I began to help him to gather information about the nature of the beast. We discovered that it was irresistible, inevitable, merciless. There was no negotiating with it. But it was not evil. He was very clear about that. In fact, it was natural.

And so I said to him, "You know, John, maybe the only thing is for you to do is to allow it to eat you." And so he did, and he went through a period of extreme anxiety, coughing, choking, screaming, shaking. Every time he fell silent I asked him "Is there something more?" and he would continue. I was saying to myself something like, "My goodness, if he dies here, how am I going to explain this?" Yet, I knew that it was right to be doing this. Gradually, the shaking stopped, and the room started to fill with a deep stillness and presence and peace. John seemed to be in great peace. We were sitting there together for a while, and then he said, "There is light; there's only light . . . I *am* light," We sat there together for a while longer, and then he opened his eyes and said, "Hey, Doc, great session! I don't feel anxious at all, that was a great session!" And of course, I was sitting there with a million questions in my mind. He said goodbye and he left.

I thought about the session for three or four days. It reminded me of some of the very innovative new books on dying and death that were only recently being published. And finally, I did something I rarely do. I called him up. He said, "Oh, I'm doing much worse." And he started to describe his physical symptoms and, sure enough, he was worse. He was calm about these major changes—yet he was a man who used to become upset even by minor physical symptoms. I pointed that out to him. "Yes," he answered, "I feel different—that was quite a session. Now I'm spending my time just thinking about things." "What sort of things?" He said, "Crazy ideas." "Tell me one." "Well, I was sitting, looking out the window watching the people on the street, and suddenly I noticed a wall just behind me. And when I noticed it, I realized that it had always been there, but I had never seen it before." I encouraged him to say more. "It gets crazier. Of course, I'm on this side of the wall. But I'm also on the other side of the wall. I don't know what that means. Do you know what that means?" I said, "No." "All I know is, I sit with this experience, and that's why I feel so good. It gives that same feeling I had in your office. Sort of peaceful and joyful." "That's a good feeling to have, let yourself have that," I told him. He began to laugh softly. We talked for a while longer, and then we bid each other good-bye and hung up. And two or three days later, he died. I like to think he died a little differently than he might have. I like to think that, but I don't know.

People come to doctors in search of healing. Perhaps we are all in search of healing from the moment we are born and incarnated. People hope to find healing in the doctor's office. Actually, of course, they bring their healing with them. They do not know that. Healing is natural and perhaps even inevitable, and it happens on many levels. Evoking healing is very simple. I can evoke healing in anyone just by sticking them with a pin. I invite you to consider ill people in this way. They are people who are more actively healing than perhaps we are at the moment. They have been stuck with a big pin and their activated healing is even more readily accessible to them in images and in words than ours is to us.

If you are interested in working with healing as a therapist, you need to find the approaches and techniques that are right for you. Imagery seems to fit me. It fits who I am, how I operate in the world. Your tools for healing are as unique to you as a therapist, as your patient's way of healing is for them. Healing is not a technique; it is a way of life and indeed may be at the core of life itself.

This paper was adapted from a talk given by Dr. Remen at the 10th Annual Meeting of the Holmes Foundation, Los Angeles, California, October 1983, and revised by the author in 2017.

Rachel Naomi Remen, MD, *is one of the earliest pioneers in the mind/body holistic health movement and the first to recognize the role of the spirit in health and the recovery from illness. She is co-founder of the* Commonweal Cancer Help Program *featured in the Bill Moyers PBS series,* Healing and the Mind, *and has cared for people with cancer and their families for almost 40 years. She is also a nationally recognized medical reformer and educator who sees the practice of medicine as a spiritual path. In recognition of her work she has received several honorary degrees and has been invited to teach in medical schools and hospitals throughout the country. Her groundbreaking holistic curricula enable physicians at all levels of training to remember their calling and strengthen their commitment to serve life. At UCSF School of Medicine Dr. Remen developed* The Healer's Art, *the innovative curriculum which is now taught at more than 70 medical school in the US and abroad.. She is founder of the* Institute for the Study of Health and Illness, *a professional development program for graduate physicians at Commonweal. She is the author of* Kitchen Table Wisdom: Stories That Heal, *and* My Grandfather's Blessings: Stories of Strength, Refuge and Belonging, *as well as the audio CD* The Will to Live and Other Mysteries.

Part II.

Self-Care

Self-Care During Dark Times

Anne Eastman Yeomans

Not in her goals, but in her transitions woman is great.
Not in his goals, but in his transitions man is great.
—Ralph Waldo Emerson

There is no birth of consciousness without pain.
—C.G.Jung

In many ways, psychosynthesis is self-care. It is both learning to care for yourself and allowing your Self to care for you. It is both learning how to consciously do the things that build confidence and trust in yourself, things that are nurturing, self-affirming, and self-clarifying, and at the same time letting go to the love and guidance of a deeper Self and to the healing forces of the universe.

The psychosynthesis perspective brings a great deal to the on-going task of learning how to attend to ourselves with both wisdom and kindness. In writing this paper, my first intention was to set out some of the tools and principles of psychosynthesis for individuals engaged in their own self-care. I thought of it as a manual on psychological hygiene, something in the psychological domain comparable to what in the health field is called preventative health care or education for wellness. I even thought it might be subtitled "flossing your soul" or "letting your soul floss you."

Yet, as I looked at the lives of my clients, many of whom were going through very difficult times, and also at my own life, for I too was in a major transition, I began to wonder if the paper I had first imagined was not, in fact, a little "too healthy." Would it really speak to the depth of the struggles I was seeing around me? I realized then, that in order to be truly useful, my paper would have to go beyond the self-care of ordinary days and address directly the deep distress and disorientation that seems to be an inevitable part of the journey through "dark times."

I knew then that I wanted to add to my understanding of self-care by thinking and reading about journeys through darkness. I wanted to reread the passages in the Bible about being in the wilderness. I wanted to remember the "night-sea journey" that Carl Jung speaks of, Roberto Assagioli's writing on "Self-realization and Psychological Disturbances," and "the dark night of the soul" of St. John of the Cross. What were these difficult crossings? Why did they come? Where were they leading? How did one survive them? Did they bring rewards, or only pain?

Rather than the more familiar word "transition," I purposely chose the words "dark times" to describe these periods in a person's life. "Transition" definitely implies crossing over to somewhere else. "Dark times" does not necessarily imply this. We know, in fact, that some people do not make it to the other side. I think that the nature of these difficult periods is that when you are really in them, you are not absolutely sure they are transitions. You are not always sure that this darkness is going somewhere, that there really will be a light at the end of the tunnel, or that maybe you are not crazy, or sick, or dying. It is hard to care for oneself during the depth of that kind of emptiness and disorientation, but we need to learn.

I mention this now, for although I will talk about what the psycho-synthesis perspective brings to self-care, I feel there also needs to be the recognition of an undercurrent that is like the voice of a chorus of doubt saying again and again, "And yet the nature of dark times is to doubt that things will work out." If you are really in that darkness, it may be comforting to hear someone say, "Crisis equals dangerous opportunity," or similarly, to know that crisis in psychosynthesis is always thought of as the breaking of something old and constricting, leading to something greater, to a higher level of integration and a more inclusive identity. But these words don't make much difference in the midst of a deep crisis. They may bring some relief for a moment, but I think there is often a sense in this kind of shift that this time these reassurances are not really true for you.

So as I talk about the principles and gifts of psychosynthesis to self-care, remember also the presence of the chorus of doubt which says again and again: "But maybe this is not true for me this time."

Personal and Global Dark Times

As I looked more closely at the task I had chosen, I saw there were two kinds of darkness I wanted to address: personal and global. Personal dark times are those crises related to loss of any kind, the death of a loved one, family or friend, a crisis of illness, or crises related to jobs or relationships. Sometimes, they are crises that the culture has named, like leave-taking from one's family, or crises at midlife or old age. Other times, they are without a name and unrelated to any outer event; yet, they represent profound shifts within the person, affecting both the inner and outer life.

What about global dark times? It seems to me that on the global level there is a darkness greater than that in any individual life, greater than that in any personal transition. I think the most powerful fact of all, and one that is now known to most of us, is that humanity has the power to destroy itself with nuclear weapons in minutes—a fact that if faced cannot help but throw us into crisis. This alone would be enough. This alone is enough. But at the same time, we can also list other facts such as teenage suicide, divorce, violence against women, violence against children, violence against men, hunger and poverty. We may not know many of these facts, but if we face even some of them as sensitive and caring individuals it is hard not to see that we are in a global dark time that is effecting us all. We are in a transition, and we do not know for certain if we will make it through. We are being asked to know more of ourselves. We are being asked to respond to the world in new ways.

It is not that this is the only dark time that the world has faced; there have been many others—floods, plagues, slavery, great wars, other dark times that somehow the world has survived. But surely we do not need to listen to the news for very long to know that we face such a time today.

So we have both personal and global dark times, and I would like to point to their interrelatedness, for certainly the personal dark times that I and many of my clients have been experiencing are part of the global situation as well. Perhaps, too, what so many are experiencing in their personal lives is a mirror of what is changing on a larger level, each level affecting the other very deeply.

My paper speaks primarily to the personal, but I wanted to mention the global because this is such an important context for many of us. I also think that if we look carefully enough at the ways in which we move through personal dark times, we may find ways to help us through the global dark times.

Psychosynthesis and Self-Care

Throughout the paper, I will be speaking about psychosynthesis more implicitly than explicitly, but before I begin to do that I would like to share a few of the basic principles that underlie what I am trying to say about self-care during dark times.

As a psychosynthesist, I assume the existence of a natural process of growth within the individual. I also assume that the process unfolds in a certain direction. It tries to move from conflict to integration, from partiality to a greater and greater wholeness.

I also assume that the process of growth necessarily goes through some very difficult times. As well as times of integration and harmony, there are also times of disorientation, of falling apart, of struggle, of darkness, of crisis. In Assagioli's words, "The process of self-realization is a long and arduous journey with many critical stages." Another way of saying this is that, at times, the process is transformational and this includes both the falling apart of old known ways of being and the coming together and reforming of new more evolved ways of being.

I also assume the existence of will and the possibility for us to discover as individuals that we are not helpless victims tossed about like boats without rudders in an unpredictable sea. We do have will and choice. We can learn to direct our attention. We can choose to strengthen adaptive patterns of behavior as well as to withdraw energy from those which are no longer working. This is not to say that we can always control what is happening to us, but we have a choice about the attitude we bring to the events of our lives.

I also assume a principle in psychosynthesis, often hard to remember in dark times, and that is that *there is help for us, both inner and outer help.* (And now, if you hear the chorus of doubt, "But in dark times I doubt all this," you will know the true reality of how it feels when you are living this.)

In psychosynthesis, what is the nature of this help? I think it can best be described by talking about the existence of what Roberto Assagioli called the superconscious, a realm of meaning, of wisdom, of higher values, of new more integrative patterns. Sometimes, we know of its existence through those moments that Abraham Maslow called peak experiences when we somehow transcend our normal way of being. The superconscious holds new patterns for us. It can be the source of our new future, or of what is emerging. In Assagioli's words, which point even beyond the superconscious to the Self, "The real you knows all about it, knows the future, will guide you," and yet again I hear the inner doubter saying, "but the nature of dark times is to doubt all this," and I think that is true. However, if we go back to the principle of there being inner and outer help for us, this help could come in many forms. For example, it might come in a dream, or in a dialogue with an inner image of wisdom, such as a wise old man, woman or child. These tools have been written about and are indeed central to psychosynthesis. Now, however, I want to speak particularly about the outer help, because I

110

think that sometimes those of us with inner tools get so involved with them that we forget the mirroring of the outer world and the gifts that it too is trying to offer us. This kind of help can be surprising, and very unexpected.

What is the nature of this outer help? Sometimes you open a book and it says the very thing you needed to hear. Or sometimes, a bird flying overhead brings the tears you have been holding back for weeks. Sometimes, the face of a child in a supermarket reconnects you to your love, even though all your trying and all your worrying have been making that love unavailable. It is that kind of experience I am talking about. In saying there is help for us, I am not just saying something about the psyche; I am saying something about the nature of the world we live in.

I want to tell you about a personal experience which happened to me, which I am still marveling at, and which deepened the faith of even the strongest doubter inside me. I was feeling terrible, having moved to a new town where I did not know anyone. It was one of those times when I could not remember anything about psychosynthesis or healing or health. I was wondering how I would find my way. I decided I would go to the health food store to buy some brown rice and vegetables with the hope that being in that lovely store might help me feel better. However, if there were a "friendly universe," there was no way it could have found me; I was so sealed off from it. I did my shopping, still feeling very disconnected from myself and the people around me in the store. As I went out the door, I noticed a journal; I think it was a yoga journal, and on the cover there was an article listed called "Parenting in the Nuclear Age." Since that topic interested me, I decided to buy it. I brought it home and put it on my desk One afternoon, a few days later, I opened it up to read the article, and in reading along, I suddenly came to a part that said, "Then a soft-spoken mother of two named Anne Yeomans said ..." and there was a quote from a talk I had given on this very topic in San Francisco. What was amazing to me was that the article quoted the one sentence that I wanted to say most of all. It was the one sentence that I thought when I wrote that short talk, "Do I dare say this?" So I said it, and someone heard it, and someone wrote it down, and it came back to me in Concord, Massachusetts, 3,000 miles away, six months later, at a time when I didn't know I was looking for it. You can't tell me that what we call the outer world doesn't want to help! Yet most of us live as if this were not true.

This reminds me of the wonderful story, which may be familiar to many of you, but it is worth retelling, the story by Hugh Prather in Gerald Jampolsky's book, *Love is Letting Go of Fear.*[1] He tells the story of a man who comes to heaven and talks to God about his life . . . and he says to

God, "Thanks for all the times you helped me," and looking down on the sands of the world, he sees the places where there are four footprints, where he and God walked together, but in remembering his most difficult times, he looks and sees only two footprints. He says to God, "Where were you then when I needed you, for I see only my own footprints in the sand?" And God answers, "Oh, that is when I carried you." I suppose that moment in the health food store was one of those times when God was carrying me, although moments before I would have sworn that I was walking alone. This is a picture of the help there is for us; it is also a picture of the nature of our doubt.

I would now like to suggest a short exercise:

> Think for a moment of a "dark time" in your life. It may be something you have already been through or something you are in now. Take a moment to feel what that time is or was like for you. See if you can remember when it began. When was the first time you began to recognize it as a dark time? Then see yourself being in it. What was or is that like? And now, if it is over, see yourself coming out of it. How did you feel? How did you recognize you were beginning to feel better? If it is not over, imagine how coming out of it might be.

> See, as you look at it, if you can get a sense of the shape of that dark time, both the entering into it, the being in it, and the coming out of it?

> What kinds of things were and are helpful to you during this time? What was not helpful?

> What is the one thing that someone could say or do which would support you the most?

> Take a moment to answer that question and when you have it, see if you can find some way to give that support to yourself right now, either through words or through cultivating a new attitude toward this time. What is it like to give that kind of support to yourself? Does it tell you anything about what people need during dark times? Take a moment to make a few notes about your experience.

De-Structuring and Restructuring

In this section of the paper, I will focus on what I call the de-structuring and restructuring process. I want to acknowledge here my friend and teacher in San Francisco, the late Angeles Arriens. She was raised in the Basque culture where there is a much greater understanding and respect for this process than we have in the West. It was her teaching as well as my own work with myself that helped me to think about dark times in this way.

As I said earlier, there are times in the process of awakening that can be described as de-structuring—the undoing, the coming apart, or the "positive disintegration" of some of our familiar ways of knowing ourselves, and of relating to the world.

Restructuring is a concept with which we are much more familiar. It describes the time when we build again, when the structure is reformed. De-structuring is something we know much less about. It is not just unknown by us; it is feared by us. It is not even a word in the dictionary. When someone is in a period of de-structuring, we say they are falling apart or breaking down. There is a critical and derogatory attitude embedded in these words. Our language indicates a lot. We rarely think of these times with respect or as a necessary aspect of the total process of growth.

As a culture, we do not understand or respect de-structuring as an essential step in our personal and collective evolution. Yet, there is really no real restructuring without de-structuring. This idea is more understood in the ancient wisdom traditions of the East and by what Angeles Arriens called the shamanistic cultures of the South (in contrast to the industrial nations of the North.) De-structuring and restructuring are interdependent and interrelated. This requires a profound new understanding for all of us. There is no new birth without the dying of the old. We need to teach and practice a new understanding that says de-structuring is essential and integral to true restructuring.

It has been said that America is a death-denying culture. And de-structuring is like dying at times; certainly it is a dying of certain ways of being and knowing ourselves, and of familiar patterns of managing our lives. We need to teach and demonstrate that so-called "falling apart" can be seen with fresh eyes. It is essential to the discovery and building of the new.

We need to know that the small deaths as well as the big ones are part of this journey, that life includes them. They are not bad, not to be feared, even though they can be frightening. We need to support our friends, our clients, and ourselves in the total process of growth. It is helpful to look at the de-structuring we see it in nature. For example, autumn is the season of de-structuring.

As well as the period of de-structuring and restructuring, there is another part of the process which I want to address here. It was written about by William Bridges, in his very useful book, *Transitions.*[2] He calls it the neutral zone. This is the time between endings and beginnings, "the time in-between," a time I would describe as often empty and flat, the time in the winter when you are not at all sure there is going to be a spring, the time when you easily feel like the man in Hugh Prather's story who asks, "Where were you God when I needed you?" It is a time when the feelings of being left and deserted are the strongest, a time when the old symbols and meanings often seem lifeless and without energy.

For the rest of the article I am going to address the issue of self-care in relationship to these three stages: self-care during de structuring, during the in-between time, and during restructuring.

Before I begin this, I want acknowledge that we are often very drawn to this kind of developmental sequence, for it gives us some sense of control and order. But in reality what I will be describing will rarely be so orderly nor are the edges between the three stages so sharp and clear. Just as Elisabeth Kubler-Ross's stages of dying do not always come in the order that she has written of them, de-structuring, the in-between time, and restructuring are not always so clearly defined. They are much more cyclical and repetitive: some de-structuring, some in-between, some restructuring, some more in-between, and then, perhaps, more de-structuring. For the purposes of the paper, I will talk about them in a linear fashion; in reality, they are much more interpenetrating.

Self-Care During De-structuring

How do we learn to care for our selves in times of crisis, or profound transition, when life feels dark and without meaning?

One of the first things that must happen is the recognition that we are in a de-structuring period, when old ways are not working, where old symbols have lost their vitality and meaning. We are in a time when our usual habits and patterns of activity do not work quite as well as they used to, where things may feel awkward and uncomfortable. We are not at one with our lives the way we might have been even a month or two before. The first step in this process is simply recognizing it. This sounds easy, but our first impulse is to continue just as before, or maybe to push even harder.

Sometimes, there is an outer event which causes the disoriented feeling—a death, a move, the loss of a job, the break-up of a relationship. But sometimes there is nothing you can point to; there is simply the experience that something within us is different, is shifting. Often, it is a multi-faceted crisis with several things happening at once. In any case, it is a time for self-care.

The first step is recognition, recognizing that change is taking place. I think that recognizing it and then naming it, naming it "transition," naming it "change," naming it "grieving," naming it perhaps even "de-structuring," will help. Giving it a name gives some sense of control and even some sense of meaning at a time when we are losing both a certain kind of control and a certain kind of meaning. I remember someone sharing that during a time of change, when they were experiencing great anxiety and terror, they used to say to themselves, "I'm in a transition now." Just quietly saying that seemed to have a calming effect. It seemed to help with the anxious feelings, and make the fearful places feel a little more secure. "Someone knows what's happening. It's a transition. I'm not out in the vastness all alone. Someone knows."

Yet, at the same time, part of self-care during de-structuring is really dealing with not knowing what is happening to you. This makes us uncomfortable, and often frightened, and anxious. I remember a time when a client and I worked to find words to help her with this kind of experience. We finally came up with the following: "I don't understand what is happening to me, but somewhere, it is known." This accomplished two things: it both allowed her to accept what she didn't understand, and it acknowledged that there was meaning and order in the universe, and that somewhere there existed a deeper part of herself that knew, even though that understanding was not available to her at that moment.

Another very prevalent feeling during de-structuring is that of shame and self-criticism. We often talk to ourselves in the following ways, "So I can't even do the old things that I used to be able to do well. I get scared when I'm away from home. I can't manage my job the way I used to. Small things that I could handle with ease seem difficult. I feel ashamed. I don't want anyone to know this about me." These are very common feelings. "I want to hide all this from others. People won't understand, and they'll be critical." And it is true: often people are critical because they don't understand, and it scares them.

However, our worst criticism undoubtedly comes from ourselves. I have found that I have been highly self-critical during times like this, when in fact just the opposite was needed. It is a time when one needs kindness toward oneself, when one needs self-nurturance and patience. It is a time when one needs to be held, comforted, and trusted.

The cultural habits of moving ahead, of pushing through, of not acknowledging de-structuring, of not allowing oneself to fall apart, are very strong in most of us. So there is a need for re-learning here, and certainly one of the things that we can do as therapists for our clients, or for friends or family who are going through such a period, is remind them of that, and offer support.

Be someone who can be called in the night by a friend. I remember a woman who had an opportunity to do some work in Africa. She did not want to go because she was afraid that she would feel alone and fearful there, even though she had been there many times before and knew how to do well what was being asked of her. One of her friends said, "Look, if you get scared, I'll come and get you!" What a wonderful gift of friendship! Of course, it turned out not to be necessary; yet knowing that there was that kind of support and trust for her allowed her to go and have things work out well.

Relationship with friends is one of the things I would like to speak more about because in such a time we do not necessarily get from our friends what we need. We are vulnerable and we are opening in new ways, and some of our old defenses do not work, so we are especially sensitive to the responses of our friends. Since we are vulnerable, we are easily hurt during this time of transition. For some people, it becomes a time to look at who their friends are and to find new kinds of relationships that are more attuned to what is happening.

I am reminded of a man who had cancer, a really extroverted fellow who was always entertaining and having big parties in the summer. When he got cancer and knew that he had a limited time to live, he found that his level of vulnerability was very frightening to several of his friends and that many of the people he had entertained so royally in the summers no longer wanted to be with him. They could not handle the life and death issues that he was now dealing with every day. Yet, of course, he needed people very much; but what came out of this was a whole different group of friends, fewer, but more intimate. A new possibility of relationship emerged for him, a depth of intimacy that he had not known before in his life.

I think that at a time like this one really needs to be open to asking the following questions: "Who or what is my environment?" "Does it support me?" "If not, how can I change it so that it does?"

I think of Roberto Assagioli's ideas in the book, *The Act of Will,*[3] on what he called *psychological breathing and feeding.* Does the environment that we draw around us support us during this time—the physical environment as well as the emotional, mental, and spiritual environments? This may well be a time for forming support groups, maybe even gathering together just a few friends that you know who have also felt something like this, or are at least respectful of this process. It is part of your self-care, and part of your self-healing to choose carefully the people who surround you.

Another part of the de-structuring process which I will just touch on briefly, though it could be a whole paper in itself, is the encounter with unknown parts of oneself. In de-structuring, we are often being asked to face and accept unknown and previously unacceptable parts of our nature. In fact, it is often because these parts are crying for attention that the crisis has come about. Consider the following:

— A man in his 30's, mentally identified, successful in the computer field, finds within himself a highly sensitive, vulnerable eight-year old boy. The inner boy is lonely and needed a friend. He needed to be included, integrated, and protected. The child, as he is befriended, brings a sense of beauty and wonder to the man.

— A woman in her 70's, competent, optimistic, positive for years, wakes one night in inconsolable grief, feeling, at last, the pain she has been denying so long. She feels that despite the efforts of her whole life, things have been difficult and there have been failures. She also knows that even though she wants so much for it to be otherwise, her children and grandchildren will suffer too. Not everything will be all right.

— A woman in her late 20's discovers fiery rage under a way of being that she had associated with doubt and insecurity, a rage that was asking to be accepted and transmuted into power, a rage against injustice in all forms.

The kings and queens and the wise men and women as well as inner demons and dragons often surface during a time like this. As we understand this, we can welcome them, and invite them in. They may appear through dreams, through new ways of behaving, through longings for new ways of living, or through an eruption of deep feelings. At first, these parts may look frightening. They must have been once, or we would not have pushed them away, but as we come to know them, and there is much in psychosynthesis about how to do this—how to deal with and welcome these disowned parts of ourselves—new relationships are possible. They bring gifts that add to our experience of who we are.

I mention both the positive and the negative aspects of ourselves because we often think that in a time like this we will only find out all the awful things. Those of us who have worked in a psychology with a transpersonal dimension know that we often fear our best parts even more than our worst. There is a terror that can be known in relationship to one's own wisdom, power and joy. Nelson Mandela has written about this.

I remember a client, a young woman, who told a story about driving in the evening to a therapy group. She was feeling alone and deeply discouraged, as if she were dying and would never find her way through this present difficulty. She began to imagine that Death, the reaper, was driving with her. It was terrifying, and then she spontaneously thought, if Death is here, why is there not also a life-affirming and positive figure? Then she imagined that there was also in the car a radiant figure of light that represented Christ. In that moment, she found that imagining the Christ figure near her was even more frightening than imagining the reaper.

We fear our best as well as our worst. Within the psychosynthesis literature, one is reminded of Frank Haronian's wonderful article, "The Repression of the Sublime,"[4] and his exploration of this phenomena.

As de-structuring continues through recognizing, naming, and accepting this phase of the process, we begin to discover that we have choice about how we respond to it. This is a profound shift. In the beginning, it feels very much like this period has been thrust upon us. We kick and scream, protesting that things are not working and that we never wanted it this way. We experience it as profoundly unfair! Why me?! Yet as recognition and acceptance occur, we can, in fact, begin to see that we do have a choice, not about what is happening necessarily, but about how we respond to it.

We are called to embrace the process that is happening within us and to realize that we have the choice to be interested in it, to record it in our journals, to paint it, to dance it, to be open to it, and ultimately to trust it.

Again, I hear the chorus of doubt saying, "And yet in the depths of dark times, one doubts all this," and I agree. Yet there are moments when help appears, when a dream comes, when a stranger smiles, when a lone swan appears on the water, that we do feel supported in a way that strengthens our faith rather than our doubt.

Self-Care During the In-between Time

What is the nature of the in-between time, best described, I think, as the time when the old is not working anymore and the new is not yet here? If de-structuring is the fall, then the time in-between is the winter. It can be a time of great darkness and despair that tests one's faith deeply. It is often experienced as a flatness, an emptiness, a time when one really doubts that there could ever be any light at the end of the tunnel.

Yet, again, as in de-structuring, naming it that, understanding that this is the way the creative process works, whether it be in the arts, or in the articles and papers we write, or in the ways we grow, naming it "the in-between time" can help a great deal.

How do we use this time once we recognize it? I think one of the best things that can be done is to use it as time to reassess values and priorities. For example, the exercise of answering the question, "If I had six months to live, how would I use them?" is a powerful way to clarify priorities. It could be that what comes as an answer to such an exercise is, "I don't know." If that is true, it is really worth knowing. To truly be with the experience of not knowing brings us to the edge of what is known. It is a profound place, and one we often avoid. I remember once hearing an Episcopal minister say in a sermon, "We are closest to God in the time we have just let go of an old understanding and before we have found the new."

Another way I remember someone using this period was as a time to gather in what was important. He started thinking about his life and tried to remember the things that seemed most beautiful, most alive to him over the years, even though he felt quite out of touch with them at present. He thought about paintings in museums that he loved and books he had read, pictures and music that had inspired him, moments in time where he had felt most alive. In his journal, he began to collect these little vignettes from his life, feeling that at some level they must all be saying something that was related. He looked through his bookcase to see the books he had carried around with him all these years. What were the common themes? Was there a common thread that was now trying to come together? So he used this in-between time as a way of gathering what was most important to him, knowing that somehow the new would build on this and be connected to it.

It is certainly a time for questions, and not answers, learning to love the questions, learning to love the unsolved. Rilke says it so beautifully in *Letters to a Young Poet*, "Be patient toward all that is unsolved in your heart and try to learn to love the questions themselves."[5]

This is no easy task for someone who likes answers and control. It is also a time for continued nurturance, kindness, and patience toward oneself. It is a time for rest. Rest gives the psyche room to rearrange itself and respond to new energies and new patterns.

A beautiful image came from a client of mine who was feeling very alone. She was in her house one day, looking out the window. She remembered a big pine tree behind the house she had grown up in as a child, and she had a fantasy that if she could just rest in the branches of that huge pine tree, she would feel comforted, and so in her imagination she did just that. She curled up, let herself be very small, imagined that that great pine tree was embracing her, that she was nestled in one of the branches close to the trunk about two-thirds of the way up the tree. What therapist would have told a client, "Climb into the nearest tree in your imagination and let yourself be held by its branches?" Somehow, this kind of self-healing had come out of a moment of darkness, of surrender. A new idea had appeared, and it became something she did whenever she needed that level of comfort. She knew that that tree would always welcome her. Later, she came to know that as well as being the child, she was also the great pine tree that could hold her. But at first, what she most needed was to be the child being held.

Part of what I love about this story is that, spontaneously, this woman opened through her relationship to the tree to the caring and comfort that exists around us in the natural world. Yet my words are quite extraneous when you think of this woman held in the arms of the tree, feeling more at peace as she opened to this deep and quiet healing process.

Another guideline that has been helpful for people during the time in-between, when the old is not working and the new is not here yet, is the idea of taking just a day at a time. To do the next thing that needs to be done, but to do it very carefully, with attention and mindfulness. It is a time to put things in order, to get closets cleaned out, to answer old letters, the way people do before they die. One is getting ready for the change, getting ready for the transition, as well as reviewing what has been before. It is preparation, like cleaning things out, and making room for the new.

I found in my year of transition that doing things carefully took the form of more attention to some of the household chores, for example, peeling vegetables or washing dishes. They were things that I might have rushed through to get on to more "important" work. As I did these carefully, I began to notice the colors of the vegetables and feel their texture, and hear the water running on the plates that I was washing, as if all my senses had become heightened, through that slowing down. It was wonderful. In a strange way, even though the meaning of the future was not at all accessible to me, the very moment itself, became alive and deeply satisfying. I learned later when I became a student of the Vietnamese Monk Thich Nhat Hanh that this was called the practice of *mindfulness*.

Another thing I want to mention briefly, though it could again be the subject of a whole paper, is understanding and working with pain, both the grief of letting go and being lost and the anger that this is happening. When we slow down, when the old does not work and the new is not here, one can expect new levels of feeling to appear. They are often related to the emerging, unknown parts of ourselves or to unknown feelings that have not been safe to experience before. To be expected are outbursts of rage, deep sobbing, being moved by stories of suffering in the news, or feeling nausea at some of the terrible things happening in the world, or suddenly finding oneself in tears while driving down the highway or upon seeing a spring blossom. This level of feeling can be very confusing for someone who is not usually in touch with their emotions. Again, here is a place where as friends, therapists, and guides we can really give a lot of support. For if one is not used to this, our first response on experiencing such depth of feeling is that something must be wrong with me. In the unfortunate words of our culture, "He or she *broke down*."

Part of letting go of the old is grieving for it, mourning it, wishing it were still here. The process cannot go on without that pain. That is the sadness that brings the moisture which is needed for the new growth; that is the sadness that unlocks the hardened parts of our hearts.

And the rage is powerful too, rage at a loss, the rage about any violations that we have experienced, rage at injustice in the world that we have felt powerless to change. Expect all this. It will not all necessarily happen, but some of it will.

Along with these feelings, there are certainly moments of deep despair and emptiness, when the darkness is very dark, when one feels that maybe this will never pass, that maybe this idea of a time in-between is something some psychologist made up to make us all feel better. "In between what and what?" one might well ask.

I had an experience in the fall raking leaves. It was one of those times when I was taking one day at a time, and I didn't have any idea where it was all leading. Suddenly, nothing made sense, the leaves, the raking, the house, the family, the cars going by, the town, the people—nothing made sense. It was frightening. At that moment, a dear friend showed up and we sat down together. I started talking, and I decided with her there I could let myself go even more deeply into my experience, terrifying as it was. It seemed as if that was the only thing to do, although I wasn't at all sure it would go anywhere. It was like falling down a deep chasm and not being at all certain that there would be any light, or any relief. As I fell, I was weeping and saying, "I believed so much, I believed so much."

I know now that I must have been letting go of a set of beliefs that had held my life together for some time. In the moment, of course, I did not understand that, nor would that kind of analysis have been the least bit useful. My friend's questions, "What makes you happy? What brings you joy?" didn't seem to help either. I no longer knew . . . I let go, because there was nothing else to do, and I let go with no assurance that I would find anything but darkness. Down, down I went, yet in the bottom of the deep chasm of blackness, there was an image of light. I could see a woman with light in her eyes and her hands, quietly walking through a hospital, offering kindness to people who were suffering. It was very simple and quiet. There were very few words. Who would have known she was there? Certainly not I. That's my story, my personal story of letting go into the darkness. I've seen that same process with my clients. When we shortcut that kind of experience, we cut off something very deep.

This is also a time to learn about balance, the balance between mind and body, between pushing and resting, between effort and non-effort. You cannot say "rest" all the time, because there are times when resting is not what works. Nor can you say, "just keep going" because there are times when keeping going is not what is called for at all. I am not sure anyone can give you advice about that balance, except perhaps to say, "You seem off balance right now, what do you need?" We are rebalancing during such a time, since our old balance is shifting.

The time in-between is surely a time which challenges our faith. The tools of prayer and meditation, and being with those people who have faith in those practices can be very helpful. It may, in fact, be a time when those who have never considered prayer and meditation, or asking for help or insight from a deeper level of themselves, may open to it quite spontaneously. As therapists and friends, we can be there to support this.

In summary of the time in-between, I would like to quote now from *The Wounded Woman* by Linda Leonard.[6] She uses the metaphor of winter to describe what I have been calling "the time in-between."

> Soon it will be winter, the time for accepting the cold outside and going inside, the hibernation and patient waiting which cannot talk of victory, but which can hold through and endure

the dark. Sometimes the stir of life is felt, but one never knows if the birth will succeed.

Here she seems to have a deep understanding of what I have been referring to as the chorus of doubt:

> In winter one has to accept that not-knowing and affirm life without results, affirm life in and of itself, and then comes spring when life buds and small green shoots appear. It would seem that this season spring would be easiest to accept, but we know that suicide rates are high in spring. If one hasn't related properly to winter, if one has fought it and not really accepted the possibility of both birth and death, or if one has gone into it too deeply, forgetting the passage of seasons, then one may not be able to accept the new and fearing change will cling to depression and the old.

Self-Care During Restructuring

If we have lived through the breaking down of de-structuring and the doubting and waiting of the time-in-between, the process will take us naturally to restructuring. Here, as Linda Leonard implies, with the first buds of spring, there are signs that the future is beginning to exist again. One gets glimpses of a new life, of the growing warmth of the sun, of buds that will be flowering, of curled leaves that will uncurl. Hope begins to return. What are the guidelines for self-care during this time?

One thing to be aware of after going through such a difficult period is that it is very natural to be so delighted when the new begins to appear that one grasps for it, and holds on to it tightly. Yet it is important to go slowly, to stay open, and receive the new, but not to close on it too quickly, for it may be that what you are seeing is only one leaf of a larger branch, one part of a larger pattern.

Do not settle too soon on what the new direction will be, but use the signs instead as a time of trial and error, and of exploration. Test the waters; experiment; don't be afraid to make mistakes. This part of the process is like all the rest—a gradual one—though our tendency is, as always, to try to settle it too quickly.

It seems to be helpful to remember that we are allowing the working of a process that is deep inside us. We need to leave time to allow the new integration to take shape. It is a process that is deeper than our conscious mind can fathom. Something new is trying to reconstruct itself within us. We need to give it space and time. This does not mean waiting passively, but being awake and present to what is emerging.

I think the two polarities to be aware of are the need to be totally sure before acting, or the impulse to act quickly and grasp immediately for the new. Knowing our own propensities in these situations, we will know what to guard against.

On a practical level, this could be a time for reviewing the journaling that one has done during the transition. As the new direction begins to become clear, we may be able to see that there was an inherent order in the process even when we didn't realize it.

One of my clients, a man in his forties who was in a mid-life crisis, took one afternoon to reread his journal and was amazed to see that this time period, which had seemed so dark, so inchoate, so seemingly random, had a deep inner order. A thread had run throughout, yet in the moment, it had been impossible to see.

This kind of looking back strengthens one's faith in the wisdom of the psyche and in the process of growth, and gives one new strength to go through difficulties as well as to stand steadily by those who are going through something similar. It brings a faith based on life's experience that is much deeper than any theory or any model of the human psyche. I think it could be considered an aspect of mature wisdom.

Self-Care in the Global Context

This paper has been primarily focused on the process of transition for the individual, but I think as we understand this process and trust it more fully in ourselves, we can apply it to a larger transition, a larger change, that some say is happening today to all of humanity and to our planet earth. For surely, the signs of de-structuring are everywhere . . . and the signs of restructuring are few, though they do exist. But probably, we would be most accurate in saying that where we are as a whole is in the in-between time, where the old is no longer working, and the new is at best faint or perhaps not yet here. It is a time that tests one's faith. It's a time of fear, a time of knowing one's pain and outrage. It is a time of feeling one's despair.

If we look back to how we dealt with the time in-between in our personal crisis, what can we extrapolate that will be helpful for self-care during this global dark time?

For the individual, we said, it is a time to reassess values, to sort out priorities, to ask ourselves what is most important to us. Certainly, facing the possibility that we could destroy civilization as we know it through our own work has already forced many to ask what is important, and how much do we care about it.

It is a time for questions rather than answers. It is a time to guard against premature closure, oversimplified solutions, and systems which offer "the truth." It is a time to learn to balance effort and letting go, work and rest, trying and not trying, personal will and trust in a higher will. It is a time to do things carefully and with attention, not to be caught up in the adrenalin rush of over-activity and urgency, but to work steadily and carefully on the task-at-hand, which might be washing the dishes or putting a child to bed, or maybe re-editing a talk you gave a long time ago.

> For it matters not how small the beginning may seem to be, what is once well done is done forever. (Thoreau, later quoted by Gandhi)

It is a time for remembering the tall pine tree of our memory, and for knowing we can always climb into its branches and rest when we need to, thus opening ourselves to the deeper healing energies of the natural world of which we are a part. It is a time for knowing the limitations of our small mind and learning how to go beyond it, to turn inward, or upward as the case may be, and ask for help through meditation and prayer. We cannot do this alone.

It is a time to face the darkness, the winter in Linda Leonard's metaphor, the despair that Joanna Macy writes about, the grieving for the planet that Helen Caldecott spoke of. Allowing this brings us closer to our connection to all beings. For pain and sorrow exist in us because there is much suffering in the human family of which we are part. We feel it because we are related to all. It is a sign of our interdependence. It is the pathway to a greater love and a deeper healing.

Author's Note, 2017

In 1983 there was an International Conference of Psychosynthesis in Toronto, Canada, and I was asked to give a keynote address on Psycho-synthesis and Self-Care. I was 42 at the time and had been involved in Psychosynthesis since the early 1970's. Later the talk was edited into an article for a book of conference proceedings called, *Psychosynthesis in the Helping Professions: Now and for the Future.* But what followed was truly a surprise. My article, "Self-Care During Dark Times," lived on long after the conference, and long after the publication of the book. It was copied and recopied and had an "underground" circulation that I was not even aware of at first.

For years—and it has been over thirty years now—I got calls from strangers who said, "I have this article, and I don't remember how I got it, maybe a friend gave it to me, and now I have another friend going through a hard time, and I want to give one to them." One said," I can hardly read this, because it looks like it was copied so many times. Do you have a fresh copy?" Or a therapist, who had found me through the internet, would contact me and say, "I give this to my clients, but I need an original. I can barely read mine."

What I came to understand was that without knowing it, I had written something that would continue to be relevant to many people's lives as they went through difficult times. One day a woman came up to me at a wedding and said, "I've read your article, "Self Care During Dark Times." Do you know the book, *Descent To The Goddess: A Way of Initiation for Women* by the Jungian analyst Sylvia Brinton Perera? It is what you have written about.[7]

Again I was surprised, yet slowly began to see that by looking very closely at my own experience and that of my clients, I had written a psychological guide to what Joseph Campbell, the great mythologist, and others like Sylvia Brinton Perera have called *the descent and return*, a powerful pattern of transformation within the psyche.

So is the paper still relevant? Yes, it definitely is.

As I write, it is October 2017. In this month, four major storms, three of them hurricanes, came ashore in this country, fires burned thousands of acres in California, mass shootings have become all too common. In Washington we see dishonesty, misogyny, political polarization, "fake news," and a total absence of mature leadership. Chaos reigns, and it is hard to find a steady place to stand, or adequate words for what is happening.

Joanna Macy, whom I quoted in the original paper, and who is still teaching and writing in her 80s, calls this time the "Great Unraveling." It would not be difficult to say we are in "Dark Times in America," and it affects us all. Yet, as I write again and again in the article, as things fall apart there is also room for the new to be born. I see evidence of this in many places, and it steadies my faith and gives me hope.

I take hope from the lives of my clients who are courageously facing themselves and the challenges of loss and disorientation that come in dark times. They are asking once again what really matters, and how can they each create lives that affirm and express what is most important to them. In the field of psychotherapy I see the new in the development of numbers of healing approaches to trauma, especially body-based, somatic oriented psychologies. I am comforted when I remember that meditation, mindfulness, and body/mind practices are available to the general public as never before.

I take great hope from a generation of young people leading the climate awareness movement worldwide. I take hope from The Women's March on January 21, 2017—the largest protest march in American history. It has given birth to unprecedented female-led activism. I take hope from the strength of the *Black Lives Matter* movement, and a growing awareness among many people I know of our unearned white privileges. We are finally beginning to look at the presence of systemic racism in our country. I take hope from the power of the internet, which has been called by some "the nervous system of the planet." As a Russian psychologist and colleague said to me recently, "with the internet we are now all neighbors." It brings us communication and learning on a global level as never before in history, and of course brings problems and challenges as well as possibilities.

It is an extraordinary time we are living in. The earth is speaking? What are we each being asked to learn? The psyche within each of us is speaking as well, guiding us toward a stronger connection to our core Self, what some have called our Soul. Can we let the inner wisdom of the deepest places within us lead us to discover, and then take our place in the healing of this world?

Notes

1 Jampolsky, Gerald G., (2010) *Love is Letting Go of Fear*. Berkeley, CA. Celestial Arts Publishing.
2 Bridges, William.(2004) *Transitions: Making Sense of Life's Changes*. Cambridge, MA. Da Capo Press.
3 Assagioli, Roberto, MD. (2010) The Act of Will. Amherst, MA. The Synthesis Center Press.
4 Haronian, Frank, PhD (1972) *The Repression of the Sublime*. New York. Psychosynthesis Research Foundation. Available as a download from The Synthesis Center at http://www.synthesiscenter.org/PDFgallery.htm download #0130.pdf
5 Rilke, Rainer Maria, (2012) *Letters to a Young Poet*. New York. Penguin Classics
6 Leonard, Linda, (1991)(*The Wounded Woman: Healing the Father-Daughter Relationship*. Boulder, CO. Shambhala
7 Perera, Silvia Brinton, (1981) *Descent to the Goddess: A Way of Initiation for Women*. Toronto: Inner City Books

Anne Eastman Yeomans, MA, LMHC, *is a psychotherapist in private practice in Shelburne Falls, MA. She has been a therapist and group facilitator for over forty years. In 1972 she studied in Florence, Italy with Roberto Assagioli, the founder of psychosynthesis. Subsequently she was a teacher and trainer in psychosynthesis for many years. The principles of psychosynthesis continue to be the foundation that underlies all her work. She has also studied and trained in Gestalt therapy, Jungian dream work, women's spirituality, authentic movement, and meditation. The Vietnamese monk Thich Nhat Hahn has been a very important teacher for her. Anne was one of the founders of* The Women's Well *in Concord, MA, (1994 to 2012), a center which was dedicated to circle work and to the healing and empowerment of women and girls. (womenswell.org) She has facilitated countless women's circles in the US, and Canada, as well as in Europe and Russia. She has taught workshops on non-violence, reconciliation, and healing dialogue. In addition to her therapeutic work Anne is a poet, a gardener, a social activist, and a grandmother of five. She has two grown sons, and is married. She lives in Colrain, MA.*

Embracing Dis-ease —
or Intercellular Peacemaking

Vivian King

Our entrenched response to any threat is to scramble for balance and control. Although our distant ancestors might have depended upon physical strength for survival, literally fighting to stay alive, it may be that we have progressed in our evolution to a point where psychological and technical sophistication protect us more effectively than does actual combat. We can, in effect, use our enhanced mental capabilities to save as well as to destroy ourselves.

Discovery of the power of nuclear energy has propelled civilization into the paradoxical position of being at once the author and the victim of force. To destroy another is to destroy oneself. In a global context, fighting for survival is anachronistic. The contemporary challenge is finding ways *not* to fight.

We require love and wisdom to match our power. We need an approach to dis-ease appropriate to our stage of development. Dis-ease infects relationships, not only among nations, but in families, between friends and associates, and within ourselves. The infection is manifested in poverty and crime, divorce and lawsuits, headaches and cancer.

Our global, social, and personal dis-ease insists that we respond. We might feel powerless to effect change on an international level, but we can begin to experiment with alternative responses on the personal level. Rather than striving for a *forced goodness*, we strive for more awareness of our choices.

This paper offers another method of handling dis-ease. I invite you to consider embracing dis-ease instead of running, fighting, or succumbing. It is my belief that every individual effort to create peace has a direct effect upon our collective life.

The Part and the Whole

A useful preparation to understanding the theory I am proposing involves experiencing the thread of consciousness that connects the smallest, subatomic unit of energy to the cosmic energy that orders the galaxies. The following imagery exercise illustrates the relationship of each unit of life to the whole:

Imagery Exercise—Find a comfortable position and relax. Imagine that you have entered a microscopic world and that you are a unit of energy. You are so small that you are not even perceived as a particle. You are in motion because of your relationship to other moving units of energy. You are moving very fast, and someone closely studying your movement would notice that you, along with the units of energy around you, form an atom.

Identify with the consciousness of this atom. You are an atom with many units of energy moving rapidly to create your atomic structure. Unknown to you, you are one atom among many comprising a molecule.

Identify with the consciousness of this molecule. You have a whole universe within you, a universe of atoms. You are the god to your atomic universe. What happens to you will directly affect each atom. As a molecule, you are unaware that you, along with many molecules, make up a cell.

Identify with the consciousness of this single cell. You are a cell with a universe of molecules within you. You are the god to this molecular universe. This universe depends upon you. As a cellular god, you also depend upon each molecule within you. What happens to each molecule affects you. Now, as a cell, become aware that you are one cell among many in a single muscle.

Identify with the consciousness of this muscle, one muscle with many cells working together. You are the god to the many cells that make up this muscle. As a muscle, you become aware that you are one muscle in a bundle of muscles and that you work with other muscle groups to form a heart.

Identify with the consciousness of the heart, rhythmically contracting and releasing as each muscle group works together to pump blood through you. You are the god of this pulsating, pumping, rhythmic universe. This universe depends upon you. Become aware that you also depend upon each muscle, cell, molecule, atom, and unit of energy. If one group of muscles is overworked or has insufficient oxygen, all your muscles will be affected. You are also aware that you depend upon organs and systems of a body. You belong to a larger universe. You are the heart of a person.

Identify with the consciousness of this person. You are a person with many systems, organs, muscles, bones, and blood vessels. You are a living universe, and your consciousness is the god to this universe. What you do, say, eat, feel, and think affects your universe. You are aware that you embody emotions and thoughts. You have a unique personality. As the god to this personal universe, become aware that you are one person among many people on Earth. You form the body of humanity.

The joys, sufferings, and problems of each person affect the whole body in some way. As the body of humanity, you share the earth with the elements, with minerals, plants, and animals. Experience the planet Earth as one part of the solar system and identify with the consciousness of the God of the solar system, the Solar God. See that all your parts and aspects depend upon each other. Each planet directly affects each life on earth. Turbulence in one area will affect all other areas.

Then become aware that you are one solar system among billions. Your solar system is one small part of the cosmos. Reflect upon the cosmic consciousness of the ONE "about which nothing can be said."

In the same way that we as individuals depend upon the God of the universe, the cells in our bodies depend upon us. The goal, then, is to become a wiser, more loving god to one's internal universe for one's own sake and for the sake of humanity. And, as we learn to be more responsive to the universe within, we find that our bodies are very helpful in alerting us to that which needs attention and integration. Dis-ease indicates that something is out of order. Its symptoms request a response leading to growth toward wholeness.

Symptoms of dis-ease are the body's way of asking its god to move toward harmony. When we perceive symptoms as *messengers*, we can learn to respond more effectively.

Responses to Dis-ease

When our security and stability are threatened, we respond with a characteristic pattern. The more aware we become of this pattern, and the more we learn about alternative responses, the greater will be our freedom to choose appropriately. All of us have daily opportunities to practice becoming aware of how we face unsettling situations and how we handle dis-ease.

We have been taught that our body mandates a "Flight or Fight" response to a threat, but this response can also be characterized as *increased energy* to confront that which threatens. While we may respond by fleeing or fighting, these are only two alternatives. Fighting or fleeing might once have been useful, but they are often too restrictive and ultimately destructive today.

The flight-or-fight response presupposes the presence of an adversary—terrorists, a spouse fighting for child custody, or a malfunctioning immune system. The moment the adversary is perceived, separation of interest is created. We learn to project our imperfection onto our enemy and then to think of it as an evil which must be destroyed. We try to escape or combat that which creates unrest in us. We forget that we are the unconscious creator or co-creator of our dis-ease.

Flight—Flight is a course of action taken by those who feel overwhelmed by the intensity of the imagined battle, or who inherently avoid fighting. Running away may take the form of withdrawal or depression. The attempt to avoid response diverts energy from living. One loses hope and abandons the perspective needed to discover alternatives.

Flight is also manifested in denial or repression. Pretending that a problem isn't there, or that it will go away, temporarily restores equilibrium. Librium, so aptly named, is an anxiety depressant which manufactures the illusion of relief. Unless one actively seeks a resolution for the cause of anxiety, medication will only mask the problem.

People who retain an element of control over the situation might consciously keep their bogeymen locked away. They sense, as a result, that they are holding down the lid on something struggling to escape. This, too, is exhausting and fear-inducing.

The euphemistic label of "peacekeeper" applied to the MX missile[1] denies its destructiveness and delivers something of a verbal anesthetic. The artificial equilibrium is short-lived, however, since we are certainly alert enough not to view our competitors' missiles as peacekeepers. We are aware of their great potential for harm, and giving them an innocuous name does little to reduce the uneasiness they produce in us.

The unspoken hope in denial, repression, suppression, rationalization, withdrawal, or flight is that the dis-ease might heal itself without our intervention. We attempt to evade responsibility—"the ability to respond." Irrationally assuming that the bogeyman will dissipate if one keeps moving and doesn't look back puts the mind to sleep, awakens fantasies, and arouses more insistent symptoms. Running from the dragon drains energy, weakens resistance, and induces fears of stumbling, being overtaken and mastered. Continuing to run invites renewed pursuit, and continuing to deny magnifies the distortion of truth.

Fight—There are those who, rather than trying to escape or deny a problem, turn and fight. The dragon appears, and one must fight or be destroyed. The supposition is that it is necessary to use the will to conquer. Fighting expresses determination to live, and fighting for life means subduing the ultimate adversary, death.

In order to "save" the Vietnamese (and ourselves), we[2] all but shattered their civilization. We maim and destroy before we are maimed and destroyed. If one must fight to survive, it is necessary to maintain a position of power over the enemy, and one is fearful if supremacy is undermined. In a fighting consciousness, the will rather than love is the guiding force.

The tendency to view dis-ease and its symptoms as adversaries is reflected in our language. We claim to be *killing* a virus, *making war* on cancer, *fighting* for our sanity, *battling* cystic fibrosis, *eradicating* disease. In this perspective the symptom is separate from us, an invader to be expelled or destroyed.

A good example of our collective orientation toward conquest is found in approaches to cancer treatment. Surgery, radiation, and chemotherapy are designed to destroy an enemy. Some of the work with mental imagery has involved picturing the bad cancer cells being engulfed, eaten, killed, or disintegrated by good cells, ignoring the disease's role as a messenger.

Physicians observe that the same treatment applied to two people with the same problem frequently has differing effects. Given the same therapy, some live and others die, apparently because of differences within the individual consciousness.

Many scientists believe that, if we can find out how a molecule is misbehaving, we will be able to design a molecular intervention, presuming that if we know enough we can find the right substance or procedure to correct the problem. It is proper that we explore all avenues of intervention, but concentrating only on the manipulation of a symptom draws attention away from the consciousness that is creating the message.

What we don't understand, we fear and alienate. The enemy becomes a projection of our disowned, distorted, or unintegrated aspects. It is the illusion of separateness that threatens civilization. The higher our military budget, the safer we expect to feel. In our military academies, the curriculum is war, the subject matter is life and death— our life, their death. The training aims to deal the enemy more death than it can deal to us. Such an approach simply fuels resistance.

If we continue to destroy our messengers, our symptoms, our enemies, without a change of heart and of consciousness, then other symptoms will manifest the dis-ease. Other enemies will appear in order to help us see where change is needed.

We have learned many ways to use power and knowledge, but power and knowledge are destructive without the leadership of love.

Losing the Race or the Battle—In the flight-fight response, if we don't win, we lose everything. If we can't run fast enough or fight hard enough, the enemy begins to dominate.

How do we respond when we seem to be losing? Some resign to defeat, in the process sacrificing the will. Losing the battle means losing hope, power, and choice. Persuaded that life is unfair, we become helpless and finally bitter. Others consciously choose to surrender, convinced that the battle is too awesome, life is too complex, but that one has done one's best. Power is retained in the action of choosing how one faces the losing battle rather than resigning to defeat.

To take flight, to fight, or to succumb are natural responses given the time-honored perspective from which they emanate. To find alternatives that do not restrict or destroy us requires a higher, transpersonal perspective. "Trans-personal" indicates movement through and beyond the personal self. A problem is seldom solved at the level of the problem itself, but is better approached from above—that is, with an awareness of its relationships. To get the big picture, we must go beyond the problem, transcend it, see it as a part of the whole, move through it.

If dis-ease is indeed a mirror of consciousness, then to fight dis-ease is to fight ourselves; to flee from dis-ease is to flee from ourselves; to succumb is to give up ourselves. The process of healing, then, begins not as a battle but as an opportunity to gain the awareness needed for physical, emotional, mental, and spiritual growth and integration. We can run from the dragon. We can fight the dragon. Or we can become larger than the dragon, believing that its heart is our friend and that it can help us in some way.

Transcending Requires Loving

The symptoms of our dis-ease ask us to be a more responsive, intelligent, and loving god to our personal universe—our body, emotions, and mind. Symptoms point to the next step in growth. *Symptoms are appropriate expressions of unmet needs.* They ask us to take time out for evaluation, for regaining perspective and readjusting our attitudes.

When we respond to the symptoms by identifying with our higher, unconditionally loving-god consciousness, we experience the contrast between this expanded awareness and our "ordinary" consciousness, and it is this contrast which enables us to perceive the needed change.

The key to transcending is love. Without the experience of unconditional love, we are trapped in the flawed consciousness which helped create the symptom in the first place. When love is blocked, withheld, or constricted, we remain at the level of the problem. Enmity toward a symptom closes the door on genuine healing. If our drain pipes are clogged, it doesn't help to pour more garbage down the drain. To relieve our symptoms, we must become bigger than they and honor their messages.

Loving precedes understanding. We can choose to love a symptom even before we know what it means, saying to dis-ease, "No matter what you are trying to tell me, I choose to love you because you are part of me and because you are trying to serve me." Understanding is a *consequence* of the embracing love, not a *prerequisite* for it. Instead of telling dis-ease, "I will love you *after* I understand what you are trying to do for me," we can say, "I love you *now* and I am willing to discern your meaning."

We consciously choose to love so that the unconscious mind, seeking to protect us from what we are not willing to hear, can safely reveal the message. The unconscious speaks through symbols, and when we are ready, we will understand them.

A Model for Embracing Dis-ease

To choose to love and to embrace dis-ease requires an open spirit and a true desire to hear our messengers. The process described below is a method of expanding awareness so that the meaning of a symptom can be perceived and the range of choices acknowledged.

Step 1—Identify an area of dis-ease or dissatisfaction. At this point, you are signaling receptiveness. The message might be a physical problem such as hypertension or pain, an emotional problem such as depression or fear, a mental problem such as confusion or pessimism, or a spiritual problem such as loss of purpose or lack of faith.

Step 2—Allow an image to emerge that represents this symptom or problem. Draw or describe the image. How does it behave? This is the proverbial picture worth a thousand words, allowing the unconscious mind to represent the problem as an image or symbol.

The right hemisphere of the brain is intuitive and synthesizing, communicating through symbols and images. It envisions the whole puzzle, the gestalt of a situation. The left hemisphere of the brain is analytical, logical, and sequential, communicating through words. It sees the pieces of the puzzle, the separate parts of the situation. The right side transmits the picture, and the left side describes it in language.

Step 2 encourages integration of the two hemispheres so that the symptom is perceived both separately and relatedly. Moreover, receiving an image of the symptom enables us to consciously disidentify from it, perceiving that we have a symptom but are greater than the symptom.

Step 3—Face the image with a positive intention and open arms. Tell it that you will not
harm it and that it is safe with you. Tell it that you are willing to listen to what it has to say.

This step requires faith that the heart (or purpose) of every symptom is good, that it has appeared because a need has not been met and something needs to be changed. Taking this step indicates willingness to assume responsibility for the symptom and readiness to discover the good intention behind it.

It is easy to resist this step, and a reminder that it is for our own well-being is in order. While we might choose to listen, we are also free to identify with the dis-ease again. We can still withdraw from it or fight it. Having seen the image of the symptom, we are now free to respond as we wish.

Step 4—Recognize that the image has intelligence. What would it like to say? What does it
propose to do for you?

You can pretend that you are the image talking to your larger self, or you can write the imagined conversation down. What is important is to empathize with the image, no matter how ugly or frightening it might be. By identifying with the dragon, we can begin to sense the need it conveys. We can discover what has been missing from the greater consciousness.

Continue to switch back and forth from the consciousness of the self to the consciousness of the symptom-image. Continue to reaffirm that you are ready to listen and discern the need that is attempting to be exposed.

Step 5—Identify with the wise, loving, effective part of the self—with the embracing
self—and begin to envision alternative ways of being, ways that would directly meet the needs of the symptom-image.

This step might be completed quickly, or it could take weeks to accomplish. The important thing is to choose to identify with the embracing self rather than the fearful, repulsed, or antagonistic elements of your consciousness.

For example, if the dragon I have imagined were to tell me that it wants to eat me, rather than becoming fearful and running or fighting, I could instead recognize its hunger and feed it as much as it could hold. Then, when it was filled, we could talk again. Perhaps it has been hungry for a long time and I have ignored its hunger. The question for me to ask myself would be, "What hunger do I have that I have not been attending to?"

Perhaps in your imagery something has been locked in a cage and wants to be released. Begin to think in terms of releasing the monsters, feeding the dragons, meeting their needs in a symbolic way. Whenever you become frightened, imagine that you are larger than the threat and that you have compassion for it. In imagery everything is possible.

Step 6—Affirm the ways in which you are willing to make changes in your life, more clearly
meeting the need to which the symptom is calling attention. How does it respond?

Continue to identify with the image and then the embracing self in a dance of consciousness, until you feel that there is agreement and understanding. Ask yourself if you are being a wise, loving, and responsible god to the image. Does the image feel loved and understood by you, its god?

Be specific in the commitment to change. If the image of your symptom was a hungry dragon, what specific change are you willing to make to satisfy your hunger? Perhaps the need is for deeper friendships, if the hunger is social, or, if an intellectual hunger has been signaled, the need might be for more challenging work or further education.

Keep in mind that, in this step, you are using the will to direct and motivate a response to the perceived need. Make a statement beginning with "I will..." to demonstrate your commitment to change.

Step 7—Imagine that you are holding the symptom-image in front of you, in your hands or
arms. Plant your feet firmly on the ground and feel the sun shining on you and on the image you are holding. Allow the sunshine to penetrate and warm you. Stand quietly, with no thought, simply being . . . self embracing symptom, god embracing dis-ease. In the silence, allow the image to be transformed as the sun shines gently on it. Sense that it is becoming harmonious with you.

Slowly bring the transformed image to your heart and allow it to merge with you. Once separate, you are now one, with unified energy serving your whole self. Feel appreciation for the symptom which came to expand your awareness, to lead you toward harmony, to make you a more responsive god to your personal universe. Affirm this new awareness and continue to sense that you are whole and symptom-free. Imagine your daily life with this degree of integration and healing.

Fear of Embracing

The idea of embracing dis-ease is resisted out of dread that if we don't fight, the problem will take over, that "it" will have license to ravage and destroy, bringing pain and ultimately death—loss of self. We fear that giving attention to the problem will encourage and empower it. If we ignore it, we hope it will go away. And sometimes it does. But often symptoms reappear or continue, insisting that we pay attention. What then?

Psychoanalysis continues to demonstrate that nothing is resolved by denial or repression. However, focusing on a problem at the level of the problem may indeed empower it. When we focus on pain, it becomes more intense, unless we move through and above the pain, imagining that we are holding the symptom in our arms, loving it, soothing it, calming and healing it. In this way, we become identified with the healer rather than the pain. The autonomic nervous system responds to the change of identification, and, since energy follows thought, the body will begin to literally heal itself.

Very few of us can face the unknown without fear. We fear our limitations. We lose control. Dis-ease, however, persists in demanding our attention and asking us to take the risk of moving beyond the known to change our images of ourselves. If we cling to an absolute, static self-image, then dis-ease threatens our stability, and we fear loss of power and choice. When fear comes, as it will, over and over again, we have the opportunity to let go and transcend it in order to see ourselves anew. We can remain victims of dis-ease, or we can identify with the healer. Fear cannot help itself, but love can transform fear.

Dangers of Responding with Enmity

The imagery practice of using soldiers, Pacmen,[3] and other opposing forces to wipe out, clean up, disintegrate, or decimate the "bad" cells makes me uneasy, and I have not used this method. I reason that if the microcosm is a replica of the macrocosm, then one must respond to one's symptoms with the same strategies for peacemaking as those necessary on international and interpersonal levels.

The enemy needs to be redefined. As long as we perceive the enemy as evil, then we can claim the right to destroy it. If, however, we see that dis-ease is not separate from us but a projection or reflection of alienated or distorted characteristics in our nature, then to kill the enemy is to kill ourselves, just as using nuclear weapons against our global antagonists will contaminate our own environment and possibly destroy us as well.

One reason for cancer's strong resistance to treatment might be that it is a part of the self that wants to grow faster than the self has been growing. The quiet, long-suffering, gentle person with cancer might need to take a more active, dynamic approach to her life, to branch out in new directions, to grow in new ways. If the uncontrolled cells are acting out what needs to occur in someone's life, then we may not be helping that person by taking over and diminishing her power. Giving up control to specialists may intensify her feeling of helplessness.

Since dis-ease is not merely an individual matter but a process shared with others, I am suggesting that those in the helping professions need to realize the importance of "the messenger," not only to the person being treated but to all those with whom she relates. One approach, in conjunction with medical treatment, would be to encourage a person with cancer to identify with the part of herself that is the embracing, loving god of her cells, thereby experiencing power, love, and wisdom. She would be directed to see the cancer cells as lost, hungry, unhappy cells confused in their desire to grow faster, needing direction for their growth. Instead of envisioning destruction of the cancer cells, she would identify with her embracing self, taking charge in imagery and directing peacemaking, healing cells to rescue each cancer cell. Delivered from their wayward existence, they would be brought together, loved, and tended by the strong, healing cells.

Because the dis-ease represents potential energy in need of direction, the person would determine how to use her energy and what she would like to accomplish. In learning to steer her own life, she would regain power and purpose.

A highly trained psychologist once conducted experiments with images and transformations of energy, intending to extract the good in an image and destroy what he perceived to be the evil elements. He ritually envisioned negative images in and around himself and his colleagues, and then, with the power of the will, disintegrated the evil parts. As time went on, he noticed more and more evil in need of destruction. The rituals became endless, but the demons seemed to multiply. The point is that resistance to force is instinctive. When change is forced from without, resistance is powerful because the change has not proceeded naturally from awareness within.

Another example of the danger in "destroying" rather than "transforming" an image is suggested by the experience of a friend of mine, a young woman who began to feel a sudden, cold constriction of her heart when she was with the man she was in love with. Her image of this symptom was that of a jackal at her heart. Believing it was trying to keep her from loving, she imagined killing it. The jackal returned in her imagery, so she killed it several more times. She continued her relationship with the man. Shortly after, the man betrayed her and "ripped her heart in two." She realized too late that the jackal was trying to protect her. Had she not seen it as an enemy, the jackal could have given her the reason for its appearance.

St. Augustine cautioned us against fighting evil as if it were something that arises totally outside of ourselves. To do so presumes that our enemy can do more harm than our enmity.

Destruction is an act of will, and the power of the will can only be used safely when guided by identification with the Transpersonal Self—the soul—which integrates love, wisdom, and will.

In practicing to be a wise god to one's personal universe, it is essential that one evoke images and qualities of harmlessness, of peace, and of loving wisdom. We can use the will to take charge, make decisions, and provide order, rather than to destroy through actions, words, thoughts, or images.

If We Embrace, What if We Die?

To live forever is not the goal of integration. To live with wisdom, love, power, and will is a noble ambition.

We may die running.

We may die fighting.

We may die embracing, loving and being loved rather than fearful and defeated.

To identify with the embracing self is to identify with a consciousness transcending death. It is the link from the physical to the spiritual: "I hold you, dear body, even while you die. I am always here for you—in life, in death."

Death is not an enemy, and the number of years we live is not as important as how well we live. As we become more committed to growth and awareness, the outcome becomes less important than the process. Gandhi reminded us that satisfaction lies in the effort, not the attainment.

What we do individually in bringing peace and loving wisdom to the dominion of our personal universe is a gift to humanity. Every effort we make on behalf of even one cell within helps heal the universe.

This article was edited to the extent that one paragraph whose content referred exclusively to political events of the 1980s has been deleted. —*Ed.*

Notes

[1] The MX ("missile experimental") missile was an intercontinental ballistic missile deployed by the USA in 1986. It had several advanced features and carried multiple warheads, and was perhaps the most lethal ICBM ever developed. The last one was removed from service in 2005.—*Ed.*

[2] "We" in this case refers to the USA during the Vietnam War. —*Ed.*

[3] "Pacman" was a popular video game in which small round figures with mouths gobbled each other, popular in the 1980s—*Ed.*

Vivian King *(1946-2000) held a BS in Nursing, an MA and PhD in Counseling Psychology. She was a licensed Marriage, Family and Child Counselor, was the Director of Education and Counseling at the Psychosynthesis Center, Pasadena, California. Her experience as a nurse, psychotherapist, and educator empowered her in her commitment to healing and synthesis on all levels of human expression. She was the author of* Being Here When I Need Me: An Inner Journey *and* Soul Play: Turning Your Daily Dramas into Divine Comedies. *She called her approach to integration "Inner Theater," which was developed after the initial publication of this article.*

Part III.

Medicine

The Emergence of a
New Paradigm in Medicine

Marco J. de Vries

Those working in the fields of science are the great
agents revealing Divinity for our present age.

When in 1980 I finished writing the manuscript for *The Redemption of
the Intangible in Medicine* (1981), I had not even begun to grasp the
magnitude and the dimensions of the paradigm shift occurring throughout the natural sciences and medicine. Moreover, I discovered to my
surprise and excitement that those who had tipped the balance, who
had pushed beyond the point of no return, were "ordinary" scientists,
some of them Nobel prize winners, who had earned their reputations
through lifelong careers of rigorous and disciplined research in the
laboratories of the traditional scientific community. They were men who
had been trained, as I was, with microscopes, radio-isotopes, spectro-
photometers, inbred mice, and the like. Here are a few of them: Albert
Szent-Gyorgi (biochemistry); Ilya Prigogine (thermodynamics and
chemistry); Paul Weiss, Conrad Waddington, Theodosius Dobzhansky,
and Brian Goodwin (cell biology, morphogenesis, genetics, and natural
evolution); John Eccles and Karl Pribram (neuroanatomy and neurophysiology); and Fred Hoyle and David Bohm (astrophysics and
quantum mechanics).

Also, I soon found out, my excitement was not very widely shared
among traditional scientists. Fred Hoyle told me that the "wall of silence"
mentioned in his latest book, *Evolution Through Space* (1981), still exists
around his studies of the infrared absorption spectrum of interstellar
dust. These studies indicate that our universe is literally riddled with
life and that life probably did not originate on earth. "Up till now they
haven't even contradicted my findings and conclusions," he comments,
referring to his astrophysical colleagues. A colleague of mine, a professor
of biochemistry, who has a personal subscription to the *New Scientist*
(1981) in which Fred Hoyle's article appeared, admitted that he had
seen the provocative title, "Where Microbes Boldly Went," but had not

read it. Another of my colleagues, a professor of neurophysiology, commenting on John Eccles's latest work (1980), said; "He deserves not one but three Nobel prizes, but now he has turned crazy." When I discussed this issue during a meeting with a Dutch mathematical physicist, he exclaimed; "Do you realize the depth of the abyss we are faced with? If we really start taking those data (of quantum mechanics) seriously and think them through we will have to accept *purpose*—and whatever may be beyond that."

Purpose in a World in Chance (1978) is the title of a book by Thorpe, a biologist and another scientist belonging to that invisible circle of "aquarian conspirators," as Marilyn Ferguson has described them.

Looking at the wealth of data that has emerged from the scientific community in recent years, I became impressed with the similarity (or using a biological term, the "homology") of the contents of the consciousness that had broken through in such diverse fields of science. To grasp what was happening in scientific consciousness, I needed to group the contents in a few categories and distill the essence of each, taking the risk of some distortion by simplification.

The Holographic Model of the Universe

The holographic model seems to be complementing the photographic model of reality in such diverse fields as physics, morphogenesis, neurophysiology, and psychology. According to the photographic model, "reality" is localized in space/time, as on a photograph; if we remove a part, like the head of a person, the remaining part of the film will reproduce a beheaded person; that is, part of the information is lost. The photograph, therefore, is a point-for-point representation of reality. Moreover, from whatever perspective (angle) we look at it, the picture (of reality) we see will remain the same.

The holographic model, on the other hand, represents reality as a hologram, where each point of the film contains all the information for reproducing the whole. The representation of the whole is, therefore, non-local (and by extension of the model, also timeless). There is no point-for-point representation, which explains why, when looking at a holographic film directly, one sees nothing, or nothing which looks like the picture for which it contains the information. The information has to be decoded, for example, by the light of a laser. Moreover, the hologram contains the information for many different perspectives: what picture one sees depends on the way (the angle from which) one observes it. This means that the hologram is a multi-dimensional representation of reality and, therefore, in a sense, transcends the dimension of itself. In the holographic projection, a two-dimensional film will actually project a three-dimensional image.

As will become clearer later, the holographic model may help us to understand, and actually link together, some of the new insights emerging, in particular, from quantum mechanics (the implicate or enfolded order as discussed by David Bohm, 1980), neurophysiology, morphogenesis, and the theory and practice of healing.

The Field Concept

Emerging in very different areas of scientific thought and investigation is the concept of fields as intangible non-local vectors, [1] which determine the emergence of forms and structures and their subsequent development. The existence of fields is already widely accepted in physics, in classical physics as well as in relativity theory, where it replaced the particle concept (the idea of separately and independently existing particles, localizable in space and time). Today, the existence of gravitational, magnetic, and electromagnetic fields is so much a part of everyone's life and experience that their intangible nature is barely questioned (e.g., one could ask the question, where in a handful of earth is gravity localized?).

The emergence of field theory is, however, relatively new in other sciences (certainly when considering its general acceptance). Fields are variously denoted as embryogenetic or formative fields in embryology and developmental biology, epigenetic fields (landscapes) or chreods in evolutionary theory, motor fields in neurophysiology, and psychological energies in psychology (e.g., Assagioli's psychosynthesis). The most general term, which we will use here, is morphogenetic field.

A morphogenetic field can be defined as a source of information for the overall order and direction of the growth and development of a living system, be it of a whole species, as in natural evolution, or of individual organisms and parts of organisms.

Traditionally, the "causes" of evolution, growth, and development were ascribed to "chance" and "necessity." Chance refers to such events as the chance combination of molecules in a "primeval soup" producing living matter, or genetic mutation and recombination in the evolution of a species. Necessity represents the physical laws and other forces and conditions of the environment where a particular system is developing the natural selection of Darwinian theory. Apart from the very high degree of improbability that life and its evolution could have proceeded from chance events and natural selection only (the probability is virtually down to zero), much empirical data has accumulated which has forced the investigators in many fields to accept a third causal factor in addition to the previous two.

As early as 1929, the geneticist Morgan described an eyeless mutant of the fruit fly Drosophila, from which he obtained a pure line by inbreeding. According to Mendelian genetics, the genetic information for "eye" must have been lost from this line. Notwithstanding this fact, eyes appeared in some specimens of this line after a few generations of further inbreeding. Genes other than those originally having the information for eye development must have "deputized" for these. The perplexing question is where those genes got the necessary information. To cite Morgan: "We are able to see how organs such as the eye, which are common to all vertebrate animals, preserve their essential similarity in structure of function, though the genes responsible for the organ must have become wholly altered during the evolutionary process."

Other examples are provided by the study of the extraordinary capacities of regeneration and repair displayed by organisms, organs, and body parts, following accidental or experimental damage. After the initial production of new cells (the fourth phase of the healing process), the exact order and alignment of many different types of cells are reproduced at exactly the right place, thus reconstituting the characteristic structure of the particular organ or body part concerned (the fifth phase of the healing process). From observations such as these, the cell biologist Paul Weiss, who as early as 1923 postulated the existence of "formative fields," concluded: "Field phenomena in supracellular systems are a firm reality to all those observers and analysts of living phenomena who have not deliberately confined themselves to the investigation of elementary and fragmentary processes in which field properties can be legitimately ignored."

Such biological miracles are daily observed by surgeons all over the world; one example is the healing of a bone fracture. Following the excessive and irregular production of new bone tissue (callus) at the site of the fracture, a process of remodeling takes place which eventually results in the exact reproduction of the original form and structure of the bone.

The question again is: Where is the information for the "blueprint" of the damaged organ or part residing? As Paul Weiss indicates, it is very hard to accept that this information is contained by individual cells or genes (this would amount to the impossibility of lifting oneself by pulling one's hair); the information must have a supracellular character and therefore transcend the parts. Moreover, the source of the information seems to be non-local, because organ regeneration occurs at sites where all the pre-existing structures have been lost, or as is seen in transplantation experiments, it occurs at abnormal sites. The information seems to have a holographic and not a photographic character.

The big problem we are faced with in the study of morphogenetic fields is precisely their intangible and non-local nature. However, the same problem is met in physics: gravitational and magnetic fields can also be only indirectly studied by their effects, such as a falling apple or the rearrangement of iron filings. On the other hand, the study of their effects has resulted in the discovery of many rules and laws, which are mathematically so consistent and have such predictive value as to have led to the numerous technical applications without which we could hardly imagine being able to live.

The "intangibility" of morphogenetic fields, therefore, does not have to prevent us from making use of them in medicine and, foremost, in the study of healing processes and the practice of healing. As Paul Weiss remarks, "This would be like saying that perfectly valid laws of optics cannot have been developed, as they have, in ignorance of the electromagnetic nature of light."

One of the questions I am asking myself in the field of cancer research is whether the growth of cancerous tissue can, at least partly, be ascribed to a loss of responsiveness of cancer cells to the morphogenetic fields which normally regulate the growth and maturation of cells and their integration into the tissues at the site of the malignant degeneration. Questions like these gain in importance when considering the possibility that "supracellular systems," such as the feelings and the mind, may act as morphogenetic fields. This is suggested by the studies of LeShan and Simonton (1978) on the role of the emotions and their repression and of images and thought-forms on the development of cancer in their patients.

Also, observations of James Lynch (1977) with patients in coronary care and trauma units have shown that the body of one person may have unexpected effects on the body of another which cannot easily be accounted for by "ordinary" physiological or psychological mechanisms. In a number of cases, Lynch observed profound changes of heart rate in deeply comatose patients when they were touched by a nurse during pulse taking. In some of these patients, a severe disturbance of the electrical impulse conduction in the heart muscle (heart block) temporarily disappeared with the nurse's touch. Is it possible that not only the feelings and the mind but also the body can act as a morphogenetic field? Questions like these may considerably broaden the perspective from which medical researchers as well as practitioners observe, think and work, thus stimulating the testing of imaginative new hypotheses and leading to strategies that might complement the more traditional ways of supporting patients in their healing process.

The Brain/Mind Interface and the (Re) Discovery of the Self

In contemporary neurophysiology, there are two main views on the mind/brain relationship. In the first, mental phenomena are seen as identical to brain activity; therefore, mental experiences are illusory. In the second view, the sheer multitude of brain cells and their complicated mutual connections give rise to mental states: the mind is an emergent property (or by-product) of the brain. In both views, the mind is secondary to the brain and causally irrelevant.

Partly as a reaction to these materialistic views, the thesis of mind and body (and thus mind and brain) as an indivisible whole has been advocated by some of the humanistic psychologies. It is interesting to note that both traditional neurophysiology and these psychologies prefer a monistic view to a dualistic one. The humanistic point of view may be a confusion of levels of reality: bodies or events which are extended in the dimension of space/time may be separate though interrelating realities, and still be projections of an indivisible reality from another, higher order dimension: the explicate and the implicate order of David Bohm's version of quantum theory.

To both camps, it may have come as a surprise that recent studies from neurophysiology and neurosurgery provide strong evidence that mind and brain are two different entities, interacting through what in computer technology is called an interface. The "modules" of the interface have even been made visible by autoradiograms of the brain (the photographs were published in 1977 in *Brain Research*, one of the leading journals in the field).

Nowhere in the different fields of biology and medicine is the paradigm shift more evident than in the neurophysiological literature. Even the titles of books and articles are revealing: *The Self and Its Brain* (a book by Popper & Eccles, 1977) and "Is Your Brain Really Necessary?" (a comment in *Science*, 1980, on the latest findings of John Lorber, a pediatrician, on children with hydrocephalus). In *The Human Psyche*, another book by John Eccles (1980), one finds in the center of a diagram of brain/mind interaction the words "The Ego," "The Self," "The Soul," and "Will." To summarize the main conclusions of the work of Eccles, Pribram, Szent-Gyorgi, and other neuroscientists:

1. We do not become conscious of sense data, nor do we act, through single nerve cells (neurones); we are not even conscious of the

neurochemical processes of entire modules of about 10,000 neurones (of which we possess four to five million). What we are "reading" or "manipulating" is the continuously changing total pattern which is formed by the alternation of closed (inactive) and open (active) modules at the surface of the cerebral cortex. We are reading an "interface," and we experience such *qualities* as "redness" or "wetness," not the electrochemical processes of nerve cells, the nature of which is entirely different from that of qualities; they are, so to say, very different languages—one, in computer terminology, being a "machine language" (the electrochemical processes), the other being a "higher level" language. Similarly, when expressing our intentions through, for example, movements, we use mental schemata (or largely unconscious images) of the entire intended action instead of manipulating single neurones at the motor cortex. These "acts of will" have been made visible by electro-encephalo-grams and appear as slow-wave potentials distributed over large areas of the cerebral cortex, which precede the much more localized firing of the motor cortex by about 0.5 seconds. Most significantly, this slow-wave potential, known as the "readiness potential" (I prefer the word "intention potential"), is also visible when a person consciously intends an action without actually following it up by a movement.

2. The brain has more plasticity than we ever considered possible. We are able to "reprogram" our brains, even after extensive damage or loss of brain tissue. Some of the children and young adults with severe hydrocephalus, studied by John Lorber, after losing more than 95 percent of their cortex, managed to function normally or even to show above-average intellectual performance. A xenon brain scan of one boy demonstrated that his visual cortical area (normally localized at the back of the brain) had disappeared and that this function had been "reallocated" to a temporal region of his cortex. What became apparent to me when watching a videotape of these children was that they all expressed a strong will to perform as well as "normal" children. (What do these findings say about us "normals?" Could it be that we use only 5 percent of our cortex and that the other 95 percent of our brain potential lies dormant, waiting for us to further develop our minds?)

This study is in line with what was already known for a long time by brain surgeons—people can lose very substantial parts of their brains (e.g., through casualties on the battle field or brain tumors) without losing their long-terms memories and without losing self-consciousness.

In addition, it confirms experimental studies by Pribram (1971) and others: to a certain extent, we can influence our brain structure by changing connectivities of neurones and re-routing pathways through the central nervous system. Remember, mental events were thought to be casually irrelevant; it now looks like that this viewpoint has to be turned around 180 degrees.

3. In his publications, John Eccles does not discriminate much between mind and self (or ego); in fact, he sometimes uses these concepts interchangeably. When looking at the data he and others have presented, it seems to me that they may reflect both the activity of the mind and that of the Self. (To me, the latter is clearest through the intention potential and the way consciousness, as well as the experience of will, can transcend the time dimension, as suggested by experiments of the neurophysiologist Libet.) I am proposing, therefore, the following extension of the "computer" model for the relationship of self, mind, and brain:

SELF <———— > MIND <————>BRAIN
PROGRAMMER <————> PROGRAM <————> COMPUTER

From the data that are now available, such as the findings with the hydrocephalic children, it looks as if the information contained in the mind may also be the nature of the brain/mind interface. It has a holographic (each part having the information for the whole) rather than a photographic character, as suggested by the model of the traditional neuroanatomical texts, with their maps subdividing the brain in numerous areas, each responsible for one specific function (point-for-point representation).

What I am hoping is that this computer model will invite medical professionals, especially psychiatrists, to have a fresh look at their rich nosological experience of psychopathology. One question which could be asked in the case of a particular patient is: At what level does it seem that this triple relationship is disturbed? Is it the computer and its interface, the program and its language, or is it the relationship (interface) between Self and Mind which has gone astray? And what could this mean in terms of the level at which I direct my interventions? An approach like this in the case of a severely brain-injured child, for example, could promote the development of much more active and supportive strategies for both the child and his parents than are current

today. All parties concerned tend to adopt a rather passive attitude—
"The child is a vegetable; we give up." It may also help us considerably
to look beyond the outer form of a severely incapacitated computer
and/or program language—one which faces us with seeming deadness
or utter confusion—to the level where a Self may be willing to "incar-
nate" and express itself. Both my wife and I have met parents and
teachers of children who have developed a sensibility to see and hear
at that level (maybe through some of the initially "dormant" parts of
their brains). This has enabled these children to evoke compassion and
respect.

The Near-Death Experience

Empirical evidence for the existence of the Self is accumulating in a
totally different direction than that of the neurosciences. Following the
initial publication by Raymond Moody in 1975 of *Life after Life*, two
comprehensive studies of individuals who had been "temporarily dead"
have recently appeared. One study is by Kenneth Ring (1980), a professor of psychology, the other by Michael Sabom (1982), a professor of
cardiology. Both studies together cover more than 200 cases of near-
death survivors (surgical cases, cases of heart arrest, life-threatening
accidents, etc.). In about half of these cases, the individuals reported
experiencing one or more phases of what is variously called the core
experience or the near-death experience. Between the two studies, and
between them and Moody's studies, there is a striking overall similarity
in the contents of the recorded experiences. The most important parts
of the core experience are:

— the entering of the darkness and the lack of fear accompanying
   this experience;
— the autoscopic or out-of-body experience in which one sees his
   or her own body and attending people like doctors and nurses,
   often overhears conversations and observes interventions (like
   resuscitation), which in a number of cases are verified as correct;
— the entering of a light or the meeting with a being of light which
   does not hurt "one's eyes" and is described as peaceful and
   comforting and of ineffable beauty; and
— the nearly instantaneous "holographic" life review in association,
   in a number of cases, with a presence which is not seen but
   intuited and on occasion is heard to speak. This presence is
   experienced as very loving and unconditionally accepting.
   Kenneth Ring interprets the being of light, or the presence, as a

projection of "one's total self, or what in some traditions is called the higher self," which "is so awesome, so overwhelming, so loving . . . and so foreign to one's individualized consciousness that one perceives it as separate from oneself . . ."

One of the puzzling facts is that "dead" people not only "see with their eyes" and "hear through their ears" but also see in terms of physical world data such as colors, music, persons, etc. To explain this, Ring assumes that the mind functions as a holographic plate on which is accumulated one's lifelong experience of brain data and thought-forms. He supposes that the Self, for a while, is still decoding information from dimensions of reality other than the physical world through this composite hologram.

One of the most important merits of these studies is that both authors have thoroughly examined a great number of possible physical, physiological, and psychological explanations of the near-death experience, such as hallucinations, brain anoxia, the action of anesthetics and other drugs, temporal lobe seizures, etc., and have found them all to be inadequate as explanations for the entire complex of phenomena. Sabom also renders highly unlikely the explanation of the effect of endorphins (opiates secreted by cells in the central nervous system). Referring to a recently published study of 14 volunteers whose cerebrospinal fluid had been injected with endorphins, he argues that both the time and the quality differ from those of the near-death experience.

I cannot escape the conclusion that these studies of the near-death experience, together with the neuroscientific data, will have a great impact on medicine. The first strongly suggests that the Self and the mind can at least temporarily exist in the absence of a functioning brain (and body). This may, to mention one example, change the face of the care for elderly, seriously ill, unconscious, and dying people. Even our consciousness of the possibility that patients in deep shock or coma, or people who have recently died, might see and hear us will totally transform our attitude and strategies at the operating table and in intensive care units. It may radically change the disputes about euthanasia. For example, the question arises of who is asking for it: the individual's Self or parts of the personality, including emotions such as fear? What is the will of the Self—to live or to die? And how are we going to hear, respect, or help someone to express that choice? Many of the individuals studied by Ring and Sabom reported that they made a conscious choice to "go back" to life or were sent back by "the presence" or "other presences;" they came back and they could share their experience with us. What about the choice of those who did not "come back?" In the future, we will have to consider and respect such choices before people have died, for example, those ill with cancer or other serious diseases. Again, this will transform our attitudes and the actions we undertake in such cases. On the one hand, we will have to know more about the ways in which we can facilitate "abstraction," the last healing transformation. On the other hand, we still have much to learn about the ways in which the morphogenetic powers of the will and the mind may be used to maintain or restore the health of the body so that it can serve the Self of the person to express itself and learn from life.

The Multiple-Body Concept

Eccles speaks of a "dualist-interactionism" theory, but I am beginning to suspect that the human individual has available more than two "bodies": a Self, a physical body and a mind.

A recent article by R.B. Zajonc (1980) in *The American Psychologist* even suggests the discovery of still a fourth "body." Reviewing experimental psychological and psychophysiological studies, including those conducted by himself, concerning the relationship between cognitive and affective functions, he concludes: "Affect and cognition are under the control of separate and partially independent systems that can influence each other in a variety of ways ... both constitute independent sources of effects in information processing." Also, cognition and affect make use of different parts of the brain. The so-called neocortex "controls" cognition, while the limbic system mediates emotional reactions. Most important, the acquisition of emotional capacities precedes mental development both during child growth and in the evolution of the species. This is reflected by the evolution of the corresponding parts of the brain: the limbic system was there before the neocortex and it occupied a much larger proportion of the brain mass.

For medicine, it is very interesting to consider the possibility that the evolution of humanity is reflected by the disease patterns from which we have suffered in certain stages. For example, I believe that tuberculosis, which had its highest incidence in the West in the nineteenth century and steeply declined at the beginning of the twentieth century (the turning point was some 70 years before the discovery of the tubercle bacterium by Robert Koch), is very much associated with the emotions. In one study by a Dutch pulmonary physician, who himself suffered from tuberculosis, about half of the patients he examined in two different sanatoria experienced the onset of their disease after a disappointing love affair, the death of a loved one, or interpersonal conflicts. The emotional associations of tuberculosis are very much expressed in the romantic prose and poetry of that period. Often, one of the central characters suffers from tuberculosis or dies from it. At that time, it was even considered fashionable to cough up some blood during an emotional experience and to waste away from a broken heart.

In our much more concrete age, the most prevalent illnesses in the West are coronary heart disease and cancer. Significantly, recent research also identifies unsatisfactory interpersonal relationships and bereavement as major contributing causes of both forms of disease.

The view of man as living through different "bodies," which in many different ways are closely interacting and influence each other by their "morphogenetic fields," may help to make medical diagnosis more discriminating and healing strategies much more focused. By broadening our view still more and including the evolutionary context of human pathology, the healing professions may contribute to the healing process of humanity as a whole. What does it mean that in our time the heart of man is so much the focus of our suffering? What broken relationships does this point to and what does this say about the qualities and values that are trying to emerge and that may help to heal that breach?

The higher a living system is on the evolutionary ladder, the more determining, it seems, are formative fields and the less determining are chance and necessity in the direction of the evolutionary process. The research I have summarized points to the fact that one of the most powerful fields humanity has available at its present stage of evolution is the mind directed by will. The final question I ask is, what does the new consciousness emerging through the sciences say about our individual responsibility, our responsibility as members of the healing professions, and the responsibility of mankind as a whole in relation to our own future evolution and that of the earth and her other inhabitants?

References

Bertalanffy, L, von (1968). *General System Theory*. New York: George Braziller.

Bohm, D. (1980). *Wholeness and the Implicate Order*. London: Routledge & Kegan Paul.

Brown, B.B. (1974). *New Mind, New Body, Bio-feedback: New Directions for the Mind*. New York: Harper & Row,

Eccles, J. (1980). *The Human Psyche*. Berlin/Heidelberg: Springer International.

Hoyle, F., & Vickramasinghe, N.C. (1981). *Evolution from Space*. London: J.M. Dent & Sons.

Hoyle, F., & Vickramasinghe, N.C, (1981). "Where Microbes Boldly Went." *New Scientist*, 91,412.

Laszlo, E. (1972). *Introduction to Systems Philosophy*. New York: Harper.

LeShan, L. (n.d.). *You Can Fight for Your Life*. New York: Harper.

Lorber, J, (1980). "Is Your Brain Really Necessary?" *Editorial Science*, 210,1232.

Lynch, J.J. (1977). *The Broken Heart*. New York: Basic Books.

Popper, K.R., & Eccles, J.C. (1977). *The Self and Its Brain*. Berlin: Springer.

Pribram, K.H. (1971). *Languages of the Brain: Experimental Paradoxes and Principles in Neuropsychology*. Englewood Cliffs, New Jersey: Prentice-Hall.

Prigogine, I. (1976). "Order Through Fluctuation: Self-Organization and Social System." In E. Jantsch & C.H. Waddington, (Eds.), *Evolution and Consciousness*. London: Addison-Wesley.

Ring, K. (1980). *Life at Death*. New York: Coward, McCann & Geoghegan.

Sabom, M.B. (1982). *Recollections of Death*. New York: Harper & Row.

Simonton, O.C. (1978). *Getting Well Again*. Los Angeles: Tarcher.

Thorpe, W.H. (1978). *Purpose in a World of Chance*. Oxford: Oxford University Press.

Vries, M.J. de (1981). *The Redemption of the Intangible in Medicine*. Psychosynthesis Mono Graphs available from the Institute of Psychosynthesis , London at https://www.psychosynthesis.org/books/

Waddington, C.H. (1976). Evolution in the Sub-human World. In E. Jantsch & C.H. Waddington, *Evolution and Consciousness*, London: Addison-Wesley.

Weiss, P. (1953). Some Introductory Remarks on the Cellular Basis of Differentiation. *Journal of Embryology and Experimental Morphology*. 1,180-211.

Weiss, Paul, (1977). The System of Nature and the Nature of Systems; Empirical Holism and Practical Reductionism Harmonized. In K.E. Schaefer, H. Hensek, & L, Brady, *Toward a Man-Centered Medical Science*. New York: Futura.

Zajonc, R.B. (1980). Feeling and Thinking, Preferences Need No Inferences. *American Psychologist*, 35,151.

Notes

---

[1] A vector in physics is a force that has both magnitude and direction.

Marco J. de Vries, MD, PhD *(1927-2009), was born and raised in Indonesia. He took both PhD and MD degrees at Leiden University, specializing in pathology. He was Professor of Pathology at Erasmus University in Rotterdam where he was inspired by the work of Dr. B. Siegel and became interested in a broader, holistic vision of the human being and introduced the bio-psycho-social model into his research. In 1988 he founded the* Helen Dowling Institute for Biopsychosocial Medicine *in Rotterdam (now in Utrecht), an institute that combined research with psychotherapy and pioneered the field of psycho-oncology. He completed training in both gestalt therapy and psychosynthesis in the US, UK and Netherlands.*

Psychosynthesis:
A Conceptual Framework
for Holistic Medicine

Robert A. Anderson

The last three decades in Western society have seen the development of aspects of medical care which do not conform to the conventional model. This trend, involving a number of concepts which I shall enumerate shortly, seems to be gaining some momentum as judged by the content of published scientific and medical data, pronouncements of traditional bodies of evaluation for various diseases, and the proliferation of "holistic" or "wellness" centers which emphasize disease prevention and health promotion.

A very practical consideration, that of cost containment, has also played a role in focusing attention on the role of holistic medicine. The enormous cost of highly technical procedures to salvage a brief bit of time for patients in the twilight of their earthly lives boggles the mind. In 1987, the cost approximated 11 percent of the gross national product in the United States. The figure for 1985 exceeded 380 billion dollars. The cost of care for terminal illness is estimated to consume 20 to 35 percent of all sickness care financial outlays. [1]

The major premises of holistic medicine include the following:

- encouraging the client (or patient or consumer) to accept significant responsibility for his or her life style and decision making;
- developing a collegial relationship between the healer and client;
- recognizing life style as a significant determinant of both morbidity and mortality;
- moving toward a "whole" view of the client/patient, including the effects of the interaction of physical, mental, and emotional aspects of the personality on each other and the transformative effect of the Transpersonal Self on all levels of energy and experience;
- recognizing that sickness may frequently be a teacher;

- allowing the dying process to occur as an expected phenomenon as free of fear as possible;
- emphasizing the sometimes tenuous but quintessential connections to life's meaning and purpose;
- focusing on Love and Will as essential personal, interpersonal, and global qualities.

The conventional relationship between the physician and the patient in Western culture in the last 40 years has been that of parent/child; top dog/underdog; dispenser/receiver; knowledgeable/uninformed. This relationship, of course, is now decidedly altered, though many established health practitioners find great difficulty accepting with comfort, much less enthusiasm, the decisions, questions, and suggestions put forward by the assertive consumer. Others, having come to the new relationship, in one way or other, actually find it a relief. Not to have to be alone in making the hard decisions regarding treatment, procedures, and prognoses, not to have to face the demand of being "right" 100 percent of the time, is a potentially healing element for the healer.

The burden of doing things to consumers bears its own stress sooner or later; the adaptive mechanisms include withdrawal and non-involvement, opting for an extremely authoritarian stance, repressing the emotions which accompany the development of a relationship, or taking a dehumanizing stance toward the patient who becomes the "case" or the "gall bladder in Room 532."

In investigating the utilitarian considerations of different models, I must say at the outset that the data are far from in. Yet the conclusions I am able to reach are not without extensive research evidence; the impact on cost-containment, longevity, and more appropriate use of the system, while not "proven" in the narrow scientific sense of the term, is quite plainly written in the experiences of many people. Yet if wellness or holistic medicine is to be embraced, it must be based on a valid theory and an understandable model, and grounded solidly in the experience of both its enthusiasts and its detractors. Psychosynthesis, because of its integral, unifying, and global aspects, is an ideal model.

A Human Function Model

At the personality level, human beings may be viewed, in many aspects, like computers, taking in data, processing them, and coming to some integration of output in the form of emotional experience and behavior. The input may be viewed as having three components; perceptions of the external world, perceptions of the inner physical world, and perceptions of recall. These perceptions may be wholly conscious or not. (See Figure 1.)

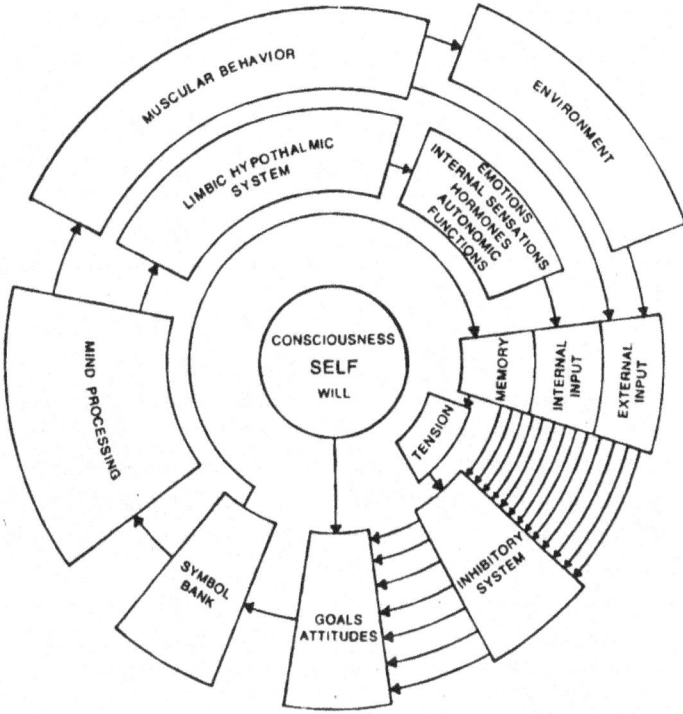

Figure 1/ A Model of Human Functioning[2]

We need to recognize that perceptions are influenced by numerous factors, including attitudes and the level of tension within the system. It is the clear experience of all observers that two individuals who have been exposed to the same visual or auditory phenomenon experience widely disparate perceptions. Health practitioners commonly encounter differing perceptions of pain in patients undergoing precisely the same procedure or experiencing the same illness.

At the outset, it is important to note that beings of higher intelligence do not respond to reality, but rather to their perceptions of reality. The two are not always the same. It is possible, roughly, to equate tension with the quantity of our perceptions. Experiments show that intelligent animals possess an "inhibitory" nervous system which prohibits input beyond a comfortable level of tension (Hernandez-Peon, Scherrer, & Jouvet, 1956). Studies also support selectivity in inhibition by a set of neurological parameters which closely conform to what psychologists call attitudes (Rosenthal & Jacobsen, 1968).

We can say that attitudes control the quality of our perceptions. Positive attitudes tend to be linked to the perception of positive characteristics in ourselves, others, and situations; negative attitudes tend to be linked to negative perceptions.

If our responses, then, depend on our perceptions, and our attitudes tend to shape our perceptions as either positive or negative, it is very important to become intimately familiar with "attitude psychology" and investigate what may appear to be optimum attitudes and what may appear to be distorted attitudes and their effects on health, sickness, survival, and costs (of all kinds) to society.

Attitudes are mind-sets. We have all come across the small sign behind the desk that reads, "The answer is no!" "My mind is already made up. Don't confuse me with the facts." Persons truly espousing this stance have fixed their attitudes, and give notice that they are determined not to change them. Yet we know that attitudes do change. They do not rapidly change as do emotions, but they do change. They change as a result of experience, insights, observations, and psychic phenomena. My attitude about mental telepathy, for example, changed when I had the experience of picking up a telephone receiver and immediately being aware of a mental picture of the home of the caller before speaking into the mouthpiece. A generically negative attitude of a man regarding women changes when he has a positive experience with an individual woman. Our attitude about mathematics may change when we have an "aha" insight regarding the theory of numbers.

Negative attitudes may be grouped around the prototypical attitude of hostility. Hostility tends to lead to negative emotional experiences of excessive anger, sadness, and fear-anxiety; to negative physiological and biochemical events at the physical level; and to negative behavior directed at oneself or others. The finger has been pointed at hostility as the pathological element in the syndrome of "Type A Behavior." In fact, it is probably more accurate to refer to this cluster of psychological characteristics as Type A Attitudes rather than Type A Behavior.

What evidence do we have that attitudes significantly alter the course of sickness, or influence longevity? The scientific evidence clusters around recent studies in which significant-sized groups of persons were followed for 20 to 25 years after completing the MMPI (Minnesota Multiphasic Personality Inventory) within which was constructed a special hostility scale. A group of medical students were given this specialized MMPI and divided into low-hostility and high-hostility cohorts. Followed for 25 years as physicians, the mortality rate of the high-hostility group was 6.6-fold greater than the low-hostility group. The incidence rate of acute coronary artery events (heart attacks) was 4.4-fold higher in the high-hostility cohort (Shekelle, et al., 1983). Similar results have been reported in studies of longshoremen (Williams, et al., 1980), indicating that both morbidity (illness) and mortality (foreshortened longevity) are significantly influenced in an adverse way by the negative attitude of hostility.

The evidence for the beneficial effects of positive attitudes is less clear at this point. Positive religious attitudes have been correlated with increased longevity. Norman Cousins is convinced that creativity, faith, and love contribute strongly to the experience of healing and engaging life-giving perceptions (1979). A life orientation of hardiness, recently shown in studies to be correlated with being able to live with high stress and little illness, seems to involve positive attitudes (Kobasa, 1979).

Conventional medicine provides no guidance regarding the importance of positive or negative attitudes in the genesis of sickness and disease, or in the promotion of health or wellness. Even Preventive Medicine, as a specialty area of expertise in American medicine, does not embrace these concepts of psycho-social medicine, much less the transpersonal aspects. Likewise, most conventional psychological schools or techniques do not mention attitudes as important in the diagnostic or therapeutic milieu. Psychosynthesis, on the other hand, offers appropriate thought forms for conceptualizing, understanding, utilizing, and teaching the emphasis of attitudes in diagnostic and therapeutic schemata.

The presence of unconditional positive regard as the prototypical positive attitude has been mentioned by many. Love is emphasized by Assagioli, as a quintessential characteristic of the Higher Self, and as having several differing aspects. The model above depends heavily on the concepts of psychosynthesis. Holistic medicine looks at attitudes, beliefs, emotions, physical being, mental/intellectual function, spiritual life, and the social, natural, and cosmic environment as essential ingredients in the balance of life/death, health/sickness, and the evolution of individuals and society.

The Human Function model has characteristics of feedback. Behavior and interaction with the environment are outputs from the system and, in turn, become inputs as we become aware of them. While internal sensations, emotional experience, and autonomic nervous system function can be considered outputs, their feedback is also input for further processing within the system. Recall (memory) is continuously available as supplied data, chiefly from the middle unconscious, but from the superconscious and lower unconscious as well. Much of the recall function may be conscious, but much more is probably unconscious.

The two entry points for changes in this feedback mechanism are from the environment and from the inner/personal self. I maintain that one of the most important functions of the will of the self is to set in place and maintain attitudes. The will has seldom been mentioned as an important factor in the theories or function of conventional psychiatry and infrequently mentioned in modern psychology until the past two decades. Psychosynthesis, through its emphasis on the will, provides a second important factor in conceptualizing a new model that embraces the ideas of Wellness Medicine.

Parameters of Holistic Medicine

Collegiality—Holistic medicine emphasizes the collegial nature of therapy, counseling, and medical care. It is becoming less and less common for the physician, or therapist, to tell the patient/client what to do or what medicine to take. Decisions are frequently made jointly. The health practitioner makes suggestions or acts as a guide to help interpret the experience, thinking, or plans and goals of the patient/client. This is done in a spirit of positive regard for the client. Disagreements can be faced in the spirit of good will. Frank (1975) has pointed out that the most significant determinant of outcomes in therapeutic situations is the quality of the relationship which develops between therapist and client. My interpretation would be that the more positive the qualities present happen to be, the better the therapeutic outcome is likely to be. The participation of the client in the decision-making process has been helpful in changing the image of health practitioners as gods on pedestals holding the choices of life and death over the patient.

Certainly psychosynthesis lays heavy emphasis on personal responsibility for choices at the physical, emotional, mental, and transpersonal levels of experience. Indeed, it not only provides convenient substance for a model of holistic medicine, but also it has probably provided impetus for its very development.

Holism—Psychosynthesis is integral. Levels of experience and energy clustered around the body, emotions, mind, personal and Higher Self emphasize the point. Holistic medicine is integral. The only comprehensively based medical organization dealing with this area, the American Holistic Medical Association, states, "Holistic medicine encompasses all safe modalities of diagnosis and treatment, including drugs and surgery, and includes the consideration of mental, emotional, physical, spiritual, and environmental aspects of the patient, and emphasizes the personal responsibility of the patient in promoting health." The first act of the President of this organization at its founding meeting in 1978 was to lead the assembled physicians in Assagioli's disidentification exercise.

Openness—Assagioli emphasized many times that psychosynthesis was not static, but an approach to therapy and to life which would embrace kindred concepts as it grew. The same could be said of holistic medicine. New techniques, insofar as they are understood to be safe, and prudently practiced, can be embraced by holistic medicine more readily than by many conventional medical disciplines which experience a certain amount of inertia in taking on new concepts. The creative quality of psychosynthesis and its contact with the collective creative unconscious in meditation enable new ideas and concepts to surface. This same approach to creativity by practitioners of holistic medicine has engendered an openness to innovative approaches in sickness treatment, disease prevention, and wellness promotion. A technique or approach is accepted when it bodes reasonable evidence of success, even though final scientific proof in the strictest sense is not yet demonstrated. At the same time, experts have written that only 15 percent of what allopathic medical practitioners do meets criteria of proof in the strictest scientific sense. In addition, there is always direction from the age-old medical principle, "Do no harm."

Emphasis on Growth—Psychosynthesis may be viewed as a growth psychology. Emphasis is placed on the evolution of the human person toward a personal and transpersonal synthesis of body, mind, emotions, and spirit. Holistic medicine emphasizes both the disease aspects and the sickness-prevention/wellness-promotion aspects of human experience. Interestingly enough, because of the tremendous cost of the highly technical and generally dehumanizing therapies of conventional medicine, there are economic pressures on the profession to simplify medical approaches and search for cost-effective prevention and health promotion. The ideal cost-effective model of holistic medicine turns out to be a model which most people in Western society would choose: a model which promotes a meaningful life, of whatever length, filled with one's share of joy, creativity, and wellness such that when one's time to leave this earth plane arrives, it is terminated quickly, without significant disability. A motto of my office practice is, "Our purpose is to help you die quickly as late as possible."

Psychosynthesis incorporates certain concepts about dying, including the naturalness of the process, the acceptability of the process, and the importance of completing certain tasks in one's relationships as the time of dying approaches. Conventional medicine emphasizes the prolongation of life at very significant cost. Part of this emphasis may be misplaced, since many persons, especially the elderly and those in scarcely controllable pain, have already chosen and prefer to die. Philosophically, holistic medicine can accommodate these situations more easily, permitting a humanitarian and dignified approach to the patient and the family regarding the dying process as an acceptable and natural process.

Change—Sickness implies change; chronic illness implies continuing change, nearly always involving deterioration, that is, movement toward a less functional state. Preventive medicine implies preparation for maintaining the status quo and, during certain periods, slowing the deterioration process. Health promotion implies movement toward greater functionality. Again, looking at these three models—interventive care, preventive care, and health promotion—few criteria for understanding the process exist (see Figure 2). Psychosynthesis embodies the philosophy of the evolution of a whole being toward balance, creativity,

Figure 2/Models of Sickness/Health Care

Interventive Care	Preventive Care	Whole Care Health Promotion
Asymptomatic healthy origins.	Asymptomatic healthy origins.	Asymptomatic healthy origins.
Early chemical changes, decrease in performance testing.	Reform/cessation of self-destructive habits: smoking, overeating, drug/alcohol overuse, abuse.	Adoption of healthy lifestyle habits: exercise, meditation-relaxation, optimal nutrition, positive beliefs/attitudes, imagery and mind-body effect.
Signs of lack of vigor.		
Symptoms of lack of vigor.	Early detection with history, physical, and lab evidence of treatable disease and degenerative processes.	High-level wellness: energy and vitality, manageable tension, satisfaction and joy, challenge and productivity.
Premature onset of disability for normal activities; high incidence of diseases.		
Health crises; surgical and medical interventions; marked disabilities.	Maintenance: Immunizations, seat belts, exercise, dietary restrictions.	Self-actualization: creativity, learning from life experiences, service to humanity, integration of spiritual dimension.
Heroic surgical and mechanical-technical interventions.	Slow onset of disability for normal activities.	
Premature death.	Reduced period of severe disability and surgical-medical interventions.	High adaptation to disabilities.
	Death.	Death as a part of life.

joy, service to humanity, and self- actualization. It is for this reason that psychosynthesis provides a model for the principle of change in holistic medical concepts.

Change is usually not accomplished without the use of the will. The contributions made both by Assagioli in understanding the nature of the will and by writers in various psychosynthesis fields in understanding its various applications have been essential to practitioners of holistic medicine. The will is back in fashion; the skillful will and the application of will through imagery are a unique combination of ideas deriving from psychosynthesis that are widely applied in holistic fields.

Emotions—The inclusion of emotions in the spectrum of important medical data to be considered by the health practitioner is not conventional. "Psychogenic overlay" is the term commonly used to relegate emotional symptoms or data to a position inferior to physical and laboratory data. Emotions, however, which are accompanied by (or perhaps representative of) certain biochemical changes deserve equal consideration. Many times a patient will be in chemical balance, as ascertained by the laboratory, yet do poorly and even die because of unconsidered emotional factors. A fearful patient, compared to a confident patient, does poorly facing surgical or medical procedures. The recent revelation of the effect of catecholamines (adrenalin and related chemicals) deserves careful attention. The breakdown products of the catecholamines contribute to the load of free radicals in the body. Excesses of free radicals contribute significantly to degeneration and to the aging process. Psychosynthesis gives full recognition to the emotions, derived from Assagioli's description of their importance: "Emotions tend to and demand to be expressed."

The self-destructive habits of substance use and abuse, improper eating, failure to use due care and caution, and smoking, have a strong basis in the emotional sphere. These alone account for the vast majority of premature deaths in Western society. Holistic Medicine addresses the whole person, including the consideration of all these life-style factors in sickness and health, and the contributing emotional factors from which they stem.

Psychosynthesis, emphasizing the three aspects of personality and the transpersonal dimension, is an inclusive model for formulating concepts of the whole person.

Global Implications

Holistic medicine includes careful scrutiny of the environment. It considers the array of assaults of the physical environment on living species. Incredible numbers of heavy metals, petrochemical derivatives, wave-form energies including ionizing radiation (x-ray and nuclear), dusts (asbestos and silicon from coal), side-effects of drugs (prescribed and non-prescribed), and smoke toxify and sensitize the environment for humans and other living species. In the consumer economy, ecological disasters are threatened, including loss of forests, habitats, soils, and exhaustion of finite reserves of minerals, to say nothing of the increasingly problematic disposal problems of the throw-away society.

Psychosynthesis speaks to the synthesis of persons, groups, and nations. It is, in short, a universal concept which has no bounds, and is not attached to narrow sectarian interests. As such, it accepts the ideas of environmental medicine and global concerns more easily. William Osler, a prominent physician in the early 1900s, is widely quoted as having said, "It is far more important to know what kind of patient has a disease than to know what kind of disease a patient has." Conventional medicine has tended to treat symptoms and diseases; holistic medicine is prone to treat persons and causes. Consider the following example as a final illustration of my premise that psychosynthesis provides the best working model to date for the concepts and practice of holistic medicine.

A woman in her fifties developed intractable diarrhea. Instead of treating her symptomatically, attempts were made to determine an organic cause for her problem. No such evidence was forthcoming after numerous tests and examinations. Attention was paid to her apparent anger. After persistent rejection of this idea for several months by the patient, continued loving contact won out, and ultimately a most vexing issue between herself and her sisters surrounding the death of their mother was recognized. The patient ultimately agreed to be led through a forgiveness exercise, and the diarrhea ceased permanently the day she completed the exercise. Concepts regarding love and human relationships which have been incorporated as essential by holistic practitioners find an ideal working model in psychosynthesis.

Healing and the Transpersonal Dimension

It may come as news to some physicians and surgeons that they have never healed a patient. A significant portion of the population, whether overtly religious or not, recognizes that healing depends on numerous factors, known and unknown, and may include spiritual beliefs and dependence on a higher power. The scientific evidence for the importance of beliefs is the wealth of placebo studies now published in the medical literature. Beliefs have the capability of changing physiology and biochemistry. To be aware of, to influence, and to cultivate and refine beliefs is part of the healing process. The vast complexity of the human frame with its one-quadrillion cells, each operating 5,500 enzyme systems all at the same time, suggests that even the hard sciences possess a tiny degree of knowledge with respect to the whole. The understanding of disease processes themselves, the possibility of "creating our own reality," and how we may have knowingly or inadvertently contributed to a sickness may hold the key to our own healing. In my experience, being aligned with an awareness of a purpose in living, and having intentions of carrying out that purpose in specific goals and projects, contributes greatly to the healing climate. Transpersonal psychosynthesis may speak much more decisively in the healing process than any deliberate balancing of biochemistry.

All physicians know numerous patients who have survived for years in what appeared to be very precarious health by having a purpose and a determination to serve. One patient I recall, 70 years of age, has volunteered at a local hospital four half-days each week, having contributed over 14,000 hours of time in the last decade. She has had three episodes of heart and vascular problems, each of which had the potential to take her life. Lying in a hospital bed, sustained by tubes and wires for several days, her question always was, "When can I go back to work?" How important it is to be aligned with the Higher Self to fully release the powers of healing of the whole being to fulfill a chosen purpose.

The energy sustaining the holistic medical movement derives from the power of concepts whose time has come. Psychosynthesis is among the most integral of those concepts. It is, indeed, an ideal model for evolving holistic medicine.

References

Cousins, N. (1979). *Anatomy of an Illness*. New York: Norton.

Frank, J. D. (1975), *Mind-body Relationships in Illness and Healing. Journal of the International Academy of Preventive Medicine*, 2(3), 46—59,

Hernandez-Peon, R., Scherrer, H., & Jouvet, M. (1956), Modification of Electric Activity in Cochlear Nucleus During 'Attention' in Unanesthetized Cats. *Science*, 123, 331-332.

Kobasa, S. (1979, January). Stressful Life Events, Personality and Health: An Inquiry Into Hardiness. *Journal of Personality and Social Psychology*, 27(1), 1-4.

Rosenthal, R., Jacobsen, L. F. (1968, April). Teacher Expectations for the Disadvantaged. *Scientific American*, 19-23.

Shekelle, R. B., et al. (1983, May). Hostility, Risk of Coronary Heart Disease and Mortality. *Psychosomatic Medicine*, 45(2), 109-114.

Williams, R., et al. (1980, November). Type A Behavior, Hostility, and Coronary Atherosclerosis. *Psychosomatic Medicine*, 42(6), 539 549.

This article was revised by the author in 2017.

NOTE

---

[1] "Patients' last two months of life cost Medicare $50 billion [in 2008] —CBS Sixty Minutes. Nov.19, 2009. In 2016, "America's total medical costs hit a new record of $3.4 trillion, according to the federal government. That's about 18 percent of the country's total GDP, meaning that one out of every six dollars we spent in 2016 went to health care. . . The cost is so concentrated, in fact, that an estimated five percent of the population accounts for 50 percent of total medical costs." T.R.Reid, *How We Spend $3,400,000,000,000.* The Atlantic. June 15, 2017. —*Ed.*

[2] Adapted from R. A. Anderson, "A Functional Model of Man," Stress Power! How to Turn Tension Into Energy, Human Sciences Press, New York, 1978, p. 104.

Robert A. Anderson, MD, *graduated with honors from the University of Washington School of Medicine. He has taught medical students in the clinical program of the Department of Medicine at the University of Washington and Bastyr University's Naturopathic Medicine program, is a diplomate of the American Board of Family Practice, and is a Fellow of the American Academy of Family Physicians and the American College of Preventive Medicine. He is past president of the American Holistic Medical Association, and founder and past Executive Director of the American Board of Integrative Holistic Medicine. He completed training in psychosynthesis in 1979. He is the author of* Stress Power! How to Turn Tension into Energy (1978), Wellness Medicine (1987) *and* Stories of Healing: A Family Doctor's Journal (2011).

Part IV.

Spiritual Life

Subpersonalities and Prayer: Psychosynthesis and Spiritual Direction

Jane Vennard

The perspective of Psychosynthesis calls people into wholeness. The experience of wholeness is validated as is the experience of diversity. We are all one and we are all many. The spiritual journey is the movement from wholeness through diversity into wholeness and back into diversity, an ever continuing spiral. This journey includes the already and the not yet.

Psychosynthesis is useful in many ways for those seeking spiritual direction: it emphasizes the use of the Will in the act of discernment, the claiming of one's own authority, the use of dream images to guide and/or make clear the unfolding journey, the discovery of patterns which block loving relationships, the discovery of our full richness to bring into ministry, the healing of old wounds that block our movement into a more complete life. The work of Psychosynthesis is spiritual work for it always holds God's loving power as a guiding force in one's life. Psychosynthesis does not exclude the power of past experiences (personal, familial, societal) in shaping behavior, but infuses these experiences with meaning by viewing them through a transpersonal lens.

In this article, I focus on one small aspect of Psychosynthesis and spiritual direction: working with subpersonalities to uncover, develop, and deepen prayer. Because spiritual direction is always done from the understanding that God, not the individual and not the director, is guiding the process of growth and unfoldment, prayer is at the heart of spiritual direction. The recognition and acceptance of subpersonalities that both block and enhance prayer helps a person to respond to the call and the guidance of God in her or his life.

Subpersonalities and Prayer

At the age of 35, I wanted to learn how to meditate. I felt called to the discipline and the peace and energy that people reported who were involved in meditation. But I could not do it. I would set a time to begin, and the time would go by. In group meditations, I would close my eyes and then begin to feel extremely anxious. During one long exercise, I left the room, for the intensity caused me to panic.

The invitation to begin meditation came in my study of Psychosynthesis. This transpersonal psychology described a perspective which granted to the human person a spiritual aspect that was as influential in the ongoing development process as one's drives, needs, and past experiences. I was finding Psychosynthesis to be intellectually and emotionally powerful in my life, but I could not move into the spiritual realm. During a session with my guide, I found the nature of my resistance.

In guided imagery, I was directed into a meadow to relax and to await the coming of the part of me, the subpersonality, that was getting in the way of meditation. In my imagination, I sat in the meadow, waiting and waiting, inviting that part to come forth. I was aware that there was a presence in the woods at the edge of the meadow. I could catch a glimpse of movement, but I could not see who it was. Then very slowly a figure began to emerge. She was about 20 years old and dressed in a gossamer gown, long and flowing. She seemed very afraid, and I reassured her, telling her I truly wanted to get to know her. She came toward me, and came to rest in front of me. She told me that her name was Esmeralda, and that she was the part of me I had left in Europe after the experience at the Ecumenical Work Camp that I had attended in Holland when I was 19. Memories of that summer flooded over me: the excitement of the many other young people from different nations and different faiths, the hard work of brick laying, the taste of Dutch chocolate melting on my tongue, the Bible reading, the singing, the prayers, and the worship. And then suddenly I was in Paris watching a man being run over by a speeding taxi and killed instantly before my eyes. Esmeralda's emergence triggered the experience that was blocking my meditation.

In talking subsequently with my guide, I relived the memories and realized that the joy of the camp and the horror of random death could not be contained in the theology I was working with at that time. Five weeks of camp had heightened my experience of a loving and all-powerful God who cared about each and every one of us. In my 19-year-old mind and heart, I could not hold both experiences. I was alone and terrified; the experience of darkness was all the more overwhelming after the experience of light. The pain was too great, and to protect myself from encountering that pain again, I closed down my religious and spiritual experiences, for I knew I could not protect myself from death. Esmeralda, the spiritual part of me, who had the will and aware-ness for meditation and prayer, had been left in Europe at the age of 19.

When I knew which subpersonality had been blocking my spiritual development, I could begin the process of education. I helped Esmeralda slowly grow up as I discovered a theology that could hold both the light and the dark. I could experiment with different forms of prayer and meditation, and integrate the spiritual into my life. All my resistance to prayer was not gone, and I have had periods of difficulty along the way. But a major hurdle had been overcome and the joys and struggles of the spiritual life opened out before me.

Subpersonalities that Block Progress

Since that time, in my work of counseling, teaching, and providing spiritual direction, I have witnessed other people discovering subper-sonalities that have been blocking their prayer life. One 40-year-old man worked with an 11-year-old boy named Rodney. Rodney was terrified of God. "The Devil was easy," he said in one session, "God was the one to fear." This man's early religious training was so filled with a frighten-ing and judgmental God that he closed God off in adolescence and had no desire to re-open the relationship. "Who would want to talk to a God like that?" he said.

"I am not worthy," a young woman said to me in a class. "How can I take myself to God? I don't expect Him to listen to me. I am so unworthy of even asking for His attention. I feel totally cut off from any of God's love or guidance. And being unable to pray makes me feel even more unworthy." This woman was not reporting a subpersonality; she was totally identified with a part of herself that was invisible, unknown, and unworthy.

Another woman reported an overachieving subpersonality that kept telling her she wasn't doing it right. "No matter how long I sat, no matter how beautiful my words, no matter how peaceful my heart, my prayer would be interrupted with the doubts of whether I was doing it as well as others, whether I was truly pleasing God. My mind held a great desire to know more and more about prayer, but all the time I was being pulled away from the experience of prayer."

Still another man talked about the part of himself that was commit-ted to social action and ending injustice in the world. Every time he began a regular prayer experience, this other part berated him, "How can you just sit there when there is so much to be done. Prayer will take you out of this world. This is the world that needs you. If you get too involved with spiritual things you will lose your power and force in the world."

All of these subpersonalities were an aspect of personality, a part of the whole. Some were developed in the past, some in adult years, but each one served to interrupt the prayer life of the people involved. By recognizing "who" was causing the problem, each person was able to begin working with that part that pulled them away from their relationship with God, and move more deeply into the life of the spirit.

Subpersonalities and Prayer Styles

Just as our subpersonalities can block prayer, they can be great helpers and friends in prayer, if we allow them to pray in ways that are most comfortable and nourishing to them. Every subpersonality has access to God, and because of the different nature of the many subpersonalities, prayer can be experienced in many different ways.

Occasionally a subpersonality will decide that he or she is the one who really knows about prayer, and so will try to make the other subpersonalities conform to a particular form or routine: "To pray correctly I have to set aside a full 30 minutes, first do my stretching activities, then quiet my mind with the use of my breathing, then I read a section of Scripture and reflect on its meaning in my life. This is followed by the cards on which I have written the names of people I wish to hold before God in my prayers. I then pray for myself, asking forgiveness and giving thanks." The person who reported this form of prayer to me also reported that her prayers were happening less often and that they were dry and routine and "just another thing to be done in the day." When I suggested that there might be other ways to engage God in her life, she was surprised, excited, and doubtful. This woman's prayer life was being controlled by a subpersonality most likely developed through her religious training.

When we honor the many different forms and styles of prayer and trust that all are acceptable to the God with whom we pray, much creativity is released. The following descriptions are subpersonality reports of experiences of prayer. I have gathered these over the years with clients and students, and use them with permission:

> River Rat connects with God in Nature. She is happiest in the wilderness where she can take off her clothes and drink in God's world with every inch of her being—the touch and the taste, the smells and sounds as well as the visual beauty that surrounds her.

The musician in me praises God with my music. When I sing out, when I write music, when I direct women's voices into harmony. I am singing, singing, singing for the glory of God.

One night when I was in distress over my mother—her health, her emotional anxiety, and our relationship—I was finding my prayers unhelpful, agitating, in fact. But then I realized I needed to pray as a daughter, and I needed to pray to a Mother of God. When I shifted my position and made specific my image of God, release, hope, and consolation began to flow through me.

Every year I make a retreat for seven days. I don't think I could get through my life without that time. The Mystic in me is so happy, and although it gets some attention during the year, only in brief moments. During that week I fully identify with Mary Ann, as I call her, and let all my other subpersonalities rest. They are as happy as Mary Ann, for they know that when I return to my busy life, the energy and love and peace that Mary Ann feels will be shared with them. Mary Ann is able to teach the others what she has learned.

I truly feel the presence of God when I serve regularly at St. Anthony's kitchen. Standing behind the tables ladling out the stew, watching all manner of folk pass before me, I am humbled and I see in each and every face the person of Jesus and hear his words: "As you do for the least of them, so you do unto me."

I was overcome with awe as my newborn infant was placed in my wife's arms. Witness to a miracle of creation. And now, as the realities of parenting are constantly before us, I still, at moments, simply stop, and the same awe overcomes me as I look at my child. To be a parent is to be constantly reminded of God.

Speedy is on the move. She laughs and clowns and wears the most comfortable clothes no matter how she looks. She is learning to juggle, and I feel as I laugh and juggle and drop the balls and laugh some more that God is laughing with me for Speedy knows that God loves to laugh even if I forget it.

Every morning when I put on my running clothes, stretch out my muscles, tighten the shoelaces, I feel as if

I am preparing to run toward my God. For as I run, I feel within my breath and my body the glory of living. My running is a prayer of thanksgiving for health and movement and energy all contained in this body I have been given. And I pray that I may use this body and this energy to further serve the God of creation.

Summer is a new subpersonality I am developing. She is quietly and comfortably in relation with God. Her spirituality infuses her being. All my other subpersonalities have a frantic quality about them. They may talk to God, but usually only in their own self interests. Summer recognizes the needs of all and trusts that those needs will be met. Her task in prayer is to listen, just listen and then share what she hears. It is amazing to me, after so many years of praying and asking and asking and praying and getting no answer. Now that Summer is praying, and praying simply by opening her heart, she is hearing. Some of my subpersonalities are a little doubtful, for Summer is so new. But many recognize her gift, for as she is more and more in charge they realize she uses love to guide herself and them, and in the light of her love, the love that comes from God, they are more accepting, less frantic, and more willing to cooperate.

Implications for Spiritual Direction

Working with subpersonalities through the stages of recognition, acceptance, co-ordination, and integration is an integral part of spiritual direction. When subpersonality work is centered around prayer, movement can be experienced within the whole personality; a reaching toward God, a deepening of the relationship with God, and the experience of God in one's life.

The descriptions of the subpersonalities that block prayer as well as the ones who have their own preference for prayer are examples of the first stage of subpersonality work—recognition. Each subpersonality is recognized, named, and explored to find out what the needs and wants are, what the gifts are, and how the subpersonality thinks and feels about life in general, and prayer specifically. The next stage is acceptance. Each one of these subpersonalities needs to be accepted as a valuable part of the whole personality. There may be blocked or distorted behavior, but each subpersonality needs to be heard and welcomed. Often when a subpersonality is discovered, another subpersonality will emerge to reject it. This rejecting subpersonality may be the judgmental type as in the case of the woman whose subpersonality felt she was not worthy to be with God; this part of herself berated her for being spineless, and although seemingly committed to building her up, was not listening to the real pain of the Worthless One.

Often a judgment will be issued from subpersonalities that believe another form of prayer is wrong or inferior. The Disciplined Mystic might say to Speedy, "That's not prayer! You're having too much fun!" Or a priestly subpersonality might tell River Rat, "For shame! Cover yourself! Who do you think you are, cavorting like a pagan?" Or Summer might be told by the Organized Doer, "All that peace and tranquility will make you lazy. On your feet, girl, there is much to be done."

In order to develop an acceptance of all the parts of the personality, the process of disidentification needs to occur. When the conflict has been recognized and named, and fully explored through imagery or gestalt chair work, the person can be invited to move to a third place where he or she is no longer identified either with the subpersonalities or with the conflict. The individual stands outside, in a place where he or she can see, hear, and bring understanding and acceptance to both parts. This third place is another subpersonality, one with a wider view that can see more, accept more deeply, and aid in both the healing of wounded subpersonalities and the mediating of the conflict between them.

From the third position, co-ordination becomes possible. With co-ordination comes the decision to share time, so that both the Disciplined Mystic and Speedy, for example, would have time to pray in their own ways, neither one insisting that there was only one way. The subpersonality that sees and values both positions can also encourage integration by helping the subpersonalities learn from one another. The idea is not for the two to become one, but rather to share some of the qualities unique to each so that in this case Speedy might become more disciplined in her playful prayer, and the Disciplined Mystic might begin to lighten up his prayer life and approach it with a more playful heart.

I have worked with clients in whose personality this third place, this loving, caring subpersonality, is readily available. In other clients, this part is not fully developed and needs to be evoked and loved into being. The subpersonality Summer is an example of one of the latter. In all the work Dorothy had done, she had recognized her many subpersonalities. All were vivid and well-formed, but narrow and self-interested. They were rich and exciting and brought her great diversity and gifts, but not one of them was willing to serve the whole personality in a loving and caring way. When she disidentified from any conflict, she stepped directly into another subpersonality that would keep the conflict going, or she would step into a judging sub personality that would defeat her with such words as "Aren't you ever going to get this together?!" In guided imagery, she called to an unknown part of herself, a part that could help her in her frenzied life. Summer appeared. The ongoing work with Dorothy is to help her get closer to Summer, to trust her, to bring her into her life. Because Summer carries and plays the flute, Dorothy uses her breathing to remind her of Summer's existence. She also uses the words of Summer: "I am spiritually content. I deserve God's love," Dorothy told me in our last session that Summer was real to her, but it was as if she was sitting next to her. Dorothy could not yet become Summer and trust that her qualities were her own.

I believe that God calls each and every one of us to wholeness. We move toward wholeness as we learn about our diversity, for we are One and we are Many. We are Whole and we are Broken. We are Divine and we are Human. Spiritual direction is a response to that call toward wholeness, and prayer is at the heart of the process. By intentionally working with the subpersonalities, particularly with their varied experience of God and their individual relationships to God, clients can discover their internal riches which they can then bring to their relationship with God. This relationship with God through prayer allows for more riches within the personality to be revealed and explored, enriching the full life which is being led. When subpersonalities are taken seriously and their fears and wants and needs and gifts and hopes listened to, the whole personality can move toward God, toward others, and toward all of life with more intention, with more awareness, with more joy, and ultimately with more love.

Reverend Jane Vennard *was called to a ministry of teaching and spiritual direction and ordained in the United Church of Christ. She recently retired from the Iliff School of Theology where she has been Senior Adjunct Faculty for thirty years. She continues to teach in other seminaries and leads retreats internationally. She has a private practice of spiritual direction in Denver, Colorado. Jane has written numerous articles and eight books on prayer and spiritual practices. Her most recent book is* Fully Awake and Truly Alive: Spiritual Practices to Nurture Your Soul.

A Theology of Blessing:
A Psychology of Growth

Joan Cannon Borton

Psychosynthesis does not aim or attempt to give a metaphysical or theological explanation of the great Mystery—it leads to the door, but stops there.
—Roberto Assagioli (1978)

Introduction

Growing up as a rebellious preacher's kid, with parents and grandparents who were teachers, ministers, and missionaries, I had a strong sense of my roots in the Christian tradition. Choosing to study religion and biblical studies in college, I explored theology and various paths to "the great Mystery." Having sworn never to marry a minister, I met a deeply seeking man, we fell in love and were married. He became a minister.

As I look back, I see myself as an intense and searching soul, whose sense of oneness with creation brought her closest to that door of Mystery. A major block to that path was my need to feel in control, my lack of trust. My psychosynthesis training enabled me to let go and trust the unfolding process of each person and all creation. I then began to open myself to the Mystery at the heart of my own tradition. I was drawn in a new way to the one called Jesus the Christ and to the way he was with people. Jesus did not use jargon when he talked with people, nor did he present a belief system. He engaged them at a level which asked for their trust. His trust was in their potential for wholeness or holiness. I responded to this Jesus who challenged people to trust, who spoke to the image of God in each person and called it forth. I wanted to learn more of him.

So I began, with gratitude to Roberto Assagioli and his conception of the human being, on a journey which led me to my spiritual home. The following article is both an expression of that gratitude and an attempt to share from the Christian tradition my discoveries on the way.

During my training I discovered the work of Meister Eckhart, a 13th-century spiritual theologian. I found myself making connections between his words and my understanding and experience of Psychosynthesis. The process of bridging the two became very exciting to me when I encountered a contemporary theologian, Matthew Fox, who was interpreting Eckhart for our time. This led me to recover for myself the spiritual tradition within Christianity known as Creation-Centered Spirituality. This theology of blessing offered an articulation of my religious experience which expanded the richness of my tradition and deepened my willingness as a counselor to engage in trust with people on their life journeys.

At a time when the Church's voice is often exclusive and is used to define someone as either "in" or "out," I find Eckhart's understanding of spiritual paths expansive and inclusive. In an age of personal and planetary threat to life, Creation-Centered Spirituality speaks of Justice and Compassion as the fulfillment of the Hebrew tradition and of the Christian gospel. It is my purpose to present the four paths of Creation Spirituality in a way that connects with the personal-spiritual growth work of Psychosynthesis. I intend to illustrate this theology of blessing with some of the principles and techniques of Roberto Assagioli's psychology of growth toward wholeness.

Meister Eckhart and the Hidden Treasure

Meister Eckhart (1260-1329) was a Dominican preacher and teacher whose holistic spiritual vision challenged the established church. His politics were also questionable for he involved himself as spiritual director with a community of lay women who worked with the poor but were not accepted by the church as nuns. They were early feminists, and so was he. Eckhart viewed all persons as "royal persons," which was an affront to the class structure of the time. He was condemned after his death by church authorities (Fox, 1980), but his sermons and writings have continued to be influential.

Mystics within the Catholic Church such as Hildegard of Bingen and Julian of Norwich drew on Eckhart's spirituality. The Protestant reformer Martin Luther and the father of Quakerism George Fox were also influenced by his thought. Carl Jung was touched by this Dominican, as were D. T. Suzuki and Thomas Merton who both saw Zen in his writings. The breadth of Eckhart's influence and his particular relevance for our time challenged a contemporary Dominican, Matthew Fox, to translate his sermons and present them with commentary in *Breakthrough: Meister Eckhart's Creation Spirituality in New Translation*. In

1985, Fox published *Original Blessing, A Primer in Creation Spirituality*, which thematically reclaims this tradition within the setting of 20th-century Christianity.

The starting place for Eckhart's understanding of the spiritual journey is one's created nature, which he calls "the treasure." His model for the spiritual traveler is the artist:

> If a skilled artist made an image in wood or stone, he or she does not place that image within the wood but chisels away the pieces that have hidden and covered it up..., Then what lay underneath shone forth. This is the treasure that lay hidden in the soil, as our Lord says in the Gospel [Matthew 13:44], (Fox, 1980, p. 412)

Psychosynthesis views the traveler as beginning the journey also by discovering that treasure which is uniquely his or her created nature. This is the beginning of healing, a moving toward wholeness. As with the process of psychosynthesis, Eckhart sees this movement not as a linear progression but as a spiral motion of four different paths that lead into and return to each other as we become more fully co-creators of our lives with God. Matthew Fox (1983) has named these paths: Befriending Creation, Befriending Darkness, Befriending Creativity, and Befriending New Creation.

Path 1—Befriending Creation

Vincent Van Gogh's painting *Starry Night* expresses in greens, golds, and blues the pulsating vibrancy of the cosmos, the aliveness of creation. The Hebrews had a word for the energy that Van Gogh expresses: *dabhar*, the creative energy of God. It is this energy that is celebrated in the psalms of the Hebrew scriptures:

> Oh Lord how manifold are thy works!
> In Wisdom thou hast made them all;
> the earth is full of thy creatures. (Psalm 104:24)

The two creation stories in Genesis proclaim through the language and context of the Middle East the sense of God or Yahweh as Creator and Giver of Life. That Life is the *dabhar*, shared with all creation, and blessed by Yahweh, "And he saw that it was good" (Gen. 102:4a). Thus the original state of creation was good and the Creator was one who blessed all forms of life.

In the first creation story, written in the ninth century B.C.E., the author's imagery expresses the loving quality of this "Lord God" (*Elohim*) who wants to create a human being. "So the Lord God took the dust of the earth and blew into it and *adam*," meaning all humanity, male or female (Kenik, 1979, p. 50), "became a living being" (Gen. 2:46). Matter, from which all creation was made, was enlivened by spirit and the creative energy of God was shared. The Yahwist whose creation story comes from the tenth century also expresses the *dabhar* enacted through the spoken word. "And God said . . . let there be light... let us make *adam* in our image" (Gen. 1). That spoken word in Hebrew is *dabhar*; it involves action. The word has the power to create (Fox, 1983, pp. 35-41).

The same word is used in the Gospel of John in reference to Christ: "In the beginning was the Word, and the Word was with God and the Word was God" (John 1:1). Creation-Centered Spirituality is a theology of creation and incarnation. The incarnation of that creative energy of God in the person of Jesus is an embodiment of God's intention for all people to realize their fullness and divinity: "I have come that you may have Life and have it in abundance" (John 10:10). This abundance was expressed by the writers of the creation stories. The Garden of Eden was a place of fullness and of blessing. "It was good" and it was enough for all creation. Wanting more than enough led to the separation of man and woman from the Creator and other creatures (Gen. 3).

This experience of separation from the Oneness that is the inheritance of humanity and from one's own true nature is often what brings a person to counseling, even though he or she may present specific problems as the initial reason. The relationship between spiritual growth and personal growth is one of interconnection. Psychosynthesis counseling recognizes this. The healing work of discovering our created nature is a form of "befriending creation," beginning with one's self. This takes place over time and is experienced in some of the following ways:

- **Touching** those transpersonal qualities, intimations of the Garden of Eden, that each of us longs to experience in a fuller way: love, courage, joy, patience, hope.
- **Holding** those qualities as affirmations for the journey while we disidentify (Crampton, 1977, pp, 22-27) from the roles and personae we have created in order to discover the "self" beneath that build-up.
- **Working** with the various subpersonalities (Brown, 1983, pp, 29-34) that have blocked the expression of the *dabhar* (God's creative energy) in us; experiencing growing communication between what has appeared to be opposing inner forces.

Joan Cannon Borton

- **Finding** the gold hidden in our most frightened parts.
- **Embracing**, as Carl Rogers observed, "the richness and complexity, with nothing hidden and nothing feared in oneself—this is the common desire in those who seemed to show much movement in therapy" (Rogers, 1984, p. 14.).

The process of befriending creation can start on a very personal level. This part of the spiritual journey is where travelers begin the life-long process of claiming the abundance of the Garden of Eden and their own state of original blessing. We begin to know that creative energy of God within themselves and all creation is enough. For enough is abundance. To realize that on a personal level, a spiritual level, and a planetary level, is the prophetic call to us as a species.

Path 2—Befriending Darkness

The spiritual heritage of Christian mystics encompasses two basic approaches. The first tradition emphasizes visions, light, images, and positive affective experiences as the way to come to know God. The second tradition is based in silence as the place of meeting God. The traveler engages in a process of emptying, which Eckhart speaks of as the second spiritual path. It involves a willingness to be open to the darkness, which is experienced in silence as a letting go of words, images, thoughts, and affections. It is a way of entering into nothingness, a trusting of empty space. The movement is one of sinking, letting go, resting or emptying. It involves a deep level of trust.

> We become a pure nothing by an unknowing knowledge
> which is emptiness
> and solitude
> and desert
> and darkness
> and remaining still. (Fox, 1982, p. 48)

This movement in therapy is very crucial. As therapists and counselors, we need to be willing to be there with another person in the emptiness, to be present at a time when he or she experiences not knowing and to let be what is (Fox, 1982, p. 48). This means that we too must have allowed ourselves to go into the darkness. This experience can be frightening. It is essential to be able to trust even when we are in darkness or to let someone else do the befriending when we do not have it in ourselves to trust.

Matthew Fox makes an important distinction regarding this part of the journey. On the one hand, there is a sinking or emptying motion in spiritual life that we can choose to follow. On the other hand, there is the experience of being emptied when circumstances outside ourselves such as loss, sexual abuse, catastrophe, or illness bring darkness and pain. When this happens, we cannot decide whether or not we want to go along with it; it is just there. Thus there is a qualitative difference between emptying and being emptied.

When I was on my back for a long period of time, working hard to heal myself, I finally recognized that the healing was taking place in the spaces between my efforts, in the empty spaces. I had to have trust that by letting go and letting be I could choose to empty myself of my effort. I could not choose whether or not I had pain. I was being emptied by the pain, and that emptying was the gift of this period of darkness for me:

> God does not ask anything else of you
> > except
> > > that you let yourself go
> > > > and let God
> > > > > be God
> > > > > > in you.
> > > > > > —Fox, 1982, p. 52

During this time, I read *Breakthrough*, Eckhart's sermons edited by Matthew Fox, and found I was helped by the process of being emptied by pain. The Japanese poet Kenji Miyazawa suggests that we can embrace pain and burn it as fuel for our journey. Fox, who also suffered from back pain, explored this further:

> We pick up our pain as we would a bundle of sticks for a fireplace. We necessarily embrace these sticks as we move across the room to the fireplace. Then we thrust them into the fire, getting rid of them, letting go of them. Finally we are warmed and delighted by their sacrificial gift to us in a form of fire and heat and warmth and energy. This is the manner in which we can and indeed must deal with our pain. First comes the embrace, the allowing of pain to be pain. Next comes the journey with the pain, then the letting go but in a deliberate manner into a fire, into a cauldron where the pain's energy will serve us. And finally comes the benefit we do indeed

derive from having burned the fuel. Pain is meant to give
us energy. (Fox, 1983, pp. 142-143)

We deal with pain as counselors. Much of our work is helping people to embrace their pain rather than denying it, pushing it away, or running from its reality. Focusing (Gendlin, 1981) is one way of strengthening a client's will while dealing with a painful thing. He or she might be asked, "Can you be with this [painful thing] as if it were a hurt child? Can you put your arm around it?" (Campbell, 1985, pp. 124-125). Gestalt methods, expressive exercises, imagery, and subpersonality dialogue are various ways of befriending the darkness. One begins to embrace the painful part and to walk with it until one can let it go, releasing its energy. This journey with a painful part of ourselves can be a long and sometimes desperate process. Yet in the depth of emptiness, we can experience the compassionate heart of God, for there is communion with God who also suffers with the darkness.

Christ on the Cross painted by Georges Roualt speaks in deep reds of the process of Jesus emptying himself in order to allow pain to be pain (Philippians, 2:5-9). The crucifixion is, for me, Jesus' willingness to go with the pain of human history and to trust in God in the midst of darkness and not knowing. This is a powerful image which can help us during our own experiences of darkness, and also enable us to be there in dark times for other people.

Eckhart said that our souls grow by subtraction, not by addition (Fox, 1982, p. 45). To trust this process while experiencing nothingness is the challenge of the second path. This experience brings us back in a spiral motion to the first path. For our willingness to go to the place of nothingness brings us to the beginning of creation; it is out of darkness that light is created. According to Matthew Fox, the relationship between the first and second paths causes a dialectic from which creative energy comes forth.

Path 3—Befriending Creativity

The third path emerges as the place of the birthing of human imagination. Being "created in the image of God" means that we, too, are image makers. In expressing the *dabhar* in ourselves, we become co-creators with God.

The colorful collages of Henri Matisse are my icons for this path. In the middle of World War II, this Frenchman felt that he had to make a statement for joy. In his later years as an invalid, he did most of his work from his bed, drawing sketches on the walls and ceiling of his room by attaching charcoal to a bamboo pole. His assistants would then cut out the vibrant shapes, which would become a mural or a stained glass window. The creative spirit of this image maker has inspired many travelers.

The creative potential of this path holds awesome power. Eckhart reminds us, "We are heirs of this fearful creative power of God" (Fox, 1983, p. 182). In similar vein, Dag Hammarskjöld asks, "Do we create or do we destroy?" (Fox, 1983, p. 178). The possibility for birthing and blessing is ours as co-creators with God. The other side of that wondrous inheritance is the power to destroy all that has been created. Both Eckhart and Assagioli were deeply aware of this potential and thus emphasized the importance of response-ability.

The Artist, for Eckhart, is that part of ourselves which expresses our deepest self. And it is the Will, for Assagioli, that motivates the expression of the Self in the world. Trusting our images is central to this process of expression, birthing, or creating the Self. Discernment is crucial at this level of trusting. As Fox said, we must decide which images we are going to ride. This involves discipline. For Assagioli, working with images is involved in techniques for developing our will. This is a training process. In both Creation-Centered Spirituality and Psychosynthesis, willing and imagination go hand in hand.

The same elements are present in the Genesis story. Man and woman were created in the image of God—with the potential to be creators themselves, using their imagination. In their freedom within the Garden, they had the choice to accept its abundance or to seek more and "be like God" (Gen. 3:5). How do we develop our creative potential (the power of our imagination) and at the same time be responsible stewards of the resources that are entrusted to us by God (the enhanced will)?

Assagioli's work with the Will is fascinating on a theoretical level as he explores the relationship between image and action in his Psychological Laws (Assagioli, 1973, pp. 51-65). More important, he translates this into very helpful exercises for the training of the Will. I often find myself returning to use the Stages of the Will (1965, pp. 125-143) for clarity in my own decision-making. I use a process of willing with clients as a tangible way to make changes on a behavioral level. Each step in the process can be valuable in itself. The total process of movement from "purpose" to "directing the action" is empowering. Assagioli places this exercise in personal willing within the greater context of Love—Transpersonal and Universal Will. Like the self-expression of Matisse, this phase of the journey is associated by Assagioli with joy. He concludes The Act of Will with the words of Evelyn Underhill:

The enhanced will, made over to the interests of the Transcendent, receives new worlds to conquer, new strengths to match its exalted destiny. But the heart, too, here enters on a new order, begins to live upon high levels of joy: that is, the sea of delight, the stream of divine influences. (1973, pp. 201-202)

This enhanced will, this conscious expression of the *dabhar*, connects us with the Transcendent. On the path of befriending creativity, we participate in the resurrection energy of Christ. With a sense of this potential, we are led to the fourth path which leads us, in the words of Underhill, toward a "new order."

Path 4—Befriending New Creation

Our creativity must be directed by compassion. This quality must guide us in all our decisions on the path of new creation. Yet as we travel, we find that the experience of each previous path is included. As we seek a just world order based on our knowledge of planetary interdependence (Path 4), we call on the birthing of the *dabhar* in all people (Path 3), which is generated by facing the darkness of possible nuclear destruction (Path 2); this experience of the darkness results from our great love and our sense of oneness with all creation (Path 1).

Deep passion for justice is expressed by Eckhart in his understanding of compassion:

> Whatever God does, the first outburst is always compassion. (Fox, 1983, p. 277)

> Compassion means justice and compassion is just to the extent that it gives to each person what is his or hers. (p. 103)

For Assagioli, the process of synthesis and expanding awareness is expressed by a commitment to "the psychosynthesis of Humanity," a realizing of interdependence, solidarity, and co-operation (Horowitz, 1984).

Eckhart sees that our vocation, what we are called forth to do with who we are in the world, is to turn the blessing that we are back into the process of creation. This movement makes available more of the creative energy of God in the Universe. It is Matthew Fox's view that all of us are potential prophets, that our task is interference and awakening for the purpose of transformation, that we should ask ourselves, "How is my work interfering with injustice? How am I planting seeds of harmony in the cosmic world?" (1983, p. 261). On this fourth path, we must trust in our prophetic vocations, not in our own ability to figure this out, but in the grace of the Holy Spirit which is available for all of us to appropriate. As Jesus met each person in his or her uniqueness, so, too, the Holy Spirit leads each of us to our unique expression of this vocation.

When I gaze at the photograph of our planet taken from the moon, I see rich blues and greens wreathed in white swirling clouds. I see that small fragile whole against the backdrop of deep, dark space. I no longer see separate land formations, continents, East or West. I see the earth in its entirety. I recognize the interdependence of all its parts and feel a longing to tend and care for this creation in its wholeness.

As we experience the life and death nature of our interdependence on this planet, we need to know that justice is "erotic," that it is intimate, passionate, and involved (Fox, 1983, pp. 286-305). When Jesus said, "I have come that you have life and have it in abundance" (John 10:10), his commitment was to become involved with all of creation.

When as a psychosynthesis counselor I am with one person who expresses despair over an inability to experience the creative life of God, or when as a Christian lay person I see the outrage of a people who may never know abundance, I confront my vocation. I feel called to draw on the creative energy of God, the *dabhar*, to care for this created world and its inhabitants in the ways that I am able so that others may experience the abundance that has been created for all of us.

References

Assagioli, R. (1973). *The Act of Will*. New York: Penguin.

Assagioli, R. (1978). *Psychosynthesis: A Collection of Basic Writings*. New York: Penguin.

Brown, M. Y. (1983). *The Unfolding Self: Psychosynthesis and Counseling*. Los Angeles: Psychosynthesis Press.

Crampton, M. (1977). *Psychosynthesis: Some Key Aspects of Theory and Practice*. Montreal: Canadian Institution of Psychosynthesis.

Campbell, P.A., & McMahon, E. (1985). *Bio-spirituality: Focusing as a Way to Grow*. Chicago: Loyola University Press.

Fox, M. (1980). *Breakthrough: Meister Eckhart's Creation-Centered Spirituality in New Translation*. New York; Doubleday.

Fox, M. (1982). *Meditation with Meister Eckhart*. Santa Fe: Bear & Company.

Fox, M. (1983). *Original Blessing: A Primer in Creation Spirituality.*
Santa Fe: Bear & Company.

Gendlin, E. T. (1981). *Focusing.* New York: Bantam.

Horowitz, M. (1984). "Psychosynthesis and World Order." In J. Weiser
& T. Yeomans (Eds.), *Psychosynthesis in the Helping Professions:
Now and for the Future.* Toronto: Department of Applied Psychol-
ogy, Ontario Institute for Studies in Education.

Kenik, H. (1979). "Toward a Biblical Basis for Creation Theology." In
M. Fox (Ed.), *Western Spirituality: Historical Roots, Ecumenical
Routes.* Notre Dame: Fides Claretian.

Rogers, C. R. (1984). *A Therapist's View of Personal Goals.* Wallingford,
PA: John Spencer.

Author's Comment, 2017:

At the edge of eighty I read this article again with deep gratitude and
only make a few minor changes. What was true for me thirty years ago
deepened my practice as a therapist during those years. More recently
the process of bridging A *Theology of Blessing* and *A Psychology of Hope*
led me into the work of spiritual direction as a companion with others
and as a traveler on the way myself.

I find our 21st century needs now, more than ever, Assagioli's call
for growth in understanding human nature and Eckhart's affirmation of
original blessing. The unknowns of aging, the precarious nature of our
planets future with climate change and nuclear threat, the movement
away from interdependence to nationalism and the closing of borders
between people and nations all challenge us to deepen our trust and to
respond to the call for compassion as a doorway to Mystery and
wholeness for all.

Joan Cannon Borton, *author of* Drawing from the Women's Well *(1992) and* Deep
in the Familiar *(2001), lives in Concord New Hampshire with her husband, Cameron.
She writes: "At the edge of eighty, I re-read* "A Theology of Blessing: A Psychology
of Hope" *with gratitude. Thirty years ago, the work of Roberto Assagioli and the
writings of Meister Eckhart converged for me to deepen my practice as a therapist
and ultimately led me into working in spiritual direction. What was true then is true
for me now. I find our twenty-first century to be deeply in need of Assagioli's
understanding human nature and Eckhart's affirmation of original blessing. The
precarious future of our planet and the divisiveness so evident in our world
challenges us to deepen our trust and to respond to the call for compassion as the
doorway to Mystery and wholeness for all."*

Part V.

Education

The Relationship of
Psychosynthesis to Education

John Weiser

Roberto Assagioli believed that the techniques and philosophy he called psychosynthesis could be applied beyond psychotherapy, which had been his primary focus, to several other fields of endeavor. He was quite explicit in naming education as one of these fields. I have attempted to gather some of his ideas, along with those of a few others, about where and how psychosynthesis can make a valuable contribution to education. I will also be adding some of my own thoughts to the picture.

It seems clear that many of the goals that are representative of psychosynthesis are shared by many people in education. In North America, these ideas seem to be shared mainly by those within the humanistic and new age educational movements. In this paper, I want to review some of the major models in humanistic education in partic- ular and to discuss how psychosynthesis seems to be aligned with or differs from these models. I believe that it is important for those of us in psychosynthesis to be conscious of these similarities and differences. It has been my experience that someone will describe a new innovation in education and say, "It's just like psychosynthesis." Sometimes, I may see the direct similarity, while at other times I feel that the program that has been described is far from being "like psychosynthesis." I have found this an uncomfortable experience, so I have attempted to determine for myself the essential principles that would need to be present for me to say, "Yes, it is like psychosynthesis." I will attempt to present these principles later in this paper.

I have had the title of this paper in mind for some time: "The Relationship of Psychosynthesis to Education." I would like to begin by sharing with you some of my process in developing my ideas about this theme. Assagioli in his book, *The Act of Will* (1973), describes several processes of meditation. He labels these processes as reflective, recep- tive, and creative, and discusses the values and purposes of each. I want to describe briefly what is involved in each meditation. In all of these meditations, the meditator is seeking to understand something more deeply.

It is fairly simple to obtain dictionary definitions of concepts that we wish to understand. However, to understand these concepts, we know that we need to think about them in order to penetrate their meaning and make them our own. Assagioli's description of reflective and receptive meditations provides an excellent guide for someone who truly wishes to pursue the meaning of a concept.

The activity of reflective meditation could also be described as thinking. By this, I mean that we bring the activities of the mind under our will and choose to use our thinking abilities to pursue a particular idea, such as "What is education?" "What is love?" "I seek to love, not to hate." Often our minds seem to operate independently of our wills. It is only when we choose to pursue an interest or idea and hold our minds to the task that we can be described as truly thinking. Assagioli states that one of the major objectives of reflective meditation is to gain conceptually a clear idea about a subject or problem. It is fairly rare to find that our ideas are truly clear about a topic. Assagioli refers to the activity of reflective meditation as turning the mind's eye in a horizontal direction.

In receptive meditation, he suggests that one turn one's mind's eye upward, seeking to discover what is to be discerned at a higher level than that of ordinary consciousness. In this activity, one is preparing oneself to receive something from the superconscious. This is often experienced as a stimulus to action. In order to remove any impediment, one must learn to develop inner silence. Again, our minds have often not been trained to come under our wills, and we need to practice silencing our everyday minds in order to receive something from a higher source. The activities of reflective meditation prepare the way for receptive meditation. The groundwork, or the structure of our understanding, is ready to receive and understand whatever occurs. In addition, one can more easily develop a contextual understanding of the message.

By creative meditation, we can take our ideas and develop a more precise understanding. We can align our feelings with the idea, and we can develop plans of action to bring the idea into form in the world and in our lives. Often we have to reduce an abstract idea into something that is both feasible and important to do. For example, from an understanding of love and its role in relationships, we can make concrete plans for ensuring its presence within particular situations in our lives.

I stated earlier that a part of my purpose here was to bring some understanding of the relationship of psychosynthesis to education. I have proceeded to prepare myself by practicing some of these meditations around the concepts of education, relationship, and psychosynthesis.

The Use of Meditation With Groups

In the first instance, these types of meditation can be used with groups or in an organizational setting and, in particular, an education institutional setting. When I began my tenure as Chairperson of the Department of Applied Psychology at The Ontario Institute for Studies in Education, I along with others believed that it was time to rethink what we were doing in our work. Many of us had concerns about admission policies, courses, thesis supervision procedures, and the need to revise our curriculum within various degree programs. For each of these concerns, members of the department had in mind specific issues, complaints, or suggestions. It seemed that in attempting to discuss any one issue, another emerged to complicate the situation. Almost always, the bureaucratic structures of the Department or the Institute seemed to discourage truly innovative or creative ideas. It therefore became important to find a place to begin our thinking in a way that was as free as possible from the history, structure, individual personalities, and special interest groups within the Department.

I decided to invite everyone in the Department—faculty, students, and support staff—to a series of meetings in which the agenda would be to practice a series of reflective meditations on the meaning of education. We proceeded to do some reflective meditations over a series of meetings in which we would meditate individually and then form into small groups to share what had emerged for each of us in the meditations. We began to include as well some receptive meditations on the theme, and eventually we were able to consolidate our thoughts into a few important concepts. We then attempted to creatively formulate these concepts into action plans for the actual situation in the Department. The reflective and particularly the receptive meditations served the purpose of removing us from our previous focus on specific concerns. We were then able to bring this higher perspective to the specific concerns we had previously identified. I found this to be an exciting process, and one that provided for many of us some important statements of our essential aims. Also, we discussed areas that we could use to guide us in our evaluation of our work and our lives together. Some of my ideas about education presented in this paper stem from these procedures.

More recently, as a member of a group studying thinking and creativity within the framework of psychosynthesis, I meditated on the meaning of relationship. I will include the results of these sessions as a part of this paper as well. Finally, I have been attempting for a good number of years to understand the meaning of psychosynthesis and I will attempt to bring together all of these ideas around the focus of the relationship of psychosynthesis to education.

Defining Education

It is difficult to define education because it is such a large concept. Perhaps it is even unnecessary to do so because all of us are so familiar with the concept from our own experiences. I think of education in different contexts at different times. Sometimes, I have a broad sense of education as inclusive of almost any deliberate learning activity. I think of this situation as unrelated to age or formal school situations. At other times, I know I am thinking more of the formal teaching structures that we have built up in North America.

In some ways, these two ways of thinking about education represent two polarities that emerged from the Department's meditations on education. On the one hand, education was related to an individual's experiences of learning and to what those experiences might imply: personal motivation, choosing one's own educational goals, personal change, the enhancement of individual potentials, and individual satisfaction. On the other hand, education was seen as related to a sociocultural perspective. Here the idea is that education is the activity of teaching the newer members of a society not only about the society but also whatever knowledge society has determined is necessary for its members if society is to benefit. So here we have the tension between the needs, direction, and maintenance of the society and, in North America at least, the needs for the personal fulfillment of the individual. In our meditations and discussions, we focused on the potentially healthy benefits of this tension for the two different value orientations.

The direction that a society's goals, needs, and future vision can provide gives the individual a sense of meaning because it gives an indication of the potential value and contribution that he or she has to the society. As a student, one may sense that one has a place, a role, and a purpose by participating in a society's educational system. That is, one senses that one is valued and is seen as potentially useful by that society.

It appears to be important for a society to support the individual talents, skills, and visions of its individual members. For some of us, it may be seen as the sole purpose of an educational system. This orientation would represent a fundamental value for a society that values the individual over the group. I know of no society which is totally devoted to such a value orientation. Rather, societies that survive tend toward one end or the other, between valuing either the individual or the group, but not to the extreme.

The benefit of accommodating the polarities is that each provides direction and support for the evolution of the other. The educational system also provides training in the developed skills of that culture. In addition, it provides a sense of direction and meaning within its system and the opportunity to positively participate in the society and to help shape the society's future. By supporting and facilitating the individual talents, skills, and values of its individual members, the society benefits from the production and advances that each individual brings as he or she expands and builds on what has already been provided. Thus, uniqueness, innovation, and creativity nurtured in the individual advances the whole society. Obviously, for each to benefit from the other requires an honest and open dialogue between the two orientations. We in psychosynthesis have come to understand the necessity of dialogue between competing interests when working with clients on their individual evolution. Roberto Assagioli (1971) has pointed out the necessity for a third and higher perspective for achieving a real synthesis between the competing interests of a polarity. I will discuss at a later time how a transpersonal orientation can provide the perspective for such a synthesis.

In Ontario, and all of North America, we have seen mild swings between the two ends of this polarity within the last twenty years. In the sixties and early seventies, we saw educational systems attempting to change to allow a much greater degree of freedom for their students. This movement included fewer required courses, more individual choices, and more alternative forms of education. A reduction in the authority of the school system over students and parents also occurred. Now we are experiencing a "back to basics" movement with more required courses in math, science, and languages. The school system is again seen as essentially providing training for a work force for society. Individuals are given support to select a career development path for themselves, but they are being asked to evaluate their individual plans and educational experiences so as to adhere to the occupational planning of the society. Swings between the competing values of individual and societal needs are probably a necessary part of the process of dialogue. However, without the action and testing components of a dialogue of this type, there can be no real progress toward a synthesis. If a true dialogue between these points of view can be achieved, it will advance a greater understanding of the goals and values of each. And as the legitimate claims of each point of view are accommodated, we will achieve a fresh understanding of their mutual interests.

The Meaning of Relationship

I want to turn now to the meaning of relationship. My comments are based on some of the ideas that emerged from my meditations in the psychosynthesis group. My first thoughts would seem to be predictable. To focus on relationship is to focus on the issues held in common between two or more concepts. These include the shared meanings, values, attitudes, contents, fears, goals, and in the case of my own meditations, the history of education and psychosynthesis. There is an experiential component to discovering relationships between concepts. The experience seems to be related to the phenomenon of starting with what one knows and experiencing something new. This experience for me was one of expansion. As I found a new sense of relationship between psychosynthesis and education, I experienced an extending and broadening of the meaning of both for myself. My sense was that I was seeing a bit of the underlying unity of everything. As I expanded my understanding of unity, I also experienced my own participation in the whole.

The experience of personally extending one's boundaries by finding similarities in two or more concepts can often include a sense of shrinking as well. The uniqueness of each is given up as the unifying elements of both are discovered. I believe that we often avoid finding relationships in order to avoid this experience of shrinking and the loss of a sense of uniqueness. The one leads to alienation and separateness, while the other leads to expansion and relatedness and the experience of unity.

What is the value then of finding differences? When we attempt to penetrate a concept in order to understand it, we are attempting to find its most fundamental essence. We can then proceed to check out the form in which this essence is manifested, expressed, and acted upon. It is in these different forms that we often find the differences between the concepts as well as their underlying relatedness. Often, we can see that the forms of expression have diluted or lost this essence. We can also see ways of changing and combining forms in order to align them with the more fundamental meaning. In addition, when finding commonalities, we may lose sight of the elements that are truly unique and valuable to each. Forms may be created to express something which combines a number of elements, some of which are common to each and some of which are not. It may be important to retain these forms rather than change them; otherwise, this uniqueness may be lost. In this paper, I do not wish to criticize or recommend changes to what others are doing in education but rather to provide assistance in finding the commonalities and evaluating the forms we see in educational practices. By doing this, we can distinguish those forms which seem aligned with psychosynthesis from those which may be valuable but which are not central to what we are attempting to do. Psychosynthesis is not education and vice versa.

The Relationship of Education to Psychosynthesis

One of the most difficult tasks in my experience has been to state briefly and clearly what psychosynthesis means to me. For purposes of this paper, I want to highlight certain aspects of psychosynthesis which seem directly related to education. In the introduction to his book *Psychosynthesis* (1971), Roberto Assagioli clarifies what he means by psychosynthesis, first by listing the similarities between his ideas and those of other psychotherapies and then by listing the differences. I have not found a clear, brief statement in his work to assist those of us who wish to share his ideas with others. I do find it reassuring that he utilized the method of pointing to similarities and differences between psychosynthesis and other models of therapy because I have chosen to do the same with psychosynthesis and education. As well, he and some others have provided several statements which are useful for an understanding of both psychosynthesis and education.

Psychosynthesis is a name for the conscious attempt to co-operate with the natural process of growth; that is, the tendency in each of us to integrate the various aspects of ourselves at ever higher levels of organization, order, and dynamic harmony. While this tendency is natural to all life, in human beings it becomes conscious. The individual feels it as an urge and strives to implement it to make its progress easier. Eastern approaches to human development have often tended to emphasize the spiritual dimension, while Western approaches have usually focused on the integration and expression of the personality. But the individual must be viewed as a whole and each aspect accorded its due importance. Psychosynthesis recognizes that each human being is spiritual in essence and, at the same time, holds that the fundamental essence, or Higher Self, is fully possible in the world of everyday personal and social existence. Assagioli (1971) adds to this concept of personal evaluation an even wider perspective. He states

> Psychosynthesis may also be considered as the individual expression of a wider principle of a general level of inter-individual and cosmic synthesis. Thus inventing

the analogy of man being a combination of many elements which are more or less coordinated, each man may be considered as an element or cell of a human group; this grows in its turn, forms associations with vaster and more complex groups and social classes, and from these to the entire human family.

I think this latter point is extremely important. It sets us in the direction of moving beyond the traditional Western individualistic concepts of human development. Psychosynthesis provides the broadest understanding of what is meant by the whole person of any model that I know of and extends and synthesizes this concept of the individual with the larger whole.

Assagioli (1971) has briefly described the functions that this holistic view of man and the universe can provide. He says, Psychosynthesis is or may become

1. a method of psychological development and self-realization;

2. a method of treatment for psychological and psychosomatic disturbances;

3. a method of integral education which tends not only to favor the development of the various abilities of the child or adolescent, but also helps him to discover and realize his true spiritual nature and to develop under its guidance a harmonious, radiant and efficient personality.

As you can see, in psychosynthesis we share the ideas of much of the human potential movement. When applied to education, these ideas are intended to assist individuals in realizing and developing their own uniqueness, but they add the understanding of a guiding source for this development from the perspective of the individual and the whole. In another place, Assagioli (1971) states that "to educate, in fact, should be to draw forth from within, that is, to develop. It is a strengthening—a reinforcement of all man's latent underdeveloped energies and functions."

I wish to turn now to more specific goals for education from a psychosynthetic point of view. Frank Hilton, who founded the Psychosynthesis Research Foundation in 1957 in New York City, included education among his formal objectives and purposes. The goals of his foundation were listed as:

1. To investigate the use of the higher psychological functions such as intuition, inspiration, mental and artistic creativity;

2. To study gifted children and genius, to develop criteria for their early recognition, and to develop methods of education and training suitable to such persons;

3. To study the nature of Will, its relation to other psychological functions, and to develop techniques for its safe development and use;

4. To develop further criteria for the classification of human types, and to ascertain and develop methods of psychosynthetic education and treatment suitable to each type; to develop and use psychosynthetic educational techniques suitable for application to family groups, schools, adult education and gifted children.

In the Psychosynthesis Research Foundation publication, *Global Education and Psychosynthesis* (1971), James Vargiu discusses the aims of psychosynthetic education. Besides those goals listed above, he adds the education of the emotions, the imagination, and the intellect. He states that we need to cultivate the more abstract thinking processes as well as those he labels the concrete. He suggests that we need to understand the stages of development of the higher functions and qualities such as intuition, beauty, justice, altruistic love, compassion, spirit of co-operation, joy, serenity, and courage. He terms this as education for self-realization. In this case, he means that in each of us we have a Higher Self and that we are working toward its manifestation through us into the world. Again, pointing to the relationship between the personal and the more general evolutionary principles, he urges the education of everyone in right human relations.

Perhaps now I can attempt to summarize the main ideas around the theme of the relationship of psychosynthesis to education. In education, the tension was seen as one between society and the individual. We saw how the individual can lose his sense of participation in the larger unity of society and become alienated. Society can, by its very nature, lose sight of individuals by seeing them only as parts to be utilized in advancing its own immediate ends. From this, we get a limited view of education as job training, for example. Even when we know that most of the job descriptions that exist today will not exist over the lifetime of our children, who are in the early years of their schooling, we persist in this direction.

Psychosynthesis shares many of the goals of other educational models that focus on the development of the student's individual talents. It shares the goals of a society that wishes to include everyone in its activities and that values the contribution of each for the mutual benefit of all. Psychosynthesis turns toward a guiding principle that sees in each individual evolution the guiding influence of a Higher Self and that sees this, in turn, as a part of a larger guiding source which provides meaning for all human activities.

Krishnamurti (1976) provides some direction for us at this point. He says that "the highest function of education is to bring about an integrated individual who is capable of dealing with life as a whole." He follows with some excellent advice for those of us who imagine ourselves as visionaries. He says, "The idealist, like the specialist, is not concerned with the whole, but only with a part. There can be no integration as long as one is perceiving an ideal pattern of action. The right kind of education consists in understanding the child as he is without imposing upon him an ideal of what we think he should be." In this examination of the effects of the tension between society's ideals and goals and those of the individual, Krishnamurti states:

> It is only in individual freedom that love and goodness flower; and the right kind of education alone can offer this freedom. Neither conformity to the present society nor the promise of a future utopia can ever give to the individual that insight without which he is constantly creating problems.

In order to achieve such an educational system, teachers and parents have to become aware of their own previous conditioning. They must be aware of their own, or society's, conditionally developed ideal model for the child. All of us know how difficult it is to obtain the type of self-knowledge that allows us to see outside of our conditioning. In psychosynthesis, we hold ourselves to be a Higher Self in the process of realization. And thus we struggle to develop consciousness of our Higher Selves. In our relations with others, we apply this same framework. We therefore see ourselves and others in a process of moving toward self-realization which is both unique and, at the moment, unknown. It is this belief which I see as the core of what psychosynthesis has to offer education. Imagine if in our daily social interactions we held to the view that we were all struggling toward self-realization and that at the level of self-realization we were all part of the same unifying order. Imagine what would happen if teachers could relate to themselves and to their students in this way, regardless of the course content or even the teaching method. Imagine the experience students would have if they were considered in this positive manner.

Those of us who have been attending to the process of human development have continued to see the positive results of an ever expanding understanding of what is human. Our concepts of wholeness, of the whole person, have been expanding over the years so that we have come to value the development and integration of feelings, body, and mind. Here in North America, we have labeled these as attempts to educate the whole child. Other labels used are affective education, confluent education, and humanistic education, all of which contain within them an expanded view of what is human and valuable. Because these expanded views have been held and acted upon, we have seen people flower and we have discovered in many the latent talents of creativity, imagination, and the capacity to realize and develop meaningful personal values. As well, we have seen people come to understand and experience the higher qualities of joy, love, and courage. It is obviously useful to support the development of these various aspects of each human being. I wish to list some of these humanistic goals because of the value they have already demonstrated and because so many are shared by psychosynthesis. As Krishnamurti warns, however, we should not set these goals as ideals. Nor, I think, should the development of feelings or imagination be seen as valuable outside the guiding principles of a Higher Self. There is a danger in this wonderful educational movement of deifying something like creativity, or the mind, or feelings in isolation from the whole. In this light, I wish to comment briefly on some of the better known movements in holistic education.

Holistic Education

One of the earliest and most influential of the humanistic education movements was led by George Isaac Brown. In his book on confluent education, *Human Teaching for Human Learning* (1971), he said, "The greatest potential for change and significant improvement in our individual predicaments and in our dilemma as a society lies in the school." By confluent education, he meant "a philosophy and a process of teaching and learning in which the affective domain and the cognitive domain flow together, like two streams merging into one river, and are thus integrated in individual and group learning." We see here the emphasis on the integrated individual, and like most of the human potential writers at that time, he hypothesized that what had been ignored or underdeveloped in the person was the affective side. His solution was to include feelings along with the mind. Many have criticized these earlier attempts for putting feelings over the mind. Perhaps this was necessary because of the imbalance at that time between the two.

In an article, "Confluent Education: Paradigm Lost?" (1983), Stuart Shapiro reviews the history of confluent education and humanistic education. He believes that the ideas of confluent education must change, but he urges that they be grounded in humanistic education. In his review of 40 humanistic writers, he found three factors that delineate the major humanistic value emphases in education. These are:

1. A general inclusive, many-faceted matrix including process orientation, self-determination, relevance, affective bias, personal growth and innovation.
2. Group approaches that emphasize participants' democracy and consensual decision-making.
3. Group approaches supporting personal growth and individualistic norms.

To avoid the criticisms of the earlier humanistic models, which have led to charges of developing the "me generation," Shapiro proposes as a title for humanistic education, "Development of the Whole Person in the World." This appears to be an effort to bring back into some balance the relationship between the individual and society. It appears to me to be an attempt at balance rather than real synthesis because synthesis requires a framework that recognizes the underlying unity of seeming polarities.

Humanistic education has been strongly associated with the process of self-actualization. Self-actualization was perhaps best defined by Abraham Maslow (1954). He proposed that self-actualization was experienced as the individual became freer of more basic needs by the process of meeting these needs to a satisfactory degree. Willard B. Frick (1982), in an article, "Conceptual Foundations of Self-Actualization: A Contribution to Motivation Theory," stated

> While there is, indeed, an impressive body of theory to suggest a belief in the presence of some fundamental energy that strives for the actualization of human poten-

tials, it becomes more difficult to explain how this primitive growth force achieves direction and expression, that is, how it can be channeled into self-actualizing activity.

He added, "Most theorists, however, do not carry us much beyond their recognition of certain innate growth tendencies or directions." I agree with his summary; most of the self-actualizing theorists were totally individually oriented in their theories and therefore unable to utilize any conceptions of the transpersonal domain. Through his study of peak experiences, Maslow was one of the few who began to reach beyond the personal. The effects of ignoring this domain were at least partially realized by him in an interview with Frick (1982).

Maslow believed that this drive for self-actualization began from a biological base but that motivation toward self-actualization became increasingly less biological as the lower needs in the hierarchy of needs were met. At the level of self-actualization, therefore, motivation shifts from a deficiency centered organism to an organism that is striving to actualize potentials at what he called the "Being" level. In this interview, Frick asks Maslow, "In other words, even with all these basic gratifications, people don't move on into any self- actualizing kind of stage?" Maslow responds, "Some do, some don't. That's quite clear. Some do not. They just get depressed at that point, or a lot of other stuff that I've described as metapathology, including value disturbances of all kinds." The symptoms that Maslow describes are common indicators of what we in psychosynthesis refer to as an existential crisis—in other words, a crisis in meaning. Most often we find that the resolution of this crisis involves an opening to the transpersonal realm for a source of meaning.

Frick's conclusion is that continued striving for self-actualization requires some conceptual model for one's own development. For this, he suggests "the Ideal Self—an image of wholeness and self- perfection, a sense of inner direction, of personal responsibility, a process conception of development and an evolving nature of personality." Frick then points beyond the earlier individualistic notions of man when he says, "This process of evolution toward greater wholeness and complexity leads us to personality developments related to the interpersonal and social realm and the transpersonal realm." Of the transpersonal, he says that "a conceptual awareness of the transpersonal, of the self-transcending potential of the human personality, is essential in moving beyond an ego-centered reality." Here we see the synthetic principle of evolution, which by expanding the concept of the individual to include the transpersonal forms the basis for a synthesis between the tension of individual interests and social interests. This principle is a fundamental one within the philosophy of psychosynthesis.

Following the lead of people such as Maslow and Brown, a number of exciting developments in holistic education have developed. John P. Miller, in *Humanizing the Classroom; Models of Teaching in Affective Education* (1976), discusses and compares 17 different models of affective or humanistic education. He includes psychosynthesis as one of the 17 models. In reviewing these models, he finds two principles that are shared by all: (1) an overall aim to reduce student alienation and (2) an effort to facilitate personal integration. The two points of tension again appear between the social and the personal. By personal integration, he means

> The personally integrated individual is committed to growth and development, to a process of change. The personally integrated person is open and sensitive to the needs of others. The personally integrated person has achieved a unity of consciousness that is a balance of heart and mind, a sense of wholeness, including the use of intuitive and imaginative faculties, faculties.

Miller's conception of the contribution that psychosynthesis is making to education is in the development of exercises and activities that lead to personal centering and consciousness expansion. In terms of the goals of Assagioli and others in education, we can see how limited Miller's conception and understanding of psychosynthesis is.

Most recently, we are seeing a rapid expansion in humanistic, holistic, new age, and affective education in the direction of expanding and developing the mind. There are two phases in this movement: the first is to assist people to develop their minds as wonderful tools for learning and creating, and the second is in the direction of opening people to the concept of a transpersonal mind. As an example of what I am referring to, I will mention some of the headings for topics covered in two 1981 newsletters (Holistic Education Network and New Horizons for Learning), both of which were aimed at holistic educators: "Mental Development," "Movement as a Teaching Tool," "Lateral Thinking," "Imaginative Play," "Visualization in the Classroom," "Relaxation to Aid Learning," and "The Brain Learns to Learn." It is clear that when we look at the latest innovations in education, we see the effect of the recent exciting research findings from brain research. Holistic educators are still including affect, the body, imagination, play, and nutrition as important elements in education; however, the mind is back in favor after almost "losing our minds" in the earlier days of the movement. Assagioli and others in psychosynthesis were emphasizing for a long time the need to develop successful and efficient methods of freeing, expanding, and training our minds, and now we are seeing a veritable explosion of developments in this direction.

We see this new phase as a natural evolutionary trend for the culture. In psychosynthesis, we have noted that the common pattern of evolution in individuals is one which proceeds from the development of the body to that of the feelings and then to that of the mind. All these developments must be integrated into the total personality. We would expect this same evolutionary pattern to be present in the ongoing cultural evolution, and it appears that this is what is happening. This new emphasis on the mind represents the next phase in our cultural evolution.

We are moving toward the development of the mind while at the same time attending to the necessity for an integration of the mind with the whole. We can look back at the early directions of humanistic education as a response to the necessity for the integration of the body and feelings with the whole, and now as this is being accomplished, we see the newer phase emerging. If we see the developments in education from this evolutionary point of view, we can see how the "back to basics" movement need not be labeled a regressive step. It seems to be an attempt to honor our minds again. If we can include this movement in the broader and more integrated evolutionary perspective, and allow it to be included rather than resisted, and seen as a positive contribution to the next step in our cultural evolution, we can bring a more harmonious sense to our overall educational efforts.

Transpersonal Education

The work that is going on in transpersonal education is also very exciting. A great deal of what has been labeled humanistic education is also included in what is being called transpersonal education. In an article in *Transpersonal Education* (1976), Thomas Roberts and Francis V. Clark state:

> An underlying assumption of transpersonal psychology is that physical, emotional, intellectual and spiritual growth are interrelated, and the optimal educational environment stimulates and nurtures the intuitive as well as the rational, the imaginative as well as the

practical and the creative as well as the receptive functions of each individual. Transpersonal psychology has focused attention on the human capacity for self-transcendence as well as self-realization and is concerned with the optimum development of consciousness.

They go on to state that "the first step in applying transpersonal psychology to education usually involves shifting the focus from external to internal awareness." The educational activities encouraged by a transpersonal perspective are those of centering exercises, meditations, guided fantasy work, biofeedback techniques, and the experience of the spiritual. The transpersonal, in the best sense, provides a larger perspective which includes the ideas of human development central to humanistic education.

Psychosynthesis is clearly a transpersonal perspective and shares this larger and more inclusive perspective. Following the direction of Assagioli, people in psychosynthesis have been able to recognize the developmental work in many fields and include these in their own practice. In light of the expanding concepts of what it means to be human, we can see how the various goals and values in the humanistic movement are shared by those of us in psychosynthesis. The definitions developed of the self-actualized person, or the fully integrated person, are also values or views of man within the psychosynthesis perspectives. In addition, psychosynthesis, because of the transpersonal perspective, includes the spiritual realm. Here, the concept of the Higher Self provides a guide to a deeper meaning of self-realization. By this, I am referring to the intentional movement toward the realization and identification with an expanded concept of self that this perspective brings.

A number of people coming from the perspective of psychosynthesis have been active in education by developing activities which promote and support the latest understandings of the capacities of the human mind. I refer here to all of the developmental work that has attempted to utilize the capacities of the two sides of the brain and, as well, has extended our understanding of the concrete and the abstract, or essential, mind. Exercises intended to promote the development of creativity, imagination, and intuition have been successfully transferred from psychosynthesis therapy to education. In addition, a number of programs which utilize the body in dance and movement, which free the mind from the concrete by utilizing music and art, have been, or are being, developed.

In psychosynthesis, we have developed a number of useful concepts and techniques which can assist a person toward self-realization. Here

John Weiser

I refer to the development of the schema of subpersonalities orienting to a center of personality. In order to assist children in their efforts to understand themselves better, we have been able to teach them to use the conceptual framework of subpersonalities. This provides a model for seeing how behavior and feelings shift from moment to moment, and from situation to situation, in relation to shifting identifications with different subpersonalities. This type of work is illustrated by Eva Fugitt (1983). Older children are able to understand that they have a constant and unchanging center to which they can refer for a sense of permanent identity in dealing with their experiences of shifting identifications. There have been several excellent methods developed to assist children in discovering this center. Three sources for such exercises are: *The Centering Book* (1976), by Gay Hendricks and Russell Wills, *The Second Centering Book* (1977), by Gay Hendricks and Thomas Roberts, and *A Peaceable Classroom: Activities to Calm and Free Student Energies* (1977), by Merrill Harmin and Saville Sax. Because psychosynthesis has utilized imagery so effectively in therapy, there have been many creative efforts to transfer the knowledge of these techniques to education. Some of these are referred to by Jack Canfield and Paula Klimek in their article, "Education in the New Age," in *The Psychosynthesis Digest* (1982).

In reviewing the history of humanistic and transpersonal education, I have noticed that two major areas are missing from a psychosynthetic point of view. The first of these relates to the concept of will. Assagioli (1973) and others in psychosynthesis appear to stand alone in Western education and psychology with their understanding of the role and functions of the will. Assagioli identified three aspects of will, 23 qualities of will, and six stages in the act of will. All of these are amenable to training and strengthening through educational activities. Here is one place where psychosynthesis is bringing an expanded view of human capacities to education.

The second area that seems to be neglected is the development of what we label transpersonal qualities. Vargiu (1971) offers some examples of these as intuition, beauty, justice, altruistic love, compassion, joy, serenity, and courage. Western developmental psychologists have generally dismissed these qualities as meaningless because they could not discover any reliability or consistency in their effects on individual behavior. However, I believe that this dismissal has been premature and that the failure to see the value of these concepts is based on a limited research design and the belief in a cause and effect mechanistic view of man. Psychosynthesis handles inconsistency in behavior through its understanding of shifting identifications. If one holds that the individual is evolving toward an integrated personality, the transpersonal qualities can be seen as playing a useful role in this evolution. We see these various identifications naturally evolving into larger and more comprehensive identifications, and these qualities, formerly only available within smaller personality identifications, becoming available for many new situations. Thus, they form the basis for more consistent behavior. In psychosynthesis, we have seen the flowering of these qualities within individuals and have marveled at the profound effect they can have on people's lives. In my own work with first and second graders, I have seen gratifying results from efforts to develop some of these qualities.

In summary, I will just restate that psychosynthesis provides a guiding principle of evolution toward self-realization, that when applied to education provides an inclusive framework for all educational activities. This same principle of evolution also assists us in resolving the tension between the individual and society that has so long plagued Western educational practices. It is by seeing how self-realization is a part of the larger evolutionary process that we can trust that our efforts to support the development of the individual are also assisting in the development of the society and the entire planet.

References

Assagioli, R, (1971). *Psychosynthesis: A Manual of Principles and Techniques*. New York: Viking.

Assagioli, R, (1973). *The Act of Will*. New York: Viking.

Brown, G.T. (1971). *Human Teaching for Human Learning: An Introduction to Confluent Education*. New York: Viking.

Canfield, J. & Klimek, P. (1982). Education in the New Age. In *Psychosynthesis Digest*. 1(11).

Frick, W. B. (1982). Conceptual Foundations of Self-Actualization: A Contribution to Motivation Theory. In *Journal of Humanistic Psychology*. 22 (4), 33-52.

Fugitt, E. (1983). *He Hit Me Back First*. Rolling Hills Estates, Calif.: Pjalmar.

Harmin, M., & Sax, S. (1971). *A Peaceable Classroom: Activities to Calm and Free Student Energies*. Minneapolis: Winston.

Hendricks, G., & Wills, R, (1976). *The Centering Book*. Englewood Cliffs, N.J.: Prentice Hall.

Hendricks, G. & Roberts, T. (1977). *The Second Centering Book*. Englewood Cliffs, N.J.:Prentice Hall.

Holistic Education Network Newsletter. (1981). Del Mar, Calif., 4,

Krishnamurti, J. (1976). From Education and the Significance of Life. In G. Hendricks & J. Fadiman (Eds.), *Transpersonal Education: A Curriculum for Feeling and Being*. Englewood Cliffs, N.J.: Prentice Hall.

Maslow, A, (1954). *Motivation and Personality*. New York: Harper & Row.

Miller, J. (1976). *Humanizing the Classroom: Models of Teaching in Affective Education*. New York: Praegers Publishers.

New Horizons for Learning: A Resource Network for Educators in the Northeast. (1981). Seattle, WA,, 1 (2).

Roberts, T., & Clark, F. (1976). Transpersonal Psychology in Education. In G. Hendricks & T. Fadiman (Eds.), *Transpersonal Education: A Curriculum for Feeling and Being*. Englewood Cliffs, N. J.: Prentice Hall.

Shapiro, S. (1983). Confluent Education: Paradigm Lost? *Journal of Humanistic Psychology*, 23(2).

Vargiu, J. (1971). *Global Education and Psychosynthesis*. New York: Psychosynthesis Research Foundation, 27.

John Weiser, EdD *(1929-2009), psychologist, educator, and psychotherapist, joined the Ontario Institute for Studies in Education at the University of Toronto in 1967, and was Chair of its Department of Applied Psychology, retiring in 1991. He was also Co-director of the Toronto Center for Psychosynthesis.*

The Inner Classroom:
Teaching with Guided Imagery

Jack Canfield

Guided imagery is a very powerful psychological tool which can be used to achieve a wide variety of educational objectives: enhance self-esteem, expand awareness, facilitate psychological growth and integration, evoke inner wisdom, increase empathy, expand creativity, increase memory, facilitate optimal performance, evoke a more positive attitude, and accelerate the learning of subject matter. In this article, I will share with you what I have learned from 15 years of exploring the application of guided imagery to the classroom.

Introducing Imagery

The first step is introducing guided imagery to your students. For most of them it will be something new, something that does not fit their experience of what school is about. There are a number of effective methods for making this transition. I have found that the most effective approach is a combination of giving them a clear rationale for its use plus a few really engaging imagery experiences right at the beginning.

I usually start by asking my students how many of them remember what they dreamed last night. Usually about a third do. I inform them that everybody dreams at least three dreams every night but we often don't remember them. We then discuss dreams, nightmares, recurring dreams, why we dream, and daydreams. I ask them where they think dreams come from. We generally then have a free-wheeling discussion based on their experience.

After a while I introduce them to the idea that their brain has two different sides, which, while they work together, seem to do different things better than each other. In school we use the left side more for things like reading, writing, and math. The left side seems to do most of the sequential, rational, linear, and logical work. The right side, on the other hand, is more oriented toward creativity, feelings, intuition, art, and holistic understanding. The right side is usually neglected in education. It doesn't get enough of a workout and therefore makes the entire brain less effective. By working with guided imagery, they will get to exercise the right side of their brain. I tell them that this will make them smarter, help them tap into their creativity, and discover aspects of themselves that they may have never known were there before. I tell them that they can use imagery to increase their memory, answer questions they have, increase their performance in athletics, get rid of headaches, and many other things. Finally, I tell them that learning to use imagery is as important a skill as reading, writing, spelling, and mathematics.

As you might imagine, many kids are uncomfortable at first about closing their eyes for a long period of time. What I usually do is to make a game out of it. It goes something like this:

> See if you can close your eyes and open them again so fast that someone looking at you would not know you had done it . . .[1] What do we call that? Right, a blink. Now see if you can close them long enough to know you've had them closed. Then open them again . . . OK, now close your eyes and see if you can see a red dot or a red ball. Once you've seen it, then open your eyes again. Take as much time as you need . . . OK, now close your eyes again and see if you can see a large blue circle. Take as long as you need and once you've seen it, open your eyes again . . . now close your eyes again and try to see a yellow triangle; as soon as you've seen it, open your eyes.

Some kids will find these introductory exercises very easy. Some will find them more difficult, seeing the shape but not the color and vice-versa. A few may not see anything at all. It is important to tell them not to worry about not seeing anything yet. They will. It is simply a matter of time and practice. I continue, after each exercise, to ask the class if there was anyone who didn't see anything. The number gets smaller with each exercise. I have never worked with anyone who didn't eventually begin to see images.

The next thing I do is ask them to close their eyes just long enough to see an animal. When all the eyes are opened again, I ask them to share what they saw. We talk about all the different animals, what they looked like, and why everyone got different animals. Next I ask them to close their eyes again and watch that same animal as if they were watching a movie and simply notice what the animal is doing. The kids report all sorts of interesting scenarios. By now, they are getting hooked on the process and I can begin to move to the next step.

For people who are having trouble imagining, I ask them to visualize their front door or some other tangible object they see every day. It is much easier for people to visualize things they see a lot than to visualize things which are abstract or things they have never seen before. The next step is to introduce a more powerful and engaging imagery experience. My two favorite ones follow below.

The Skyscraper Fantasy—This exercise is designed to demonstrate to your students just how much power the images they hold in their minds have over their experiences in the world. There is an important psychological law which comes into effect here. That law, simply stated is: All images or mental pictures tend to produce the physical conditions and reactions which correspond to them.[2] Every image or picture which we hold in our mind will create a physical reaction in our body and will thereby affect our experience and our behavior. Let's demonstrate that principle with the following exercise.

Ask your students to sit up straight in their chairs and close their eyes. Ask them to take a few deep breaths and relax. After a few seconds elapse, take them on the following guided fantasy:

> Imagine you are standing in the middle of a small terrace on top of the tallest skyscraper in the entire world. Also imagine that this terrace has no railing . . . As you are standing there, look down at your feet and notice what the terrace is made out of. Are you standing on marble, tile, concrete, asphalt, wood, stone, or what? . . . Notice what the weather is like. Is it warm or cold, sunny, or overcast? . . . What noises can you hear? Maybe there are some pigeons or other birds up there. Maybe you can hear a helicopter flying by or the street noises below . . . Now, I'd like you to walk to the edge of the terrace and look down at the street far, far below . . . (pause) . . . As you are doing that, notice what you are feeling in your body and choose to remember whatever it is . . . Now, I would like you to slowly walk or crawl back to the center of the terrace . . . When you have reached the middle of the terrace, I'd like you to open your eyes and come back into the room at your own pace. Take as much time as you need to make that transition. There is no hurry.

Once the students have all opened their eyes, ask them to share with you and the class what they experienced in their bodies as they walked to the edge of the terrace. Tell them that you are not interested in what they saw or heard, but what they felt in their bodies.

Almost all of the students will report some physical reaction. Possibilities include increased rate of heart beat, sweaty palms, shallow breathing, constriction around the chest, dizziness, nausea, a hollow feeling in their stomach, shakiness, a tightening of the legs, and clenching of fists. I have even had some students who have opened their eyes in the middle of the experience because the images were so scary.

Some students will start to tell you what they saw or will say things like, "I couldn't walk to the edge; I had to crawl. " Just politely cut them off and say something like, "That's neat, but what I'm more interested in now is what you were feeling in your body during the experience. " Some students will say, "I felt scared," or "I felt excited." Ask them, "Where in your body did you experience the fear?" or "What did you experience physically that you are calling excitement?" They will usually respond with something like, "I felt a tightness in my stomach," or "I felt tingling all through my body."

After a few minutes of this sharing, ask them to consider the following questions: "Where was your body really?' (Here in the room, sitting on your chair.) "So what was your body responding to?" (The image you created in your head.) "Who created the image?" (The students did. All you, the teacher, did was to say the words: they created the images!) "So, who created the experience you had in your body?" (You did! And, what's more important, we do this all the time.) "Can anyone think of other examples of images you create that produce physical reactions in your body?" (Examples would be butterflies before a football game, muscle tension when you think of your boyfriend with another girl, physical excitement when you think of somewhere you are going to go, a hollow feeling when you imagine being rejected, salivating when you think of eating a lemon—you can actually have them do this one—and so on.)

The Apple Fantasy—This fantasy experience is a lot of fun and acts as a subtle diagnostic test to see how well students can control their imagery. We need to learn to control our imagery so that we do not become the victims of our imagination, but rather the masters of this aspect of our mind:

Again, I'd like you to close your eyes and let your body find a relaxed position . . . Take a few deep breaths and with each breath allow yourself to become more and more deeply relaxed . . . Now take whichever hand you normally eat with and hold it out in front of you as if you were holding an apple in it. Notice, what color is the apple? Is it red, yellow, green, or multicolored? . . . Notice what kind of apple it is. Is it a Macintosh, a red Delicious, or golden Delicious, or maybe it's an organic apple with little scars on it . . . Now, notice the temperature of the apple. Is the apple cold, like it just came out of the refrigerator, or is it hot, like it's been sitting in the sun? . . . See if you can feel the weight of the apple in your hand . . . Lift the apple up to your nose and see if you can smell it. What does it smell like?

Now, I'd like you to keep imagining the apple, open your eyes, and, without talking, trade apples with someone near you. Use both hands, just as if you had real apples . . . Now, close your eyes again and look at the apple you received in the trade . . . What does this apple look like? What color is it? What shape? What kind? . . . Notice how you feel toward this apple . . . Do you have any judgment about it? Is it a better apple or worse apple than the one you gave away? . . . Look at it from all different angles. Turn it upside down . . . Look at the stem; is it there, or is it broken off?

Now, open your eyes again, and once more, without talking, trade apples so that you get your original apple back . . . When you've got your own apple back, close your eyes again . . . Make sure it's the same apple, that they didn't cheat you or dent it or take a bite out of it . . . Notice how you feel having your own apple back . . . Now, still keeping your eyes closed, I'd like you to stop imagining the apple . . . (pause) . . . okay. Whenever you're ready, just open your eyes and come back into the room.

After the students have completed this imagery experience, ask them the following questions:

- Did any of you have any trouble in stopping imagining the apple? Raise your hands . . . Does anyone want to share what happened?
- How many of you preferred *your* apple, somehow felt more comfortable with it?
- How many of you felt that the apple you gave away was better than the apple you received in the trade?

I then tell the students to consider the following ideas: We become attached to our images of ourselves, other people, and how the world is. We only had the image of the apple for a minute or two and many of us had trouble making it disappear. This is what we do with our self-image. I may have an image of myself as a klutz or an awkward person. Even when the data begins to change, I may still cling to the old image because it is comfortable and familiar. Many students have self-images of being an A, B, or C student. Just like the skyscraper image, these images control us unless we learn to control them.

Classroom Atmosphere

After the basic idea of imagery has been introduced, there are some general guidelines to follow that will facilitate the best results.

1. **Creating a Safe Space**—When students are participating in a guided imagery experience, they are in an altered state of consciousness. Their brain wave activity is slowed down. They are highly relaxed. It is therefore advisable to minimize potential distractions. If your classroom is prone to a lot of interruptions, place a sign on the door which says "Do Not Disturb," "Concentration Training," or "Testing." If necessary, assign different students on a rotating basis to be door guards to intercept any potential disturbances outside of the door. If you have the ability to turn off your intercom, do that also, or alert the office to hold back all messages for the next 15 minutes. Do not start a guided imagery experience right before the bell is about to ring. A school bell can be extremely jarring to the nervous system in the middle of a guided imagery experience.
2. **Lighting**—It is easier to visualize in a room where the lights have been dimmed and/or the shades drawn. Be careful, however, not to totally darken a room. This can frighten some people. So, keep at least a night-light on or a candle lit.
3. **White Noise**—If your classroom is in a noisy area, you can use what is called "white noise" to block most of it out. White noise is some constant sound like that produced by a fan, air conditioner, or electric motor. This is especially helpful in urban settings. Soft, relaxing music can also be used or a recording of natural sounds like the seashore or the rain.
4. **Timing**—It is best to avoid conducting imagery experiences immediately following a meal or late at night. The usual result of ignoring this guideline is that most of your students will fall asleep. I should also point out here that it is okay for someone to fall asleep during a guided imagery session. It simply means they needed sleep more than they needed awareness at that point in time. Snoring, however,

is disruptive, so I instruct my students to gently reach out and nudge someone who has started to snore. This usually stops it. Sleeping can usually be avoided by periods of active physical exercise before the imagery experiences.

5. **Positions**—There are three positions which seem to work best for guided imagery. The first is lying down in a comfortable position. My experience is that the position you normally wake up in is the best one. This works best in a carpeted classroom. The next position is called the taxi driver position. It is done sitting up, hands relaxed on the thighs, and the head tilted slightly forward, like a cabbie asleep at the wheel. The third position is done sitting at a desk with the head resting on the arms which are folded on the desk.

I have found that the following rules contribute to effective guided imagery sessions:

1. Students are to keep their eyes closed. You will find, however, one or two students in a hundred who actually visualize better with their eyes open. For them it is okay to have their eyes open. It is advisable for people with contact lenses to take them out if the imagery session is going to be a long one.
2. No talking during the imagery experiences. This disturbs others. Also, no touching others unless they are snoring.
3. It's okay to fall asleep; it is not okay to snore.
4. It's okay to go on your own trip. Often the unconscious mind will take over and the students will find that they imagined something entirely different from the images described in the instructions. This is generally okay because the unconscious will often create its own priorities. There are, however, times when we are practicing control over our images. In these cases, we would encourage concentrated effort. In other, more open-ended experiences, it does not make any difference. In these cases, it is best to trust the natural process of the unconscious mind.
5. Raise your hand if you need assistance. Occasionally a student will have a scary image. They need to know that you will be there to comfort them if they do.
6. Students may go on a *detour fantasy* to a favorite place if they find the imagery becomes scary or evokes uncomfortable feelings. Students should practice detour fantasies ahead of time.
7. If students ever find themselves stuck or blocked, they can send to central control for whatever they need to get unstuck—a magic ring, a ladder, a magic wand, a space car, wings, an elevator, a companion,

a guide or whatever would be helpful. They are to know that whatever they need is immediately available from central control by wishing it or by snapping their fingers.

8. Do not compare, judge, or analyze other people's images.
9. There is no pressure to share verbally afterwards—just an "invitation."
10. If there is an interruption from the loudspeaker, just pretend it is like a TV commercial. Remember the information if it is personally relevant; forget it if it isn't.

Relaxation

It is useful to start each guided imagery with a brief period of relaxation. There are many types of relaxation exercises. I shall describe a few of them here and then refer you to several books which contain a great deal more. The first three, Breath Awareness, Breath Imagery, and Breath Control, are breathing exercises.

1. **Breath Awareness:**—Now that you have your eyes closed, simply become aware of your breathing. Notice how your stomach and chest rise and expand as you inhale and contract and fall as you exhale. Just concentrate on the rising and falling sensation, over and over again, like the waves of the ocean rolling gently in and out at the beach . . . now place your awareness at the top of your nose. Notice the feeling of coolness as you inhale and the feeling of warmth as you exhale . . . now place your awareness on the place where your breath stops coming in and starts going out, on the transition from inhaling to exhaling. Notice what happens there. What do you feel?
2. **Breath Imagery:**—Imagine breathing in a beautiful white light. Imagine that with each breath you take, your whole body is beginning to fill up with this radiant white light. After several breaths, you can begin to feel your body becoming bathed in a warm (cool) glow. You can feel yourself growing very calm. This white light is dissolving any tension, anxiety, fear, doubt, worry, or negativity that you may have been experiencing in your mind or your body. Just continue to imagine breathing in this wonderful, soothing, relaxing white light. You can feel yourself growing more and more relaxed with each breath.
3. **Breath Control:**—Close your eyes and become aware of your breathing. In a moment, we are all going to begin to breathe together. We are going to inhale for the count of four, hold our breath for the count of two, exhale for the count of four, and hold our breath out

for the count of two. We will then repeat that pattern for a minute or two, Okay, let's begin. Inhale, two, three, four. Hold, two. Exhale, two, three, four. Hold, two. Inhale, two, three, four. Etc. Be sure not to count too fast or too slow. Practice beforehand.

The next two exercises are Stretching and Progressive Relaxation:

4. **Stretching:**—There are a number of stretching exercises which range from simple exercises like bending over to touch one's toes, to more complicated yoga postures. The simplest ones are *slowly* bending over to touch the toes, slowly rotating the neck, stretching the arms overhead, and bending over to the side. There are numerous books available on yoga exercises for adults and children which can be used successfully in the classroom. They are listed in the resource guide at the end of this article.

5. **Progressive Relaxation:**—Get into a comfortable position and relax. Start by tensing all your muscles in your feet as tight as you can. Keep them tight and notice the tension. Then relax them. Now tighten the muscles in your calves as tight as you can. Keep them tight. Now relax them. Now tighten the muscles in your hips and buttocks. Keep them tight. Then relax them . . . (continue this process with the lower back, stomach, chest and upper back, hands, arms, shoulders, neck, and face). This process can also be done in a wavelike fashion. Start by tightening the feet, then calves, thighs, hips, stomach, chest, back, hands, arms, shoulders, neck, and face. Then starting with the feet again, relax each part of the body in the same order. It is like a wave of tension washing over the body and then a wave of relaxation. Once kids learn to do it, they can relax themselves very quickly with this method.

There are numerous other methods of relaxation. They include autogenic training, meditation, sensory awareness, chanting, biofeedback, Feldenkrais, massage, movement, and polarity awareness. See the resource guide at the end of this article.

Sometimes our students need to be awakened and enlivened rather than relaxed. There are also numerous activities to accomplish this. They include running, jumping, dancing, bioenergetics, calisthenics, and new games. By far, the most fun are the new games, which are creative, non-competitive play experiences. I have listed several sources of new games in the resource guide.

Part of the art of being a master teacher is knowing when to use a relaxation technique and when to use an energizer. Trust your own intuition and ask your students for feedback, too.

Induction Techniques

Once the students have been appropriately relaxed or energized, it is time to begin the actual imagery experience. The first step is called the induction. This is simply the transition phase from regular consciousness to the imagery state. There are basically two techniques for this—deepening images and music.

Deepening images are images which are designed to deepen the state of consciousness of the students. They are simply relaxing and repetitive images which include visualizing the waves on a lake growing calmer and calmer until the lake is as smooth as glass, visualizing clouds drifting slowly by, visualizing sand falling from the top half to the bottom half of an hourglass, or boats drifting slowly by on a river or lake.

Music can be used in two ways. You can use relaxing classical, oriental, or New Age music to deepen the relaxation state, or you can use instrumental or vocal music to create a certain mood or theme for the imagery.

Music for relaxation includes calm, classical pieces, Japanese *koto* music, certain Indian ragas, flute and harp music, and some of the electronic and New Age compositions by such people as Steve Halpern, Iasos, and Ron Dexter. Music that I have used to create a certain emotional mood or effect includes "Theme from Rocky" (courage), "Ali's Theme" (caring and love), "You've Got a Friend" by Carly Simon (during an imagery experience exploring friendship), Greek music (during a visit to ancient Athens), and "The Ultimate Seashore," a record from the Environment Series (for a visit to an island). [3]

The Main Imagery Experience

Further on in this article, I will describe several classroom applications of guided imagery and give you detailed scripts which you can use. At this point I want to discuss some of the general principles that you will need to be aware of in creating and guiding imagery experiences.

Use all of the senses in an imagery experience—visual, auditory, kinesthetic, olfactory, and taste. This will allow all students, no matter what their dominant perceptual system may be, to relate deeply to the imagery. Referring to all the sensory systems will also heighten and sharpen the imagery experience for everybody. The tendency for most people when they are just beginning to use imagery is to only use words like "Imagine you see . . . ". This is very limiting. Let me give you some examples of how to incorporate the other systems. Suppose you were guiding a fantasy trip through a meadow. It might sound like this:

Imagine you are walking through a beautiful meadow on a warm summer day. The sky is blue, the sun is shining a bright golden yellow, and you can see one or two small, fluffy, white clouds (visual) . . . As you walk along, you become aware of how free you feel in your body. There is nowhere to go, nothing to do, and no right or wrong way to do it. Maybe you even run, skip, or turn a somersault or two. Notice how your body feels (kinesthetic) . . . As you walk along, you can feel the warmth of the sun on your face and arms; however, there is a slight breeze so that you do not become uncomfortably hot (kinesthetic) . . . As you look off to your left, you see the edge of a forest. You can hear birds singing there and the sound of a babbling brook (auditory) . . . As you continue to walk along through the meadow, you notice that it is filled with beautifully colored wildflowers. Stay a moment and smell their beautiful fragrance (olfactory) . . . As you continue to walk through the meadow, you notice a very special flower, different from all the others. You stop, reach down, and touch the flower, noticing how soft and delicate its petals are (kinesthetic) . . . As you are looking at this flower, feeling its petals, and smelling its special fragrance, you realize that you, too, are special, just like this flower. You are one in a million. There has never been another person on earth exactly like you and there never will be. How do you feel, knowing you are so special? (mental insight, emotional response) . . . As you stand up to say goodbye to your special flower friend, you see a beautifully gift-wrapped box nearby. It has been left for you by a fairy that lives in the nearby forest. It contains a gift to help you remember how special you are. Go over to it and pick it up. How much does it weigh? (kinesthetic) . . . Now carefully open the box and see what is inside . . . Look at the gift carefully from all sides (visual), pick it up, and feel it (kinesthetic), and see if it makes any sounds (auditory) . . . You may keep this gift forever to help you always remember how special you are . . . In a minute, I am going to ask you to return to the room, gently open your eyes, and draw a picture of your gift. Before we do that, just notice what sounds you can hear inside and outside of the room right now (auditory) . . . Good. Now just gently stretch your body a little bit and feel what that feels like (kinesthetic) . . . and, then, when you're ready, just open your eyes and look around the room for a minute (visual) . . . Welcome back.

So, as you can see from the above example, you can integrate all of the various sensory systems into the imagery experience. We could also have integrated taste by adding something like, "Off to one side, you see an apple tree. As you approach it, your eyes are drawn to one apple in particular that you can easily reach. Let yourself reach up, take the apple, and bring it up to your face. How does it smell? What does it look like? Now let yourself take a bite out of the apple. What does it taste like?" or "You notice that it tastes a little sour." You can also add dimensions of temperature, texture, weight, hardness, softness, and so on. The more richly you create the images, the richer the experience will be for the students.

There are two ways of presenting these sensory experiences. One I call directive and the other non-directive. A directive instruction tells the student what to experience—what sounds to hear, what smells to smell, what feelings to feel. The non-directive approach asks the student what she hears, smells, feels, and sees. An example of a directive instruction would be, "As you are walking through the forest, you can hear the birds singing and the wind blowing through the leaves." A non-directive instruction would be, "What sounds do you hear as you are walking through the forest?" You may also combine the two approaches. For example, "As you are walking through the forest you can hear many sounds. Perhaps there are some birds singing back and forth to each other, maybe the sounds of animals scampering away as you approach. What other sounds do you hear?" My experience is that for most imagery trips some mixture of the two works best.

Changing perspectives heightens the imagery. Let's say you ask your students to close their eyes and let an image or symbol appear that represents a quality of courage. After they begin to see the image (perhaps a heart, a sword, a lion, or a warrior), ask them to look at it right up close, to thoroughly examine it. Then ask them to step away from it and view it from a distance—with more perspective. Look at it from above and below. Go inside it and look at it from the inside. Also listen to it, smell it, touch it, feel it, taste it. This process will heighten imagery that is vague or fuzzy. It will also add new dimensions of insight to the meaning of the symbol and its relationship to the student's life.

Whenever you take a student *up* in an imagery experience (via stairs, escalators, elevators, clouds, magic carpets, ski-lifts, airplanes, rockets, climbing, a giant bird or butterfly, a balloon, magic), you will be encouraging the student to move into a higher level of consciousness which is generally associated with emotional and spiritual upliftment, inspiration, creativity, insight, healing, transmutation, transcendence, inner wisdom, the transpersonal, and alignment with the higher qualities of love, joy, courage, perseverance, justice, peace, tranquility, harmony, integration, and synthesis. On the other hand, taking a student *down* (via stairs, elevators, escalators, submarines, diving gear, magic turtles and fish, into caves, tunnels, and below the sea) will likely take the student down into the lower unconscious part of the mind, which is associated with negative emotions, the past, repressed traumatic experiences, unresolved conflicts, repressed aspects of the personality, darkness, monsters, and fear. It is therefore a good idea to avoid taking students below the ground unless you have a clear psychological purpose and are adequately trained in psychodynamic techniques of counseling such as gestalt, transactional analysis, psychosynthesis, or neurolinguistic programming.

This doesn't mean to never go down. For instance, if you have been studying in a science class how rabbits live or have been reading *Watership Down* in an English literature class, you may want to take your students on a guided imagery trip through a rabbit warren. However, if you do, be very directive rather than non-directive, provide a source of light in your description so they can safely see, be sure to remind your students of their detour fantasy before you begin the imagery experience, and remind them about using a magic wand or suggest that they surround themselves with light. Afterwards, make sure that you ask them if any of them had a bad trip, had a negative experience, got in touch with anything scary, or would like to help in sorting anything out.

Any time you leave ground level in a fantasy journey, *always return to ground level* before you ask the students to open their eyes and return to the classroom. If you don't, you may find that some of your students will seem "spaced out," ungrounded, not quite all present, or overly euphoric if you elevated them, or tired, sluggish, or depressed if you took them underground or underwater.

When working with students who have apparent physical handicaps such as blindness or loss of limbs, you will need to adapt consciously some of your verbal instructions. For example, with blind students don't use words like *see* or *visualize*. Instead use words like *imagine, sense, pretend, feel* and the other auditory, kinesthetic, olfactory, and taste words suggested earlier. With paraplegic and quadriplegic students, use images such as elevators, ski-lifts, flying, floating, magic clouds, magic carpets, and driving to replace climbing a mountain or walking along a road.

Voice and pacing should be relaxed, calm, rhythmic, regular, and slow—but not so slow that your students wander or fall asleep. The best delivery will be developed over time with practice and feedback. When developing your timing for a specific guided imagery script, practice by speaking into a tape recorder. Afterwards, close your eyes and play the tape back to yourself and see how the images, voice, and pacing work for you. Are the images rich enough? Do you use enough different sensory modalities? Is the pace so fast that you don't have time to develop an image before the next instruction is given? Is the pace so slow that you get bored, wander, or start creating your own images? Is the voice tone so dead, unanimated, or hypnotic that you begin to nod off or fall asleep? Is the voice too high or grating? Do you need to add or eliminate anything? You can also practice on a friend, your spouse, or your own children. Also, and probably most important, ask your students for feedback. Remember, you do not have to be perfect the first time you do it. Guiding imagery sessions is an art, and like any other art, it takes time to become a master. I have been using guided imagery for 15 years and I am still learning more about it every year.

Most noise distractions can be "incorporated" into the imagery experience. If a loud plane flies by overhead, just say ". . . and imagine you hear a loud plane flying by overhead." This will work for most interruptions of sounds. Another method for dealing with predictable sounds is to tell the students that each time they hear the sounds, their imagery will grow deeper and more clear. For instance, "Every time you hear the lawn mower come by the window, just let the sounds carry you deeper into the land of courage. Each time you hear the sounds it is a signal to your unconscious mind to make the images stronger and clearer."

Coming Out

After the imagery experience is completed, you need to bring the students back to normal waking consciousness. There are basically two methods for doing this. One I call *organic* and the other *numeric*. You can experiment with both ways of doing it. I prefer the organic method for imagery sessions that are especially deep or long. Some people will need more time than others to make the transition and this method allows for that.

The organic method would sound like this: "In just a minute, and there's no hurry, taking as long as you need, just honoring your own internal rhythm, perhaps on one of your exhalations, just gently open your eyes and bring your visual awareness back into the room. There is no hurry; just take as much time as you need." It is important when you do this to wait until all eyes are open before proceeding onto the next stage. If there are one or two students who seem to be taking an inordinately long time to return, you can say something like, "OK, is everybody back? I'd like to move on now." That will usually get everybody to open their eyes in a few seconds.

The numeric method looks like this: "In just a moment I am going to count from 1 to 10. When I reach the number 5, I'd like you to join me in counting out loud. When we reach 10, I'd like you to return to the room fully alert and awake, rested from the experience and remembering everything that you have experienced . . . 1 . . . 2 . . . 3 . . . 4 . . . 5,., everybody counting out loud with me now . . . 6 . . . 7 . . . 8 . . . 9 . . . 10. Eyes open, fully alert and awake, feeling refreshed and rested . . . Welcome back." This method, as you can see, is more directive and uses more suggestion, "You will feel alert and awake, refreshed and rested, and you will remember everything you have experienced."

Another aspect of the coming out stage is what I call *anchoring*, which is the process of recalling or returning to a visual, auditory, or kinesthetic cue which has been previously established. This can greatly aid the transitional process. I use three types of anchors— external, physical, and imaginal.

External anchors can be visual or auditory. For the visual anchor, I ask students to gaze around the room until they find an object that attracts them. I then ask them to continue to look at that object and to study it carefully. I let this continue for about 30 seconds. Then I ask them to close their eyes and I proceed as usual with a relaxation exercise and the imagery experience that I have planned. At the end of the experience, after the students have opened their eyes, I ask them to once again find the same object and study it carefully. This helps refocus their awareness back into physical reality.

I use music as an auditory anchor. You can use the same piece of music at the beginning and the end of an imagery experience. This provides an auditory bridge into and out of the imaginal state of consciousness.

Physical anchors are any physical sensation that you can have the students focus upon, such as the rise and fall of their stomach and chest as they breathe in and out or the sensation of their back against the floor or the back of their chair. You can use physical anchors at the beginning and at the end or you may introduce them at the end simply to ground the student's awareness back into his or her body. I have used all of the following anchors with great success—taking a deep breath, feeling your stomach rise and fall as you breathe in and out, listening to the sound of your inhalation and exhalation, rubbing your hands together, wiggling your fingers and/or toes, rubbing the soles of your feet together, stretching your arms and legs, feeling yourself in your body, feeling your back against the chair, and feeling your feet on the floor.

Imaginal anchors are images that you establish in the beginning of the experience and return to at the end. These imaginal anchors provide an artful transition and sense of closure to any imagery experience that you create. For example, let us say that you begin an imagery experience by asking the students to imagine they are in school and they get up and walk out of the school and find a magic carpet waiting for them in the playground.

They take a ride to a special land and have some sort of adventure there . . . At the end, have them get back on the magic carpet, return to the playground, walk back into the school, into the classroom, and back into their own seat. This is a use of an imaginal anchor. Other examples are a trip on a cloud, a plane ride, a boat ride, riding a school bus, and walking out of and back into the school. Whenever you take the students up (a mountain, stairs, an elevator, etc.), first have them look down at the ground beneath their feet and see what is there. Is it carpet, grass, dirt, rocks, cement, asphalt, a wood floor, or what? When they come back down, have them look down at what they are standing on again and look at it once more. This acts as an anchor for the normal plane of waking consciousness.

Paula Klimek and Hans Poulsen, two colleagues of mine, have designed the most creative sequence of anchors I have ever seen. They call it "The Magic Island Sequence." They design a room to look like the deck of a sailing ship, complete with ropes and sails. To get into the room, each student walks over a gang plank and is greeted by the captain of the ship. Once they set sail, they hear the Sailboat/Country Stream record, one side of which is an actual recording of the sounds of a sailing ship. The students are also treated to cider, grape juice, cheese and crackers. Along the way, they all sing "Ship-a-Sailing," a song which Hans has written and recorded on *The Wonderful Family Singalong Songbook*.[4]

As they approach the magic island, on which they will take several imagery trips—on the beach, at the waterfall, and at the mountain top—they begin to see slides of a south sea island projected upon the wall. As they leave the island, the sequence is repeated in reverse. They re-enter the boat, hear the sailing sounds, see the slides in reverse order, eat more cheese and crackers, drink more cider and grape juice, sing "Ship-a-Sailing," and disembark over the gang plank. It is quite a thrilling and fun experience and one that is artful and complete in its design.

Grounding and Processing

After the students have returned to normal waking consciousness, there needs to be some form of "grounding" or processing of the imagery experience. Like dreams, imaginal experiences have a tendency to be lost from memory if they are not quickly recorded or acted upon in some fashion. We have all had the experience of unsuccessfully trying to remember a dream that we experienced so vividly only an hour earlier. It is the same with imagery.

There are numerous forms for grounding an imagery experience. They include drawing the image or images you saw, writing about it in a journal, writing a poem about it, discussing your experience with a partner (or in a small group or with the whole class), acting it out with other members of the class, making what you saw (a statue, a mask, embroidery, etc.), and creating an affirmation for whatever message you received.

I like to use a combination of drawing, writing, and discussion for most imagery experiences. I first have the students draw what they saw (5 minutes), write about it (5 minutes), and then share their picture and discuss their experience with a partner or in a group of three (5 minutes). This seems to be a very effective combination for grounding. It involves all three of the perceptual systems—visual, auditory, and kinesthetic. It also gives the student a visual and mental record of the event as well as an opportunity to share the experience and hear from one or two others.

It is possible to create more elaborate and integrative forms of grounding such as the radiant body and mandala processes which Paula Klimek and I have written about in our paper "Discovering Your Radiant and Creative Self: A Transpersonal Arts Approach to Expressing One's Potential"; it is also contained in my book *100 Ways to Enhance Self-Esteem in the Classroom.*[5]

When discussing or processing the students' images (what they saw, heard, felt, and otherwise experienced), there are several guidelines that are useful to follow:

1. Don't interpret. Let students discover their own meanings for their symbols and images. Based upon their unique experiences, a symbol may mean different things to different people. Also it is important to let the students learn that they have their own answers. Students in America have been over trained to look outside of themselves for the answers to their questions.

2. Don't judge people's images. Students may come up with bizarre, weird, negative, sexual, violent, unexplainable, discontinuous, or otherwise confusing or unusual images. The unconscious mind will sometimes take over and attempt to bring unresolved psychological material to the surface of one's consciousness. It is important not to judge whatever comes up as bad or unacceptable. Judging will only create lying, non- participation and possible withdrawal.

3. Don't grade any guided imagery experience.

4. Don't allow students to get into comparing their images. Obviously, they can share them with each other. However, comparing them as better or worse can be a negative experience. Some people may have beautiful, cosmic, three-dimensional, superscope, color images. That is fine. Tell them both that it doesn't make any difference. You get what you get and it will change from time to time. People image differently.

5. If students don't understand what the imagery means, tell them not to worry about it. Some of the methods they can use to extract more meaning from their images and symbols are to imagine having a dialogue with a particular image or symbol and asking it what it means or why it is there or what it is trying to tell them. They can also just go back and observe the imagery at greater length, for the symbol or image may start or continue to change and move. Often a theme will emerge from the flow of images. They can also reflect or meditate upon an image. Also, the process of grounding it—writing, drawing, and talking about it—will elicit greater clarity of meaning.

There are several process questions that are helpful in getting students to talk about their images. These are:

- What did you see?
- What did you feel?
- What did you think?
- What did you do?
- What did the imagery mean to you?
- What did you learn from it?
- How can you use what you learned?

If the imagery session was focusing upon some aspect of personal awareness or growth, it is important to encourage the students to act on any new insights they may have received. It is helpful to use questions such as, "How can you use what you have learned in your everyday life, in this class, at home, or with your friend? What would you say or do differently now that you know that? Are you willing to choose that? What would you have to give up? What support do you need? How can you get it?" It is also helpful to have the students set action goals that are measurable and that have deadlines.

Let us turn now to some of the different uses for guided imagery and some scripts of imagery sessions that you can use with your students.

Imagery for Self-Awareness

In one sense all guided imagery leads to greater self-awareness but the two that follow, The Motorcycle fantasy and the Rosebush fantasy, are especially useful as a type of diagnostic instrument to assess how one really "sees" oneself.

> Imagine that you are a motorcycle . . . What kind and color are you? , . , How old are you . . . Where are you kept when you are not being ridden? . . . What kind of condition are you in? . . . What do you sound like when you start up? . . . Do you start up easily or with difficulty? . . . Imagine you start up and you are driving along a road . . . What is the road like? . . . How is the traffic? . . . How fast are you going? . . . Now imagine that you have a rider. Look back and see who it is . . . Now have a dialogue with this person. Just carry on a conversation with each other . . . (long pause) . . . Now let yourself go anywhere you'd really like to be. Once you get there, just stop and park yourself. . . Let yourself enjoy being there for a while . . . Whenever you are ready, I'd like you to gently open your eyes and return to the room.

After you have done this exercise, ask your students to find a partner and describe themselves as the motorcycle, starting each sentence with, "I am . . .". This will give them a lot of insight into themselves. I have had students realize that they don't like how they are being taken care of, that they are not self-starters, that they are afraid of being run over by other people, and that they have a feeling of being driven too hard by someone in their life. The images are indeed a metaphor for their lives.

This next guided fantasy has a similar purpose and is taken from John Stevens' book *Awareness* (New York: Bantam Books, 1973).[6]

> I'd like you to imagine you are a rosebush. Become a rosebush and just discover what it is like to be this rosebush . . . Just let your fantasy develop on its own and see what you can discover about being a rosebush . . . What kind of rosebush are you? . . .

Where are you growing? . . . What are your roots like? . . . and what kind of ground are you rooted in? . . . See if you can feel your roots going down into the ground . . . What are your stems and branches like? . . . Discover all the details of being this rosebush . . . How do you feel as this rosebush? . . . What are your surroundings like? . . . What is your life like as this rosebush? . . . What do you experience, and what happens to you as the seasons change? . . . Continue to discover even more details about your existence as this rosebush, how you feel about your life, and what happens to you. Let your fantasy continue for a while . . .

In a little while, I'm going to ask you to open your eyes and return to the class and express your experience of being a rosebush. I want you to tell it in first-person present tense, as if it were happening now. For instance, "I am a wild rose, growing on a steep hillside, in very rocky soil, I feel very strong and good in the sunshine, and little birds make their nests in my thick vines" or whatever your experience of being a rosebush is. OK, whenever you feel ready, open your eyes, find a partner and express your experience of being a rosebush.

Imagery for Self-Esteem and Learning

Most students have been programmed by their past educational experiences to believe that learning has to be difficult, boring, or even painful. It certainly is not supposed to be easy and fun! But if you will look back on your own life, you can no doubt remember times when you enjoyed learning something new—something that was fun, challenging, self-satisfying, perhaps even exhilarating. Maybe it was learning to swim, water ski, or ride a surfboard, or learning to fish, cook, or do macramé. No matter how young or old your students may be, they have all experienced moments of positive learning.

There is a psychological law which states we can create any desired feeling state simply by vividly re-creating in our imagination any prior event in which we experienced that same feeling.[7] As teachers, we can use this psychological phenomenon to our benefit. We know that our students will learn better in a state of relaxed anticipation of a positive event. The desired mental state is, "We are about to learn something new and we know that learning can be easy and fun . . . so let's go!" You can evoke this state by using the following exercise, which I first learned from Jolene Somsky, who is a very creative elementary school teacher in Sioux City, Iowa.

The Positive Learning Recall—Ask the students to get into a comfortable position and to gently close their eyes. Ask them to concentrate on their breathing for a moment . . . to focus on the rising and falling of their chests as they breathe in and out. After a brief moment of relaxation, ask them to imagine the following:

> Imagine you are walking through a spring meadow . . . You can feel a light breeze against your face and the warmth against your back . . . You can hear the birds singing nearby and you can hear the buzzing of honey bees in the air . . . You feel comfortable and relaxed. Only peace and harmony is here . . . You're enjoying the flowers that are here, taking in their beautiful colors and smelling their wondrous fragrance . . . In the meadow there is a special flower that is different. It is special and unique . . . You find it. You're going over to it. You observe its petals and smell its fragrance. This flower is truly unique in all the world . . . You are this flower. Find a way to become this flower . . . You are special, unique, very caring, great and powerful . . .
>
> Everyone in the room is like this. You feel very good now and very relaxed . . . (longer pause) . . . Now go to a time when learning was fun for you, perhaps when you were a little child—learning to tie your shoelaces, camping with friends, or learning to fish or cook—maybe it was later, but find a time when learning was easy and fun for you . . . (longer pause) . . . When you have that time, raise your hand . . . (wait until all or almost all of the hands are up) . . . You can put your hands down. Now, become aware of who you were with . . . What did you feel in your feet . . . stomach . . . hands . . . and face? Let that good feeling spread through your whole body and let it spread through the whole room . . . (longer pause) . . . In a moment we're going to open our eyes and everybody will be coming back into the room with that very special feeling that they are unique in all the world and that learning can be easy and fun. Will you open your eyes now and return to the room relaxed and alert?

When the students have returned, they are ready to begin whatever lesson you have prepared.

Beverly Galyean, the former Director of the Confluent Language Project in the Los Angeles City schools, developed a similar guided imagery experience which she used to help students in an inner city high school Spanish class to reduce negative behaviors such as lateness, disruptions, and put-downs and to increase positive behaviors such as affirmative communication with other students and oral and written participation in learning activities. The activity was used daily during the first five to seven minutes of class for a period of three months. The results were highly positive. Students exhibited increased attentiveness, increased involvement with the lessons being taught, an increase in the number of supportive interactions among the students themselves, and an increase in the number of supportive responses to the teacher. Here is the Perfect Student[8] exercise:

Close your eyes for a few minutes and relax. Take a deep breath. As you breathe in, imagine yourself taking in all the most beautiful, wholesome, helpful, and good energy around you. As you breathe out, see yourself breathing forth any tension, worry, doubt, or negativity you might be feeling. (pause) Take another breath, breathing in the good around you. This time, as you breathe out, feel yourself floating away . . . floating gently away from this room. (pause) Float away now to a place where you really like to be. This is a favorite place where you feel really good. Go there now . . . gently . . . floating to your place . . . (pause) When you get there, just enjoy being there . . . (pause) Now, while at this place, look into the sky and see the sun . . . warm . . . brilliant. Ask the sun to descend upon you making you feel very warm . . . comfortable . . . secure. Notice how the sun warms but doesn't burn. The sun seems very friendly today . . . (pause) Now, call the sun to enter your body through the top of your head. See how it lightens you . . . makes you feel weightless. Gradually, it descends through your head . . . releasing all tension from your eyes . . . jaws . . . neck . . . shoulders. Then it quietly descends through your shoulders . . . arms . . . chest . . . stomach . . . hands . . . thighs . . . legs . . . and feet. Notice how light you feel. Experience the good that is you . . . (pause) Now see yourself as absolutely perfect . . . capable of achieving anything you want. You have all the ability to succeed. See yourself as perfect. (pause) What do you look like as perfect? How are you behaving? How do others think of you? . . . (pause) See yourself as absolutely perfect. Now see yourself as perfect in this class. You have all the knowledge . . . all the ability to be a perfect student. It's up to you. What do you look like as a perfect student? What are you doing in the class? How are others responding to you? (pause) Now, take a moment to say some things to yourself to remind yourself that you are, indeed, perfect, and that you can be perfect any time you wish. Repeat to yourself: I am a perfect person . . . (pause) I am a perfect student, (pause) The others are here to help me continue to be perfect . . . (pause) I am here to help myself continue to be perfect, , . (pause) Say this to yourself three times . , , (pause) Now, take the sun that has descended through you and slowly draw it back up through your body . . . leaving you with a feeling of lightness and brightness. Send the sun back into the sky and feel your body so light . . . so gentle . . . so cared for . . . (pause) Take a deep slow breath . . . hold it at the top . . . and slowly let the air out and feel yourself floating back to us here in the room . . . (pause) Open your eyes and enjoy the deep feeling of relaxation.

Imagery and Remedial Reading

Dr. Gerald Jampolsky, Director of the Center for Attitudinal Healing in Tiburon, California, has successfully developed and implemented a guided visualization for remedial readers at the elementary level. The seven-step process is as follows:

Let your body find a comfortable position either lying down or sitting up. Let yourself begin to take long, slow, deep breaths and just let yourself become more relaxed with each breath. There is nowhere to go and nothing to do except become more and more relaxed with each breath that you take . . .

Let yourself open and close your eyes until you become comfortable with having them closed . . . Notice that with each breath that you take that you become more and more relaxed . . .

Now, imagine entering an elevator on the first floor of a building. As you look up above the door, you can see the number 1 is lit up. After the door closes, the elevator begins to ascend one floor at a time. You can see the numbers above the door changing from 1 to 2 to 3 and so forth . . . You can feel yourself becoming more relaxed as the elevator ascends . . . more relaxed as each floor goes by . . . until you are finally at the tenth floor . . .

Now, imagine that you reach up to the top of your head and you find a long zipper that runs from the front of your head to the back of your head. Go ahead and unzip the zipper and gently remove your brain and place it on the ground in front of you . . . Now, imagine you have a hose in your hand and begin to wash out your brain with the hose . . . Get rid of all the dirt and grime in your brain . . . Wash out all the old painful memories of having difficulty with learning to read . . . Wash out all of the old ideas that are in your brain that interfere with your reading. Wash out all the ideas and phrases like, "I can't." "It's too hard." "I'll never be able to do this." "I'll try." "If only . . . " and "But . . . " These words and phrases only create negative pictures in your mind that will make the past repeat itself. As you wash your brain out, you are replacing these words with, "I can." "It is easy." "Reading is simple and fun." "I like to read. " "I am successful at everything I do." You are washing away your old negative belief system about your ability to read. You are replacing it with a new one that will help you to read easily and quickly. You will be surprised and delighted to see how easily you can read now that you have washed away these old ideas from your brain . . . You will be pleased with yourself and very proud . . .

Now, very gently reach down and pick up your clean brain. Notice how clean it is now. All the negative thoughts and memories have been washed away . . . Now, very gently place it back in your head and zip the zipper closed again . . . Very good. .

Now, imagine that you are sitting at your desk at school . . . Think of your most favorite subject in the whole world, the thing you most like and are the most interested in. Now, imagine that you are writing a small book about that subject . . . Think of all the things that you would say in such a book . . . Realize how easy it is for you to write the book. You know all the words that you need to know and you know how to spell them correctly. You are really enjoying writing this book. It is fun and exciting . . .

Now, imagine that you are reading the book you have just written. You can read all the words easily because they are all words which you wrote earlier . . . Imagine that you are reading the book out loud so that you can hear each word. Listen to how your voice sounds . . . You are able to read each word fluently and easily . . . See yourself flipping the page over as you go onto the next page. Notice how the pages feel in your hand . . . They are very smooth and crisp . . . Also notice how the cover feels. It is stiffer than the pages . . . You feel very confident and joyful as you read because you know that you can recognize, pronounce and understand all of the words without any problem . . . You can feel a big smile come onto your face as you continue to read.

Now, imagine that you are sitting in front of a big motion picture screen. On the screen you see a movie of yourself reading a book. You can see that you are reading with pleasure and ease because there is a big smile on your face. You are reading successfully, fluently, and without effort. All of the words come very easily to you. Just watch and listen as you see yourself reading out loud with ease . . . (long pause) . . . Now, imagine that there is a door right in the middle of the motion picture screen. Let yourself stand up, open the door, and walk right into the movie and climb right into your own body on the screen . . . You are now that person who reads successfully, without effort, and with a big smile on your face . . .

Now, take this picture of yourself reading with ease and put that picture in your blood cells. Just imagine every cell of blood as it pumps through your heart being filled with the picture of your reading with a big smile on your face . . . Now, see all of these blood cells going to all the organs and your skin . . . You have become one with the picture of yourself reading well . . .

Now, imagine yourself entering the elevator on the tenth floor again. See the door close and look up at the numbers above the door. You see them changing from 10 to 9 to 8 to 7 to 6 to 5 to 4 to 3 to 2 to 1. As you reach the first floor, you see the elevator door open and you step out into the lobby . . . Now, focus on the rise and fall of your chest and stomach as you breathe in and out . . . Feel your feet on the floor and your back against the back of the chair.

When you are ready, taking as much time as you need, for there is no hurry, just begin to bring your awareness back into the room and open your eyes when you feel like it.

After the students returned to normal waking consciousness, Dr. Jampolsky had each student record the same guided experience on a cassette tape in his or her own voice. They were then instructed to play the tape and do the visualization experience for five to ten minutes at night before going to sleep, and in the morning for five to ten minutes before coming to school. The parents of the children were encouraged not to be involved in the children's reading program and not to try to get them to read. The teachers were encouraged to develop positive mental pictures of the children reading more fluently and pleasurably, to feel a lightness and fluidity in their relationship with the children, and to stop all critical statements.

The results of this experiment were that during this one-month period students in the experimental group showed an average increase in their reading skill of one and one-half years as compared to an average increase of one month for the control group. There was also a tremendous increase in the experimental group's self-esteem. The parents reported that they felt much closer to their children, that they were less tense and driven. The teachers not only reported a difference in the children in this project, but they also reported that they felt more relaxed and less tense with all their students. They all reported more energy at the end of the day. The students were retested one year later and, compared to the control group, were continuing to make excellent progress.

Imagery and Inner Wisdom

To me, the most interesting use of guided imagery is the evocation of the wisdom that lies deep within each of us. The most exciting experience I ever had with this grew out of a discussion of the television show *Kung Fu*[9] with a group of sixth graders. We were discussing how it was that Cain always knew the right thing to do in any situation no matter how difficult or hopeless it may have appeared. They told me that each time he was in an emergency situation, he could close his eyes and flash back to a time when his teacher had told him something very wise and important. I asked them what this was called. One girl said, "It was like meditation." I agreed and said that it was. I then asked them what kind of teacher Cain talked to. Was he like their sixth grade teacher? They all agreed that he was a different kind of teacher, somehow special, wiser, and more trustworthy. They all agreed they would like to have a teacher like that,

I then asked the kids if they would like to have a wise old teacher whom they could consult for advice in times of pressure and confusion. They all said yes they would, but they weren't sure where they'd find one. Most of them decided they'd have to go to China or Japan or India. I asked them where David Cain went when he needed help. They finally realized that he had closed his eyes and gone inside himself. At this point, I suggested that we all try that and see if we could find a Wise Old Teacher inside our minds who could share his or her wisdom with us. They excitedly agreed to try. Here is what I asked them to visualize:

> Close your eyes, take a few deep breaths to relax. I want you to imagine that it is a pleasant day and you are walking in a friendly foreign land, a place where you've never been before. What does it look like there? . . . Can you feel the ground underneath your feet? Look down and see what you're walking on. What does it look like? What sounds do you hear? What smells are you aware of? . . . Off in the distance to your left, you see a very tall mountain. What does it look like? . . . As you look at the mountain, you begin to feel drawn toward it. As you approach the foot of the moun-

tain, you see a path going up the side of the mountain. It is an easy path with no obstacles or difficult places and you begin to walk up this path toward the top of the mountain ... As you reach the half-way point, you stop and look back and see that you have come a long way up the mountain. You can see very far in all directions ... Then you turn around again and continue up the mountain.

... Eventually you begin to reach the top ... When you get to the top you notice a temple—a very special building. As you approach it, you can feel the solemnity and sacredness of this place. You decide to go inside, but before you do, you carefully remove your shoes and place them beside the doorway ... Once inside, you notice thousands of candles burning, creating a great light inside. At the far end of the room, you see a very kind and wise old person. As you approach this person, you see a very loving smile and bright, happy eyes. As you get closer, you realize that there is a question about life—your life in particular or life in general—that you want to ask this wise old person. When you are ready to ask, ask your question and let him or her respond. If at first you don't understand the answer, ask for more clarity. Have as long a conversation as you need to understand the answer. (Long pause— about one minute) ... OK, now, realizing that you can always come back to this place and ask your wise old teacher any question you have about anything, say goodbye for now and begin to leave the temple ... Once outside, remember to put your shoes back on and begin to come back down the mountain ... As you're coming down the mountain, feel the warmth of the sun on your skin and feel the ground beneath your feet as you walk ... When you reach the bottom, look down again and see the ground beneath your feet. What does it look like? How does it feel? ... Okay, when you're ready, and taking as much time as you need, take a few deep breaths again, open your eyes and come back to the class.

I gave them about a minute to get back and then I asked them to share their experiences. It was incredible listening to them. They had been given wisdom as old as time, things like: "If you're nice to people, people will be nice to you." "You can only be happy if you decide to be happy." "Things would be easier if you didn't try so hard." One girl had asked the wise old woman the question, "What is the meaning of life?" She said that her wise old woman didn't say anything, but held up a mirror to her. I asked her if she understood what that meant. She said, "Yes, it means to me that life is what I choose to make it." That's an amazingly sophisticated insight for a sixth grader.

Another boy said that he did not see a wise old man or woman but that he had felt "a nice strangeness." I asked him what he meant. He said it was a strange feeling—one he had never felt before—and yet it was very nice. When I asked him what was nice about it, he said that he felt relaxed—"like no hassles. "

Everybody was very eager to do it again. And everybody also agreed that there were very few times that they didn't feel hassled and uptight. It's very difficult for students to learn, let alone be creative, when they're uptight. It is necessary to be relaxed for the unconscious mind to work. (That is why so many inspirations and solutions to problems come in the morning, right after waking up from a relaxed and calm sleep.)

The Life Purpose Fantasy—Paula Klimek developed this guided imagery session. We have used it with kids in the sixth grade and with adults. It is a very powerful experience which can help students become aware of their essential nature, their highest potential, their unique gift to the world, and their life purpose. Especially as kids enter adolescence, they often become confused and are usually unable to get clear answers from their parents or their teachers about many basic questions of life, such as, *Who am I? What difference does my life make?* and *What do I really want to do?* My experience has been that when those core questions are addressed from within and when students experience recognition and affirmation of their essence, their core self, and their inner wisdom, remarkable transformations occur.

Before conducting this guided fantasy, you will need to conduct a class discussion of what is meant by the term *life purpose*. Just have the class brainstorm on what the concept means to them. After you are satisfied that they have an adequate understanding of the concept, ask them to find a comfortable position, close their eyes, and relax. Then you can begin the session.

> We are about to review your life. As you begin to experience yourself going backwards in time, begin by thinking about this day. Go back to when you woke up this morning . . . What have you done all day? . . . Now, look back at the past week . . . the past month . . . the past year . . . Review the significant events of this time . . . What did you look like? . . . Who were you with? . . . Where have you been? . . . . If you get caught up in any particular event or find yourself being judgmental, just allow yourself to let that go. Allow your life to pass by as if you were watching a movie . .

. Now, go back to your previous grade . . . To your elementary grades . . . To the primary grades . . . To the time you first entered school . . . To being a young child . . . A two-year old . . . a baby . . . to the time of your birth and the time you were in your mother's womb . . . And now go back to the time before your conception. You are about to meet a special guide, your own special guide, A guide whom you may ask what the purpose of your life is. . . Meet this guide and pose your question . . . Feel your guide's unconditional love and strength and beauty . . . Let whatever happens happen . . . communicate with your guide in whatever way possible, (pause) As you continue to listen to your guide, the guide hands you a beautifully wrapped box. The guide tells you that it contains a gift to represent your purpose, your essence, your unique gifts, your genius . . . Open the box and see what is inside . . . Now it is time to begin your journey back. Say farewell to your guide, knowing you may visit your guide at any time . . . Begin to make your journey back bringing with you both your life purpose and the gift from your experience. Make your journey through time, through your birth, your infancy, your childhood, and finally to the present moment in this room . . . When you are ready, open your eyes, remain silent and draw and write about your experience. We will share our journey after a few minutes.

The responses from the students to an exercise such as this are usually quite profound and moving. Subsequent drawings of the experience have included rainbows, the sun, the light, contact with another being, mountains, meadows, flowers, birds, and animals. The students' writings have been poetic, creative, beautifully simplistic, and yet full and rich, as in the following response: "When I met my guide and asked my question, he gave me a great big smile and held my hands. It was like he was saying, it's real neat. Try it. It's a great thing to be a person. He gave me a sense of wanting to be just by holding my hands. My guide seemed like a real nice person, the kind people would like to know. When we were holding hands I thought, 'Wow, I hope everyone's like this.' When I was leaving, I looked back. It seemed as though he was saying, 'It's OK, go ahead,' just by looking at me. We met in a place full of nothingness."

Imagery for Empathy

Guided imagery can be used to increase empathy. It allows the student to enter into the experience of another, to literally walk a mile in their shoes. It can be used to increase empathy for pets, other students, parents, someone you are afraid of, a student you are having a problem with, a person of another race, nationality, or even another time in history.

One class that I worked with had a tendency to treat the class gerbil much too roughly without the proper concern for the gerbil's comfort and safety. Rather than a lecture, which would turn the students off, I asked them to close their eyes and participate in the following guided fantasy:

> Imagine you are a gerbil in a cage in a fourth grade classroom. How does it feel to be in a cage all day long? How does it feel to be totally dependent on others for food, water, and adequate warmth and love? . . . Imagine that it is early in the morning and you are simply sitting around and relaxing. All of a sudden the fluorescent lights switch on and you run to the side of the cage to see what is happening. It is the teacher. She comes in and sits down at her desk. Several minutes later you hear a lot of noise and you look up again. A whole bunch of people are running into the classroom pushing and shoving and shouting loudly . . . Several of them approach your cage. You see these two big hands reaching down and grabbing you. Then you hear a loud shout and two other hands reach out for you. They seem to be fighting over you. Your skin hurts as they pull you in two different directions at the same time.
>
> All of a sudden you find yourself falling. You land on the hard cement. How does that feel? . . . You quickly run and hide under the radiator. But now there are all these big hands reaching in to get you . . . etc.

Imagery and Subject Matter

A number of researchers have now shown that imagery can be used to accelerate the learning of subject matter. The students learn the material more quickly and retain the material over a longer period of time. Studies have shown that with each additional psychological function that is utilized in a lesson -body, mind, emotions, imagination, and intellect—there is a geometric progression in the rate and retention of learning.

I will give you a few examples below. The possibilities are endless.

The Bee Dance—Suppose you are teaching science and the subject for the day is how bees communicate with each other. You are planning to show a film on the bee dance, which German scientist Karl von Frisch discovered and studied. Before discussing the bee dance or showing the film, you take the students on a guided fantasy.

> Imagine you are a bee. You are flying along over fields and through valleys looking desperately for flowers that are in blossom. There has been a drought recently and flowers and blooms have been hard to find . . . Finally you spot a field of color. You fly down closer. You are very excited by your discovery. You fly back to the hive where you live and find that most of the bees are there . . . Without talking—since bees can't talk—how do you communicate to the rest of the bees where the flowers are located? . . . OK, in a minute, when you are ready, come back to the room with your eyes open and we'll each share how we did it.

After the students have had a chance to share, show them the film. They are much more curious now than they would have been otherwise. After the film has been shown, repeat the guided fantasy and this time have them imagine doing a dance to communicate the location of the flowers to their fellow bees. To heighten the experience, once the students have their eyes open again, have them actually get up and do a bee dance similar to the one they just did in their fantasy. You have now engaged three functions— the intellect, the imagination, and the physical. They will definitely remember the material.

Electronics—Here is an example of how to use guided imagery in an electronics course:

> Imagine you are an electron . . . What does it feel like to be such an incredibly small piece of negatively charged matter? . . . Imagine as you are moving along through space that you encounter two very large coils of wire. Notice how large the coils are . . . As you get closer and closer, you begin to realize that there is a huge and rapidly changing force field around the coils . . . As you enter this force field, you can feel the effects of it . . . Next, imagine that you are entering the wire of the coil . . . You see thousands of other electrons moving within the coil. How are these electrons affected by the rapidly changing force field?

You could continue this experience by telling the students that another coil of equal size and strength has come toward them, that the two fields begin to interact, that the interactions become very violent as the coils come closer to each other, and so forth. Again, you could follow this up with a movement exercise.

Spelling—There are several imagery techniques I have used with helping children to spell better. I will share two of them with you here, The Magic Carpet and The Magic Blackboard. These are both methods for dealing with misspelled words.

> Imagine you are standing on a sandy beach. You can hear the sound of the waves rolling rhythmically onto the beach. You can see the blue sky, the bright sun, and lots of seagulls flying overhead. The sun feels warm upon your skin . . . All of a sudden, you look up and see a flying carpet flying toward you. It lands on the beach and you get on . . . Very gently it takes off and flies you across the ocean to a very special island—the island of words . . . As you begin to land, you notice the word *judgment* (j-u-d-g-m-e-n-t) waiting for you on the beach . . . Each of its letters is a bright blue, like a neon sign. One by one the letters flash on and off (j-u-d-g-m-e-n-t) . . . As you look down at your feet, you see a box that has been carefully wrapped. Inside the box is a gift from the word judgment to help you remember to spell it correctly in the future. Open the box and see what is inside it . . . Thank *judgment* for the gift and get back onto your magic carpet . . . As you wave goodbye to *judgment* on the beach, your magic carpet begins to fly and take you back home . . . Pretty soon, you are back again and ready to open your eyes.

When the students have returned, have them open their eyes, write the word judgment in large blue letters on the top of a piece of paper and then draw the gift they were given underneath. This could then be added to a folder or book of spelling words, which could be reviewed later for reinforcement.

Every student can be taught that they have a magic blackboard inside of their head. This blackboard can be used for math, spelling, remembering dates and other facts, and for writing down affirmations. Here's how it could be used for spelling.

> Visualize your magic blackboard. On it see the word judgment misspelled as "jujment." Visualize your own hand reaching out and placing a big X through the misspelled word . . . Now, take your magic eraser and erase it . . . Now, again with your own

hand, reach out and write the correct spelling, j-u-d-g-m-e-n-t . . . Now, look at what you have spelled . . . Imagine now that the blackboard becomes framed by a beautiful and brilliant white light . . . Once again, visualize yourself spelling the word correctly j-u-d-g-m-e-n-t . . . When you are ready, open your eyes and write the word *judgment* three times on a piece of paper.

Mathematics—I learned this one from Robert Rose, an elementary school teacher in San Bernardino, California.

> Imagine you have a whole lot of numbers with decimal points that need to be added together. Visualize each decimal point as a glowing bead which flashes on and off like a Christmas tree light. Visualize all the beads hanging down in a straight line as if they were suspended on a string. All the colored beads should always be in a straight line. You may need to help put them in their places. Then when all the numbers are lined up, you can add them . . . Remember this every time you have numbers with decimals in them.

You can also use the Magic Board technique for math tables, formulas, and so on. Another technique is to have the students imagine they are floating in a balloon above a beach. From the balloon, they watch as people draw math tables (i.e., 2 x 2 = 4) in the sand with a large stick.

Social Studies and English—Social studies and English are probably the two easiest subjects in which to utilize guided imagery. You can have the students take visual trips to ancient times and places (Egypt, Greece, Rome, Colonial America, and feudal England), visualize being a great figure from history (Benjamin Franklin, Napoleon, Lincoln, Joan of Arc, St. Francis, Martin Luther King), visualize participating in a process you want them to understand and remember (coming through Ellis Island for immigration, working in a meat packing house in the Chicago stockyards for unionization, being a dust bowl migrant for *The Grapes of Wrath*, etc.), and visualize how they might have acted if they were in a particular situation (a slave in the old South, a soldier called to war in one of Shakespeare's plays or a novel, a juror in the Scope's trial and so on).

Final Thoughts

So as you can see, there are innumerable possibilities for the use of guided imagery in teaching and counseling. I hope you will attempt some of the suggestions that I have presented here. If you do, you will embark upon a new and adventurous journey in your teaching. You can expect some profound changes to occur in your classroom. At the very least, you will have regular periods of silence in your classroom, and in these days of stress and burnout, that's a nice thing to look forward to.

Resources

There is a quickly growing field of literature on imagery and education. I will list here books, organizations, and people that have been most helpful to me. Good luck with your future quest.

1. Books on Guided Imagery

Bagley, M. T., & Hess, K. (1984). *200 ways of Using Imagery in the Classroom*. San Francisco. Trillium Press.

Canfield, J. (1986). *Self-Esteem in the Classroom: A Curriculum Guide*. Pacific Palisades, CA: Self-Esteem Seminars.

DeMille, R. (1973). *Put Your Mother on the Ceiling. Children's Imagination Games*. New York: Viking Compass.

Eberle, R. R. (1971). *SCAMPER: Games for Imagination and Development*. Buffalo, NY: DOK Publishers

Galyean, B. C. (1983). *Mind Sight: Learning Through Imagery*. Long Beach, CA: Center for Integrative Learning. (Available through Zephyr Press)

Harmin, M., & Sax, S. (1977). *A Peaceable Classroom: Activities to Calm and Free Student Energies*. Minneapolis, MN: Winston Press.

Hendricks, G., & Wills, R. (1975). *The Centering Book*. Englewood Cliffs, NJ: Prentice-Hall.

Hendricks, G., & Wills, R. (1977). *The Second Centering Book*. Englewood Cliffs, NJ: Prentice-Hall.

Hills, C,, & Rozman, D. (1978). *Exploring Inner Space*. Boulder Creek, CA: University of the Trees Press

Murdock, M. (1988). *Spinning Inward: Using Guided Imagery with Children*. Berkeley, CA: Shambhala Press.

Rapkin, M. (n.d.). *The Power of Pretend*. Available from Maurice Rapkin, 10480 Santa Monica Blvd., Los Angeles, CA 90025.

Rozman, D. (1975). *Meditating With Children*. Boulder Creek, CA: University of the Trees Press.

Rozman, D. (1976). *Meditation For Children*. Millbrae, CA: Celestial Arts.

Samuels, M., & Samuels, N. (1975). *Seeing With the Mind's Eye: The History, Techniques and Uses of Visualization*. New York: Random House/Bookworks.

Vitale, B. M. (1982). *Unicorns are Real: A Right-Brained Approach to Learning*. Rolling Hills Estates, CA: Jalmar Press.

2. General Books on Imagery

Gawain, S. (1978). *Creative Visualization*. New York.New World Library

Lorrayne, H., & Lucas, J. (1974). *The Memory Book*. New York: Ballantine Books

Nichols, R. E. (1978). *Picture Yourself a Winner*. Lakemont, GA: CSA Press.

Sherman, H. (1978). *How to Picture What You Want*. New York: Fawcett Goldmedal.

3. Books on Relaxation

Davis, M., Esheiman, E. R., & McKay, M. (1980). *The Relaxation and Stress Reduction Workbook*. Richmond, CA: New Harbinger Publications.

Mason, L. J. (1980). *Guide to Stress Reduction*. Culver City, CA: Peace Press.

Walker, C. E. (1975). *Learn to Relax*. Englewood Cliffs, NJ: Prentice-Hall.

White, J., & Fadiman, J. (Eds.). (1976). *Relax*. New York: Dell.

4. Books on Energizers

Fleugelman, A. (Ed.). (1976). *The New Games Book*. Garden City: Doubleday/ Dolphin.

Ichazo, O. (1976). *Arica Psychocalisthenics*. New York: Simon & Schuster.

Weinstein, M., & Goodman, J. (1980). *Playfair*. San Luis Obispo, CA: Impact Publishers.

Notes

1 Whenever three dots appear in the guided imagery exercises, they indicate a pause of about 5 seconds. Whenever a longer pause of about 15 seconds is appropriate, I have written the word "pause" in parentheses. *Editors' note: Readers will notice that ellipses points are used conventionally in the other articles in this book to indicate material that is left out.*

2 See Assagioli, Roberto, *The Act Of Will.* Chapter 5, Psychological Law I.—*Ed.*

3 *Environments 1: The Psychologically Ultimate Seachore* is availoable on CD from Atlantic.—*Ed.*

4 Apparently no longer available as of this re-printing—*Ed.*

5 Second edition 1994. New York: Pearson Educatsion —*Ed.*

6 Also Eden Grove Editions, 1989—*Ed.*

7 See Assagioli, Roberto, *The Act Of Will.* Chapter 5, Psychological Law III.—*Ed.*

8 Note: Some introduction may be needed so that students know that there are different variations of "perfect;" i.e. blue jays, robins and cardinals are all "perfect" birds. Some students may have emotional histories around the word "perfect" that may need to be defused before using this exercise.—*Ed.*

9 *Kung Fu* was a popular American television series 1972-1975 which followed the travels of a Shaolin monk who traveled the American old west of the 19th century, searching for his half-brother, armed only with his spiritual training and his skill in martial arts. Many or most of the aphorisms used in the show were derived from the Tao Te Ching.—*Ed.*

Jack Canfield, MEd, *first taught high school in Chicago, then worked for the W. Clement and Jessie V. Stone Foundation, which provides grants for child development and education. He became a therapist, and founded The New England Center for Personal and Organizational Development in Amherst, Massachusetts. The center focused primarily on Gestalt Therapy, Psychosynthesis, and a number of other modalities including Rolfing, Feldenkrais work, massage therapy, and Kundalini yoga. He is the author of numerous articles and books, including the* Chicken Soup for the Soul *series, and founder of the* Canfield Training Group *in Santa Barbara, CA and the* Foundation for Self-Esteem *in Culver City, CA. He holds an honorary PhD from the University of Santa Monica.*

Part VI.

Environmental Design

Nature as Healer

Anita R. Olds

In over a decade of designing educational and therapeutic environments, I have found that even where the integration of organic, psychological, social, and spiritual factors is appreciated, there is consistent failure to include the physical environment as a fifth, essential component of holism. Administrators and helping professionals are insensitive to the ways in which their work settings contribute to poor performance and illness; nor can they fully comprehend what a powerful ally the environment can be for growth and recovery.

Yet, work with psychosynthesis and dreams, both of which draw upon images of persons, events, and places in the subconscious, made me suspect the existence of environmental sensitivities outside daily conscious awareness. I therefore created a workshop entitled "Spaces Can Heal" to explore whatever latent knowledge helping professionals might have of the relationship of external space to physical and emotional well-being.[1] In describing the outcomes of the workshop, I hope to convey that nature is perceived as a primary agent of healing and therefore should be used more widely. I will then discuss various qualities of nature that make her a healer and suggest ways those qualities can be incorporated into health-care settings to improve their healing capacities.

Background

I have conducted the workshop for several years with over 300 people, in groups of 6 to 60. Participants have included architects, designers, social workers, psychotherapists, nurses, parents, students of the humanities and social sciences, and teachers of normal and handicapped persons at all grade levels. Most have been helping professionals; only a few have been identifiably active clients or non-professionals.

The workshop consists of two visualizations, one related to wound-edness, the other to healing. After a brief relaxation, participants are encouraged to see themselves as strong and whole, standing in the center of their own awareness. They are asked to recall a time when they, or someone close to them, felt helpless, wounded, or in pain. Still feeling their own power, they are encouraged to re-experience that time as deeply as possible. Then they are directed, by my questions, to pay close attention to the physical setting in which the helplessness, pain, or wounding occurred:

> How large a space was it? What colors were prominent? What odors? Were there any sounds or textures that felt important? What was the quality of the light? Were there any enclosures and safe places, any exposed and unsafe zones? Did the setting help or hinder attempts to relieve the hurt and wounding?

The incidents evoked by this intense and frequently painful visualization have included physical, emotional, and social wounding in both indoor and outdoor settings. For example, outdoors, a woman was stung on the head by a swarm of bees; a mother and her young child were rejected by neighboring women with whom they had to share a common outdoor play space in their housing development; a man broke a limb while skiing down a mountain.

People have also recounted experiences of wounding in a wide range of indoor settings (e.g., hospital bedrooms, corridors, emergency or treatment rooms, falling down a flight of subway stairs, or being burned by hot liquids or frying oil). The situations they have described vary from receiving a frightening diagnosis from a physician, or an unfavorable decision from a judge, to learning of the death of a loved one, or being told by one's spouse that he or she is leaving.

No one injured outdoors has ever recalled the exterior setting as affecting the wounding, although they have recounted the negative impact of interior spaces they had entered for treatment and recovery. Thus, outdoor settings seem to be perceived as neutral or benign (even when they are the scene of great pain), whereas interior spaces are experienced as exacerbating the pain.

Discussion of the painful feelings, and of the impact of the physical setting on the wounding, is followed by a second visualization in which participants "envision an environment that would be healing for the person previously wounded." Participants are guided to place the wounded person—and then themselves, as observers—in the healing space, to watch what happens, and to improve the healing qualities as seems appropriate. But no guidelines are given for the design of the new setting except to "make it as rich and embellished as you wish, in order to best achieve the healing desired."

After opening their eyes, each person is given a large sheet of paper and a box of crayons with which to "draw the healing environment envisioned." The pictures are then placed in an open circle to be appreciated and discussed by others. They obviously vary in artistic skill, sensitivity to aesthetics, and attention to detail. But the ways in which they do not vary—in content, color,[2] and thematic concern—are the reason for writing this paper.

Basic Findings

The unexpected outcome of the exercise is that over 75 percent of the healing spaces drawn are of outdoor scenes with many common elements. The remaining 25 percent, or less, are interior settings, which always contain elements related to the outdoors—a prominent window through which are visible sky, trees, sun, a garden, or yard—and indoor potted plants, flowers, and growing things. Thus, despite a seeming insensitivity to environmental factors, helping professionals do have images of healing spaces. Most often, these are outdoor settings, and they always involve nature as the healing agent. Below, I will consider the salient features of the healing spaces that have come out of these workshops and discuss their significance for the design of therapeutic settings.

Motion

All the healing spaces are described as quiet, meditative, and comfortable, yet replete with change and motion: water is flowing, breezes are blowing, and the sun's heat and light are pervasive; there may be swings, rocking chairs, waterfalls; people walking, swimming, sliding down a hill, watching birds fly, and so on. In addition, all sensations (odors, sounds, textures, light, and space) are perceived with heightened awareness and pleasure, as if the stimuli from nature were especially comforting and supportive rather than forceful and overpowering. Movement, which is so apparent in the settings, is important in two respects. First, movement is the *sine qua non* of life. Second, the senses, and ultimately all feelings of comfort, require motion for optimal functioning.

Gross Bodily Movement

When something moves, it is alive. When it moves easily, in accordance with its own structure, it is healthy and functioning well. Motion permits an organism to freely locate itself in space, assume different body postures, create its own boundaries, have access to diverse territories, manifest power, and fulfill its potential. Thus, motion is an essential manifestation of health and well-being, and in both sickness and health is necessary for maintenance of the body's integrity.

The need for movement, so superbly supported by nature and outdoor spaces, is, however, severely restricted in institutional settings by the intervention of rules, the withdrawal of materials, and the reduction of the territory available for action. The presence of many bodies moving in unpredictable ways is felt as intolerable indoors. Also, because motion is more apparent in small spaces and at the same time makes space "feel" more congested, it is not encouraged when square footage is limited or focused attention required.

Generally, employees have the greatest freedom to move (which increases with increasing status) and to demonstrate their status when they know their way around and have access to spaces off-limits to clients and to persons who are lower on the social hierarchy. Hence, nurses, doctors, and therapists come and go freely while clients sit passively in waiting rooms until called for treatment.

Some control of movement is necessary. But gross bodily activity is essential for recovery, as it prevents atrophy and honors the life force in each individual. Opportunities for movement, which are usually the most sorely neglected, should therefore be the primary design goal of any therapeutic program. The well-being of staff and clients alike requires that every means be found to utilize capabilities that are strong while exercising those that are disabled. And since the ability to move freely in space is particularly well-supported by nature, helping professionals also need to actively create and use outdoor places as a fundamental part of therapeutic practice.

Movement in the Environment

As we go from outward manifestations of bodily movement to inner conditions of sensory awareness, it is apparent that the senses must also move and receive changing stimulation from the external environment in order to function. The eyes "see" by virtue of scanning a visual field, but are reduced to "blindness" when forced to stare at a stationary image. The ears "hear" when sound waves strike and vibrate the ear drum. Changes in air currents bring us odors which would go undetected in a static, enclosed space.

When the environment provides rhythmic patterns of predictable sameness, combined with moderate diversity, the senses are able to maintain optimal levels of response, and we experience what is known as "comfort." Unlike rigid, built environments which defy destruction and dare users to modify them, nature is healing because she possesses the type of movement that generates basic comfort. Natural elements such as "blazing fires," "babbling brooks," or "gentle breezes" are always in motion, with fairly predictable yet varied transformations (a flicker or flare, a new pitch, a cooler or warmer draft). The transformations prevent boredom and withdrawal by periodically reawakening the nervous system.

Since we seem to require a continuous yet moderate array of signals and stimuli to stay tuned in (our focus outward and our interest charged), the monotonous quality of most institutional settings exacerbates feelings of dis-ease. A poorly designed or impoverished environment forces those who live constantly with pain and discomfort (and have reduced tolerance for the extreme levels of arousal of the typical therapeutic context) to be doubly disabled—first by personal and then by external circumstances. For a healthy existence, difference-within-sameness, exquisitely present in nature, needs to be simulated in the creation of meaningfully rich interior designs.

The old adage "variety is the spice of life" is the best guideline for creating comfortable and functional interiors. They should include (1) varied sensorial and physical parameters (changes in scale, lighting, and floor, ceiling, and boundary heights; visual, auditory, olfactory, textural, and kinesthetic interest) and (2) varied spaces and activities—spaces that are large and small, private, intimate, semi-private, and public; and activities that are fast- and slow-paced, messy and clean, noisy and quiet, and, above all, enable each client to be involved as an active protagonist in his or her own daily life. Both these requirements are amply fulfilled by outdoor settings. Variation along these lines indoors could transform a stark, stressful institution into a comfortable place to be (see Olds, 1979).

Everyone benefits from comfortable settings because they reduce anxiety and self-consciousness. Clients become more amenable to treatment, better able to focus, and more playful and creative, while staff are less impersonal in dealing with human needs. Such sensory-rich surroundings optimize the ability to perform by making handicaps appear less formidable, by minimizing disabilities aggravated by tension, and by creating an expectation of possible future health. Most of all, by inviting clients to pause, attend, and be nourished by the world's richness, comfortable settings help them feel connected yet free, bringing them closer to the Higher Self, their ultimate source of recovery.

Control

Despite the public nature of outdoor settings as well as the potential for intrusion of interior ones, a noteworthy characteristic of healing spaces is the degree of control one feels able to assume over self, territory, and intrusion. Environmental control results from (1) being able to make predictions about territories and events beyond one's immediate spatial sphere and (2) being able to assume a safe orientation.

Prediction

Participants recalled that a painful part of wounding was the unpredictability of who might enter their room or what might occur. In the healing spaces, on the other hand, a wide vista, or a position on top of a rock or hill, enabled them to see great distances, to anticipate future events, and to gauge their safety in relation to the surrounding terrain. Such predictability, often provided by outdoor settings, depends upon access to information, whereas womb-like enclosures and disorienting interior layouts induce arousal and uncertainty. Since many things take on a different perspective when viewed in light of vast expanses of land or water, broad vistas can provide a perspective on personal misfortune that is also healing.

Broad vistas are difficult to achieve indoors, particularly in buildings designed with rooms along the corridors. However, interior windows or walls of glass, bold graphics, informative lighting which does not create mysterious shadows, and balanced acoustical control can be intentionally employed to provide the "extension of the senses" that is required. For new or renovated construction, a good example is illustrated by the Hyatt Hotels which place the life of the facility—registration desk, bars, lounges, restaurants, escalators, and glass elevators—within an open central "hub," or core, that is visible from a variety of levels. All spaces orient to the hub. The bedrooms, requiring seclusion, are then located off short, amply spaced corridors on the periphery. Thus, the traditional relationship between public and private zones is reversed, and users are given an open, informative locus to which to refer.

Orientation

Because we do not have eyes in the backs of our heads and cannot protect ourselves from attack from the rear, control and physical security also depend upon having something solid at our backs, with the ability to see and hear what is approaching head-on. Thus, people move across beaches, fields, and parks, and stand still only when their backs are against a wall, a tree, a bench, et cetera. If protection at the rear is impossible, security may also be achieved by sitting or lying close to the ground, or attaining a position of height from which to survey the surrounding terrain.

Enclosures, such as huts, small houses, lean-tos, caves, arches, and clearings in a forest, are a common feature of healing spaces. But, always, these are partial or three-quarter structures, never encapsulating wombs. One woman built herself an eight-sided house of glass, on a hill, from which she could see everything while feeling protected from the elements.

Participants derived security outdoors from sitting inside these enclosures, standing in front of trees and boulders, traversing open spaces, lying on the ground, or sitting on rocks and hill tops. Occasionally, being embraced by land, space, light, earth, water (e.g., the curve of a wave), a friend, or an animal was also described as protective. Indoors, beds and chairs with high backs, positioned to provide a view of the door through which an intruder might enter, created a similar sense of safety. These interiors featured materials (quilts, drapes, carpets, hammocks, pillows) capable of enclosing a space or enveloping the body while responding to movement and changes in posture.

Protection at the rear is frequently absent from therapeutic settings because professionals instinctively place their own backs against the walls, or take the most protected corner of the room, and locate clients in exposed zones, making them accessible to caregivers at all times. Ideally, all parties should have protection at their backs, perhaps by each being positioned so that they are perpendicular to the door, or in a right-angled, L-shaped orientation to one another. If there are few protected areas, it is essential that the client, not the guide, feel in control of the spaces beyond by being given the position of greatest environmental security. Group leaders should place the group members in the most secure zone, perhaps on tiers, or risers, in a corner so they can see and hear one another more readily. Leaders themselves should sit in the more exposed spaces.

Light

Since light, depicted as both yellow rays and the sun, figured prominently in the drawings, it is instructive to examine its relationship to healing. Natural light changes continuously. It enables us to experience the passage of time, to estimate the time of day without recourse to mechanical devices, and to enjoy an implicit form of variety as our perception of objects and spaces changes under different conditions of illumination. It therefore provides many components of healing, including motion, change, difference-within-sameness, variety, information, and orientation.

Next to movement, light is the variable most sorely neglected in interior design practices. Yet, according to Richard J. Wurtman, a nutritionist at the Massachusetts Institute of Technology, "it seems clear that light is the most important environmental input, after food, in controlling bodily function."[3] Experiments have shown that differently colored lights affect blood pressure, pulse and respiration rates, brain activity, and bio-rhythms, and can be used to cure neo-natal jaundice, psoriasis, and herpes sores.

Ott (1973) argues further that the trend for people to spend increasing hours behind windows and windshields, eye and sunglasses, in front of TV and display terminals, and under the partial spectrum of fluorescent bulbs affects the incidence of headaches, arthritis, stunted growth, diabetes, cancer, hay fever, infertility, hormonal imbalances, tooth decay, obesity, hyperactivity, and delinquent and criminal behaviors. Thus, time spent outdoors, or in the presence of sunlight streaming through an open window, may indeed be critical to health.

Recently, a relationship between depression and increased positive ions in the air has been suggested.[4] Less well-recognized is a possible connection between depression and light. This connection works as follows: On sunny days, the world outside our window is brighter than the interior spaces, while at night, the interior is more brightly lit than the out-of-doors. On gray days, because of reduced exterior illumination, we use more artificial light inside, thereby approximating night-time conditions during day-light hours. As a result, our biological clocks are thrown off balance and we feel depressed (Lam, 1977). This effect also exists in interior spaces without windows, where nighttime conditions prevail continuously. Sadly, the more wounded the individual in this society, the more likely he or she is to be placed in settings lacking access to natural light.

Professionals can moderate their own and clients' reactions to the depressive effects of gray days by providing more direct access to the outdoors, by choosing therapeutic spaces which have windows, and by installing fixtures which vary the intensity and sources of interior illumination.

In nature, one is surrounded by luminousness. Indoors, one is bombarded by intense waves of fluorescent radiation interspersed by shadows. Daylight outdoors is rarely insufficient, but interior lighting is usually either too intense or inadequate for the task at hand. This is because architects tend to treat artificial lighting as unidimensional, rather than task-specific, and as unrelated to the natural light entering through windows.

For biological and aesthetic reasons, lighting must become part of architecture, and a variety of forms—natural and artificial, general-ambient and task-specific—must be provided. Varied sources of lighting (floor, desk, ceiling, wall) can be easily added to most therapeutic spaces. Wall-mounted, reflected-light fixtures, in place of overhead fluorescents, simulate the experience of light in nature by "washing" the light down a wall and up over the ceiling. Instead of standard bulbs, full-spectrum lights, which approximate the range of wavelengths provided by sunshine, may reduce disturbances caused by inadequate exposure to the ultra-violet and infra-red ends of the spectrum (Ott, 1973).

Beyond this, therapists should use every means possible to give clients access to natural light. Perhaps they should even dictate that, except for instrument-related restrictions, no space without windows will be used for therapeutic purposes whatsoever!

Privacy

Whether indoors or out, a person in a healing space is usually depicted alone—walking, seated, or lying; on land, on elevated terrain, or in the water. Occasionally, a trusted friend (never more than one or two and never a therapist or professional) is present as well. More often, pets (a dog or cat, or birds) are the person's only companions. Despite this aloneness, participants often felt a sense of connection and belonging to the setting and to life. The striking absence of people, including therapists, contrasts sharply with the togetherness and professional intervention mores of our society, suggesting that perhaps privacy, expanded to include animals, is essential to healing.

Wolfe and Laufer (1974) distinguish four types of privacy: (1) controlling access to spaces/having a place of one's own; (2) controlling access to information/being able to tell secrets; (3) being free from distraction and the bother of others; and (4) being alone or by oneself.

These were honored by the healing spaces, but violated in the circumstances of wounding.

In terms of the fourth type of privacy, that of aloneness, two observations seem relevant. First, a special quality of nature seems to be her capacity to be a "friend" and to support an aloneness that is experienced as connection rather than isolation. Feeling one with, in private, nature's "varied sameness" may enable clients to achieve a personal centering that is a prerequisite for tackling the social domain. Second, a source of wounding in society, both in daily life and in the way therapy is provided, may be an overemphasis on togetherness at the expense of private time. Keeping in touch with one's deeper sources of wholeness and individuality, and with the healing forces of the universe, requires some privacy and solitude. Thus, a gift of any therapeutic process would be the space, time, and encouragement for the client to be alone both indoors and out.

Institutional settings often fail to honor the client's need for all four types of privacy because professionals, who "own" the space, permit their need for access to the client to take precedence over the client's need for control and solitude. The addition of natural outdoor spaces to the therapeutic milieu would obviously give clients and staff more places to be alone. But therapeutic routines and interior spaces also need reshaping so clients can find solitude, "personalize," and have territorial control over at least those spaces where therapy does not occur. A striking feature of the interior healing spaces described by the participants was the presence of artifacts of sentimental or historical value that enabled them to make a space their own. Similarly, waiting areas, lounges, libraries, recreational rooms, intimate dining facilities, meditation and worship spaces, shops, laundries, kitchens, and personal bedrooms can all be designed to respect needs for personalization, territorial control, and solitude so that clients can come and go as they please, execute self-care tasks, and carry forward their own healing during the hours outside the therapeutic encounter.

Pets

Recent psychological research into the human-animal bond reveals that caring for a pet is a significant deterrent to depression, loneliness, and alienation.[5] Thus, victims of heart attacks recover more rapidly with fewer reoccurrences and the elderly suffer less from disability and depression when given something as seemingly insignificant as a parakeet to care for. For infection-control reasons, many institutions currently restrict the presence of animals. But potential dangers need to be weighed against the animals' healing benefits. The oncology waiting area of one pediatric hospital has a huge aviary and a fish tank, while the chief of oncology sports a hamster in her uniform pocket because she believes it helps children want to live. A nurse in a major city hospital confided that breaking hospital rules to allow a critically ill boy's dog to visit was ultimately the factor that saved the child's life. Someday, Feeling Heart dogs may well do for mental health programs what Seeing Eye dogs do for the blind. Meanwhile, as the drawings of healing spaces suggest, animals very much need to be acknowledged as natural healing agents and given a more significant place in all types of therapeutic practices.

Beauty

In *What We May Be*, Ferrucci (1982) devotes an eloquent chapter to the regenerative, self- transcendent, and revelatory effects of beauty. By contacting the aesthetic dimension, he argues, people seem to experience themselves as more beautiful and seem to open more fully to the experience of beauty in the environment around them. Both sets of feelings, in turn, assist the healing process.

Undoubtedly, "beauty is in the eye of the beholder." Yet, the opposite notion, that pleasant settings can entice us from ordinary concerns to a sense of greater personal harmony and vitality must also be emphasized. In the drawings, the wounded and ugly were placed in natural settings which aroused powerfully therapeutic feelings of joy and love for self, life, and beauty. It is as if the embrace of nature's physical wholeness and harmony transmitted psychic wholeness and tranquility. This itself provides an argument for taking advantage of the beauty which nature provides and also for the therapeutic benefits of creating mere beauty around us.

While beautification of dwellings preoccupies many a homemaker, comparable consideration is rarely given to the urban landscape, the work place, or the therapeutic milieu. These settings, by virtue of their anonymous ownership, become an aesthetic no-man's-land designed more to assist the custodians who maintain them than the users who must grow and heal within them. Aesthetic considerations, termed "luxuries," invariably rank last or are totally ignored, due to the presumed monetary expense involved.

However, "beauty is as beauty does," in the built as well as social world. Far from being a luxury, one must question whether modern man, bombarded by chaotic, artificial, poorly integrated, and ugly settings can afford *not* to devote more energy to the creation of aesthetically pleasing work and communal places.

The entrance to every healing space should be graced by a *torre*, a Japanese arch signaling the transition from profane to sacred territory, from that which is spontaneous and ordinary to that which is spiritually and aesthetically integrated. Passage beyond the torre would then surround each individual with beauty, wholeness, and care, proclaiming that he, too, however wounded, belonged to the sacred domain and that by his very presence in it he was graced with inner and outer loveliness.

Natural Features

The natural features most common to the outdoor scenes were earth, sand, and mud, trees, grass, sky, open space, water, sunlight, rocks, ledges, hills, and mountains. In *The Sacred and the Profane* Eliade (1959) argues that, for religious man, "nature is never only 'natural'; it is always fraught with religious value and expresses something that transcends it." Perhaps, then, the choice of nature as a healing agent is symbolic of spiritual needs also related to healing.

For example, trees symbolize the transcendence of the human condition by the sky, the home of God, and by the powers of creation. Earth symbolizes fertility and fullness, while rites of lying or being placed on, or in, the ground represent desires to wipe out a sin, cure a malady, promote regeneration, or be reborn as a new man or woman. Sky and land together represent the primal forces of creation. Thus, the presence of trees, sky, and land in the drawings could reflect desires for contact with spiritual and creative forces beyond the wounded individual, desires to be purified, desires to fill oneself with the earth's richness and energy, and desires for "re-creation" and regeneration as the ultimate form of healing.

Similar meanings can be attributed to other natural features of the drawings. Water, which implies both death and rebirth, abolishes form, washes away sins, purifies, and supports regeneration. Its presence may reflect inner wishes to be washed clean of all illness and anxiety, and make contact with the untarnished essence of one's being.

Stones and rocks, which represent power, hardness, permanence, and the irreducibility of existence, may affirm the continuity of one's life despite any wounding as well as the paradox that one is whole while becoming more so. Structures such as buildings, dwellings, huts, or temples mark a place and symbolize our assumption of an existential position in the cosmos. In the drawings, enclosures clearly marked the person's location and provided a secure locus from which to survey and interact with the world. Like stones and rocks, they could also reflect desires for the stability and permanence that are absent from the rapidly changing, mobile existence of 20th-century man.

In the healing spaces, some individuals are depicted as walking, while others are stationary. Walks sometimes symbolize a search for one's soul or for greater meaning in one's life. Perhaps those walking are searching for self-knowledge, which heals by resolving conflicts and giving meaning to the wounding.

A "timeless" quality of connection and belonging, yet of freedom, was also attributed to the healing spaces. This type of time is characteristic of ritual and ceremonial time, meditative states, and moments when the loss of self-consciousness results in heightened external awareness and the merging of self with the universe. For centuries, in order to establish harmony with the world, Chinese esthetes have meditated upon miniature gardens set up in pottery bowls inside their houses. Perhaps participants who are in environments possessing these same features—water, trees, a mountain, and a grotto—experience a "moving meditation," thereby establishing a similar healing harmony.

Concluding Thoughts

Although few helping professionals explicitly evaluate the therapeutic impact of their working environments, the visualizations clearly indicated that everyone is intuitively aware of a healing setting. Most participants, who had never thought of an environment as having healing capacities, were reassured to have their intuitions about space made conscious. The similarity of their healing spaces gives them a universal significance, perhaps as archetypes of the collective unconscious, and draws attention to natural features often viewed as commonplace, or simply taken for granted. If tapped, this common knowledge could empower professionals to promote collectively sorely needed institutional renovations and refurbishments. Few endeavors are more powerful in uniting a staff than joint participation in a successful renovation project.

For us all, the subconscious images of nature as a primal source of nourishment and rejuvenation are probably laid down in childhood when our perception of the environment is immediate and holistic. Children have little sense of part/whole relationships, or of the self as a separate entity, and so live according to the information provided by their senses and activity, feasting upon the nuances of color, light, sound, and touch by which they come to know the world.

The pursuit of purposes and goals, and the achievement of order and success in adult life, requires a focused and narrow vision which takes precedence over awareness of the whole, driving it underground, while freeing conscious behavior for performance-based tasks. Hence, adults tend not to see the impact of the physical environment on their work, even when it is right under their noses.

Yet, although we simply absorb stimulation mechanically and without real attention throughout the day, or fail to accompany our daily transactions with a wider vision, each of us is sensitive to all qualitative aspects of the environment: movements, sounds, volumes, textures, visual and kinesthetic vibrations, forms, colors, rhythms, ideas, et cetera. As the Hindus claim, "*Sarvam annam.* [Everything is food.]" Thus, it is both illusory and potentially harmful to assume that an environment can be neutral. Environments, like human beings and all other aspects of life, are potent purveyors of stimulation, information, and effect, be it the ill effect of neglect, poverty, and disorder or the beneficial effect of beauty, unity, and positive attention to detail.

Thus, helping professionals need to care for and judiciously design all therapeutic contexts. They also need to explore with clients the ways in which the environment was experienced developmentally, or *is being* experienced as part of their current work, living, and healing circum-stances. As is done in our workshop, clients can be encouraged to envision a healing setting for themselves and to identify the physical parameters (perhaps the very ones described here) that might be modified to support individual growth and change.

However disillusioned, modern man has clearly not wiped out his primal connections to the earth, sky, water, and all living matter. Indeed, if "the unconscious offers him solutions for the difficulties of his own life and in this way plays the role of religions" (Eliade, 1959), then these visualizations, drawing upon collective unconscious material, may even yield one solution for mankind's recovery and renewal: nature and the outdoors are powerful healing agents, to be created, preserved, and used as part of all healing and therapeutic practice.

The Knowledge is Rarely Used

In this culture, because relief from distress is believed to come primarily from professional and pharmaceutical sources, few persons view nature, or physical circumstances, as relevant to cure, or use the outdoors specifically as a therapeutic agent. In contrast, the healing settings in the drawings were devoid of technical/professional elements and the inclusion of other people depended solely upon their relationship to the wounded individual, not upon their professional expertise. Thus, there is an obvious discrepancy between the ways in which we behave when wounded and our intuitive sense of alternate routes to recovery.

Although the workshop has revealed that nature is the healer, clearly she is far from available for such purposes. Current architectural practices and models of therapy require that one spend time almost exclusively inside buildings and interior spaces such as hospitals, offices, clinics, treatment rooms, pools, jacuzzis, steam rooms, and massage parlors, all of which maintain predictable year-round conditions defying the vicissitudes of nature and our relationship to her. Only rare treatments, usually involving extra cost, occur outside: hot water spas, clay pits, mineral springs, sanitaria with beautiful grounds for walking.

In addition, primary determinants for the location of a therapeutic site involve proximity to target populations, public transportation, and energy sources; thus, hospitals, clinics, and therapeutic centers are generally located with little regard for site conditions and rarely in areas where natural features are present. In fact, the simplest and most cost-effective construction method is to raze the land, build a regularly shaped building, and then put in a few young trees to make the structure less of an eyesore.

Sophisticated technology may now enable us to use large expanses of glass to distribute natural light to interiors. But the tendency to build horizontal structures, spreading great distances on each floor, results in buildings with a select number of rooms with windows and views to the outside and with many interior spaces that never see the light of day. Dense building-proximity in urban areas tends, similarly, to limit light penetration to the front and rear of buildings, or to skylights in the upper stories, and to restrict all views of the outside.

In addition to the absence of nature in therapeutic centers, nature-related places that could be used for purposes of informal healing and rejuvenation are clearly absent from the daily experience of most city dwellers. This is due to limited urban planning practices, economics, and lifestyles. The lack of a regular relationship with nature may, in fact, be a major reason why urban inhabitants experience stress. According to Alexander (1974), if natural spaces are to be used frequently for their physiological benefits, they must be an integral part of the urban territory (i.e., within three-minutes walking distance, or about 750 feet, of every house and workplace). Easier access to natural spaces, and a greater abundance of them, might nip in the bud many problems requiring professional intervention later on.

While city planning and architectural practices will not change easily or quickly, the power of citizen pressure should not be underestimated. In Canada and Japan, for example, citizen pressure has led to the establishment of "sunshine laws" entitling each person to a minimum number of hours of sunshine per day and banning the construction of buildings taller than 33 feet (2 stories) in residential areas. A Tokyo court ruled that "sunshine is essential to a comfortable life and therefore a citizen's right to enjoy sunshine at his home should be duly protected by law."[6]

At the very least, the presence of natural elements within interiors should be given greater attention by those interested in promoting health. Windows to natural light, ideally a good deal of sunlight, are essential. If vistas to lawns, trees, and sky are impossible, window boxes filled with evergreens in winter and geraniums in spring would provide some relief. Moderately expensive structural changes such as balconies, porches, courtyards, window wells, lowered window sills, windows which can be opened, greenhouses, and clearstories could all assist in providing vital links between the indoors and outside. And, when weather permits, professionals could definitely experiment with the effects of conducting therapeutic sessions outdoors.

Numerous biofeedback studies (Benson, 1975, 1979; Samuels, 1975) affirm that restful, natural settings envisioned by the mind's eye can produce meditative states and reduce the physiological effects of environmentally and psychically induced stress. The same nerve and muscle pathways involved in real action are also involved when a person pictures that activity in his mind. And the more vividly the situation is envisioned, the more the body reacts as if it is actually happening. By having participants move from an assumption of physiological balance to envisioning the setting that would create it, our workshop may have simply reversed the standard stress-reduction technique.

However, in putting the focus on visualizations and meditative states, both of which utilize nature as the healer, an important component is still forgotten. For, if merely imagining a healing space can have a strong regenerative effect, how much more healing might be the experience of being physically located in a natural, healthy setting? Indeed, it could be that healing spaces, in and of themselves, would suffice for recovery in certain instances, without any medical and professional intervention whatsoever.

Sacred Islamic architecture intentionally manipulates the acoustical properties of a mosque to create harmonious sound patterns for aligning the chakras and assisting in the attainment of spiritual connections with God. Who is to say, then, that similar attention to the impact of the environment on other energy levels would not lead to physiological and emotional rebalancing as well as spiritual re-alignment? If something as seemingly innocuous as an increase in negative ions in the air can "cure" allergies, headaches, dizziness, depression, and asthmatic attacks, then how much more powerful must be light and sound waves, minerals in water and a sea breeze, and the organic compounds in sand and earth!

The overwhelming tendency to see nature as the agent of healing suggests a new vision of therapeutic settings and practices which would include the outdoors as a part of the program and incorporate natural features in interior spaces. Someday, all therapeutic centers may have gardens, lawns, trees, ponds, and hills where clients can wander or be escorted on walks as part of their recovery regimen. Hopefully, these features will eventually be seen to be as critical to site selection as square footage and other location criteria.

Meanwhile, therapists should experiment with making nature integral to the therapeutic process, creating pleasing and supportive interiors, and encouraging clients to spend more time outside as an important means of grounding their personal change and discovery.

Fortunately, the healing spaces described by participants in our workshop still exist outside urban areas as public lands which are available free, or at low cost, to everyone. All that is required is the effort and means to get to where they are. The preservation of such lands, and of open space and natural terrain in and around urban settings, should be the task of all conscientious citizens.

The simple exercise described here suggests that we ignore the environment at our own and our clients' peril. Failure to utilize our implicit knowledge of nature as a healer both perpetuates our ills and denies our own resources for recovery. From this knowledge of nature's role in health, those of us who have responsibility for the healing of others may draw inspiration and courage to create and use the new types of settings so critical to individual and societal well-being.

References

Alexander, C., et al. (1977). *A Pattern Language.* New York: Oxford University Press.

Assagioli, R. (1974). *The Act of Will.* New York: Penguin Books,

Benson, H. (1979). *The Mind Body Effect.* New York: Simon & Schuster.

Eliade, M. (1959). *The Sacred and the Profane.* New York: Harcourt Brace.

Ferrucci, P. (1982) *What We May Be.* New York: Jeremy P. Tarcher/Putnam

Lam, W.M.C. (1977). *Perception and Lighting as Form Givers for Architecture.* New York: McGraw-Hill.

Olds, A.R. (1978). Psychological Considerations in Humanizing the Physical Environment of Pediatric Outpatient and Hospital Settings. In E. Gellert (Ed.), *Psychosocial Aspects of Pediatric Care.* New York: Grune & Stratton.

Olds, A.R. (1979). Designing Classrooms for Children with Special Needs. In S. Meisels (Ed.), *Special Education and Development: Perspectives on Young Children Talk Special Needs.* Baltimore: University Park Press.

Ott, J. N. (1973). *Health and Light.* New York: Simon & Schuster.

Samuels, M., & Samuels, N. (1975). *Seeing With the Mind's Eye.* New York: Random House.

Wolfe, M,, & Laufer, R. (1974). The Concept of Privacy in Childhood and Adolescence. In D. H. Carson (Ed.), *Man-Environment Interaction.* Milwaukee: EDRA (6:29-54).

Notes

---

[1] I am indebted to Pat and Larry Sargent, co-founders of Dream Arts, Box 981, Taos, New Mexico, for the initial conception of this workshop.

[2] In all the sketches, greens, yellows, and blues predominate, and earth tones convey the "felt sense" of the spaces. Purple (a healing color) is generally reserved for elements of key importance. Red can depict flowers, demarcate a remaining zone of pain despite the healing, or, in abstract representations, symbolize the core of the healing energy. Most drawings are curvaceous and filled with much energy and motion.

[3] See *New York Times*, October 19, 1982.

[4] See D. W. Pihlcrantz, "Creating a Healthier Worksite" (*Industry*, January 1984)

[5] See L. Gal ton, "Best Friend Best Therapy?" (*Parade*, June 3, 1979)

[6] See *New York Times*, July 17, 1975

Anita R. Olds, PhD, *(1940 -1999) held a doctorate in Human Development and Social Psychology from Harvard University, and taught in the Eliot-Pearson Department of Child Study, Tufts University and at Wheelock College, Lesley College, and the Harvard University Graduate School of Design. She pioneered and specialized in the innovative design of many environmental facilities, especially for children. She founded and, until her death, directed The Child Care Institute, and summer program co-sponsored by Harvard and Tufts Universities that taught the complex needs of a well-designed child-care center. She was the author of* Designing Developmentally Optimal Classrooms for Children with Special Needs *(1979),* Perspectives on Young Children with Special Needs, Environmental Design Class *(1987), and* Child Care Design Guide *(2000).*

Part VII.

Organizations, Communities, and Society

Inquiring Into Organizational Systems: Psychosynthesis Spawns a Methodology

Bruce McBeath

Psychosynthesis principles long useful for the understanding of individual psychodynamics have recently been incorporated into a methodology for discovering how organizational systems are perceived and experienced by individuals within them. This methodology represents another step in a continuing effort to understand the interrelationship between individual and organizational dynamics. In this article, some of the efforts to understand the linkages between individual experience and organizational dynamics are profiled followed by a description of a psychosynthesis-related methodology for understanding the individual /organization interface.

In his recent contribution to organizational theory Stakeholders of the Organizational Mind (1983), Mitroff identifies the key roles played by what he terms the "internal stakeholders" of various organizational members. Internal stakeholders look very much like what we, from a psychosynthesis perspective, identify as "subpersonalities." Mitroff speculates about how various relationships between an individual's internal stakeholders come together to form the culture of an organization. Mitroff draws on Jung's concept of the archetype to develop the idea that organizational archetypes emerge that interact with and variously reinforce individual patterns of stakeholding in the system of the organization.

I found Mitroff's work particularly helpful in developing an integration of the principles of depth psychology with those of systems science (McBeath, 1986). Human systems theory has characteristically been expansively conceived to describe the dynamics of collectives apart from the subtleties of individual experience. Depth psychology, and here I would include Psychosynthesis, has placed phenomenal importance on the intrapsychic character of individual experience. (Assagioli [1965], calling Psychosynthesis a "height psychology," referred to it as making a major contribution to the "depth psychology" of Freud and Jung.) Generally depth psychology has disregarded the impact of larger collective, or conjoint, experience. There are few theoretical constructs that incorporate depth (or height) psychology into systems perspectives, though Mitroff does so to some extent using Jung's typology, as does Maccoby (1976) who turns his attention to the psychological dynamics motivating organizational leaders. The often quoted though perhaps little understood Bateson (1979) has provided the source for several recent forays into systems discussions that touch on individual dynamics (e.g., Maturana and Varela, 1980). These are useful but essentially theoretical stabs at understanding the individual-within-the-system.

I sought to generate a methodological approach that would describe from a subjective point of view the relationship between intrapsychic process and group or larger organizational process. Assagioli's techniques, related to images, symbols, and metaphors, were key aspects in my effort to capture the conjoint experience of persons united within a common organizational system.

Purposeful Imagination Within the Organization

Assagioli (1965) described the "purposeful imagination" and its role in the integration and spiritual synthesis of the personality. Assagioli, Jung (1955), and more recently Lifton (1976) characterized the imaging process as an important aspect of an internal guidance system that influences the ongoing development of the individual. The systems philosopher Jantsch went even further in developing the idea of a "guiding image" that functions as a universal archetype in influencing the development of persons, societies, and the evolution of culture (Jantsch & Waddington, 1976).

At the individual level, Assagioli's "ideal model" exercise[1] elaborates a psychosynthesis technique that uses images to enhance individual development. This exercise illustrates how the imagination can function as a mirror reflecting one's internal psycho-spiritual "condition" at a given moment in time. Subjective images are taken that reflect both deflated and inflated experiences of the self as related to self-perception and the perception of others. The ideal model exercise "catches" these various subjective impressions so that they can be harmonized and integrated within an emerging positive image of the self. In the exercise, even inflated images have a particular relationship to the model that is finally evoked. As with most experiences with imagery work related to personality development, the ideal model becomes real as it becomes the focus of sustained creative mediation; that is, as it is incorporated into oneself and the essence of that image is expressed in everyday life.

The use of imagery to reflect group process is a fascinating new area of study. At this point, organizational applications of a reflective imaging process have been only partially developed and are often used haphazardly. Thus the development of an ideal model process for larger systems might help us tap into the subjective experience of persons and systems. This would seem a useful extension of Assagioli's earlier applications with individuals.

The structured use of mental imagery as described in the ideal model exercise provides a starting point for the design of a larger methodological framework to explore the person/system interface within organizational settings. The larger approach described below uses imagery and other facilitative processes to characterize organizations in ways that capture both the depth of subjective individual experience and the breadth of the collective system.

Bridging Psychosynthesis and Systems—Individuality and collectivity come together at the juncture of person and system. Jantsch (1980) uses the analogy of a stream to describe the boundaries that the individual maintains between self and other in a particular system. Covering the perspectives identified by Checkland (1981), Jantsch says that one can observe the stream, or ride its surface (experience the flow "on the stream"), or become the stream itself (identify oneself "as the stream"). From this last perspective, identification with the system becomes an expansion of self-identification and a definition of a larger experience of "self."

The fundamental construct of the egg diagram designed by Assagioli (1965) has permeable boundaries that suggest transpersonal possibilities for the further expansion of the identity of the self. The diagram can be extended to describe the purposeful, evolutionary nature of the interaction between individuals as members of a larger constellation of relationships. Images help us explore how an individual's subjective experience of connection to others colludes with the subjective experience of others to form images of the larger system. This evolving network of inter-individual images becomes what Jantsch and Waddington (1976) refer to as a "guiding image" that determines the composition and evolution of the system (i.e., relationships, families, or organizations). Theoretically, these system images influence the development of the individual's self-image as well.

Description of the Methodology

Inspired by Assagioli, Jung, and others regarding the power of imagery (especially Assagioli's methodology relating to the progressive clarification of an image as an ideal model) and augmented by Checkland's description of an interactive systems methodology, I designed an approach that integrates imaging into a broader interactive systems methodology. This methodology was further developed and refined through its application in several organizations. Assagioli's view of how a network of images constitutes the experience of the self is reflected in the methodology; its purpose is to evolve a conscious description of a system as it is experienced by its members (the image of the system as-it-is) and to use this description as a link to the evolution of the system in the future (the image of the system as-it- might-become). The stages in this methodology are outlined below in an abbreviated fashion.

Before beginning the systems characterization process, an individual "base line" or starting point is established for exploring the self/system interface. An abbreviated form of Assagioli's ideal model exercise is used here to evoke images of self. First, individuals reflect on self-image distortions in both a positive and negative direction, and then they are led to evoke a more realistic yet positive self-image. This becomes the individual's baseline image characterizing his or her subjective experience before moving into his or her experience in relation to the system. The three individual images of the self—as deflated, as inflated, and as functioning well—comprise a subjective scale that can be used to rate how well an individual perceives his or her relationship to the system at various points in the systems characterization process.

Following the formation of an individual baseline image, a fourth image is tapped that reflects an individual's general experience with the organization. This is also a baseline impression, without regard for any particular problem situation within the organization.

After the initial "image taking," a process of characterizing person and system is employed that relates systems images to personal images. This is an interactive, dialogic process through which the subjective meanings of individual and collective images are amplified and examined. Finally, a realistic and positive ideal model image of the organization is elaborated. [For a more detailed presentation of this methodology, see McBeath (1986)] The ideal organizational model that results becomes a basis for designing action strategies to make the ideal image an actuality. This process is similar to grounding in work with individual ideal model images. Its purpose is to make an organizational image or model viable and real.

Example—The following example illustrates how this process was used with one particular organization. The participants were the management staff of a small company that had experienced very rapid growth. The company president was aware that the growth spurt had created job stress for the managers. The management staff had no previous familiarity in working with imagery techniques, nor had they previously attempted to look systemically at organizational problems. They also had little familiarity with group process techniques, although they had been meeting as a management group for over two years.

Imagery was used to help make conscious and available for discussion aspects of individual experience with the system that might not have otherwise emerged. At the first meeting, the managers were asked to generate a series of images of how they experienced themselves functioning in general; then they were asked to evoke personal images that characterized how they functioned in relation to a particular subsystem (the management staff) and to the organization as a whole. They were also asked to generate images which characterized their relationship to organizational issues that were drawn from responses to a set of pre-structured questions (a part of the methodology). Initially, they "imaged" their individual relationship to these issues with some difficulty and awkwardness, possibly related to their unfamiliarity in accessing and sharing internal perceptions with each other and the uncertainty they had about trusting this kind of information in the group.

During the second meeting, the managers began to fashion a definition of a system that would contain the issues they had elaborated at the first meeting. In accordance with the methodology I was using, I introduced a focused discussion that was intended to characterize these issues systemically. I wanted this discussion to result in problem-solving strategies which would address the more systemic problems, not simply the symptoms of those problems (which is what usually happens when organizational issues are not systemically addressed).

In attempting to help the managers think systemically about the issues they had identified, I was aware of their high level of fatigue, which was only enhanced by our late afternoon meeting. In order to enliven the session, I invited the managers to play with organizational images which captured their perspectives regarding the interrelationship of the various issues they had described. A rush of energy arose when they began to synthesize individual images into "corporate images" that integrated their collective personal experiences of the organization. One manager who had imaged herself "tiny" and "intimidated" began to view the organization as an infant whose needs were overwhelming her capacity to supply them. Through continued discussion, the organizational images began to coalesce around one particular theme—that of the developing child. The organization was characterized as a child experiencing a growth spurt. Parts of the organization's development (growth, co-ordination, capacity to make decisions, ability to manufacture its own resources) were out of balance with other parts. The managers used the language of the image to talk about how a rebalancing of the organization would allow development to even out.

The use of this organizational image prompted managers to identify personal images that characterized their individual experience with the organization in relation to this theme (i.e., issues generated by the growth spurt). Personal images were shared that related to being "expected to run when I'm just learning to walk, " or "a small child with a head full of curiosity who is still trying to get his body to work right. "

These images stimulated an elaboration of the organizational ideal model. The managers decided that the organizational climate needed to be a safe one for the "child's" continued development to occur. This led to a discussion of how a nourishing work climate and appropriate staff expectations could be structured. Earlier the managers had abstractly (and metaphorically) described the need for a management focus on establishing a nourishing work climate; now they saw that such a climate would have to provide direction and support for the "child" (organizational staff) if it was to help it through a stressful time in its development. Providing appropriate nourishment translated into revising staffing patterns and job performance expectations and providing sufficient preparation and on-the-job training so that a well-developed (or developing) staff would result. Thus, the image of the developing child became the basis for an organizational model that presented a unified perspective on how the organizational system would appear if it were providing an appropriate, nourishing environment.

This collective image of the organization captured a particular insight for managers because it conveyed the idea that the organization was a developing business and that it had different needs from a developed business. The managers determined that a legitimate need for external assistance existed in the short run, and broadened their consideration of strategies to support the development of such assistance. Imaging themselves as a developing organization altered their perceptions both of how they actually "were" as a system and of the strategies they might employ to move from unbalanced development to greater maturity. For example, the managers' stance regarding available external sources of contract funding softened. They had formerly been unwilling to consider various loans and government-sponsored business-assistance programs that were available to the newer, more fledgling divisions, preferring to demonstrate their capacity to run each of the divisions "solidly in the black." This pervasive emphasis on fiscal independence had in part resulted in a restrictive and punitive reaction to issues resulting from "down time" (mechanical or human in origin), even when employee errors could be simply viewed as an expected part of the process of learning to do the job. Management's punitive response contributed to the staff morale issues that were captured metaphorically in the image of the child "running before he can walk." This image helped the managers characterize a systemic issue (the need for the appropriately supportive development of the organization's capacity to "grow" into its expanded services) rather than focus on an isolated symptom like down time or staff morale. Further, the image was a model that provided some direction about possible and desirable changes that would contribute to a systemic "solution" to this problem.

Further Discussion

Several authors (Assagioli, 1965; Campbell, 1972; Hillman, 1983; Jantsch & Waddington, 1976; Jantsch, 1980; Jung, 1959, 1961; Lifton, 1976) attest to the power of the image as a vehicle that can both contain and communicate to others essential elements of the psychological or, more appropriately, psycho-spiritual experience of the self. From the perspective of human systems, images are tools that capture the emerging nature of a system as well as the evolving nature of the self.

Self and system demonstrate an interconnected pattern of mutually reinforced, reciprocal development that has been theoretically described by writers demonstrating the breadth of systemic approach (e.g., Churchman, 1977) and those probing the depth of the structural foundation of the human psyche (e.g., Assagioli, 1965; Jung, 1959). Both the breadth of the systemic perspective and the depth of human experience are contained in the collective and intersubjective experiences as represented in the corporate images of organizations. Guiding images or ideal models serve as vehicles for achieving shared understanding regarding complex problems and can illuminate the steps in the transition from problem to resolution, from today's issues to tomorrow's potential.

Afterward 2017

Since the original publication of this article there has been some sustained focus on "spiritual development" within large organizations. Mitroff has remained a pioneer in this area, incorporating the spiritual values of managers into the process of establishing a corporate culture and mission. His practice of employing "spiritual audits" with organizations is captured in several recent volumes, and in particular, in Mitroff & Denton (2008).

The use of an imaging process to construct and articulate the interface between the subjective experiencing individual and conjoint collective organizational images continued to develop through repeated applications in a variety of contexts. This methodology gained considerable strength through the contributions of James Bugental, a leading American existential depth psychologist and my long time mentor and colleague. As both teacher and friend, Bugental helped me deepen the process of tapping into "guiding images" and "ideal models" that, while formed through qualities related to intuition and imagination, also "lived in the body." Bugental's (1987) constructs of "presence" as a whole body-mind-spirit process of moment-to-moment mindful awareness, and his careful exploration of "subjective searching" (Bugental & McBeath, 1995) as a vehicle for focusing subjective attention, awareness, and choice, were designed for application within the context of depth oriented psychotherapy. Judiciously applied to individual subjective experience within an organizational context, these constructs augmented and enriched the effective use of imagery. Expressing an interest in and understanding about psychosynthesis, Bugental described an important visit and conversations with Assagioli at his home in Florence that helped him further refine his perspective regarding existential, depth-oriented psychotherapy.

Finally, I would acknowledge the important contemporary contributions of neuropsychiatrist McGilchrist (2009). His comprehensive description of the functions of the hemispheres of the human brain highlight the power of intuition and the imagination in developing human potential, and their importance in transforming human culture. McGilchrist presents an integrated amalgam of science, philosophy and literature that identifies how these "right hemisphere-oriented" capacities carry the seeds of transformation and transcendence for the developing human being. Assagioli's psycho-spiritual perspective favors the full flowering of our human potential. McGilchrist offers documentation that those qualities, so well described in psychosynthesis, lie resonant within each of us as individuals and reside also in the "in-between" in our relationships with one another. Like Assagioli, McGilchrist advocates the application of these qualities as vital for the further transformation of human life, individually, organizationally, and as planetary citizens.

References

Assagioli, R. (1965). *Psychosynthesis.* New York: Viking.

Banathy, B. (1973). *Developing a Systems View of Education.* Seaside, CA: Intersystems Publications.

Bateson, G. (1979), *Toward an Ecology of Mind.* New York: Ballantine,

Bugental, J.F.T.(1987). *The Art of the Psychotherapist.* New York: W.W. Norton.

Bugental, J. F. T., & McBeath, B. (1995). "Depth existential therapy: Evolution since World War *II.*" In B. Bongar & L. E. Beutler (Eds.), *Comprehensive Textbook of Psychotherapy: Theory and Practice* (pp. 111–122). New York: Oxford University Press.

Campbell, J. (1972). *Myths We Live By.* New York: Bantam.

Checkland, P. (1981). *Systems Thinking, Systems Practice.* Chichester: John Wiley & Sons.

Churchman, C. W. (1977), *The Systems Approach and its Enemies.* New York: Basic Books.

Hillman, J. (1983). *Healing Fiction.* Barrytown, NY: Station Hill.

Jantsch, E., & Waddington, C. (1976). *Evolution and Consciousness.* Reading, MA: Addison-Wesley.

Jantsch, E, (1980). *The Self-Organizing Universe.* New York: Pergamon Press,

Jung, C. G, (1955). *Modern Man in Search of a Soul.* New York: Harcourt Brace Jovanovich.

Jung, C. G, (1959), *Aion: Researches into the Phenomenology of the Self.* Princeton, NJ: Bollingen Series, Princeton University Press,

Jung, C, G. (1961). *Memories, Dreams, Reflections.* New York: Random House.

Lifton, R. (1976). *The Life of the Self.* New York: Simon & Schuster.

Maturana, H., & Varela, F. (1980). *Autopoiesis and Cognition.* Boston: Reidel Publishing.

Maccoby, M. (1976), *The Gamesman.* New York: Simon & Schuster.

McBeath, B. (1986), *Exploring the Interface Between Human Systems and Human Beings: A Methodology for Characterizing Human Systems.* Saybrook Institute: San Francisco.

McGilchrist, I. (2009). *The Master and his Emissary: The Divided Brain and the Making of the Western World.* New Haven & London: Yale University Press.

Mitroff, I. I, (1983). *Stakeholders of the Organizational Mind.* San Francisco: Jossey-Bass

Mitroff, I & Denton, E., (2008), *A Spiritual Audit of Corporate America:*
a   *Hard Look at Spirituality, Religion and Values in the Workplace*. San
     Francisco: Jossey-Bass.

This article was revised by the author in 2017.

NOTE

―――――――――――
[1] *See Assagioli (1965) Chapter IV "Techniques" —Ed.*

Bruce McBeath, PhD, *is a clinical psychologist practicing in St. Paul and Red
Wing, MN. He has been active in the developing field of "psychology of aging,"
serving as a consultant to organizations and as a speaker and author. He was
previously a cofounder of the Psychosynthesis Institute of Minnesota and an
adjunct professor of psychology and human development at St. Mary's University
of Minnesota. His recent book* Reflections on Aging *is available through
Amazon.com.*

Setting the Captives Free:
A New Approach

Kathleen Denison

Individuals who have been imprisoned are usually thought of as society's untouchables. Persons convicted of crimes such as murder, rape, child abuse, drug sales, theft, and embezzlement are incarcerated with little expectation of rehabilitation, let alone healing. The "lockup" serves its purpose and removes the offender from the streets. Until released, the offender is far removed from the mind and heart of the average person.

My work as prison chaplain the last few years has brought me into the heart of the reality that exists behind the bars. Not only have I walked into the physical environment that is called "prison," but I have also walked into inner prison cells, and explored the depths of the psyche imprisoned there. This has been an exploration of the heart and of healing.

My work with prisoners has led to profound and dramatic changes in men and women who have been labeled "unredeemable." As I developed this work, I found that principles of Psychosynthesis assisted them in a process of psychic "liberation" which opened their inner selves to healing and enabled them to step from the darkness of their inner cells.[1]

In reflecting upon the relationship of the prisoner to the prison, it became clear that the outer prison environment actually mirrored the inner psychic environment of the inmates. Similarly, the inner psychic environment was reinforced by the outer setting.

The Outer Prison

A typical jail or prison environment is characterized by isolation from the outside world. Most jails or prisons are located in secluded spots and are surrounded by high barbed wire fences which clearly define the area that is set apart from the rest of society. Most inmates cannot see outside the prison building itself, since the bars on the windows and the frosted glass are intended to prevent any visibility to the outside. This seclusion is even more pronounced in some facilities which are designed to provide "outside recreation" in an entirely enclosed courtyard. Areas within the prison setting are securely locked and movement is limited. Visits from immediate family members are arranged for only a few hours on set days and phone calls are restricted. Incoming and outgoing mail is carefully monitored.

Inmates are classified according to their crimes and behavior, and are assigned to different levels of security. As an inmate becomes more threatening to the system, through a disregard of certain rules, greater isolation is imposed. A high security facility, for example, imposes the greatest isolation so that the risk of escape is minimized. Within the correctional system, segregation provides maximum seclusion as a form of punishment. An inmate is placed in a cold, dark cell with only a bed and a toilet. Visits from family are denied.

Almost all jails or prisons are devoid of beauty and natural light. Visually, prisons are ugly. Inappropriate color combinations assault the eye upon entering. A building may be painted yellow with black trim, or walls may be painted bright orange. Generally there are no trees, plants, or flowers within or around the building. The inmates are encased within smoke-filled rooms, surrounded by steel, concrete, and fluorescent lighting. There is no access to the healing aspects of nature. There is no room for beauty.

The sounds within the prison setting also assault the senses. The bang of steel doors or the loud clang of the bars sliding back into a locked position is constant. The barrage of abusive language is continual. Noise blares endlessly from multiple TVs. Loud speaker announcements successfully interrupt any meaningful speaking or listening. The buzz of fluorescent lights is constant. Solitude is not an option.

The prison environment is highly structured and highly controlled. Security is primary. Rules which safeguard this security dominate the needs of individual persons. The guards enforce the rules. These officers are predominantly young with minimal education and undeveloped social skills. They take their power seriously. In order to safeguard their own security, their power must be equated with control. The guards control the movement and monitor the behavior of the inmates. They carry the keys which can open or lock an area. The degree of an inmate's freedom, therefore, is dependent upon the cooperation of the guards. The inmates must acquiesce to the defined structure of rules and power in order to survive.

The prison culture is characterized by a lack of the feminine—a lack of feelings, sensitivity, and compassion. This is true for the inmates as well as the guards. Caring and sensitivity are considered a sign of weakness. Since such "weakness" results in the loss of power and status, toughness and hardness become the norm. Guards who are too compassionate cannot enforce the rules and are disdainfully considered by colleagues to be "inmate lovers." Inmates who do not have a tough exterior are easy prey to the demands of the tougher inmates. Their few commissary supplies are stolen and they are subject to constant harassment by other inmates.

Key to the prison culture is the attitude of the "keepers" toward the "kept." The attitude toward the inmate is often punitive and demeaning. Little respect is shown the inmate. Incarceration is seen as a just punishment. Verbal abuse and physical abuse between inmate and inmate and between guard and inmate are common. The inmates are treated like children, punished for the slightest disregard of a rule no matter how insignificant it is. Since everything is taken away from the inmate, anything needed must be requested from the guards or administration. There is no room for initiative or autonomy. The inmate is constantly told what to do and how to do it. The inmate no longer has to make any choices. All food, clothing, and shelter are provided. Dependency is fostered. Autonomy is neither encouraged nor tolerated.

As I worked with inmates, I discovered that although the dehumanized and dependent setting of the prison system is on one level highly uncomfortable, on another level it is familiar. Such a destructive and regressive environment is chosen by the individual on an unconscious level because it is familiar and therefore safe. Most inmates have experienced profound dehumanization in their own families, and the prison environment simply replays that history. Dependency is also chosen on an unconscious level because it means that care is finally being provided. In addition, the external pressures of life are temporarily removed. The inmate no longer has to deal with paying the rent or negotiating family and child demands.

The Inner Prison

Mirrored in the external environment of the prison setting, the inner prison begins to take shape. The parts of the individual that are considered unacceptable are repressed, isolated, and locked up. As in the external environment, the more threatening the aspect of the personality, the more restricted it becomes. The most dangerous subpersonalities are locked away, doing time in segregation and isolated from other aspects of the personality.

The inner prison environment is also highly structured and controlled. The inner psyche sets up rules to guarantee safety and appoints guards to monitor and enforce the rules and maintain control. Just as in the outer prison, the degree of freedom becomes dependent upon co-operation with the guards and acquiescence to the rules.

The inner guards take their positions very seriously. They will not allow themselves to experience compassion and sensitivity lest they lose power or become too identified with the "prisoner." In order to keep the prisoner in line, the inner guards may be punitive and demeaning. Internal verbal abuse may go on constantly.

Consequently, the core attitude toward the Self becomes punitive, restrictive, and harsh. Self-hate is predominant, and guilt and fear reinforce the hate. There is no room for compassion. There is virtually no real sense of self-worth and no experience of self-acceptance. There is also an innate distrust of Self, just as the prison guard distrusts the inmate.

Because the psychic guards carry the keys and hold the power, they become the "visible self" of the inmate, which is tough, macho, and intolerant of weakness, In essence, the outer system, the prison guards, and the inner guards collude to keep the "inner self safe." Ostensibly, the world is being kept safe and protected from the inner "monster."

But who lives in the inner cell? Each of my experiences with inmates has demonstrated that a Wounded Child lives behind the bars. This child is in pain. As I have progressed through this work, a consistent pattern has emerged. The inmates have usually experienced some sort of profound loss, rejection, abuse, or abandonment at a point of critical emotional vulnerability. This usually occurred when the inmate was a small child or young adolescent and experienced feelings of loss, abandonment, loneliness, terror, rejection, or emptiness. The psychic pain became so overwhelming that this part of the self was locked up to be kept safe from pain; the ability to feel was, and continues to be, anesthetized. The Child becomes isolated behind a wall of frozen feeling. He or she is placed in segregation. No one comes in and no one goes out. The Child is trapped and held hostage by the psyche's fear of pain. The walls are thick, cold, and unfeeling. The inner cell is dark and lonely.

Just as the inmate in the outer prison environment is subjected to a constant barrage of noise and abusive language, so too the inner child is constantly harassed by inner messages taken from parents and society. These messages interrupt any positive sense of worth and reaffirm feelings of worthlessness. The inner child begins to connect only with other psychic inmates who are also imprisoned and who have grown up with the same inner messages. The messages from the psychic prison culture are clear and consistent: "You are no good;" "I will not let you forget what you have done;" "You do not deserve to be trusted, loved, or cared for;" "You are worthless;" "You get what you deserve;" "It was something you did that got you here;" "You are an animal."

Time and time again, however, as I work with the Child imprisoned within, I discover that the Child is basically good—sensitive, spontaneous, and linked to the positive aspects of the Self. The Child is not a monster, but a victim who has been traumatized at a crucial development stage. In fact, it is acute psychic sensitivity that made the early formative experiences so traumatic.

In order to ensure the Child's survival, a Benevolent Judge orders protective custody. The original intention is one of survival and concern. The Child is put in a place where it will not be hurt again. This action is a direct indication of the psyche's drive toward health and wholeness. Although the protection is originally a loving act, what protects eventually imprisons. The protective mechanism cuts the Child off from further nourishment and he or she cannot grow. The positive aspects of the Self cannot be sufficiently developed.

The jailers, or guards, in the psyche simply carry out the sentence issued by the Benevolent Judge. The inner cell is tightly monitored so that the Child cannot leave, lest the pain be touched again. Security is primary and the jailers are constantly on guard for danger to the system. The Benevolent Judge is removed from the scene and the Child has no advocate.

My work with Philip, a 24-year-old man in prison, helps to illustrate the power of the jailer and the vulnerability of the Wounded Child within. I first met Philip in segregation. He was a victim of repeated beatings by his alcoholic father. He witnessed his father rape his mother and sister—both at his father's insistence that he watch. When Philip was 8, his mother turned her children over to the state since she planned to remarry. From that point on, Philip lived in numerous children's institutions. As he grew older, he began skipping school regularly. He became a chronic truant who was continually ordered by the court to spend time in a center for juvenile delinquents. He would escape from the center, steal a car for a joy ride, and then end up serving additional time in the correctional center. This pattern matured into incarceration for car theft and drug usage. At the time I met him, Philip had served more than two years in medium security at a state prison. Shortly after we began to work together, he wrote me:

> I don't really know if I can write you without you or myself getting into trouble. See, I've been here for two years and ten months and all of the time I never talked to anyone about my problems because I am scared to get

279

close to anyone in here ... I can write my problems and my feelings down on paper better than I can talk about them. Because I am so used to it and after I write them down I read it over and over and then I throw it away so no one will find it. Some of the time I feel like crying but I hold it in, and hide it. And now that I am down here in lockup, I can think a lot better now because I'm alone and if I don't want to talk to anyone, I can just lie here and pretend like I'm sleeping.

I don't really know why I am writing you this letter 'cause I've been here so long! Have you ever heard of the saying that when you get hurt so many times you put up a wall so no one can get in? Well, my wall is up so high that it even scares me because if I don't open up to someone, then when I get out of here, I'm still going to have everything still inside of me, and believe me, I don't want to come back to this place.

After Philip was returned to the prison dorm, I was able to meet with him in a private room. I was concerned about his appearance. He looked hardened and unkempt. He explained that he had stayed in bed the last three days—not wanting to eat or even take a shower. He talked about his rage at his father. He had just learned that his father was coming back to live with his sister (the one the father had raped). All he could do was think about getting out and beating up his father. Nothing else mattered.

Philip and I began to work in meditation and guided imagery. He imagined an 8-year-old boy who was kept in a room by an older angry youth who would bully him. The younger boy felt lost, lonely, and rejected. He was sitting slumped in a dark corner. The younger boy wanted to talk to the bully, but his attempts were met with anger and physical abuse. The bully didn't want anyone to get near the boy. He kept him in the room and made it impossible for him to get out.

Philip's story is very typical of those told by the men I encountered at the prison. It illustrates the premise that the positive aspects of the psyche are imprisoned within inner cells, just as the individual is imprisoned within the institution. The wounded parts of the person contain incredible potential but he is too fearful and feels these parts are too despicable to approach or retrieve.

Another inmate, sentenced for selling drugs, wrote:

I feel like crying a lot, fighting back the pain and hurt I feel so much of . . . not willing to deal with the parts in me that are rotten, that I feel ashamed of . . . The guilt is so overwhelming, so terrifying . . . I'm always thinking, can I find what of me is lost, or what is broken? I'm really just a child with so much to learn, so much to do, with no time, no freedom.

Given the main components of the inner prison, it becomes quite apparent that the setup of the prison not only reinforces the inner wound but also makes real rehabilitation almost impossible. Ironically, the prison system seems to successfully recreate the inmate's past childhood environment of severe confinement and abuse. It gives credibility to the voices of self-negation, and encourages the power of the inner jailer. The inner child feels that the abuse is deserved. The prison system acts like a magnetic pull dragging the inmates back into what is most worthless and condemned within themselves. They are not trusted or believed. They are kept in their place within the inner prison. One 30-year-old male in a high security facility asked, "Why does this place put so much energy into making you feel like a nobody—an animal who can't escape his past? Why don't they put energy into making you feel human—giving you another shot? It's so frustrating in here because even though I change inside, I'm still treated the same way."

The Healing Process

Since the early world of the inmates was so unsafe, the introduction of a new inner environment which is safe is essential to the healing process. Inmates are first taught to imagine an environment where they feel safe and accepted. Often built upon childhood memories of a favorite place, their new place becomes a haven to which they can return, through imagination, at any time. Because it's safe, eventually this place becomes the inmate's "home base." As one inmate put it, "I'm in touch with who I really am. There are no cons. Wherever I am inside, I'm faced with it immediately. In this place I can only be myself."

Many imagine this place to be outside, in a setting of natural beauty such as at the ocean, or on a mountain. Others remember grandfather's attic, or their own bedrooms. The place provides a protective, serene environment where an individual can be alone, if desired, and content, without fear of intrusion. The unmasked self begins to have a place to "be." The place provides the security previously found only within the inner cell. Unlike the prison environment, the safe place emerges with color, light, warmth, and beauty.

Once the safe place is established, the inmate can begin to explore memories of past pain and rejection. What is wounded within can begin to be faced. Structured imagery sequences and attention to feeling begin to evoke this.

Working with inmates, I discovered that following a feeling was essential to the process of finding a wound. The frozen feeling, or wall of pain, insulates the wound within the psyche. As long as feelings are shut down, wounds can be ignored, even if life continues to be controlled by them. In an accepting environment where feelings are welcomed, the pain can begin to be experienced. Through the attention of compassionate listening, the frozen wall of feelings melts and flows to the source of the wound like a healing stream.

In ministering to individual inmates, I listen to the feelings under their words and their stories. I then invite them to explore a particular feeling such as anger, guilt, or loneliness, and encourage them to express it through words, images, or drawings. For example, the inmate is invited to explore an image evoked in response to the question, "What is the hurting part of you?" or "Who is the part of you that feels guilty, angry, lonely, etc.?" Invariably, the image evoked is that of a hurting child or adolescent. The inmate is then encouraged to dialogue with the hurting part and to listen to the feelings of the Child who has been isolated within the psyche.

Eventually, when it is safe enough, the inmate is able to actually feel the feelings and not just identify them. The use of imagery gives the inmate a means to explore the intensity of feelings that have long been buried. At the same time, imagery bypasses a mental exploration, which can define but does not feel. The combination of feeling and image is a very powerful means of arriving quickly at what is most in need of healing and acceptance within the psyche.

Part of the structured imagery process also involves recreating former experiences of loss, abandonment, and rejection. Through guided imagery, the inmate is taught to step back and to begin to feel compassion for the part that is hurting. The inmates are given very explicit directions on how to take the Wounded Child to the safe place, and to image holding him, allowing tears to come. They are told to "give the child what is needed." The Child guides the inmate in the healing process.

After the inmate has identified the Wounded Child, he or she is taught to form a relationship with the Child. A bond is established which is compassionate and tender. After this relationship is firmly established, a new relationship is introduced. The inmate is invited to call in a Divine Friend to work with the Wounded Child. This Friend is experienced as unconditionally loving and accepting. The Friend will be either masculine or feminine depending upon the inner psychic needs of the individual. The gender is not prescribed but emerges through the meditation exercises. The Divine Friend image reinforces the channel of love developed through the relationship with the Child.

The Divine Friend becomes an outer figure which offers unconditional acceptance and love. The Friend is unafraid of feelings, encourages their expression, and makes no judgment about the outer self. Most frequently, the Divine Friend is experienced as Jesus or as Mary, the mother of Jesus, or as an angel. Many of the inmates have had early Christian training, and the request to call the Friend evokes these images. Crucial to this process is the visualization of a personal divinity.

This figure is not equivalent to the traditional guide in Psychosynthesis. The Divine Friend brings love rather than wisdom. It is an image used to reinforce a healing relationship and to evoke a renewed relationship to divine energy. The divine is invited to enter the core of the wounded self. The Divine Friend is able to model an ideal of loving acceptance. Healing proceeds as that core is further energized. The Divine Friend brings both light and warmth to the darkness of the inner prison. The inmate experiences the healing, the light, and the warmth. Change takes place from the center outward.

The impact of this work on inmates has been striking. Most noticeable is the melting effect outlined above. The Divine Friend provides a deeper dimension of safety so that frozen feelings can be softened. An example of this is shown in the story of Karen.

Karen, an inmate in a women's correctional facility, was charged with sexually molesting her child. As is usually the case, she herself was the victim of incest. Through imagery, Karen visualized the 7-year-old victim of incest who was imprisoned within her. This child felt dirty, guilty, and unlovable. Since Karen was in need of feminine support and understanding,

I suggested that she invite Mary the mother of Jesus to come and be with her. Karen agreed to this. Mary came as a Divine Friend and gently invited Karen to allow herself to feel the guilt and pain of the child. As she began to cry from experiencing the pain, she also experienced the love and tenderness of Mary who held the 7-year-old child in her arms.

Previously, Karen had had difficulty getting close to the pain within her. With Mary present, she could let herself feel it because she felt safe. Tears came as they had never come before. After this experience, Karen struggled with why Mary would love her when her own mother hadn't. I encouraged her to express her struggle to Mary directly. She did this and her relationship with her Divine Friend deepened. On her own, she began to spend time with her inner 7-year-old in her safe place. Often she asked Mary to be present. Over a short period of time, Karen became less anxious, more connected to feeling, and more at peace with herself. She began to possess a new inner strength and softness. Equipped with a new sense of self-worth, she began to ask her Divine Friend to explore with her the parts of herself which she had imprisoned because they were unacceptable.

Later she wrote to me,

> I learned that there are many parts of yourself you can count on when you need them. They are always there and you cannot try to suppress them or pretend they do not exist . . . I have met many of these personalities and I have found I enjoyed meeting them and getting to know them. I saw that if I cannot like them, I can at least accept them. I grew to like these parts of myself and in doing so, grew to like me.
>
> I have never trusted a woman completely before this time. It was surprising for me to trust a woman. I also learned that I could trust myself, that there are limits to my anger and other such emotions. In dealing with what I have always considered violent emotions, I now figure I can deal with all the emotions. The most important thing I learned is to feel. Sometimes I do not like what I am feeling hut I could never go back to not feeling at all. I have found a freedom and peace I have never had before this time.

There is no question that this system evokes deep inner healing. The core is found, brought to a safe place, and engaged in a process that allows feelings to be felt. The reactivation of the feelings allows the inmate to move into a healing relationship with the wounded self. The introduction of the Divine Friend reinforces that healing relationship and evokes connection with the core self. The net effect is liberation from the inner prison.

Externally observed positive changes in behavior are corroborated by the inmates' own experience of themselves. Each of them has reported a significant improvement in the ability to accept who they are and what they have done. Since it is the deepest core which has been energized, the process does not stop with the end of the actual work an inmate may have done with me. The process continues with the life of its own that comes from the inner relationships to the Wounded Child and the Divine Friend. The inmates speak, "When you open, you get pain

... but you feel the warmth and love that is inside ... Who could go hack? Something else is coming out ... it cannot be stopped because it is so real."

Postscript (2017)

After many years of working within this approach I realized that it isn't just prison inmates who can most benefit from it. Granted, it's important to note that the psyches of the incarcerated are particularly receptive to the "bright shadow" waiting to be liberated within them. Yet work with people in recovery from addiction, clients who have known childhood trauma, and even seemingly well-adjusted folks seeking greater spiritual connection, are all similarly empowered by this process.

When an inner safe place is established and a personalized form of Divine Love is then invited to emerge from within the psyche, all aspects of the imprisoned, unacceptable parts of ourselves can be graciously received. This personalized love models how to attend to the feelings and needs of these captive aspects in us in healing and healthy ways. Over the years I have witnessed this Spiritual Friend take the form of a religious figure from a myriad of spiritual traditions, an animal, or even an aspect of nature. This Spiritual Friend always embodies a presence of love and healing in a form that the client can most easily and deeply receive.

My website www.findinghealingwithin.com offers online courses and a structure for this process.

Note

¹ This is not to say that major systemic penal reform is not also necessary. Rather, my intention in this article is to focus upon the inner prisoner who can be touched, healed, and liberated. This can be achieved through the use of imagery, drawing, careful attention to feelings, the establishment of an inner safe place, and a relationship with an inner Divine Friend.

Kathleen Denison *received her Masters degree in Applied Spirituality from the University of San Francisco in 1979. Her background includes spiritual direction, prison chaplaincy, teaching, and group facilitation. She is a certified clinical hypnotherapist. Ms. Denison is a gifted teacher with a visionary commitment to the development of unique healing tools combining spirituality and guided imagery. She is the originator of the* Finding Healing From Within *process, which has been taught to groups and individuals over the last three decades as a way to facilitate emotional healing. Kathleen currently works with individuals to help them connect to their own inner spiritual resources in order to experience well-being and joy in their lives.*

Birthing and Rebirthing
Peace-Building Communities:
Experiments in Social Psychosynthesis

Judith Bach and Helena Davis

In *Psychosynthesis: Individual and Social* Assagioli wrote:

> All human individuals and groups of all kinds should be regarded as elements, cells or organs (that is, living parts) of a greater organism which includes the whole of mankind. Thus the principle of, and the trend to, synthesis carries us from group to group in ever wider circles to humanity as an integral whole. The essential unity of origin, of nature and of aims, and the unbreakable interdependence and solidarity between all human beings and groups are a spiritual, psychological and practical reality. It cannot be suppressed, however often it may be negated and violated through the numberless conflicts in which men, foolishly and painfully, squander their precious energies and even deprive each other of the sacred gift of life. (1965, p. 9)

As spiritual beings, we are devoted to peace on an inner level. We have skills and knowledge which enable us to move toward peace within ourselves and, in a small way, to promote world peace by contributing positive attitudes and qualities to our global environment. Yet our experience shows us that this alone is not enough to create a peaceful world.

We who have begun to learn to create inner peace can apply our knowledge to wider foci; we can use these same skills and experiences to help families, communities, and institutions create peace.

We have chosen to write this article because we strongly believe that the most effective way to bring peace to our world is through the principle of synthesis. Ferrucci (1982) describes synthesis within the psyche as the harmonization of diverse elements into successively greater wholes. Through the process of attaining inner wholeness through "balance and synthesis of opposites" (Assagioli, 1965), we attain not only a state of inner harmony, but also the capacity to do our work more effectively in the world.

We have worked with this principle of synthesis within individuals and in process groups. We are convinced that it can be applied to promote peace in families and communities as well. Thus, our present endeavors involve the development of models and interventions which will help communities grow and flourish in the direction of greater creativity and harmony:

It is imperative that we encourage the growth of peaceful communities in order to promote world peace. If we are to achieve world peace, we cannot address our problems on a few levels and ignore the remainder. We cannot teach the skills of peace just to ourselves or to mediators and government leaders; education must take place at all levels, from the smallest child in a poor rural village to the most powerful heads of states. The global transformation we are trying to achieve can only take place if the values of peace are woven into the fabric of Earth's cultures. If such systemic change is to occur, skill levels and awareness must increase from the grass roots upwards—from the intrinsic motivation of ordinary citizens to the moral imperatives they can engender in the heads of state. (Davis, 1986, pp. 1-2)

As we move toward synthesis in our own lives, sooner or later we feel the need to transform the context in which we live; we yearn to transform it to support continued synthesis for ourselves and others. As we and our immediate environment move closer to synthesis, the energy released creates a ripple effect that is felt through the other systems to which we belong: from self, to family, to community, to town, to state, to nation, to planet.

If we are to transform our communities to support further synthesis, how do we assess success? How do we discriminate which segments of the environment have evolved toward synthesis? Once we have identified the "evolutionary state" of a particular segment of the community at large, can we set realistic goals for transformation or determine the most effective interventions to achieve those goals?

This article explores the use of a model to study the evolution of communities. The model is briefly described and case studies are presented to demonstrate how it works.

Theory

In the same breath that we offer this model, we want to caution the reader about the danger of "pigeon-holing" or categorizing that is so prevalent in the field of psychotherapy these days. This same danger exists in relation to social systems. As we attempt to understand and work with communities, we must approach each group of people, not only with our skills and knowledge, but also with awe and humility as we join with others to reach toward the best within all of us.

Our model is based on Assagioli's (1965, p. 17) map of consciousness: the lower-unconscious realm, the personal or self-conscious realm, and the transpersonal or superconscious realm. It is not such a great stretch to parallel the unintegrated, lower-unconscious primitive and instinctual drives of an individual to a community in which the dominant mode of relating includes unconscious, unreflective, impulsive expressions of basic human drives. The self-conscious level is equivalent to consciousness, awareness, and the capacity to function adaptively and reflectively in daily life. For a community, it is the ability to mediate conflicts, to take responsibility, and to plan and achieve goals. The transpersonal level for a community is its capacity to uphold a value system that speaks to and lives a consciousness of the whole. Such values as co-operation, sharing, and good will are implicit in such a world view.

We must also be able to determine the "ego strength" and personal will development of a community. Ego functioning can be measured by how the community carries out its daily business. Does snow get removed? Are potholes filled? Is the mail distributed efficiently?[1]

The community psychosynthesist is, most effectively, a small group whose role is to evoke the creative spirit within the community in order that it may design its own future in the direction of stronger ego-functioning and spiritual psychosynthesis. From this perspective, the "design group" can be seen as the temporary I-consciousness of the community, with the capacity to observe, reflect, and choose appropriate courses of action without being caught up in limited identifications (Assagioli, 1965). Throughout this process, it is essential for the design group to encourage continually the development of a healthy community I-consciousness. We are defining "community I-consciousness" as the capacity of a critical mass of the members of the community to disidentify from their own narrow viewpoints and to work toward the betterment of the whole.

It is through the process of design itself; that is, through creating new organizations and reorganizing old ones, that peace building can happen. Through consensus methodologies and group creative thinking, each member of the community not only has the opportunity to participate in the process of design, but also to learn how to achieve harmony in group interaction. For such a transformative process to happen, it is essential that the initial design group hold the attitude of sensitivity and concern for the inclusion of all of the members of the larger group. Decision making must be approached with creativity and concern for the whole and the process of decision making must be considered as important as the product.

The group's concern must be that everyone experiences freedom of action and thought. Each point of view must be contained within the whole. There must be a wise tolerance of each person's beliefs. No one has the right to interfere with even the humblest person's belief system or to influence personal opinion. Any other attitude will lead to distortion and dissension. The end must never justify the means. The secret behind such an "ideal" group model is that it is precisely the differences that, if handled creatively, can lead to harmony, not only in relationships, but also in terms of purpose and goal orientation. So long as unity exists on the level of purpose, differences in details can—and must—be worked out. As the design group learns to work harmoniously and creatively, it becomes the model for the rest of the community as different groups take over parts of the design process that pertain to their own interests. We believe that the process of self-organization, using consensus methodologies, is self-empowering for people and is truly transformative on both group and individual levels.

Once the community has achieved a relative degree of personal (ego) integration and the potent organizations or subsystems within the community are reaching higher values, then the community has begun to move into a state of self-transcendence, or spiritual psychosynthesis. By this time, there are enough individuals to take responsibility for the spiritual direction of the community. A critical mass has been achieved that, in the long run, can affect all of the members of the community, whether or not they are consciously participating in this evolutionary process.

Case Studies

From Chaos to Co-operation—The first case study looks at an elementary school selected in 1982 as the pilot site for a training program to provide teachers and students with conflict management and mediation skills. This pilot program acted as the catalyst which enabled the school to strengthen its I-consciousness and thereby synthesize its diverse elements into successively greater wholes. As synthesis occurred, harmony and creativity increased. In two years, the school's ambience changed from chaotic, rugged individualism to joyful co-operation.

The school is located in a low-income urban neighborhood and students come from modest, single-family dwellings and city-subsidized apartments known as "the projects." Students and staff represent approximately 15 nationalities or ethnic groups and speak an equal number of languages. At first glance, one is immediately aware of a great many Latinos, Blacks, Filipinos, and Pacific Islanders.

The youngsters are very active and the playground is too small to adequately accommodate their energy. In perpetual motion, students often bump into each other; they seem like molecules bounding in a hot frying pan. The noise is almost deafening. It is no wonder that the principal reports that more conflicts occur on the playground than anywhere else.

Upon returning to class, students find it difficult to settle down and work because they are still carrying the frustrations from incidents which occurred outside. It is difficult to do anything more than to survive one day at a time when classrooms are crammed with 35 to 40 active youngsters, all of whom have special needs, Children compete for space and scarce materials, as well as the teacher's attention. Many children lack adequate nourishment and sleep; they need far more affection and security than they can hope to get at home. Spending 30 minutes on the campus evokes such phrases as, "law of the jungle," "every man for himself," "sink or swim," and "survival of the fittest."

This community had little to offer its members in 1982. Physically, the building was adequately lit and heated; there was ventilation, there was pleasing visual stimulation. However, there was a severe lack of playground and classroom space. Texts and basic tools such as pencils, crayons, and scissors were also in short supply.

Emotionally, this community needed help. Most feelings emitted were negative. Many adults and children felt isolated, irritated, discouraged; they perceived themselves as being harassed by peers, other community groups, and the central administration. Conflict among students and between students and teachers happened in almost every classroom, every hour. In the teachers' lunchroom, faculty gathered in small cliques to gossip and complain; some sat by themselves. There was no positive sense of community; there was no sense of hope. Students' behavior at lunch and recess was similar. There seemed to be no sense of co-operation or belonging to a community. There was only survival.

For the most part, planning and decision making took place at the administrative level. While some effort was made to include staff in decision making and cooperative projects to improve the school, these overtures were often met with cynicism and apathy. A small handful of staff did most of the work. Planning in the classroom was reactive; it often took place in a moment of crisis or a few minutes before "zero hour" because life in the classroom seemed to be one crisis after another.

Many staff and students felt isolated from the community at large and, in fact, did not feel that there was a community. Communication, for the most part, was either manipulative or aggressive and was delivered in the form of verbal put-downs or memos. Normal conversation between adults and students or among adults tended to be superficial. Staff seemed to have little sense of purpose other than their common goal of trying to survive one more day by getting all the paperwork done and going home without a splitting headache.

The spiritual aspect of the school was not apparent. There seemed to be no sense of common purpose or cooperation. One observer was reminded of a saying: "When you're up to your eyeballs in alligators, it's hard to remember that the initial objective was to drain the swamp." At this stage in its development, Assagioli might have said this community was dominated by lower unconscious dynamics, without a strong "I," or centeredness, and without a sense of alignment with superconscious qualities and values.

In 1982, we convened a meeting to introduce the staff to a training program. After formal introductions, teachers participated in an exercise in which they described what school was like for them. All descriptors were negative. Next, teachers offered descriptors about how they would like the school to be. Finally, as we reviewed the second group of statements with the group, they identified which things could be changed and which things they most wanted to change. Increased discipline and less fighting were at the top of the list. Faculty also expressed a strong need for affirmation for staff and students and the need to feel like part of a community. A short time later, the principal and a small group of teachers were trained as leaders for the new conflict management program. In effect, this group became the I-consciousness of the school community.

After intensive work with students and staff during the 1982-83 school year, not only did the training program flourish and begin to function independently, but the school community as a whole used its new skills to create a community that worked interdependently to fulfil common needs and goals. Indeed, the entire school environment seemed far more positive than it had in the fall of 1982.

According to final program evaluations, the most notable changes occurred in the types of goals set by individuals and the community at large. People were no longer interested just in their own survival; they wanted to improve the quality of life for everyone. Students and staff, alike, expressed wants and needs assertively about 80 percent more frequently than in 1982. Listening skills improved almost as much. On the playground, which once seemed like an armed camp, student mediators complained about not having enough work to do. Adult playground monitors looked a little bored rather than frazzled. Classrooms were calmer and students settled into the business of learning. Relationships between students and teachers improved significantly and classrooms seemed more like cohesive groups than mere collections of individuals. On the whole, staff responded to adversity in pro-active, problem-solving modes rather than complaining or gossiping and feeling powerless. Faculty and student groups spent less time arguing and complaining; they devoted time and energy to thinking of new ways to improve the school environment so that it would support everyone's growth efforts. This school became a community where individuals and groups could determine their own needs and initiate their own changes in response to those needs.

In Search of Spiritual Identity—Our second case study is about a small New England village community which we will call Cranfield. Cranfield, with its population of 800, can be viewed as a community that is in search of its spiritual identity and collective consciousness, reflected in such values as good will and cooperation.

If you drive into Cranfield, you are likely to be on the other side of town before you know it. The ambience is New England white clapboard (with a few brown and green houses thrown in for variety), the obligatory spartan white church, general store, and post office. Next to the general store beside the river is the library.

The community is rural-residential, with several working farms. There are two lakes which attract a summer population, increasing the town size to about 2,000 each summer. This population is a strong subgroup, coming primarily from New York City and the Boston area. Cranfield is in one of the major cultural areas in the East, featuring music, dance, and theatre in the summer. As a result, the area contains a heterogeneous population of intellectuals, artists and writers, and "old-timers," leading to a greater level of sophistication among the villagers than one would find in otherwise similar New England towns.

In the business district of the village, there is a general store; a luncheonette, managed by a therapeutic farm community for former mental and drug patients; a New Age bookstore, a car repair garage, and a combination health food and wooden toys store. There is also a thriving cottage industry in the community. For example, one young couple runs a successful goat cheese farm. Another family sells maple syrup, makes and repairs musical instruments, and plays for dances in the area. There are also potters, artists, odd-job men and women, carpenters, teachers, psychotherapists, secretaries, store clerks, and construction workers.

At this point in the town's life, there is an integration process happening between the various factions of the community. Fifteen years ago there were schisms between the oldsters and the newcomers; today such separations have been largely healed. At a planning board meeting recently, an old-timer was heard to say that the community must be open to the fact that the town is changing and that new people are moving in. This statement was in dramatic contrast to what this resident said five years ago when she was very fearful about change and resistant to alterations in the town.

If we hope to cooperate in the evolution of our communities, we must reframe our attitudes about instability, or crisis. These crisis points happen organically in all living systems and almost invariably precede and accompany growth (Jantsch, 1980). How the system responds to crisis or instability determines whether or not pathology or synthesis will result. For example, pathology can occur when the pain from crisis is suppressed. Conversely, when pain and difficulty are acknowledged and consciously worked with, there is an opportunity for integration and synthesis. While a small community allows for more cohesive decision making and action than a large complex social system, it is also more subject to shock waves generated by crisis situations.

In most communities, when crisis occurs, the ensuing polarizations often take years to heal. This was also true of Cranfield, until one person, the minister, moved to town. How he helped heal one crisis and contributed to the evolution of the community to a new level of con-sciousness is a powerful example of the positive power of one individual in a community. In the early seventies, a group of young people moved to town who were interested in buying land and becoming self-sufficient. The old-timers had become paranoid toward these young people, fearful that they would introduce drugs into the community. Had this situation run its course without the intervention of the minister, the healing, if it had happened at all, might have taken years. With his intervention, the illness was aborted. He invited the young people to participate in a monthly "alternative life-style supper" in the church basement in order to meet and inform other community members of their intentions and plans. He then invited everyone in town to attend these suppers to discover what "alternative life style" was all about. After about six months, a monthly community supper evolved out of this idea which,

15 years later, continues. It is a time for old and young, traditional and non-traditional members of the community to eat together and participate in a program after the supper.

Since that time, such active, conscious interventions in the ongoing life of the community have been applied in a fairly regular manner by a design group. As community designers, our approach has been to identify, draw forth, and enhance the most evolutionary possibilities that exist in the community and, at the same time, facilitate the integration of these possibilities into the community as a whole.

Our first intervention was to invite 40 people to a community-building meeting. To our astonishment, 42 people showed up on a blustery, rainy evening. This group ranged in age from 11 to 90 and included both those whose families had lived in town for generations and newcomers to the community.

First, we asked each person to share what he or she felt about the community. The effect was a warm, group-building experience. We then asked people to think about the values they would like to see upheld and worked for in the town. "Brotherhood," "sharing," "the spirit of cooperation" were some of the statements expressed. And, finally, we asked the group to respond to the question, "What do you think needs to happen in this town as an expression of these values?" Ideas such as a community garden, transportation for the elderly, a community bulletin board, and a children's play group emerged in response to this question.

We then created working groups around each of these central initiatives. These groups met over a period of time to actualize these projects. Some of the projects materialized quickly, some more slowly, and some have yet to be realized. The most powerful aspect of the meeting was the message that we could effect change if we mobilize the will of the group in relation to a stated value system, a phenomenon often experienced in psychosynthesis psychotherapy.

Another intervention of the design group was to initiate an annual "I Love Cranfield Day"—an event that was built around a theme that expressed some aspect of good will. The first such event was called "A Festival of the Earth." This was a day of celebration of the planet, ecological principles, and sound energy use and planning. The seed was planted. Just one month later, the Cranfield Energy Committee was formed, which became one of the most effective in the state.

Within the community, there has grown an increasing sense of global consciousness, linked to concerns about nuclear proliferation and peace-education efforts. At a meeting of community members in 1985, it was suggested that this group of 20 people focus prayers and healing visualization on Ethiopia. The issue was raised by several people that perhaps we had better concern ourselves with poverty at home. The discussion continued all evening. The questions raised and the ongoing discussions were crucial to the establishment of seeds of global consciousness within the community.

One of the most important dynamics happening in the community accords with Banathy's (1984) statement that "traditional values, transcendent values, and individual values are dynamically interrelated with design to form unique amalgams of humanly purposed systems" (pp. 3-23). The current challenge in Cranfield is to integrate the emergent values, as represented by the New Age group, with individual and traditional values. The New Agers introduced a new crisis and opportunity for growth when they started moving into town about seven years ago. Although their belief systems are divergent, they are principally united around a suspicion of traditional religious practice and a commitment to a holistic lifestyle, such as health food, meditative practices, and alternative forms of healing. They have a deep commitment to spiritual growth, whatever form that takes for them individually. Many traditional-thinking townspeople have had their ideas stretched throughout this process; the New Agers are also learning that they can be as "dug in" and separative as anyone else. However, the integration is beginning to occur.

An example of how this polarity became resolved on a higher level of integration is the general store. (See *The Balancing and Synthesis of Opposites*, Assagioli, 1972.) A good general store must be a confluence of all the strands in the community, satisfying material needs from cleanser to soup to nails. Fifteen years ago, an elderly couple ran the store. It was a traditional old-style country store. When they retired, it was sold to a young man who ran it very ineptly. People stopped coming. To walk inside was a dreary experience. Then, with the first wave of New Agers, the store was bought by several members of this group who tastefully remodeled it, threw out the cleanser and the nails, installed health food and a restaurant, and waited for customers. They never came. An angry relationship developed between the owners and many of the villagers who refused to support it because they just weren't interested in health food; those who wanted health food were in the minority and couldn't support the store by themselves. It became clear to the design group that the store was not representing the community.

We tried to talk to the owners, who stubbornly defended their position, angered that the community was not supporting them. The position of many townspeople was, Why should we support a store that refuses to carry what we really want? Ultimately, the new owners gave up, and it was bought by a man in town who was committed to the needs of the whole village. The general store now stocks sugar and health food and is serving the needs of the whole community. This is a concrete expression of good will.

Another arena for the integration process has been the church itself. With a long tradition of community involvement, the church is one of the most powerful social forces in town. When the minister retired several years ago, the church was thrown into crisis. Up to that point, many newcomers had not felt that the church met their more eclectic spiritual needs, and so had stayed away. In order to take advantage of the possibilities for growth, we inaugurated a series of three meetings with the parish council, the governing body of the church. Through an envisioning process, members were encouraged to create their ideal church (See Assagioli, 1965, on the "ideal model"). These images were separated into spiritual images, such as purpose and values, and structural images, such as forms of worship and placement of pews. There was so much enthusiasm generated at these meetings that the church council itself became the design team that facilitated moving the process out into the larger church community in order to generate more communication and feedback. Small "cottage" groups met several times, led by members of the council, to discuss desired changes in the church, Out of these discussions, one of the members of the council put together the results, which became the basis of the "profile" provided to applicants for the ministry.

The primary effect of this process was to suggest to the church community that it could design its own future. The result was an unparalleled amount of energy and creativity in the group, the development of a lay ministry, and a series of weekly discussions before and after church services engaging the entire congregation. Discussions ranged from questions of whether or not baptism should be optional to deep spiritual sharing. The more traditional members of the church community and the New Agers began to discover in each other the same spiritual commitment, even though their forms of worship differed.

Further evidence of value-based changes in the community can be seen in the annual town meetings. A new spirit of good will has entered this process. For example, a bridge collapsed in the village. The issue arose about whether to use available state funds to build a concrete bridge or to raise money to build a more ecologically sound, aesthetic bridge. Five to ten years ago, this issue would have led to heated and probably explosive exchanges at the town meeting. The discussion during this particular meeting was good-humored and polite, each side presenting its case with clarity and reasonableness. The implications of the fact that the townspeople voted state funding down by a two-thirds majority are that the community must develop self-sufficiency, not as a retreat from the world, but so that it can cleave to the values that are important to it.

Another crisis was presented by a woman who moved to town with a long history of psychosis. She began to act out, wandering into people's houses, creating havoc in the stores, and disrupting meetings. Instead of calling the police, people tried to respond in a caring way. When this didn't work, an informal support network was formed. For example, the clerk in the store would call a psychotherapist in town to get advice, or just to vent. Finally, a group of community members, along with the woman, went to a family therapist outside the community, who demonstrated how to set the boundaries that she obviously needed. His comment to her when she complained about us to him was that this was his first experience of a community reaching out to try to resolve such a situation rather than just throwing her out. The learning for the community was "tough love."

At this time in Cranfield's history, the original design group has been absorbed into the community. There is now enough I-consciousness so that whenever there is a new crisis (and there are always crises), there is a spirit of willingness to work with it and learn from it. The people of Cranfield are becoming more open to facing their pain and vulnerability and, thereby, learning to become more loving and caring.

Conclusion

As we look at communities in general, it seems that they consist of fragmented aspects of the whole, much like an individual. What is often lacking in the dysfunctional community is an "I" with sufficient strength and knowledge to transform and integrate distorted subpersonalities or fragments. If psychosynthesists can intervene and facilitate transformation and I-consciousness on a social level, then other community members, through their own involvement and evolution, can nurture the growth of the community as a whole.

The implications of applying social psychosynthesis to disenfranchised communities, such as refugee groups, the rural or urban poor, and villages in the Third World countries, are far-reaching. The possibilities for empowerment of the most powerless are tremendous. The positive transformation of several small communities in a given area would certainly have a potent effect on the region in which they exist, and as regions change, their wider contexts change as well. Such change can occur peacefully through evolution rather than violently through revolution.

Where there is true good will, where people learn to co-operate in designing their own future, the ground is prepared for the emergence of a consciousness of the whole. One can no longer think only of self, but experiences the self as part of a greater landscape in which all of us are intimately connected, pulsing with the one Life that lies hidden within our hearts. It is when we move more into relation to that Life that we experience our connection with everything on earth. Imagine the effect of communities around the planet expressing these values of good will!

References

Assagioli, R. (1965). *Psychosynthesis: Individual and Social.* New York: Psychosynthesis Research Foundation. (Available as a pdf download from The Synthesis Center, download #0116.pdf at http://www.synthesiscenter.org/PDFgallery.htm —*Ed.*)

Assagioli, R. (1972). *The Balancing and Synthesis of Opposites.* New York: Psychosynthesis Research Foundation. (Available as a pdf download from The Synthesis Center, download #0129.pdf at http://www.synthesiscenter.org/PDFgallery.htm —*Ed.*)

Assagioli, R. (1977). *Psychosynthesis.* New York: Penguin.

Bach, J. (1985). *A Systems Study of the Psychology of a Small Community.* Unpublished Master's thesis, Saybrook Graduate School, San Francisco.

Banathy, B. H. (1984). *Systems Design in the Context of Human Activity Systems.* San Francisco: International Systems Institute.

Davis, H. (1986). *Culturally Relevant Conflict Management Training: A Participatory Design Approach.* Paper presented at the Third National Conference on Peacemaking and Conflict Resolution.

Ferrucci, P. (1982). *What We May Be.* Los Angeles: Tarcher.

Jantsch, E. (1980). *The Self-Organizing Universe.* New York: Pergamon.

Miller, J. G. (1978). *Living Systems.* New York: McGraw-Hill.

---

[1] Miller (1978) has developed a comprehensive scheme which derives from the assumption that all living systems, from the cell to the supra-national system, have sets of common properties, even though each system occupies a different hierarchical level. His Living Systems Theory provides us with an approach which is useful in assessing the ego strength of a social system (Bach, 1985).

Judith Bach, PhD, *co-founded the Psychosynthesis Institute of New York and the Berkshire Center for Psychosynthesis in Massachusetts, and presented seminars in the United States, Austria, Switzerland and Germany. In addition to her long-time private psychotherapy practice and her work as a Psychosynthesis trainer, Dr. Bach is a writer and artist, now retired.*

Helena Davis is a teacher, trainer, and pioneer in the field of conflict management and mediation training for children and youth. She explored ways to integrate psychosynthesis principles and techniques with both systems theory and interpersonal communications techniques to heal dysfunctional families and communities. She also has taught non-violent parenting workshops.

Four Questions for Guiding Peacework

Molly Young Brown

Let us imagine that we are sitting together at some sort of planetary conference. We have decided to consult our inner wisdom with some fundamental questions in order to better focus our deliberations. To prepare, we each assume a comfortable position, relaxed and alert, and take a few minutes to focus attention within ourselves. We close our eyes and breathe slowly and deeply. We gently move our awareness to a place deep inside where we each feel safe, private, quiet. In these inner places, we can ask questions and receive responses from our deepest wisdom. The answers may come in words, but more likely they will come in impressions of various kinds, such as visual images, sounds, sensations, emotions, tastes, smells, or combinations of these. So we prepare to be receptive, patient, and non-judgmental, simply observing whatever happens inside in response to each question.

We will ask ourselves four questions.[1] The exact wording is not so important as is the general direction of the inquiry:

1. The first question we ask is, "Where are humans now in our life as a species?" Or, "Where are we in the industrialized world now in relationship to our planet Earth?" After observing our inner responses, we attempt to draw or write about them.
2. Then we return to our meditative state and ask a second question: "What is our highest vision for ourselves as a species?" Or, "What is emerging for us now; what is our next step in growth?" Again, we draw or write out our responses.
3. Now, holding a sense of that vision, we ask a third question: "What is getting in the way of moving toward that vision or next step? What might hold us back?" After observing our responses, including our feelings about them, we draw or write them out once again.

4. We now prepare for the fourth and last question, taking time to quiet any emotional upsurges from the previous questions. Now we ask: "What do we need to develop, collectively, to move toward our potential? What qualities do we need now to move past our blocks?" Again, trusting whatever comes, we record our responses in drawing or writing.

If we were indeed sitting together at a planetary conference, we could now create a very rich synthesis of our wisdom, visions, and perspectives by sharing our various responses to the four questions. We could go on to brainstorm ways of developing needed qualities, and plan an array of activities to do so. These four questions can form the framework for peacemaking and transformative projects, just as they do for individual psychosynthesis.

This process can be used to address more specific situations, adapting the questions accordingly. For example, we might ask, Where are we Americans now in our relationship to Russia or North Korea? Or, Where is the peace movement now? What is our next step (Questions 1 and 2)? The four questions could also address one's personal involvement in peacework: Where am I now in my contribution to world peace? What is emerging for me in this work? What holds me back from a more effective or satisfying contribution? What do I need to develop?

These four questions represent an attitude toward growth which is of far greater significance than the specific methodology described here, however useful a tool it may be. This attitude is the willingness to perceive and work with all aspects of a situation—its here-and-now totality, its potentials, its problems, and its inherent growth challenge. Almost any problem or situation, from personal to planetary, may be elucidated by approaching it with this attitude and with these questions. Let's look at each question in more depth to discover its special value to the process of growth, and to see how its perspective contributes to a whole, balanced, and effective transformation.

Question 1: Where Are We Now?

The first question begins the process of conscious growth by exploring where we are now; its purpose is to expand and clarify our awareness of the scope, quality, and interrelationships of the current situation. We cannot hope to find solutions to problems—or even to know clearly what the problems are—unless we first give our attention to "where we are now." All too often, we react to a life crisis by putting on Band-Aids without apprehending the whole situation. Political leaders often react this way to national and world crises (sending arms to prop up an unpopular government or making threats against another nation). Personally or politically, the Band-Aids often do more harm than good because the needs and dynamics of the whole have not been taken into account.

Along with understanding the whole, we also need a sense of acceptance of the present situation, with all its pain and beauty. This does not mean resignation, only a realistic recognition of things as they are and a willingness to work from that base. Acceptance is always the first step, so that we begin from *where we actually are now*, not from where we would like to be.

I know from my own experience that the complexity and profound dys-functioning of our present world situation are part of what make it so difficult to acknowledge and accept where we are now as a species. It seems that whenever I begin to explore this question, to find out more about what our world situation is, the information I gather is so painful to accept that I often turn away from knowing more. So it seems important to balance the bad news with the good, to include in our explorations the sustaining, creative, and healing forces which are alive in our world as well as the forces that are destructive and confused. It is also necessary to breathe, to open our hearts, to take our time, and to return often to our inner place of quiet and peace.

There is a great deal of useful literature on the state of the planet that can be consulted as part of exploring Question 1. I recommend Naomi Klein's *This Changes Everything* and her follow-up book, *No Is Not Enough, YES! Magazine,* any of Richard Heinberg's books, *State of the World* reports from World Watch Institute, among many more books, articles, and videos.

Whatever study materials are used, it is very important to bring the information within oneself and to allow the unconscious to expand and synthesize it all. Only in this way can we create the living images we need to guide us intuitively and imaginatively toward new perspectives and commitments.

Question 2: What Is Our Vision for Ourselves?

The second question addresses an often neglected step, one that is essential to creative transformation. Our tendency seems to be to burrow into our problems without first noticing where it is we want to end up. What is on the other side of the problem? What is our vision of what is possible? By asking for a vision of our potential, or even more specifically for our next step, we allow ourselves to connect emotionally with a purpose or goal. A vision or sense of purpose can energize the problem-solving process; it gives us a positive reason for going through the often painful or tedious steps that lie before us.

Few of us have a coherent vision of what is possible for humanity. We tend to think in terms of absence of problems rather than holding visions of positive potentials. We may imagine peace, for example, as the absence of conflict rather than as an exciting, enjoyable arrangement in which conflict is used creatively. Of course, there are various ideological visions in the world, but many of these tend to divide and alienate one group from another. We need to synthesize our visions of the future and create images for the dynamic possibilities which a peaceful and sustainable world could hold, images which transcend particular socioeconomic systems or religions. Now, for perhaps the first time in history, large groups of people are becoming capable of this scope of vision. More and more people are awakening to the perception that our common humanity makes us more alike than different, and that our differences can enhance our world rather than threatening to destroy it.

So, like Question 1, Question 2 is worthy of time and attention. Resolving the problems which might come up in actualizing the visions comes later. First we must create and energize the visions, and commit ourselves fully to making them possible. Only then will we have the fire within—the will— to meet and resolve the inevitable problems.

We can create images of our potential in various areas of concern. We can imagine a world without war; we can imagine a world without hunger; we can imagine a world of self-reliant people living side by side within their own communities of faith and culture. We can create images of an adequate water supply for everyone, or of mobility without traffic noise and pollution. We can imagine people of the First, Second, and Third Worlds learning from one another and sharing resources equitably. One source of inspiration here is the quarterly journal *YES! Magazine,* that describes itself as "a cooperative project exploring and clarifying just what is involved in a humane sustainable culture—and how we can get there." Each thematic issue inspires hope and vision for me.

Broadly brushed images seem to work better than those tied closely to a form. Believing that we can only save the world through capitalism, for example, may prevent us from seeing the value and truths in other systems and approaches. At this early stage, we need to focus on qualities and flavors more than mechanisms and structures. And this is not easy for those of us trained to be "practical" by a technologically oriented educational system.

Our images need to be "realistic" as well, but we cannot limit our creativity with pessimism. It is better to have to revise an overly optimistic plan than to labor along under the limitations of "can't" or "that won't work." Unfortunately, realism is usually based on our collective past experience, which in turn has been determined by our collective beliefs of how the world works. The challenge of the second step in this process is to break free of our past limitations of belief and create new inspiration and hope for ourselves and our world.

Question 3: What Might Get in Our Way?

The third question now moves into the "problem" by uncovering the blocks to growth and change. Notice, however, that the question "What gets in our way? What might hold us back?" focuses the exploration on the specific blocks to the vision or goal of Question 2. This is very different from asking, "What's wrong with me (or us)?" When we ask what's wrong, we open up a "can of worms;" self-criticism, guilt, fear, self-blame, and denial can come wriggling out. By asking what gets in the way, on the other hand, we address patterns, beliefs, or problems which block the immediate path. There is no need for us to worry about limitations or faults which are not holding us back from our purpose.

Moreover, the question of what gets in our way implies no judgment; a pattern, behavior, or belief which blocks us in one endeavor may actually help us in another, or it may be a carry-over from the past when it did indeed serve our welfare. So we don't need to feel bad about ourselves; we only need to observe dispassionately what may be getting in our way and take steps to change that within the current circumstances.

It is a temptation for many of us when asking this question of ourselves to look for external conditions beyond our control to blame for our dilemma. Many people in the U.S., for example, apparently have used "peace is not possible as long as Muslim fanatics exist." Unfortunately, this brings the process to a dead stop and puts us into a position of constant belligerence. It is far more empowering to consider the ways in which we hold ourselves back. These can be changed; we have power over the ways we act and respond to life's demands. And generally when we take the responsibility (not the blame) for our self-imposed limitations, we find many of the external blocks disappearing as well. We can also often find ways to use constructively the blocks which don't disappear, or at least we can work around them.

About two years ago, I saw a television documentary about a small town in India which demonstrated these principles dramatically. The town transformed itself from a starving village into a thriving agricultural community. If the villagers had been asked several years before what had gotten in the way of their making an adequate living for themselves, I imagine they would have blamed the rocks in their fields and the monsoon floods. The vision of one man inspired them to use those hated rocks to build a dam and to store the flood waters of the monsoons to irrigate their crops year round. Their own sense of hopelessness and impotence had held them back.

This example demonstrates another principle as well. Had the leader criticized the villagers for their hopelessness, had he lectured them about their shortcomings, it is doubtful that any positive change would have resulted. They would have either resented his scolding or felt even worse about themselves—or both! The same is true when we examine our own patterns of self-limitation; we need to hold an attitude of compassion and detachment. "Yes," we might say to ourselves, "this way of acting or this belief seems to be getting in my way now; it is probably time to change it."

It seems to be an enormous undertaking to examine the collective beliefs and behaviors which are now getting in the way of planetary peace. We need to address the question a little at a time, noticing at each step on our journey what gets in our way rather than trying to encompass all at once our collective shortcomings.

When we examine our inner blocks, whether individually or collectively, a lot of painful feelings are likely to be brought to the surface; we might become aware of hurt, fear, grief, anger, and other uncomfortable emotions which we have been suppressing. As we begin to notice the many ways we as a species have stood in our own way of growth, have held ourselves back from our potential, we may feel very badly about it all. A very necessary part of this third step is to experience these feelings fully. I am convinced that when we cut off our feelings of grief and anger and anguish about our situation, we cut ourselves off from our strongest source of energy to change. We may need to weep and wail together in order to experience our common humanity. Joanna Macy and others leading the *Work That Reconnects* workshops have found collective expression of pain to be a powerful release of commitment and power (Macy & Brown, 2014). Figuratively speaking, we need to create a planetary self-help group, like Alcoholics Anonymous, to acknowledge our common despair and to commit ourselves collectively to healing.

The third step in the process of conscious growth is to recognize without blame or negative judgment the beliefs, patterns of behavior, and attitudes which hold us back and get in the way of our collective growth. The step includes the experience and appropriate expression of the feelings which may arise through this recognition. Often, the very process of recognition and emotional release allows the beliefs and behaviors to change spontaneously; they have been held in place only by our denial and ignorance. Sometimes, however, we need to explore these patterns in more depth, seeking their origins within our history and unraveling their complex interrelations with the various dynamics of our lives. Then, the fourth step can facilitate the needed transformation.

Question 4: What Do We Need to Develop?

The fourth question asks, not what we should do, but what we need to develop. It seeks a needed quality rather than a specific plan of action. This is a departure from the way many of us have traditionally solved problems. We tend to ask what's wrong and what should we do about it. In this psychosynthesis process, we ask what is possible (Question 2) and what needs to change or to grow within ourselves to remove the blocks to the possible.

If what gets in the way to peace is hopelessness and a sense of impotence, what qualities do we need to develop in ourselves to move forward? Logically, it would seem we need hope and self-empowerment, and these indeed may be on the mark. But sometimes the contemplation of this question yields surprising responses. We may need courage, or love, or commitment. We may need faith.

Often, when confronted with words like "courage," "hope," or "faith," we feel embarrassed or inadequate. Just as we have tended to suppress our feelings of fear and pain, we also suffer from "the repression of the sublime" (Haronian, 1967). We may fear that we will fail if we strive for such ideals, or we may have been disillusioned as children by the preachings of hypocritical adults. Yet as we look around us, we find inspiring examples of these admirable qualities in action, and we can see the benefit they bring to the world. If we look within, moreover, we find deep yearnings to realize higher values in our lives.

We need to learn more deeply and fully the meaning and scope of the qualities we see as valuable to our world. What is courage, for example? How does it feel to be courageous? What is its opposite? What kind of experiences tend to develop courage in people, and what experiences discourage people? Who are some models for courage in our world, either historical or living now?

Question 4 is based on the premise that, once we have identified qualities we need, we can develop them within ourselves through study, meditation, imagery, imitation, and practice. We can begin by examining what we already understand about a quality and how we have experienced it in our lives. Just thinking about a quality in this manner begins to activate it within us. And we can expand what we already know by reading, talking, listening, imagining, imitating others, and by trying things out. Roberto Assagioli observed that whatever we give energy to, grows; the simple act of giving attention (energy) to desirable qualities brings them more actively into our lives. Attempting to teach others about these qualities, and how to develop them, can also help us do the same for ourselves.

Question 4 challenges us to identify what qualities we need to develop as peacemakers or as Americans or as First World citizens, and to set about doing so. Of course, just as an individual can only develop something which already lies latent within, so the qualities we need are already in existence in humanity and in some cases are highly developed. Each culture of our human family has special qualities and gifts to offer as well as undeveloped dimensions and limitations. So Question 4 may be answered differently for different people. And, in many cases, we may need to seek the help and guidance of another culture to help us develop certain qualities within our own culture. We see this recognition, for example, among young non-native people in the United States who are eager to learn from Native American traditions. This process promises to bring together the various peoples of the world on new terms.

The mechanisms for developing such qualities already exist within our social structures: schools, media, churches, social and service organizations, to name a few. Projects that endeavor to develop qualities may even experience a greater sense of success because they are not fixed on specific quantitative goals. Moreover, we can carry out our qualitative education without threatening political structures because our strategies need not be focused on them. Few governments would object to their people developing courage, for example; yet as their people became more courageous, changes within the political structure would surely follow. Such changes would tend to be evolutionary and harmonious rather than sudden and violent; they would occur at all levels of life and not be aimed at just one particular institution. I offer this process to groups and individuals seeking to generate transformation in our world today—transformation vitally needed for our common survival and for improving the basic living conditions for most of our human family. Such transformation will also inevitably lead to the flowering of our vast human potential. I believe that many human projects naturally follow these principles and that our work can be made more effective and more joyful by using them consciously. Whether or not the questions are formally addressed as outlined here, projects can be planned with the same steps in mind. As we work with them together, we will no doubt expand and refine them so that this process too will evolve in the service of planetary synthesis.

Author's Note, 2017

This essay was written many years ago, before I became fully aware of the global climate crisis or the extent of systemic racism and oppression in the United States. This essay describes how to use four psychosynthesis questions for peacework; they can be used equally well to address the challenges of racism, climate crisis, and inequality.

References

Brown, M. Y. (2004). *Unfolding Self: The Practice of Psychosynthesis*, New York: Skyhorse Press.

Brown, M. Y. (2009). *Growing whole: Self-realization for the Great Turning.* Amherst, MA: Psychosynthesis Press.

Haronian, F. (1967). *Repression of the Sublime.* New York: Psychosynthesis Research Foundation.

Klein, Naomi. (2014) *This Changes Everything: Capitalism vs. the Climate.* New York: Simon & Schuster.

Macy, J. and Brown, Molly. (2014) Coming Back to Life: The Updated Guide to the Work That Reconnects. Gabriola Island, BC: New Society Publishers.

YES! Magazine, http://www.yesmagazine.org/

NOTE

---

[1] A description of these four questions applied to individual psychosynthesis work appears in my books *Unfolding Self* (2004, pp. 102-104) and *Growing Whole* (2009. pp. 21, 56-57, 66, 118-119)

Molly Brown, MA, MDiv, *brings psychosynthesis, ecopsychology, and the Work That Reconnects to her work—phone coaching and counseling, writing books and essays, teaching online courses, and giving talks and workshops. Her six books include* Growing Whole: Self-realization for the Great Turning *and* Unfolding Self: The Practice of Psychosynthesis. *She is editor of* Deep Times: A Journal of the Work That Reconnects *and, with Joanna Macy, she co-authored* Coming Back to Life: The Updated Guide to the Work That Reconnects. *Molly co-directs and co-teaches an online international Facilitator Development Program in the* Work That Reconnects. *She lives in Mount Shasta California with her life partner Jim Brown; together they take frequent long walks in the woods.*

Part VIII.

Psychosynthesis Theory

The Three Dimensions of Psychosynthesis

Thomas Yeomans

This article proposes a change in the theory of Psychosynthesis, namely that the process of psychosynthesis be conceived as having three rather than two dimensions and that these be termed "personal," "transpersonal," and "spiritual." This innovation entails drawing a distinction between "transpersonal" and "spiritual" and more fully delineating the issues of spiritual psychosynthesis. The change is proposed in the hope that it will shed light on the process of psycho-spiritual development and Self-realization as we are coming to understand it now.

Psychosynthesis, like all other theories, is a way of seeing human development and, so, is at best only an approximation of that reality.[1] Further, given the advance in our understanding of human development in this century, some of the ways of seeing within Psychosynthesis may be less useful in 1988 than they were in 1910 or 1937. This article seeks both to honor the early work in Psychosynthesis and to propose a modification in one aspect of its theory—a change which I think will help us better understand, and co-operate with, the process of psycho-spiritual development as we see it now. Time will tell the degree to which this new idea is useful; here I will only attempt to articulate it clearly so it can be examined more widely by fellow practitioners and theorists.

Background

When Roberto Assagioli first formulated Psychosynthesis, he posited two dimensions of human development—the psychological and the spiritual, This way of seeing and thinking about growth was powerful in that it acknowledged the full spectrum of human experience and supported the integration of these two dimensions in one lived reality. In 1910, this was an innovation in thought which did not achieve popularity until nearly 50 years later. Most work in the field of Psychology had stressed the psychological dimension and it was not until the advent of new thinking in the fifties and sixties that this way of seeing human development found some kin. Jung's work was, of course, the major exception to the general disregard for the spiritual dimension, as were some other minor schools of thought that developed during the first half-century.[2] But the dual formulation held up well over time, for it seems to describe accurately the process of growth that most people follow quite naturally—development along the personal dimension followed by an opening to the spiritual and subsequent growth in this realm. What begins to make this theoretical distinction less precise and useful is the advent in the seventies of Transpersonal Psychology.

The development of the Fourth Force in Psychology has had several effects. One very positive outcome is a much fuller acknowledgment of spiritual development as an aspect of Psychology—an acknowledgment that has led to a far broader acceptance of spiritual phenomena within our culture. As this has happened, the terms "transpersonal" and "spiritual" have come to be understood as synonymous, and, in Psychosynthesis, for example, the Higher Self is now sometimes referred to as the "Transpersonal Self" or as the "Spiritual Self. " Schools of thought and practice have emerged that recognize and seek to organize the phenomena of these two dimensions of growth as conceived in Psychosynthesis and in the spiritual disciplines of the East and those of native peoples around the world. This wealth of insight and practice has been the major contribution of Transpersonal Psychology to Psychology in the last 20 years.

Another effect of the development of the Fourth Force, however, has been less positive. As the seventies wore on and the eighties began, the term "transpersonal" was used increasingly to describe phenomena that were not necessarily spiritual in the sense that that term is used by psychosynthesists, and, in fact, by the early transpersonalists. These phenomena include psychic powers, trance, and shamanic states of consciousness, regressive and past life experiences, collective and archetypal material, channeling and sensitivity to mediums, and the opening to powerful superconscious energies. In the many versions of psychic healing and "energy" work, these are often confused with the energies of the Self. As the exploration of the human unconscious expanded, "transpersonal" increasingly became a catch-all for this vast spectrum of experience, with little attention paid to the different sources of experience within the unconscious and little discrimination as to their relative value and, at times, counter-indications for use. Specifically, the distinction between the Self and the Superconscious became blurred, if not lost, and the emphasis in therapeutic work was placed increasingly on awareness and the contents of consciousness. Less attention was paid to the development of the personal will and its alignment with the "higher" will, or will of the Self, which is a central aspect of spiritual psychosynthesis as Assagioli conceived it. In this context, spiritual work is reduced to transpersonal work in the sense that emphasis is placed on opening oneself to higher states of consciousness, or going deeper into the collective, thereby obscuring the very real issues around personal and spiritual direction, namely meaning, choice, and responsibility. The result of this confusion is that the Self, as portrayed in the traditional oval diagram, tends to become mistaken for, and merged with, the energies of the Superconscious, and the "I" overshadowed by the dynamic forces of the Psyche and the Collective Unconscious.

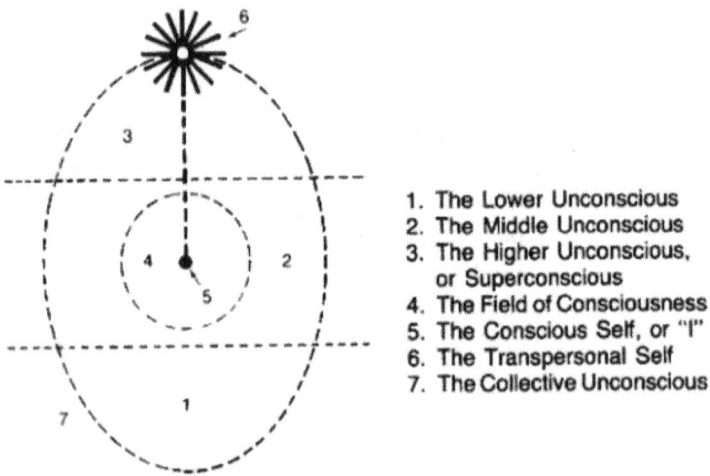

1. The Lower Unconscious
2. The Middle Unconscious
3. The Higher Unconscious, or Superconscious
4. The Field of Consciousness
5. The Conscious Self, or "I"
6. The Transpersonal Self
7. The Collective Unconscious

Assagioli's "Egg Diagram" of the Human Psyche

This is perhaps an overstatement, but I think it points to a growing confusion about the spiritual dimension of work with clients. I would like to address this confusion here quite simply by proposing that we think of work with the process of psychosynthesis as differentiated by three, not two, dimensions—personal, transpersonal, and spiritual. In order to co-operate with the process of psycho-spiritual development, we need to make this distinction, both to acknowledge and to limit the transpersonal and to ensure that the spiritual dimension is honored and addressed in its own right as the core of the whole endeavor, "'Transpersonal" can remain a more general term; we can still say Psychosynthesis is one of a number of transpersonal psychologies, but "transpersonal" in its use here is no longer synonymous with "spiritual," It is limited to describe work within the psyche, not with the Self.

The Personal Dimension

In the scheme I propose, the personal dimension is much as before. It contains the work of integrating the personality around a stable center of identity and will, the "I, " Work here is with subpersonalities, body, feelings, and mind identification, disidentification, and the development of the observing self. It also includes work with more unconscious aspects of the personality, early object relations and trauma, and an analysis of the functional and dysfunctional aspects of the personality as they are expressed in attitudes and behavior. Training of the personal will is also a central aspect of work in the personal realm.

The purpose of work in this dimension is to construct and/or cohere a personality structure and dynamic that is healthy and effective in both coping and expressing in the given environment.[3] Assagioli was clear that this work needed to precede opening oneself to the spiritual dimension—a conviction he shared with Jung. Western psychoanalytic and psychodynamic schools of thought concurred in this assessment, the difference being that they did not propose anything beyond this, as did Jung and Assagioli. Unfortunately, some forms of psychosynthetic practice ignored the need for thorough personal work and leaped prematurely into the spiritual. This was particularly true in the seventies when Psychosynthesis tended to be identified with the counter-culture in North America. Hopefully, this time is now past and a better balance exists between the personal and spiritual dimensions—a balance that honors the necessity of sound personality development as a foundation for spiritual opening and expression.

The Transpersonal Dimension

This is the new distinction. Previously this would have been subsumed under the spiritual dimension, but in the last 15 years the understanding of the realms of the psyche has grown and it seems more precise to differentiate this dimension of work from the others. Transpersonal work, as I am using the term, has to do with the expansion of consciousness beyond its normal limits into any realm (unconscious, personal, or collective). It entails the disciplined exploration of the various dimensions of the psyche, as portrayed in the egg diagram, for example, or work with the birth pattern and perinatal matrices as described in Stan Grof's (1985) work. Also included is work with what Jung termed the

Shadow or with the Anima and Animus and their integration. It includes as well work with transgenerational patterns and past life phenomena, the emergence of psychic powers and parapsychological phenomena, altered states of consciousness, and the cultivation of superconscious qualities.

In short, the transpersonal is the realm of development that literally enables a person to know him or herself more fully and deeply, to become aware of aspects and energies that were not previously available to consciousness, and to integrate these into a more inclusive sense of identity. In all cases, the focus is on the expansion of awareness and the contents of consciousness. Obviously, a sound personality and personal will are prerequisites for doing this work safely. Neglect of the personal and a premature opening to transpersonal energies can generate further imbalance in the personality, ego inflation, and regression in behavior. Conversely, rightly used, the energies of the psyche can greatly enhance one's life, bring a fuller degree of self-knowledge, and heal, support, and foster the further development of the personality.

The Spiritual Dimension

As distinct from transpersonal work with the contents of the Unconscious, this dimension works directly with the energies of the Self, the energies of synthesis, the will of the Self, and the alignment of the personal with the spiritual will. The experience of the Self and spiritual will is central here, and this is distinguished from the transpersonal in that there is no content to this experience. The Self, this "contentless being," "suchness," "creative void," "Big Mind," whatever name the nameless is given, is seen as the context and guiding principle for the psyche and personality. Whereas psyche has content, and personality has dynamic structure, the Self is pure being which infuses the other two, much as the sun infuses atmosphere and earth. Self is not superconscious, it is not even soul, which is the experience of Self and psyche taken together, but it is an energy that permeates the entire life system and is the context for that system (see Hillman, 1975; Vaughan, 1986).

Work with the spiritual Self and its will has its own dimensions and issues, some of which I will speak of below. Spiritual work, in this sense, then, is not a matter of expanding awareness to get more content, high or low, but simply a matter of intensifying essential being, of removing obstacles to that being, and of making choices that allow that being to shine more clearly and brightly through the "lenses" of the psyche, of the personality, and of the body. Assagioli said that "the basic purpose of Psychosynthesis is to release, or let us say, help to release the energies of the Self" (1971, p. 65). The spiritual dimension works directly with these energies as they affect psyche and personality and with the experience of the will of the Self and its expression in life as a whole.

A simple model may help to clarify this distinction. If we visualize three concentric circles and posit that the innermost is the Self, the middle the psyche, and the outer the personality and if we hold that the Self is context for the psyche and the psyche is context for the personality, then we can see that the "light" of the Self will shine more fully into the world in proportion to the coherence of the "lenses" of the psyche and personality (see Figure 1). If the personality is disorganized, or the psyche chaotic, then the spiritual light of being will be blocked, distorted, or fragmented. Conversely, as the work of healing and growth goes on in the dimensions of the personality and psyche, this light will shine forth more coherently and the energies of the Self will be constructively released into the world.

The work of the personal and transpersonal dimensions is that of cohering and harmonizing the lenses, or inner systems, through which the light of being shines. The work of the spiritual dimension is that of affirming the reality of the light of being and reorganizing, through the personal and spiritual will, the outer environment so that this energy is fully released and expressed in the world.

Figure 1/ Self, Psyche, and Personality

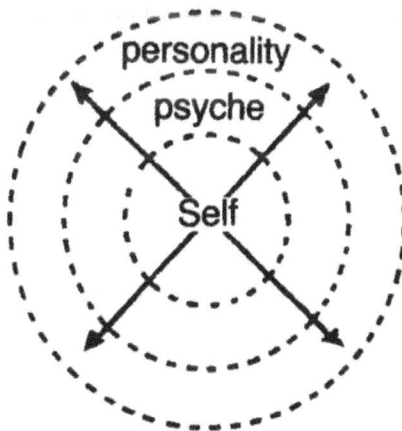

Implications

Some of the value of this distinction is immediately clear. First, because the Self is set at the very center of work in Psychosynthesis, it becomes the context and the fruit of work in the other dimensions. Second, the distinction limits the work of expanding awareness within the psyche for what it is, and lessens the confusion between transpersonal phenomena and the experience of Spirit itself. Third, the distinction makes the will, both personal and spiritual, central to the work of Psychosynthesis. Rather than being relegated to something other than the two original dimensions, will is set at the center of the whole process and endeavor of Self-realization as the thread of continuity that unites all three dimensions.

The distinction also allows for a more balanced conception of the process of psychosynthesis as a whole, honoring more fully the complexity and beauty of Life. Obviously, in actual work, the three dimensions are present, but at any particular time one will be in the foreground. Issues in the personal, transpersonal, and spiritual dimensions are different and should be treated differently, and when one is mistaken for the other, problems occur.

Below, I want to speak to some specific issues within spiritual psychosynthesis as it has been redefined here. As noted above, these issues in the past tended to be lumped together with transpersonal issues when in fact they are of a very different order. Coming up again and again in psychosynthetic clinical practice, they give a sense of the spiritual dimension of the work and its importance to the overall process of psycho-spiritual development. They are set under the headings of being, orientation, relationship, responsibility, and service.

Being—The experience of being is central to both the "I" and the Self. At moments of being in touch with these, there is no particular content to the consciousness, no coloration, no qualification, but simply a beingness that is both powerful and pervasive. This beingness is often accompanied by an experience of radiance, of being a source of light and life, an energy that permeates every aspect of psyche and personality and extends to others and the world. There is often an experience of being both universal and unique, having transcended all aspects of one's everyday self and yet at the same time being oneself more fully than at any other time.

This experience is radically different from being in touch with a superconscious quality, or a subpersonality. It has no content and yet it seems to hold, and be the context for, all content. It is the light out of which the coloration and the drama of the psyche and personality spring, the "unmoved mover" that is the guiding and organizing principle of inner and outer life events. Also, there is no "where" to go to have this experience; it is here/now. This contrasts to transpersonal experiences in which one journeys into a dimension of the unconscious, and seems to go far away or deep within. Being is present now/forever and is not dependent on change, growth, development, circumstance. In working with people, it is crucial to recognize and affirm this difference; otherwise, this central experience is reduced to just another aspect of the psyche.

Obviously, many spiritual practices, particularly those associated with some schools of Buddhism, aim directly at this revelation of being and bypass all content as simply "thinking, thinking; feeling, feeling." In Western psychotherapy and education, where there is more focus on content, this experience is only beginning to be recognized and cultivated (see Deikman, 1982). In Psychosynthesis, it is, and always has been, a touchstone for healing and human development, but it can be overlooked, or confused with very "high" content in the psyche.

Orientation—This issue concerns the basic life direction of the person or how the personality is oriented as a whole. It entails work with the alignment of the personal and spiritual will and the making of choices that energize and realize the deepest sense of direction, calling, destiny, and value that the person is aware of. It does not have to do with gaining more awareness— this is the work of the personal and transpersonal dimensions—but with choosing to choose on the basis of what one is aware of, to act in accord with what is felt as deepest and truest within one's soul. Many people avoid the issue of orientation by continuing to do personal and transpersonal work, mistakenly thinking that more work on expanding their awareness will help. Such work does not in and of itself help. What they need, rather, is encouragement to make real choices that will align their daily behavior with their spiritual will and help them recognize the intent of the Self so that they may give themselves to it fully. Issues of sacrifice, surrender, voluntary suffering, and self-forgetfulness all come to the fore here, and need to be treated seriously as spiritual struggles, not reduced to psychic or psychodynamic problems. A growing number of people who have integrated their personalities and have an ample amount of self-knowledge are struggling with these spiritual issues, and are hard put to find a therapist or counselor who will acknowledge these issues in their own right.

A second area where orientation is of concern lies in what is sometimes termed a crisis of expression. Developmentally, this crisis tends to come after the growth crises of earlier life and the existential crises of mid-life, and it occurs when a person begins to recognize an expanded arena of expression that he or she is called to enter, leaving behind a familiar and often successful one. Again, this crisis is not resolved through expanded awareness, though some reworking of psyche and personality may be necessary to support the move, but rather through a series of choices that effect a move into this larger arena. This move entails personal sacrifice, but there is also a recognition of the "rightness" of the choice and a resultant increase in the flow of energies of the Self into the world. Accompanying the move is often a clearer sense and a fuller acceptance of one's place in the world, of one's strengths and limitations, and a recognition of one's involvement in and responsibility to the larger community. People in this crisis need support that recognizes these issues for what they are, and deals with them accordingly.

Relationship—As contact with the Self and the flow of the energies of synthesis grow, a new experience of relationship begins to emerge. Whereas earlier relationships involved a particular person or thing, often excluding others and reflecting some degree of attachment (or cathexis), at these moments the experience of relationship is of both detachment and kinship to all people and things, all aspects of creation. This lends an almost impersonal quality to relationships, even as they become, paradoxically, more immediate and intimate. For most, this is a matter of a moment only, an experience that comes and goes quickly; for a few, it becomes a fairly consistent experience. But the point is that it is different, whether it is built upon a relationship with one person or a number of people and things. It brings with it a realization of being inextricably interconnected with all Life and an awareness of the implications for "normal" relationships which tend in themselves to be exclusive and polarized. A common example of this realization is the recognition that occurs after intense work with one's own suffering as a child that "all children are my children."[4] The experience has no particular quality or specific focus, but it is an aspect of the touch of the Self and the inflow of a spiritual love that Dante had characterized as that which "moves the sun and all the stars." The experience needs recognition and validation in and of itself; it is an indication of the inherent participation of the Self in all life and of the universal aspect of identity.

Responsibility—The issue here concerns taking a stand in your life and doing your part in the world. It involves acting on what you know best at any particular time, being willing to make a mistake and to learn from it, and recognizing that only through choice and behavior can the energies of the Self be fully expressed. Responsibility is based on consciousness, but a response requires the transformation of consciousness into action. The action may be inner or outer, highly visible or known only to Self, but without it the process of psychosynthesis is blocked. Only by taking personal and spiritual responsibility, as expressed in behavior that is in line with one's calling, can the Higher Self express itself in the world.

If issues around taking responsibility are interpreted on a psychodynamic or transpersonal level and are treated as such, the opportunity for expression is delayed and the release of the energies of the Self impeded. Often work needs to be done at other levels to support taking spiritual responsibility, but this work is not the same as that of making choices, acting, and learning from the experience of Self-expression, The spiritual response requires a direct confrontation with the world, with those forces within and without that resist this action, and a willingness to be seen and heard in the light of one's deepest values. Taking spiritual responsibility in the world is the final flower of the process of psychosynthesis.

Service—The fruit, then, of the endeavor is service. Yet there is a great deal of confusion about the word and the experience. The most common mistake is to introduce service as a concept before work has been completed at the personal and transpersonal levels. This results in a forced experience of service, rooted in guilt and shame, inner or outer coercion, and intellectualized goodness, or its rejection as oppressive and arbitrary. The true experience of service is the deepest instinct and need of the Self. As a person matures, the impulse to be of service to others and the world naturally emerges, not as an arbitrary thought or as a concept imposed from a belief system, but as a natural outcome of life's development. The experience of service is rooted in one's being, in presence to all life, a balance in the giving and receiving of love, and a recognition of the sacredness of all lives, including one's own. It is completely natural to the human being, and is the outpouring of the energies of the Self. That it is blocked in so many of us is only a measure of how disconnected we have become from the Self.

Service is seen quite often in children who are still connected to their deeper nature, in mature adults who have reconnected, and intermittently in the rest of us at those moments of Self-connection when we open to the reality of Self and "see the world" through its perspective. The need to serve is a spiritual issue involving the alignment of personal and spiritual will and the sustained release of the energies of the Self into the world. Work on personal and transpersonal issues is clearly prerequisite, but these issues are not to be confused with the experience itself and its acknowledgment and careful support.

Synthesis

The above gives a brief idea of the distinct clinical issues encountered in spiritual psychosynthesis. Clearly, the three dimensions, personal, transpersonal, and spiritual, are inherently interconnected and in actual work all three are present in some proportion. But developmentally one is usually foreground, and if one dimension is mistaken for another, then difficulties arise in the work and the process is not fully supported. Conversely, if we can recognize each dimension for what it is, and address directly the issues that properly belong to it, then we greatly increase the precision of our co-operation with the Self in our work, and in this way are able to help release the energies of synthesis within the person for healing, growth, and service. The three dimensions, I believe, also apply to the development of couples, families, groups, organizations, and perhaps nations and the planet as a whole. For the moment, however, they are most clearly grounded in clinical practice with the individual. Should the distinction prove useful, then work can proceed in testing it at these other levels as well.

Psychosynthesis, like all systems of thought, all theories, or ways of seeing, is evolving, and I offer this one change as an aspect of its evolution. My hope is that it will allow us to see more clearly what is true about individuals and their development and to be of greater help in healing and nourishing both person and planet. If the idea is of use, then it will illuminate work in Psychosynthesis in a natural and common-sense way. What is needed now is the testing of its validity within the context of clinical and educational work. I invite fellow practitioners to this task and to the continuing examination of how we "see" and what its impact is on both our practice and our lives.

References

Assagioli, R. (1971). *Psychosynthesis.* New York: Viking.
Dante, A, (1961). *The Divine Comedy.* London: Oxford University Press.
Deikman, A. (1982), *The Observing Self.* Boston: Beacon Press.
Grof, S. (1985), *Beyond the Brain.* New York: SUNY Press.
Hillman, J. (1975). *Revisioning Psychology.* New York: Harper & Row.
Vaughan, F. (1986). *The Inward Arc.* Boston: Shambhala.

Author's Commentary—2017

This article, when I wrote it in 1988, was rooted in a response to Roberto Assagioli's distinction between the Higher Self and the Superconscious, and was an attempt to clarify and amplify this important difference further. In re-reading it now almost thirty years later, I am struck by how well it still holds true. It does so by making the distinction between personal, transpersonal, and spiritual dimensions of human experience rather than just between personal and spiritual, and also by bringing the Higher Self forward and foreground in the distinction between its energy of Being and "transpersonal" phenomena. The reasons for this are stated clearly and the tripartite schema I propose makes the distinction, I believe, even clearer than the two dimensions do. Certainly, it is food for thought.

One change I would propose, in order to highlight this distinction further, would be to replace the term "transpersonal" with "psychical", as I actually did in my later writing and teaching. The three dimensions would then be "personal, psychical, and spiritual", and these together would constitute a three dimensional differentiation of the experience of psycho-spiritual development, or what Assagioli termed, "the process of psychosynthesis".

The other change I would propose, and have also made subsequently in my writing and teaching, is to be bolder in bringing the Higher Self to the very center of psychosynthetic work and to posit its existence and guidance from the very beginning of life and development—an influence that is always present, but with which we lose touch, out of unconsciousness, identification, distraction, enculturation, trauma—a host of reasons. I would make it very clear that the Higher Self does not lose us: we lose it, and then we need to set out on a journey to find our Selves again—a journey that, paradoxically, it guides us on.

For both changes I would highlight Assagioli saying " the basic purpose of Psychosynthesis is to release, or, let us say, help to release the energies of the Self", and, drawing on this statement, I would recommend that work in Psychosynthesis focus more directly from the very beginning on the existence and presence of the Higher Self in our immediate experience. I would also emphasize that the core of the work is the release of Higher Self's being, vitality, and force through the patterns and forms of psyche and personality. This would include, of course, studying, and working with, all the ways in which these two dimensions (psychical and personal) obstruct and impede the flow of that force into the world, as well as exploring how psyche and personality can in time come to be coherent instruments of expression of the Higher Self. From this perspective psyche and personality come to be seen as serving the Self rather than as ends in themselves, and human spiritual maturity becomes characterized by the steady infusion of these "instruments of expression"—psyche and personality-- by the light and force of the Higher Self.

The last thirty years have brought us much more understanding of the experience of the Higher Self and its centrality in psychological health and human development. Hopefully these energies will continue to be unlocked and utilized in psychological work and in time the Higher Self restored to its rightful place in the concept of the human being. The differentiation of the three dimensions, I believe, can contribute to this goal.

NOTES

---

[1] It is useful to remember that the word theory is derived from the ancient Greek theorem, which means "to see." A theory, then, is a "way of seeing" a topic, and different people will have different theories, depending on how they experience reality. Some theories will be more general, some more specific. All theories are biased and limited in some way. Therefore, the work of developing theory is to find a way of seeing that seems to fit the phenomena under observation and at the same time can gain enough consensus among fellow "seers" to be generally accepted. All theories are at best approximations and therefore never true in an absolute sense. They can, however, help us see what is "there" to the best of our knowledge at the time. As we "see" more clearly over time, we can modify our theories or we can reject them as they cease to be useful. At any point in time, certain theories will inform the "seeing" of the majority while other theories will have a more marginal existence, either because they are becoming obsolete or because they have not yet been recognized as holding a way of seeing that reveals reality, Examining a theory, then, involves studying how people see certain phenomena and assessing how useful this way of seeing is in its capacity to illuminate and explain the aspect of reality under scrutiny. At the moment in Psychology, a number of ways of seeing human development, function, and dysfunction exist side by side, The broad schools of thought in this century have been psychoanalytic, behavioral, humanistic, and transpersonal, but within each there have been many subschools with methods and techniques based on their particular ways of seeing. On the one hand, this has generated a fragmented and often conflicting array of possible approaches to healing and development. On the other, it points to the eventual emergence of a unified theory that will be capable of helping us see how the schools of thought are interrelated. This theory has yet to be found, but there are people working toward it. By the end of the century, we may have made a solid beginning toward a unified way of seeing human development in all its dimensions.

[2] Viktor Frankl's logotherapy is one example; Rudolf Steiner's thinking on education another.

[3] In recent years, psychosynthesists have paid greater attention to psychopathology, recognizing that techniques for the various neurotic disorders were not appropriate for more severe dysfunction within the personality. This has led to the development of new techniques, still consonant with the principles of Psychosynthesis and appropriate for dealing with this level of pathology, and a consequent expansion of the dimensions of work in personal psychosynthesis.

[4] It is interesting to note that clinically this experience almost always follows the experience of the client's own particular pain. This is true also of outrage at world conditions, which follows from the release of personal anger about issues in one's own life. This would indicate that a true experience of "larger love" is rooted in a confrontation with personal suffering. Without this, the claim to this level of love can easily become platitudinous, superficial, and eventually used as a reaction formation to repressed and denied personal material.

Thomas Yeomans, PhD, *is the founder and director of the* Concord Institute *and co-founder, with Russian colleagues, of the* International School, *a post-graduate training institute in St. Petersburg, Russia. In 1974 he completed training in Psychosynthesis, which included work with Roberto Assagioli in Florence, Italy. Since then he has worked as a psychotherapist, teacher, and trainer of professionals in psychosynthesis and spiritual psychology throughout North America and in Europe and Russia and, more recently, as a spiritual guide/mentor. He has published writing on psychosynthesis and spiritual psychology, as well as three volumes of poetry. He is also a painter and musician. Currently he maintains a private practice in spiritual guidance/mentoring in Shelburne Falls, MA and teaches occasional training workshops.*

Appendix.

What Is Psychosynthesis?

In its most basic sense, psychosynthesis is simply a name for the process of personal growth: the natural tendency in each of us to harmonize or synthesize our various aspects at ever more inclusive levels of organization. In its more specific sense, psychosynthesis is a name for the conscious attempt to cooperate with the natural process of personal development. All living things contain within them a drive to evolve, to become the fullest realization of themselves. This process can be supported consciously, and psychosynthesis is one means to do this.

Cooperating effectively with this process can be assisted by a conceptual understanding of the nature of this evolution, and by practical techniques. Psychosynthesis provides these and integrates them into an inclusive and ever-growing framework designed to support the individual, groups, and the planet in their process of unfolding.

As an inclusive approach to human growth, psychosynthesis dates from 1911 and the early work of Roberto Assagioli, MD, an Italian Psychiatrist. Though one of the pioneers of psychoanalysis in Italy, Assagioli maintained that Freud had not given sufficient weight to the "higher" aspects of the human personality, and recognized a need for a more inclusive concept of humanity. From this beginning Assagioli and an increasing number of psychotherapists, educators, physicians, social workers, clergy, and others have worked to develop and refine this inclusive view of human growth. The task is considered to be an open one, one that will never be finished. Each year, new discoveries in psychology, new developments in education, religion, anthropology, physics and other disciplines add to the principles and to the techniques of psychosynthesis. Psychosynthesis, by its very nature, is always open to new approaches to human development.

Over the past sixty years, a number of conceptual points and a number of methods have proven themselves to be fundamental. These provide a working structure for psychosynthesis.

A Synthesis of Many Traditions

Any comprehensive psychological and educational approach to the development of the whole person must draw from many traditions. While Eastern disciplines often have tended to emphasize the spiritual side of being, Western approaches usually have focused on the personality level. But humanity must be viewed as a whole and each aspect accorded its due importance. Psychosynthesis recognizes that we have a transpersonal essence, and at the same time holds that the individual's purpose in life is to manifest this essence, or Self, as fully as possible in the world of everyday personal and social existence.

Stages in Psychosynthesis

Every person is an individual, and the psychosynthesis of each person follows a unique path. At the same time, the overall process of psychosynthesis can be divided into two stages: personal and transpersonal. In personal psychosynthesis, the integration of the personality takes place around the personal self, and the individual attains a high level of functioning in terms of work, relationships, and general living that is meaningful and satisfactory to the individual.

In the transpersonal stage the person learns to achieve alignment with and to transmit the energies of the transpersonal Self, manifesting such qualities as responsibility, the spirit of cooperation, global perspective, love and purpose, and having access to inner guidance and wisdom.

Often the two stages overlap: there can be a considerable amount of transpersonal activity long before the stage of personal integration is complete.

Methods Employed in Psychosynthesis

Any method that assists in the personal evolution of a human being is a method useful in psychosynthesis. To be maximally effective, we clearly need to have a broad range of methods and techniques to meet the needs presented by different situations and people. As each person must be treated as an individual, an effort must be made to choose the methods best suited to each person's existential situation, psychological type, goals, desires and path of development. Some of the methods more commonly used include guided imagery, movement, subpersonality work, disidentification and self-identification, creativity, meditation, will development, symbolic art work, journal keeping, ideal models and development of intuition, and many more. The emphasis is on fostering an on-going process of growth that can gain momentum and bring a more joyful and balanced actualization to our lives.

As this process goes on, we gain the freedom of choice, the power of decision over our actions, and the ability to regulate and direct many of the personality functions. This entails developing the personal will—the will of the personal self. Through this development we free ourselves from helpless or preprogrammed reaction to inner impulses and external situations and expectations. We become truly "centered" and gradually become able to follow our own path, guided by our inner knowing, or true Self.

As we reach toward the transpersonal Self, we can liberate and encourage the synthesizing energies that organize and integrate the personality. We can make ever increasing contact with the Will of our transpersonal Self, which provides clearer and clearer meaning and purpose in our personal lives and our social tasks. We become able to function in the world more serenely and effectively, in a spirit of cooperation and good will.

Psychosynthesis is a powerful and effective mode of holistic growth and is rapidly gaining recognition in the psychological and transformational fields. It is also a positive and dynamic framework from which to view the evolution of our planet. Psychosynthesis principles and techniques have been used effectively in education, medicine, politics and business, as well as in all forms of counseling and psychotherapy and personal, business and group

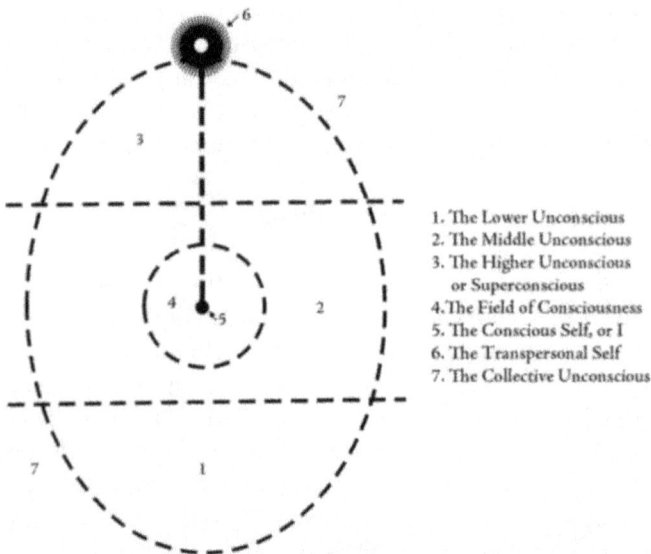

1. The Lower Unconscious
2. The Middle Unconscious
3. The Higher Unconscious or Superconscious
4. The Field of Consciousness
5. The Conscious Self, or I
6. The Transpersonal Self
7. The Collective Unconscious

Dr. Assagioli's "Egg Diagram from his Book: *The Act of Will.*
This is the basic psychosynthesis map of the Human Psyche

coaching. It is rapidly growing in its sphere of application, range of techniques, and depth of understanding.

The two most well-known diagrams that Dr. Assagioli created to depict the makeup of the Human Psyche and its psychological functions, the "Egg" and "Star" diagrams can be seen below.

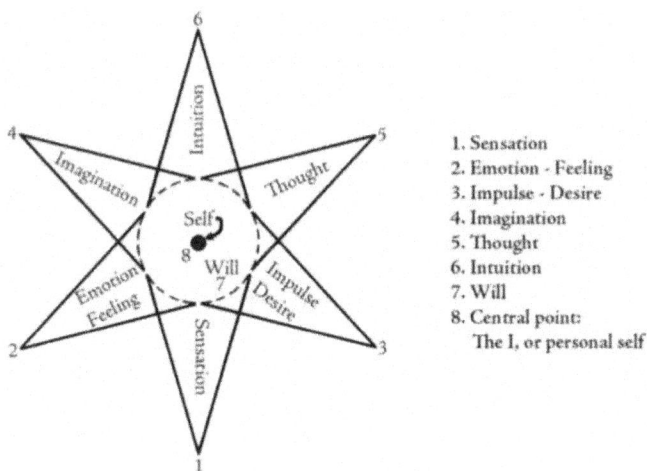

1. Sensation
2. Emotion - Feeling
3. Impulse - Desire
4. Imagination
5. Thought
6. Intuition
7. Will
8. Central point:
   The I, or personal self

Dr. Assagioli's "Star Diagram"
from his book: *The Act of Will.*
Showing the relationship between self, will
and the psychological functions.

—adapted from the website of **The Synthesis Center** at
http://www.synthesiscenter.org/ps.htm
More about how these diagrams can be interpreted and used
can be found in the "Resources" at the end of this book.

Selected Resources

Books on Psychosynthesis

Assagioli, Roberto, (1974), *The Act of Will*. London: Turnstone Press. Numerous other editions are available including one currently available from The Synthesis Center published in 2010.

Assagioli, Roberto, (1965), *Psychosynthesis: A Collection of Basic Writ ings*. New York: Dorman   & Co. Inc. Numerous other editions are available including one currently available from The Synthesis Center published in 2000.

Brown, Molly Young, (2004) *Unfolding Self: The Practice of   Psycho synthesis*. New York: Helios Press.

Ferrucci, Piero, (1982). *What We May Be*. New York: Jeremy P. Tarcher.

Firman, John, and Ann Gila (2002). *Psychosynthesis: A Psychology of the Spirit*. Albany: SUNY Press.

Firman, John, and Ann Gila. (2010). *A Psychotherapy of Love: Psycho synthesis in Practice*. Albany: SUNY Press.

Hardy, Jean, (1987). *A Psychology With a Soul: Psychosynthesis in Evo lutionary Contact*. London: Routledge & Kegan Paul

Nocelli, Petra Guggisberg (2017). *The Way of Psychosynthesis*. Lugano: Nocelli.

Parfitt, Will (2003). *Psychosynthesis: The Elements and Beyond*. Glas tonbury: PS Avalon.

Parfitt, Will (ed.) (2009). *Psychosynthesis: New Perspectives*. Glaston bury: PS Avalon.

Sørensen. Kenneth, (2016). *The Soul of Psychosynthesis: The Seven Core Concepts*. Gentofte: Kentaur Publishing

Articles on Websites

Assagioli, Roberto, MD (N.D.) and others. Numerous monographs and articles are available online at the following websites:

Archive.org.
https://archive.org/details/SomeCollectedWorksOfDr.RobertoAssagi oliM.d

Assagioli Archives. http://www.archivioassagioli.org/
Association for the Advancement of Psychosynthesis. https://aap-
    psychosynthesis.org/
Institute of Psychosynthesis. https://www.psychosynthesis.org/
Istituto di Psicosentesi. http://www.psicosintesi.it/
Istituto di Psicosentesi (in English):
    http://www.psicosintesi.it/english
Psychosynthesis Resources.
    http://psychosynthesisresources.com/index.html
Psychosynthsis.net. http://www.psynthesis.net/ps/index.htm
Psychosynthesis Palo Alto. http://www.psychosynthesispaloalto.com/
Psychosynthesis Trust. https://psychosynthesistrust.org.uk/
Kenneth Sørensen. http://www.psykosyntese.dk
Molly Young Brown. http://mollyyoungbrown.com/
Synthesis Center. http://www.synthesiscenter.org/
Will Parfitt. http://www.willparfitt.com/
Will Project. https://willproject.org/

Psychosynthesis Organizations—
Training, Therapy, Coaching, Information

North America

Association for the Advancement of Psychosynthesis. https://aap-
    psychosynthesis.org/
Bring Out the Best. http://www.bringoutthebest.com/
Center for Awakening. http://www.centerforawakening.org/
Centre Psychosynthèse du Bas-St.Laurent.
    http://www.psychosynthese.ca/
Connecticut Institute for Psychosynthesis.
    http://synthesisjourneys.com/connecticut-institute/
Counseling and Human Resources Cunsulting.
    http://www.michaelbrown.org/
Emotional Medicine RX. http://www.emotionalmedicinerx.com/
Huntington Meditation and Imagery Center.
    http://huntingtonmeditation.com/
Kentucky Center of Psychosynthesis.
    http://www.kycenterofpsychosynthesis.org/
Molly Young Brown. http://mollyyoungbrown.com/
New York Psychosynthesis Institute.
    http://www.newyorkpsychosynthesis.org/
Psychospiritual Coaching. http://psychospiritualcoaching.com/

Psychosynthesis Palo Alto. http://www.psychosynthesispaloalto.com/
Synthesis Center. http://www.synthesiscenter.org/
Synthesis Center San Francisco. https://synthesiscentersf.com/
Synthesis Coaching Philadelphia.
    https://www.synthesiscoachingphiladelphia.com/
Synthesis International. http://synthesisintl.com/
Vermont Center for Psychosynthesis. http://synthesisvt.net/

Central and South America

Centro de Psicossíntese de São Paulo. http://psicossintese.org.br/

Europe and UK

Aeon. Zentrum für Psychosynthese und Ganzheitliches Heilen.
    http://www.aeon.ch/
Centre for Soul Psychology. http://www.soulpsychology.fi/
Centre Source France. http://www.psychosynthese.com/
Circadian Psychosynthese. https://www.circadian.de/
Deutche Psychosynthese Gesellschaft.
    https://www.psychosynthese.de/
European Federation for Psychosynthesis Psychotherapy.
    http://psychosynthesis.net/
Harmony Institute for Psychotherapy and Counseling.
    http://eng.inharmony.ru/1
HumaNova. http://www.humanova.no/ and
    http://www.humanova.com/
Institut Français de Psychosynthese. http://psychosynthese.fr/
Institut für Psychosynthese.
    http://www.saltiel.at/Aron/Willkommen.html
Institute of Psychosynthesis. https://www.psychosynthesis.org/
Instituto de psicosintesi. http://www.psicosintesi.it/
Instituut voor Psychosynthese. https://psychosynthese.nl/
Instytut Psychosynttezy. http://www.psychosynteza.pl/
Kenneth Sørensen. https://kennethsorensen.dk/en/
Norsk Institutt for Psykosynthese. http://psykosyntese.no/
Norsk Psykosynteseforening. http://www.psykosyntese.net/
Psykosyntes Akademin. http://psykosyntesakademin.se/psa/
Psykosyntesförbundet. http://psykosyntesforbundet.se/
Psykosyntesföreningen. http://psykosyntesforeningen.se/
Psykosyntes Institutet. http://www.psykosyntesinstitutet.se/
Psychosynthese Academie. https://www.psychosyntheseacademie.nl/

Psychosynthese Haus. https://www.psychosynthesehaus.de/
Psychosynthese Vereniging.
    http://www.psychosyntheseVereniging.org/
Psychosynthesis Ireland. http://psychosynthesis.tel/
Psychosynthesis Trust. https://psychosynthesistrust.org.uk/
School voor Imaginatie. https://www.imaginatie.nl/
Societa Italiana si Psicosintesi Tedrapeutica.
    https://www.scuolapsicosintesi.com/sipt/
Société Française de Psychosynthèse Thérapeutique.
    http://www.psychosynthese.com/
Synthesis Coaching Italia. https://www.synthesis-coaching.com/
Will Parfitt. http://www.willparfitt.com/psychosynthesis-distance-
    learning/
Zentrum für Psychosynthese. http://www.psychosynthese-bern.ch/

New Zealand

Institute of Psychosynthesis N.Z. http://www.psychosynthesis.co.nz/
PANZA. http://panza.org.nz/

Australia

Good Therapy Australia.
https://www.goodtherapy.com.au/flex/psychosynthesis/739/1
Inner Harmony Center. http://innerharmony.com.au/
Jodie Gale. http://jodiegale.com/
PANZA. http://panza.org.nz/

Index

www.ingramcontent.com/pod-product-compliance
Lightning Source LLC
Chambersburg PA
CBHW020241030426
42336CB00010B/569